In this book Mary McAuley explores the political reactions of elites and society in the Russian Federation in the years following the collapse of communist party rule and the break-up of the USSR. Spanning two republics and four regions, the book offers the first in-depth study of the impact of change in the regions as well as at the centre. Using first-hand research including extensive interviews and personal observation, this book provides a unique study of the response of a society to the break-down of the established political order. Mary McAuley traces Russia's search for new identities, institutions, and rules of political behaviour. Her book will appeal to students of comparative politics generally, as well as to all those interested in transition in Russia.

Russia's politics of uncertainty

Russia's politics of uncertainty

Mary McAuley

The Ford Foundation, Moscow

CAMBRIDGE
UNIVERSITY PRESS

PUBLISHED BY THE PRESS SYNDICATE OF THE UNIVERSITY OF CAMBRIDGE
The Pitt Building, Trumpington Street, Cambridge CB2 1RP, United Kingdom

CAMBRIDGE UNIVERSITY PRESS
The Edinburgh Building, Cambridge CB2 2RU, United Kingdom
40 West 20th Street, New York, NY 10011-4211, USA
10 Stamford Road, Oakleigh, Melbourne 3166, Australia

First published 1997

Printed in the United Kingdom at the University Press, Cambridge

Typeset in 10/12 Plantin

A catalogue record for this book is available from the British Library

Library of Congress cataloguing in publication data
McAuley, Mary.
    Russia's politics of uncertainty / Mary McAuley.
        p.   cm.
    Includes bibliographical references (p. 000) and index.
    ISBN 0 521 47452 3 hbk   ISBN 0 521 47976 2 pbk
    1. Russia (Federation) – Politics and government – 1991– –Public
opinion.   2. Public opinion – Russia (Federation).   3. Russia
(Federation) – Social conditions – 1991–.   4. Post-communism – Russia
(Federation).   I. Title.
JN6690.M38   1997
320.947′09′049–dc21   96-45554 CIP

ISBN 0 521 47452 3 hardback
ISBN 0 521 47976 2 paperback

To Vadim Volkov, his colleagues, and students
at the European University, St Petersburg

Contents

Acknowledgements

Studying Soviet politics used to mean long hours in libraries reading the press and analysing official data. Research visits meant staying in hotels or student hostels in a few major cities, carefully controlled meetings with academics, and, if one was lucky and the time was right, using archives or observing official Soviet practices. Yes, one went mushroom picking or skiing with close friends, but there was no way a western academic could study the subterranean politics of those years at first hand. Pages were written about party secretaries but no one could conceive of interviewing them in their faraway fiefdoms or, even more unbelievable, of their participating in open political meetings and discussions. By 1990 all that became possible. The politics were changing, systems of control were unravelling, and no one knew what the rules were or what the future held. A politics emerged, open to analysis by whatever means one chose to use.

My first and greatest debt is to those who made this possible. Some of them feature in this book, but I wish to acknowledge all whose actions prised open a closed society and allowed an open politics, however blemished, to emerge. Citizens regained their rights and academics acquired extraordinary opportunities. I cannot thank by name all those who helped me to take advantage of those opportunities. I owe a debt I can never repay to colleagues and friends, both old and new, in St Petersburg, my home while I worked on this book. The Institute of Sociology of the Russian Academy of Sciences in St Petersburg, under its director Boris M. Firsov, and in particular its Sector on Social Movements, headed by Vladimir Kostiushev, was the base from which I ventured far afield and to which I returned to think, to learn, and to discuss my findings. My thanks to all the sector's members and associates: Elena Alekseeva, Aleksandr Duka, Vladimir Gol'braikh, Leonid Kesel'man, Nikolai Kornev, Boris Maksimov, the late Sergei Rozet, Anna Temkina, Olga Tsepilova, Viktor Voronkov, and Elena Zdravomyslova. I owe a special debt to two among them: Andrei Alekseev, archivist and friend, who not only guided me to sources in the archive and first introduced to me to Krasnodar krai, but whose wise counsel was a constant in an ever-changing environment; and

Vladimir Gel´man, whose unrivalled knowledge of political developments is matched by his ability to explain and analyse them cogently. Singling out those among the political activists, parliamentary and soviet deputies, members of the administration, academics, journalists, ex-party secretaries, enterprise directors, and social activists who gave me their time and shared their expertise is never satisfactory but, in St Petersburg, Feliks Yakubson and the members of the F-seminar, Leonid Romankov, Oksana Dmitrieva, and those who helped with the elite and the interview project contributed in important ways to my understanding of developments. Galina Lebedeva and El´mar Sokolov provided the kind of support that accompanies thirty years of friendship.

Working and living in the regions would have been impossible without the unstinting help and hospitality of very many people. Again I cannot thank them all. My gratitude to Oksana and Elena Oracheva, and Oleg Podvintsev in Perm; to Inessa, Gennadii, and Liuda Tarusin in Tomsk; and to M. Zakiev and Talgat Bareev in Kazan. I would never have explored Sakha-Yakutia without Vilen Ochakovskii as guide and companion. I owe thanks for hospitality to Aleksandr and Alla Anikeev, to Natasha and Oleg Prosapov, and in Irkutsk to Gennadii and Tania Khoroshikh. In Krasnodar and the Adygei republic my debt is to Oleg and Nina Khuazhev, and to A. Khagurov. I am grateful to the help given me everywhere by the librarians: at the Academy of Sciences library and the newspaper collection of the public library in St Petersburg, at the regional public libraries in Kazan and Krasnodar, the library of the cultural centre in Perm, the university library in Tomsk, the town library in Mirny, and at the archive of the Institute of Humanities and Political Research, Moscow. All roads lead back to Moscow. For me that meant departing and returning, often at short notice, to my second home in Russia, at Valentin and Marina Peschanskii's apartment.

If all the above helped realize the project, the British Academy provided the financial support. I owe a special debt to the Academy, not only for the award of a research Readership which enabled me to spend 1992–4 living and working in Russia, but also for earlier funding which allowed me to begin the research in 1990. My sincere gratitude to the Academy for its support throughout my career, which has been important not only financially but also psychologically. I am also particularly grateful to the Nuffield Foundation, whose small grants programme, with a minimum of fuss, made possible both research assistance and travel within Russia.

My colleagues in Oxford put up with the inconvenience of my absence with their customary good grace, and subjected my ideas to their usual criticism when I returned. I am particularly grateful to Rachel Walker, Eugene Huskey, and Michael Urban for reading the manuscript and drawing my attention to errors and weaknesses. Needless to say any errors that remain are my responsibility. I am well aware that this could be a better book had I the time to read and absorb recent contributions to post-Soviet politics by western colleagues; at times I fear I may only be repeating what others have already said better. But the pressures of a new job, in Moscow, have meant choosing between putting an exploratory analysis before the reader or leaving it somewhere in a drawer. I am grateful to Michael Holdsworth of Cambridge University Press for his encouragement throughout.

All interviews cited in the notes were conducted by the author unless otherwise specified; in some cases I do not spell out the name or names of interviewees for protection of their privacy. I use a modified Library of Congress transliteration system: ia and iu but not ie; I use Ya, rather than Ia, at the beginning of names, and an -ia rather than an -iia ending, e.g. Yakutia; soft and hard signs are denoted by ´ and ´´ respectively; they are omitted from the text when they appear at the ends of words. Publishers' names have been omitted for books published in Russia and the former Soviet Union; they are not important for the locating of a book. Part of chapters 6, 7, and 8 appeared in two earlier articles 'Politics , Economics, and Elite Realignment: A Regional Perspective' in *Soviet Economy*, 8 (1992), pp. 46–88; and 'The Politics of City Government: Leningrad/St Petersburg 1990–1992', in T. Friedgut and J. Hahn (eds.), *Local Power and Post-Soviet Politics* (New York: M. E. Sharpe, 1994), pp. 15–42. They appear here with acknowledgement.

My debt to the members of my family for their forbearance with an errant wife and mother, and for their welcome when I return from my travels, needs no stating. But on this occasion I would like to express my particular gratitude to my mother-in-law who, well over ninety, is the only member of the family who shows the slightest inclination to read any of the books I write and always wants to hear about Russia.

Glossary

All-Union or Union	the adjective describing the USSR
ASSR	Autonomous Soviet Socialist Republic
CPSU	Communist Party of the Soviet Union
DemRossia	the political movement Democratic Russia
DPR	Democratic Party of Russia (leader: Travkin)
Gazprom	the gas industry
GKChP	the 'putsch' committee in August 1991
gorkom	Communist Party city or town committee
Gossnab	State Supply Administration
gubernii	regional administrations under tsarism
edinonachalie	one-man management
ITAR-TASS	government press agency
Ittifak	Tatar nationalist party
KKV	Kuban Cossack Unit (leader: Nagai)
Komsomol	Communist Party youth organization
KPRF	Communist Party of the RF (leader: Ziuganov)
krai	region with an external border
kraikom	Communist Party krai committee
LDP	Liberal Democratic Party (leader: Zhirinovskii)
nomenklatura	personnel appointed by the Communist Party (CPSU)
obkom	Communist Party regional committee
oblast	region
OFT	United Workers' Front
orgnabor	the system of labour recruitment
PRES	Party of Unity and Accord (leader: Shakhrai)
propiska	residence permit
raikom	Communist Party district committee
RDDR	Russian Movement for Democratic Reform (leaders: Popov, Sobchak)
RF	Russian Federation (from January 1992)

RSFSR	Russian Socialist Federal Soviet Republic (until January 1992)
TOTs (VTOTs from 1990)	Tatar Social Centre (United Tatar Social Centre)
trudiashchiesia	labouring masses
VKV	All-Kuban Cossack Unit (leader: Gromov)
vnebiudzhetnyi fond	extra-budget fund
VR	electoral bloc, Russia's Choice (leader: Gaidar)
Yabloko	electoral bloc, then party (leader: Yavlinskii)

Abbreviations

Chelny izv.	*Chelny izvestiia*
Gorod. gaz.	*Gorodskaia gazeta*
Izv.	*Izvestiia*
Izv. Tat.	*Izvestiia Tatarstana*
Kaz. tel.	*Kazanskii telegraf*
Kaz. ved.	*Kazanskie vedomosti*
Kaz. vesti	*Kazach´i vesti*
Komsom. Kub.	*Komsomolets Kubani*
Komsom. pravda	*Komsomol´skaia pravda*
Kr. znamia	*Krasnoe znamia*
Kras. izv.	*Krasnodarskie izvestiia*
Kub. kaz. ved.	*Kubanskie kazach´i vedomosti*
Kub. kur´er	*Kubanskii kur´er*
Kub. nov.	*Kubanskie novosti*
Len. pravda	*Leningradskaia pravda*
Mirnyi rab.	*Mirnyi rabochii*
Mol. Tat.	*Molodezh´ Tatarstan*
Mosk. nov.	*Moskovskie novosti*
Nar. trib.	*Narodnaia tribuna*
Nev. kur´er	*Nevskii kur´er*
Nev. vremia	*Nevskoe vremia*
Nezav.	*Nezavisimaia gazeta*
Nov. gaz.	*Novaia gazeta*
Nov. vremia	*Novoe vremia*
Perm. nov.	*Permskie novosti*
Pol. monit.	*Politicheskii monitoring*
Polis.	*Politicheskie issledovaniia*
Res. Sakha	*Respublika Sakha*
Ross. gaz.	*Rossiiskaia gazeta*
Ross. vesti	*Rossiiskie vesti*
Sots. Yak.	*Sotsialisticheskaia Yakutiia*
Sov. Adygeia	*Sovetskaia Adygeia*

Sov. Kub.	*Sovetskaia Kuban*
Sov. Ross.	*Sovetskaia Rossiia*
St Pbg ved.	*St. Peterburgskie vedomosti*
Svob. mysl´	*Svobodnaia mysl´*
Tom. trib.	*Tomskaia tribuna*
Tom. vestnik	*Tomskii vestnik*
Vech. Kaz.	*Vechernyi Kazan*
Vech. Perm´	*Vechernyi Perm´*
Vech. Pbg	*Vechernyi Peterburg*
Vol. Kub.	*Vol´naia Kuban*
Vop. fil.	*Voprosy filosofii*
Yak.	*Yakutiia*
Yak. ved.	*Yakutskie vedomosti*

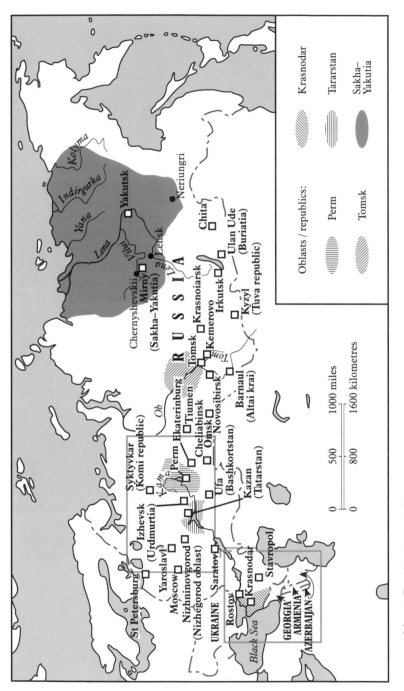

Map 1: Russia, 1991–1994

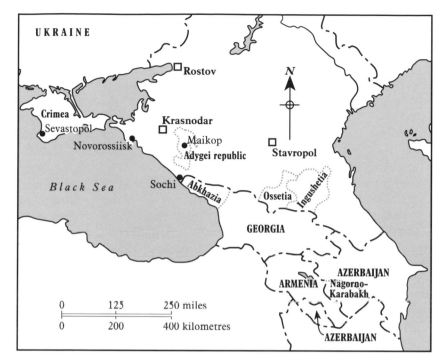

Map 2: Krasnodar krai, 1991–1994

Map 3: Perm oblast and Tatarstan, 1991–1994

Introduction: the politics of uncertainty

As I observed developments in Russia in the early 1990s I began to feel that I was being offered a snapshot introduction to politics. Understanding what was happening was extraordinarily difficult, but I was learning a great deal about the politics of other countries. The living seemed to be recreating or reenacting the politics of their own and other societies, both past and present. The poorly educated young Tatar nationalist, in his black leather jacket, sitting in the unheated committee room he and his followers had wrested from the educated, more moderate Tatar leadership, suddenly made real one type of civil-war Bolshevik. As Diakonov, the big, self-confident construction engineer from Krasnodar, who took on the apparatus in 1991 and lost, recounted his version of events, I began to understand the battles of the Khrushchev period in a new way. The diamond-town of Mirny, in the Far North, made real the company towns of Alaska or South Africa. Election campaigns brought *The Pickwick Papers* or Japan to mind. Clan-politics suggested comparisons with Southern Italy; Mayor Daleys from Chicago ruled provincial cities. And with the storming of the White House in October 1993 CNN treated millions of viewers to a siege of a medieval castle.

The reason why developments in Russia presented themselves in this way gradually became clear. With the breakdown of an existing order – state, empire – the stakes are high, the struggle begins to retain or claim control over valuable resources, to redistribute power and decision-making. So much is common across time and space. The citizens find themselves facing a series of basic issues. The resolving of these lies at the heart of any political community. There is the identification of the community: who *are* its citizens? There is the question of who is to make authoritative decisions and of their implementation. This involves deciding how conflicts are to be resolved and order ensured. There is the question of how interests are defined, and can be defended. These provide an extremely contentious set of issues, and there are no ready-made answers to them. In established political regimes they may well undergo continual

1

renegotiation at the edges, but with the collapse of communist party rule and the dissolution of the USSR they appeared *ab ovo*.

How do people – rulers and ruled – react when long-established rules of the game governing political behaviour are radically altered? Most of the time political change occurs gradually. There are frameworks which define power and authority, mechanisms which uphold them, rules which govern behaviour. People know these; they may attempt to change them – indeed, we can say that politics involves the continual renegotiation of the rules – but political life has an order, a predictability about it. Sometimes the rules are rudely changed, as under a coup d'état. With a revolution the whole framework is demolished. In this, the most extreme case of all, the existing distribution of political, economic, and social power within a society changes dramatically. Substantial sections of society are involved, existing hierarchies are overturned, the privileged displaced, and a new social and economic order emerges. Russia in 1917 witnessed such a revolution. Tsarist rule went, and then the Provisional Government. The army fell apart and was reconstructed as a White and a Red. Factory workers in key cities took over their factories, peasants dispossessed land-lords. A civil war ensued. Rough class rule drove the privileged classes into exile, prison, or subordinate status. The new rulers, the Bolsheviks, introduced state ownership of property, new patterns of distribution, and one-party rule, and new social hierarchies emerged.

The ending of communist party rule in Russia saw no such revolution.[1] On this occasion, in August 1991, a last-ditch attempt by members of the Soviet government to preserve communist party rule and the Soviet Union failed. In some of the outlying republics, both 1990 and 1991 had seen violent clashes between troops and civilians or between different ethnic groups, but the attempted putsch of August 1991 cost only three lives on the streets of Moscow. Large demonstrations had become part of the political landscape in a few of Russia's key cities but, with the exception of the miners, there were no organized challenges to the government or employers. Some of the press had broken free of party control, and in a

---

[1] M. McFaul, in 'Russian Centrism and Revolutionary Transitions', *Post-Soviet Affairs*, 9 (1993), pp. 196–222, and at the introduction to his 'State Power, Institutional Change, and the Politics of Privatization in Russia', *World Politics*, 47 (1995), pp. 210–43, raises the question of whether today's events qualify as revolutionary, and suggests that they do. I would argue that the way communist party rule ended was sufficiently different from the revolutions that have occurred since the French – which introduced the political phe-nomenon of revolution – that we should put it in a separate category. I suspect the ending of communist party rule marks the end of an era in which the distribution of power and authority in a society can be changed by revolution; it announces the coming of a 'post-revolutionary world', in which change will be of a different kind and for which we shall need to develop new categories of analysis.

few cities elected soviets with democratic majorities were competing for control of decision-making, but the August events caught the population and the new political activists largely by surprise.

The unforeseen consequence was the collapse, with indecent speed, of the most powerful and coercive system of rule the world has known and the break-up of the last of the great modern empires. The Communist Party was banned and its property seized. Within a matter of months the fifteen republics of the Union had dissolved their ties and gained international recognition as independent sovereign states. The existence of elected republican governments, only too willing to take over the reins of power, allowed for a smooth transfer. In Russia, where Boris Yeltsin, the popularly elected president, had led the opposition to the putschists from within the parliament building, there existed an unchallenged political leader and ready-made institutions of state. The Russian government welcomed the statements of independence by the Baltic republics and, once it became clear that Ukraine also was going to declare its independence, moved to dissolve the Soviet Union. The Union ministries and agencies, based in Moscow, came under Russian jurisdiction and the contentious issues of the allocation of federal property, responsibility for USSR debts, and, most sensitive of all, of control over nuclear weapons and the armed forces formed part of a new political agenda. On 31 December 1991 the red flag that had flown, night and day, in a man-made breeze over the Kremlin was hauled down, and the red, white, and blue of the Russian Federation was raised in its place.

This was an unusual situation in which state institutions, previously under the control of a ruling party, could begin to function as the real loci of power and authority. Their incumbents or sometimes new appointees took over the institutions of the state with a minimum of violence. Much could continue as before, at least in the short run. In the autumn of 1991 there was nothing in the shops, but there was expectancy in the air. In the towns a feeling of liberation was tinged with disbelief that communist party rule could have shrivelled away so fast. The KGB faded into the background. Fear disappeared. Access to state offices became easy, officials anxious not to offend. Coercion and repression, both hallmarks of the Soviet order, evaporated. A closed society burst open. The range of published opinion, including western ideas, and television coverage became wide. There were no parades to mark 7 November; the banners, placards, and red bunting had been bundled away. Somehow the state, and its trappings, seemed to have disappeared. Yet, at the same time, everyday life continued much as before: institutions, enterprises, local authorities, and the media continued to be financed from the state budget; the huge state infrastructure that supported all aspects of existence remained in place. Work relations within factories, universities, trade and services, and the army did not alter; nothing changed on the farms. Those who had managed all these institutions remained in command. They were no longer bound by instructions from higher party authorities – whether on personnel appointments or on policy – but, with the exception of those running the media, they continued to operate in the accustomed way. Factory workers did not dismiss their directors, university students their rectors, nor did peasants dissolve the collective farms.

Yet, if the Communist Party had left the scene with barely a whimper, its going could not but herald far-reaching change. In 1991 the words that were ringing in the capitals of Central Europe and the former republics of the Soviet Union were those of sovereignty, independence, democracy, and market reforms. In Moscow the Yeltsin leadership spoke of the future of the Russian Federation as a sovereign state, reincorporated into the world economy on a market basis, part of the world of democratic states. The translation of these words into practice would mean radical change for Russia. Its identity as a state would need to be clarified. The Russian Federation, the huge republic that stretched from the Finnish gulf to Vladivostok, had been the heartland of the Soviet Union. It now gained its independence and lost an empire. What was it that would hold the Federation together, provide a basis for citizenship? The USSR and one-party rule, bound up together and perceived as part of the natural order of things, had disappeared (equivalent in American terms to the disappearance of the office of the presidency, the flag, the Constitution, together with California, Texas, and New Mexico; or in Britain to the loss of the Monarchy, the Houses of Parliament, Scotland, Wales, and Northern Ireland), and with them went the country's past.

If communist party rule had provided an answer to the question 'how should society's rulers be chosen?' as a self-recruiting, hierarchical, political organization, the new rulers offered another: electoral democracy. The old order had been based upon centralized, unitary political leadership of state institutions and of the legal system, and a federation in name but not in reality. The new rulers advocated the separation of powers, an independent legal system, and national self-determination. Communist leaderships had seen censorship, repression of any opposition, and tight controls on travel to be essential for guiding and controlling social developments; the new leaders advocated freedom of speech and the press, and open borders. Communist party rule had introduced state ownership of key resources, and state management of all collective activ-

ities; the new democrats were arguing for the introduction of private ownership, market mechanisms, the encouragement of private initiative, and
reducing state involvement in society. The implementation of measures
such as these would necessarily transform the relationship between state
and society, the social structure, and social hierarchies as well as political
regime. But, argued its advocates, the process should be a peaceful one,
marked by neither violence nor bloodshed, a democratic process involving the people.

For rulers and ruled the situation was entirely novel. Those in the
government now had real responsibility for policy. The new rulers,
whether at the centre or in the regions, faced a future in which they would
be accountable for their actions, through elections. The process, begun in
1989, had empowered the people. They were free to act, to make
demands, to hold their representatives accountable. This was as strange
for them as it was for the rulers. In this situation how did rulers and ruled
conduct themselves? How do people react when key features of their
environment disappear, when the ground on which they tread becomes
uncertain? This was the question I found myself asking, and which I
attempt to answer in this book.

How though to approach it? If for the participants 'these times are times
of chaos; opinions are a scramble; parties are a jumble; the language of
new ideas has not been created . . . the world has jumbled its catalogue'
(Lamartine),[2] scholars should expect to feel disoriented. Their intellectual baggage may be as little appropriate to the task in hand as some of the
political ideas of the participants. 'When history "suddenly accelerates"',
Hirschman has argued, it has more than its share of 'highly improbable
events'.[3] It does not lend itself easily to analysis through the prism of a
social science that is interested in prediction. Periods of social and

---

[2] Taken from C. Geertz, *The Interpretation of Cultures: Selected Essays* (New York: Basic
Books, 1973), p. 221.

[3] A. Hirschman, 'The Search for Paradigms as a Hindrance to Understanding', *World
Politics*, 22 (1970), pp. 339–42. He gives us a nice quote from Lenin, taken from
Althusser, on 1917: 'If the revolution has triumphed so rapidly it is exclusively because, as
a result of a historical situation of extreme originality, a number of completely distinct
currents, a number of totally heterogeneous class interests, and a number of completely
opposite social and political tendencies have become fused with remarkable coherence.'
So much for the laws of history. Writing more recently about Soviet developments,
Hirschman has made the point again: 'if the events which are the points of departure for
their [the specialists'] speculations were so hard to predict, considerable caution is surely
in order when it comes to appraising their impact': quoted and commented upon by
G. Di Palma, in 'Legitimation from the Top to Civil Society: Politico-Cultural Change in
Eastern Europe', *World Politics*, 44 (1991), p. 78.

political turmoil and even less turbulent transition periods are often chaotic, and collective action is fragmented and changeable.[4] An uncomfortable thought arises. If the ending of communist party rule signifies the beginning of (or is part of) a major shift in the way communities organize their politics – and hence of the world order – then the kinds of questions we ask at present and existing approaches to studying political change will soon begin to date.[5] Just as the theory of war and of international relations had to adjust to the fact of the First World War, and then to nuclear weapons, so major an event as the end of communist party rule will surely lead to changes in the way we think about states, political order, and society. But an academic community cannot be intellectually *prepared beforehand* for a paradigm shift. What we can do is to start asking: how might approaches to the study of politics be rethought in the light of the collapse of the USSR and subsequent developments? Recognizing that this takes time, and that our understanding of the political processes of the post-communist period is still rudimentary, we need to begin by experimenting imaginatively with different kinds of comparative frame-

---

[4] M. Olson, 'The Logic of Collective Action in Soviet-Type Societies', *Journal of Soviet Nationalities*, 1 (1990), p. 8, suggests that because demand curves, *ceteris paribus*, everywhere slope downwards, just as water always runs downhill, behaviour in a Soviet-type society will follow certain common rules of collective action. The difference, however, is that *ceteris* are so patently *non paribus* at times of such dramatic and rapid change, and human behaviour is not like water; different rules may well be operating. A. Przeworski, 'Some Problems in the Study of the Transition to Democracy', in G. O'Donnell and P. Schmitter (eds.), *Transitions from Authoritarian Rule*, 3 vols. (Baltimore: Johns Hopkins University Press, 1986), vol. I, p. 55, stresses the difficulty of predicting actions 'when expectations of success shift rapidly', and suggests we should think of 'uncertainty' as a key characteristic of democracy, but I am claiming much more than this for Russia in the 1990s. Whether such periods, marked by instability, can be studied by methods devised for looking at stable systems has not been ignored (see S. Mainwaring, 'Transitions to Democracy and Democratic Consolidation: Theoretical and Comparative Issues', in Mainwaring, G. O'Donnell, and J. S. Valenzuela (eds.), *Issues in Democratic Consolidation: The New South American Democracies in Comparative Perspective* (Notre Dame, Ind.: University of Notre Dame Press, 1992), pp. 329–31), but there remains the further issue of the kinds of questions we should be asking of politics at times such as these.

[5] Take the debate over the role played by economic factors or by culture in influencing institutional development, or the discussion over institutional choices and strategic decisions in promoting or maintaining a democratic order. I have in mind the presidential versus parliamentarianism debate (see below, p. 233, n. 3, or contributions to G. Marks and L. Diamond (eds.), *Re-examining Democracy* (London: Sage, 1992) with particular reference to that by P. Schmitter, 'Interest Systems and the Consolidation of Democracies', pp. 156–76, as well as the classic by D. North, *Institutions, Institutional Change, and Economic Performance* (Cambridge University Press, 1990), and the more recent work by R. Putnam, *Making Democracy Work* (Princeton University Press, 1993)). Only long-term analysis will be able to make a serious contribution to the debates but, by the time we have the answers, will the questions that prompted them any longer seem interesting ones?

works, by posing questions that will prompt the exploration of unfamiliar themes, and encourage us to be catholic in the collection of different kinds of data.[6]

These, however, are pleas to the profession, not a claim about this book. In it I simply take one set of actors and look at the way they reacted in this new environment of uncertainty. I could have taken any one of a number of sets: the new government, the military, the procuracy, the cultural intelligentsia, or the press. The ones I have chosen, for several reasons, are the rulers in a small number of regions and republics. Why the choice of rulers rather than ruled? Although 'the people' will appear as political actors, in these years the new rulers held centre stage. There are periods of politics when the centre of action seems to lie in society, others when it shifts to the political elite; if pushed to characterize the years 1991–4 in Russia, I would call them a time of elite accommodation. It was a period of awakening to political and independent activity and, perhaps not surprisingly, it was those with resources who were the most active. Why focus on the regions? Because this allows us, first, to move away from Moscow and out into the vast hinterland, with its sharply contrasting regions, which for the great majority of the population is Russia, and about which little is known. Secondly, it allows us to compare and to try to explain different reactions to a similar set of circumstances, and

---

[6] It is noticeable that those working on post-communist developments have taken their inspiration primarily from the political science literature (on the USA, and on Western Europe), or have turned to the now-mainstream transition literature, but have rarely looked to Africa, Asia, or Japan. Rather differently, the new opportunities for data collection have resulted in a boost to survey analysis, supported by the assumption that our task is to bring the study of these societies into 'mainstream political science'. Sovietologists used to reflect mainstream concerns with about a ten-year lag (see the literature on interest groups, political culture, and comparative policy-making). Are post-communist studies repeating the pattern? I am not here advocating an area-studies approach versus a discipline position. See the debate between S. Meiklejohn Terry, 'Thinking About Post-Communist Transitions: How Different Are They?', *Slavic Review*, 52 (1993), pp. 333–7; P. Schmitter with T. Karl, 'The Conceptual Travels of Transitologists and Consolidologists: How Far to the East Should They Attempt to Go?', *Slavic Review*, 53 (1994), pp. 172–87; and V. Bunce, 'Should Transitologists Be Grounded?', *Slavic Review*, 54 (1995), pp. 111–27. I am on the side of Bunce here. I would argue that we should be thinking of our task as *changing the mainstream, creating a new intellectual agenda*, not simply adopting mainstream concerns. An example: the study of values and the influence of culture on political change (and vice versa) is still an untapped area, partly because of the way political science has developed (with an emphasis on quantitative measurement and hence the claim that only survey data 'counts' as evidence of values); partly because, after a flurry of interest in political culture, scholars turned away from the task of analysing the cultural dimension of politics to aspects which interested them more. It remains probably the most interesting, and difficult, question on today's agenda (see pp. 16–17 for a brief further discussion of this point).

hence to contribute to the literature on how political change occurs. In this sense it is a comparative study as well as a country study.[7]

In August 1991 the regional and republican authorities found themselves facing a new set of opportunities and constraints. As regards their relationship with the federal centre, all began from very much the same starting position: subordinates in a hierarchical chain with very little control over resources or decision-making. The federal centre had, however, passed into the hands of a new Russian government, a self-proclaimed democratic government bent on economic and political reform. The regional elites now had a real opportunity to renegotiate their relationship with Moscow, and to oversee the redistribution of economic resources. Secondly, the office-holders found themselves subject to new institutional rules, based on a separation of powers. They became electorally accountable, and needed to establish a new basis for their legitimacy in the eyes of the population. Legislation on the freedom of the press now appeared. None of this had featured in the previous political system, the only one of which they had experience, and which had its own conventions of behaviour. Hence, as regards the opportunities they faced, the institutional arrangements, and past political practice, all were operating in the same environment.

However, those who found themselves in charge in the regions did not share a similar set of ideas on how the new political order should operate and what kind of policies they should pursue. The post-August environment was peopled with conservatives, centrists, and reformers. Regional authorities differed in their political complexion, as did their populations. The resources at their disposal, whether raw materials or strategic location, and hence their bargaining position, varied too. Now choices had to be made. Our regions include the two national republics of Sakha-Yakutia and Tatarstan, the one a huge territory in the Far North, the other a landlocked Volga region in the heart of Russia. We shall look first at these, at the very different strategies employed by their elites to redraw the repub-

---

[7] I shall not address the questions raised in the new literature on elites during transition (see, e.g., J. Higley and R. Gunther (eds.), *Elites and Democratic Consolidation in Latin America and Southern Europe* (Cambridge University Press, 1992)), because I am dealing with the initial reactions of regional rulers to a new government. If I were to place the regional elites of Russia in a broader comparative context, I would start by looking to Africa and the break-up of the great empires of the past. See the article by J. Forrest, 'Asynchronic Comparisons: Weak States in Post-Colonial Africa and Mediaeval Europe', in M. Dogan and A. Kazancigil (eds.), *Comparing Nations: Concepts, Strategies, Substance* (Oxford and Cambridge, Mass.: Blackwell, 1994), pp. 260–96, which prompts several points of comparison with developments in the countries of the former Soviet Union.

lic's relationship with Moscow, and then at their relationship with their populations. From there we move to the border region of Krasnodar krai, down in the south of Russia, to observe the way in which a conservative elite came to terms with a new democratic regime in Moscow, and its reaction to open borders. We then turn eastwards to the Urals and to west Siberia to contrast the way two very different sets of rulers – the centrist, cautious elite in Perm and their divided counterparts in Tomsk – reacted to the new situation. Finally we turn back to St Petersburg, source of many of the new ideas, the city in which the democrats were already in power when Russia gained its independence.

I am firstly interested in the strategies the rulers chose in negotiating with the centre, and in negotiating new systems of regional government among themselves and new electoral relationships with their populations. I ask what governed their choice of strategies: was it their political complexions, the ability to command resources, inherited political conventions, or pressure from below? The participants were struggling to grapple with basic issues. My task is to illuminate the way the issues presented themselves and were fought over. I want to understand why particular groups of people acted as they did, and to see what light this sheds on the way people construct or reconstruct relations of power at a time of change. Studying politics in Russia during those years was like watching a play in the making. At times of stability the tracks are worn, roles so formalized they become taken for granted. The members of the British Parliament play their parts without thinking about them; institutions live on. But at a time of crisis and change, the actors are struggling to write a script. Like children making up a play, the script is often impromptu; fairy stories feature along with scraps of television dialogue, and words borrowed from schoolteachers. An old hat becomes a crown; we see hierarchy, quarrelling, appeals to fairness, passionate involvement, and storming off the stage. My concern is with the scripts as they emerge, with the rehearsals, and the ongoing performances for what we can learn of politics and Russia's neo-politics from them. I am as interested in the intentions, the failures, the false starts as in anything else: the script in the making.[8]

I also want to try to explain outcomes. By 1994 the balance-sheet, for

---

[8] C. Geertz, *Local Knowledge: Further Essays in Interpretative Anthropology* (New York: Basic Books, 1983), p. 23, has suggested turning our attention to 'following a rule, constructing a representation, expressing an attitude', rather than 'isolating a cause, determining a variable, measuring a force, or defining a function'. I suggest that we shall not be able to explain political behaviour unless we begin by doing the former, but we then want to identify which factors, or combination of factors, are responsible for outcomes.

Russia as a whole as well as in individual regions, was one nobody had foreseen. In the world of international diplomacy the Russian Federation existed as a sovereign state, and one in which the federal authorities could, with impunity, send in the army to regain control over a small and wayward republic, Chechnya. But the federal government could not monitor the country's borders, nor secure implementation of its rulings throughout the vast territory. Until December 1994, when the army went into action in Chechnya, relations within the Federation were remarkably peaceful. This had, however, been achieved by the federal authorities' simply not taking action against those republics within the Federation, Chechnya and Tatarstan, which had refused to sign a new Federal Treaty. The war with Chechnya sent out a message to other republican leaderships, but it did nothing to resolve the question of federal–republic–regional relations.

The presidency and the government, flanked by the state apparatus, had emerged as the dominant political institutions, but only after armed confrontation with the Parliament in the autumn of 1993. The representative bodies, whether the Duma and Council of the Federation at central level, or the soviets and assemblies at republican and regional level, had lost ground since 1991. The attempts to create a new executive–legislative arrangement had all too often led to stalemate, conflict, and high-handed intervention by the executive. Nor could federal or regional politicians pride themselves on having gained the confidence of the electorate. Barely 50 per cent of the population turned out to vote in the federal elections and for the new constitution in December 1993, and even fewer in the subsequent regional elections. Political parties were failing to put down roots.

The authorities seemed unable to halt the rise in organized crime and the wave of lawlessness, crime, and violence that was sweeping the country. The police, procuracy, and courts were riddled with corruption, and lacked the means with which to tackle the breakdown in law and order. The economy had been opened to the world economy and the ruble had lost steadily against the dollar as domestic production continued to decline and inflation rose. By the end of 1994 GDP was only two-thirds that of 1991. The shops in the major cities, now privatized, were stocked but largely with foreign goods. The cities were full of foreign cars. The 'new Russians', a thin stratum of the wealthy, had appeared, travelling the world as part of a consumer elite. For much of the population, however, and especially in the countryside and small towns, the only change was a worsening in their standard of living as wages and pensions failed to keep pace with prices. Privatization of trade and services in the towns was real enough; privatization of industrial enterprises, while realized on paper, had to a large extent meant the acquiring of assets by the existing directors or government institutions, reorganized as corporations. Banks, insurance companies, and holding companies had sprouted up in their dozens – the financial sector and, oddly enough, the civil service showed the fastest rise in employment. Despite the cutting back on health, education, and the privatization drive, the state sector continued to grow. Welfare, pensions, salaries, subsidies to industry and agriculture (where almost no privatization had taken place), funding of education and of the press – all still came within the state budget. A strange new quango-land[9] of corporations and agencies linking state and society had emerged.

The relationship between rulers and ruled had clearly changed. If earlier an unaccountable elite ruled a mute society, now a partially accountable elite ruled a noisy one. Both authority and repression had gone, to be replaced by freedom and lawlessness. Society had given birth to new social and political institutions and associations: organized criminal associations, business and industrial lobbies, issue-oriented groups, religious and ethnic associations, and tiny political groups, while some of the original 'state' associations (the unions, veterans, youth) still survived, but in new forms. Yet the citizens seemed to have failed to make the rulers accountable to them in any meaningful way or the rulers to establish their authority.

I shall not attempt to offer a comprehensive explanation for this very complex set of developments. But I shall address three issues: the reassertion of the executive, the failure of the representative assemblies to hold their ground, and the inability of political movements or parties to sustain themselves or to attract a following. Regardless of the different starting points of our regions, in these respects by 1994 all had evolved in the same way. The situation was not identical in each, and this allows us to try to identify those factors that were responsible for a similar pattern of development, and those that accounted for the differences. Was it, for example, the institutional arrangements themselves that were at fault, or the strength of political conventions? Was it the lack of political ideas, or the consequences of policy choices? What influences behaviour at a time of stress and the renegotiation of rights? We shall get no definitive answers from a study of politics in six regions over a short time period. We can, however, identify certain common patterns of behaviour and then suggest

---

[9] The term 'quango' or 'quasi-non-governmental organization' was coined in the late 1960s to refer to a new type of private/governmental institution that had appeared in Britain.

which factors played a role in their appearance.[10] And, furthermore, an analysis of developments in the regions helps shed light on similar processes occurring at the federal level.

To understand the negotiations that took place between those who in August 1991 found themselves to be rulers in the regions, their publics, and the federal authorities in Moscow, we need to set our players within a context. This was Russia, situated in the world of the end of the twentieth century. Rulers and ruled met each other carrying the baggage of the past, shopping baskets of home-grown produce, and brief-cases of imported goods. They inherited certain state institutions, and long-practised conventions of political behaviour. Some held traditional positions of authority, others new; some controlled valuable resources, others now had a right to them. They did not sit down around a table in a western conference centre with blank pads of paper and finely sharpened pencils in front of them. On the contrary, they met in a familiar Soviet conference room with its heavy furniture, and on the table was a new agenda. Different actors held very different ideas as to how the basic issues should be resolved. Some were long-time party officials or soviet administrators, others perestroika activists or free-thinking intellectuals. The global environment of the late twentieth century, with its economic, technological, and cultural features was pushing at the door. This was the context within which they would negotiate for the next three years. I begin with the world they were leaving behind – the Soviet world – then look at the ideas that had come to the fore as the Soviet Union and party rule crumbled.

[10] During 1992–3 I explored the feasibility (and sense) of attempting a regional classification of political regimes for all the regions of the Russian Federation and a model which could explain it; initially I had hopes that a combination of variables including the resource base, strategic position, ethnicity, and party conservatism might work, but it became clear that there were far too many wild cards to make this kind of approach meaningful at that point in time. For an early attempt at a regional political classification, see N. Petrov, et al., 'Sotsial'no-politicheskii monitoring Rossii', in *Politika i mysl'*, 1 (1992), pp. 10–41; and for an economic classification, E. Yasin, et al., 'Regionalizm: zlo ili blago', *Rossiia*, 16 December 1992, p. 14.

1   The negotiating table

The political inheritance

Although in the USSR, formally, the people were sovereign, the right to rule was claimed by the Communist Party, the CPSU, in whose hands power lay. Its apparatus formed the nucleus of, and administered, a system of appointments (the nomenklatura) to all leading positions throughout society. Party officials either followed careers within the apparatus itself or moved in and out of the apparatus to posts in government administration, industry, culture, and education. Others, who had never worked in the party apparatus but had risen to factory directorships or ministerial posts, or who had become rectors of institutes, owed their appointments to party secretaries and were part of the nomenklatura circle. The soviets, the elected assemblies, played a largely decorative role; their executive committees, staffed in the main by full-time officials, were responsible for administration but policy decisions were taken by the party. Its apparatus controlled communications, allowing no criticism of communist party rule, and employed the KGB to limit and curb any dissident behaviour. Its control over appointments, communications, and coercion enabled it to act as policy-maker or to intervene where it wished, to amass huge resources and award itself and others within the ruling elite privileges of all kinds.

Formally the USSR was a federation of fifteen soviet socialist republics, among which the Russian republic was by far the largest. These, the Union republics, outranked a second tier of autonomous republics, each of which existed within a Union republic as the administrative unit in those parts of the country where a minority nationality happened to be concentrated – for example, the Tatar ASSR in the Russian republic, or the Abkhazian ASSR in the Georgian republic. In the Russian republic the most common administrative sub-unit was, however, a region, based simply on territory. All were orchestrated and held together by the apparatus of the CPSU, whose central leadership controlled the fourteen republican party organizations and those of the regions and autonomous republics of the Russian republic. Unlike the other republics Russia had no separate party organization; its provincial party secretaries reported directly to the Central Committee of the CPSU.[1]

The Central Committee and the All-Union ministries – henceforth referred to as the Union authorities – disposed of the territory's resources as their officials thought appropriate, both through central agencies and through rulers appointed from and loyal to Moscow. The armed forces and an array of law-and-order institutions – the KGB, the Ministry of Internal Affairs, and the procuracy – funded without difficulty by a state that could extract huge resources from society, accepted unquestioningly that their loyalty was to the Union. The country's resources were state-owned and -administered through central direction; welfare, culture, education, and leisure all came under party and government control. In ideological terms 'state' was privileged over 'private'. Associations and organizations were all created by and overseen by the state. Lines of control ran vertically, from the centre, downwards. The consequence was a state-structured society and a state-dependent population. It was a closed society vis-à-vis the outside world and in its communications with itself. This was the world, the only world, known to rulers and ruled.

Over time the centre's policies had the effect of producing republican and regional elites equally as interested in defending their own interests as those of the Union. The management of economic policy was partly responsible. The central authorities determined the economic profile of each region, allocated the resources, and took what they wished. The centre levied taxes, redistributed resources between regions, and fixed the size of republican and regional budgets. The wealth or poverty of a region bore little relation either to its natural resources or to levels of productivity. But while the centre thought in terms of the USSR as one unit, it administered the territory by dealing individually with each republic and region – a separate line went down, as it were, to each, which lived its own life, unrelated to that of its neighbours. Republics or regions were self-enclosed territories, their elites blind to their neighbours, their eyes ever looking up to Moscow. The road network within a region stopped at its borders. Some regional party secretaries were attracted by the idea of growing a forestry belt round their territories. Horizontal links between regions did not exist, and where goods moved between them it was by administrative order from the centre. Verticality and parcelization of activities characterized the system.

The republic or regional party leadership was responsible for its territory and its population. It had to see that the taxes were paid, the population fed, and law and order maintained. It was directly responsible for

---

[1] I deal with the situation in the Russian republic in more detail on pp. 29–30.

agriculture. The existence of huge enterprises, often part of the military-industrial complex, meant the presence of heavyweight directors whose funding came from Moscow and who took their orders from their industrial ministries. Local party and soviet officials needed to establish good relationships with the directors both to ensure the region's targets were met and because enterprises provided much of the housing and local services. By the 1980s a deal was in place between centre and localities. In return for running the regions, for ensuring that the centre received the bulk of the resources, and for maintaining the status quo, the local leaderships received a share of local profits, and of party dues, and disposed of them as they thought fit. To what extent the deals involved the mafia need not concern us here: the point is that the 'surplus' at republic and regional level was in the gift of the local authorities and – increasingly as the Brezhnev period moved on – was used as conspicuous consumption, both public and private, by the elite.

In the Union republics the political elites were beginning to emerge as forces in their own right. The way the party organized its affairs (the inclusion of key officials from different institutions in the republican Central Committee, for example) and party control of government appointments had always encouraged the formation of closely knit party–soviet local elites. One way to counteract this was by moving personnel between regions, but the Brezhnev policy of leaving people in place and, when necessary, making new appointments from within the local republican or regional party organization strengthened the tendency towards localization. In addition, a policy of affirmative action towards members of the titular nationality in the republics meant that the party and soviet, but not necessarily the industrial, elite was increasingly composed of individuals of that nationality. Their career horizons rarely extended to Moscow: for them the republic leadership was the ceiling. This was true for those both in the Union republics and in the autonomous republics within the RSFSR. In this environment the long-standing party practice of operating on the basis of personal followings – the patron with his supporters – flourished.

Although, without doubt, the central party leadership was responsible for policy and did indeed take action, as for example over the Afghan war or over dealing with dissidents, it had become increasingly slothful and corrupt under Brezhnev. It is also doubtful to what extent the political authorities were determining the direction, let alone the management, of the economy. The huge state bureaucracy, dominated by the military-industrial complex, ran the industrial sector; interlocking networks of party and state officials ran their republics and regions. The consequence of political practices and economic policies was that lines of loyalty to the centre became fainter both for party and soviet officials and for those in the federal agencies, including the procuracy and KGB. Their fortunes and careers became more subject to influence exerted by republican party bosses than by their Union superiors. The phenomenon of family circles, of links and corrupt dealings within the republican party and soviet elite, began to come out into the open from the mid-1970s on. In both Georgia and Azerbaijan, a KGB official was appointed to the first secretaryship to cope with the problem, but the occasional scandal also broke over a regional first secretary in Russia.

Although the phenomenon of localism was as marked in the Russian republic as elsewhere, there was an important difference in the way officials in its regions viewed the centre. For those in other republics the Union was run by Russians; for those in the Russian regions this distinction did not exist. Furthermore, although the Russian republic had its own government structures, centred in Moscow, they were overshadowed by the Union institutions. In some cases there were no separate Russian institutions, simply Union authorities. Thus Russia and the USSR were merged in a way that was not true of the other republics. Although, within the RSFSR, those of the smaller nationalities might identify with their national republic, for the Russians who ran the regions the USSR was their state and the Central Committee of the CPSU the legitimate ruler. They could look for promotion right to the very top and that meant to posts in Union structures. Hence any disentangling of Russia from the USSR was going to be something very different from a seemingly similar process involving the other republics.

The institutional framework and political guidelines created specific conventions of political behaviour. Those who rose through the ranks knew the rules, knew what was required to advance a career or stay in post. Although writers sometimes touched on the theme, and a few western scholars attempted to analyse the organizational culture of the communist party state, we have no substantive analysis of this less formal aspect of the Soviet political system.[2] Although the impossibility of doing

[2] Literature, throughout the Soviet period, has shed light on different aspects of official behaviour. A post-glasnost novel, *Svoi chelovek*, by G. Baklanov (published in article form in *Znamia*, 11 (1990), pp. 7–120), offers a telling description of Brezhnev officialdom. Western scholars drew attention to the patron–client relationship but few went further than this. An exception was K. Jowitt, 'Soviet Neotraditionalism: The Political Corruption of a Leninist Regime', *Soviet Studies*, 35 (1983), pp. 275–97; for the cultural legacy, see his *New World Disorder: The Leninist Extinction* (Berkeley: University of California Press, 1992), pp. 287–94. An earlier, rather different, attempt to tackle the question of administrative behaviour was M. Urban, *The Ideology of Administration: American and Soviet Cases* (Albany: State University of New York Press, 1982).

anthropological research probably contributed, the cultural dimensions of politics have not been high on the agenda of those studying political institutions or behaviour in the post-Second World War period, whatever the country. Political conventions are not quantifiable, measurable, written down on paper, and scholars have been interested in other things.[3] But if we wish to understand political behaviour, we need to be aware of conventions and attitudes which govern responses. This requires identifying the cultural conventions at work, and trying to assess the role they play in determining outcomes.[4] This narrower aspect of Soviet political culture is not a topic either western or Russian scholars are particularly interested in, and it is one that it is difficult to incorporate into existing frameworks of analysis. But, we might hypothesize, at a time when political structures are demolished and new rules introduced, the informal conventions governing behaviour will provide the only element of stability in an uncertain world. We cannot ignore them. Anyone who has observed or participated in political activities in post-communist Russia will have quickly become aware of conventions and attitudes carried over from the Soviet past. How they have been affected by the changes – the resilience or feebleness of different parts of the Soviet inheritance when faced with change – would be a topic in itself. I touch on this, but only in passing,

---

[3] In relation to communist party systems, the often lively discussion over political culture tended to get diverted either into debates over 'what is political culture' or into irresolvable disagreements over whether Soviet culture represented a continuation of traditional Russian culture or not. S. Welch, *The Concept of Political Culture* (London: Macmillan, 1993), offers a detailed analysis of this literature and its weaknesses.

[4] Although a question high on the agenda of Russian scholars is whether the cultural behaviour we observe today owes its existence to seventy years of Soviet rule or to earlier, pre-Soviet, Russian cultural patterns is interesting and important in its own right, it is not central to assessing the role played by the cultural inheritance (regardless of its origins) in influencing political behaviour in the immediate post-communist period. Intuitively we would expect seventy years of a specific and repressive type of rule to leave strong traces on behaviour, but the distinguishing of a Soviet from a pre-revolutionary influence will require historical and cross-cultural research of a new kind. Unfortunately the tendency of some Russian scholars to advance unverifiable assertions of a vaguely specified 'Russian culture' does little to take the intellectual agenda forward. The issue of verification has not engaged those who have taken up sides in the debate. As of now the arguments consist of interesting hypotheses. See, e.g., the debate 'Rossiiskaia modernizatsiia: problemy i perspektivy', *Vop. fil.*, 7 (1993), pp. 3–39; V. Bocharov, on traditional political culture, in R. Ganelin (ed.), *Natsional'naia pravaia prezhde i teper'*, 3 vols. (St Petersburg, 1992), vol. II, pp. 43–65; A. Akhiezer, 'Sotskul'turnaia dinamika Rossii', *Polis.*, 5 (1991), pp. 51–64; Akhiezer, 'Rossiia kak bol'shoe obshchestvo', *Vop. fil.*, 1 (1993), pp. 3–19; and his *Rossiia: kritika istoricheskogo opyta*, 3 vols. (Moscow, 1991); A. Kara-Murza, 'Chto takoe rossiiskoe zapadnichestvo', *Polis.*, 2 (1993), pp. 90–6; V. Shapovalov, 'O kategoriiakh kul'turno-istoricheskogo protsessa v Rossii', *Svob. mysl'*, 6 (1993), pp. 68–78. See also V. Sergeyev and N. Biryukov, *Russia's Road to Democracy: Parliament, Communism, and Traditional Culture* (Aldershot: Edward Elgar, 1993), where some interesting analysis of political language is accompanied by strangely sweeping assertions on European and Russian cultural history.

because my focus here is on post-Soviet behaviour and I am interested in the conventions for the way they influenced that behaviour.

Republic and regional elites relied heavily upon closely knit local and personal networks both for advancement and for safeguarding their interests in the face of demands from Moscow. An ambitious individual with a patron in Moscow might split the ranks but, in the regions, elites had emerged whose members had grown up and worked together all their lives. Deference to the centre was a rule of survival. All, including regional officials, enterprise directors, or ordinary citizens, viewed 'the government in Moscow' as being immensely powerful and the dispenser of limitless resources. The regional elites were middlemen, serving the centre but ruling their populations. Whether party or soviet officials, industrial directors, or farm managers, they were responsible for managing the state's resources. This placed a heavy burden on their shoulders and, in their eyes, justified their privileged position. Giving orders, changing policy in accordance with instructions from above, and managing a bureaucratic administration constituted their job. They were used to doing this without being queried publicly, without the fear of opposition, without public accountability. The legal institutions dealt with the everyday civilian and criminal cases, but party interests took precedence over legality. By the 1980s these often meant the personal interests of members of the nomenklatura: for them the public good and private interests were difficult to disentangle. They controlled the media. Much of the political reporting, and all the public political discussion, had acquired a standard format. Central Committee materials were reproduced in the regional press; changes in the policy line from above were announced, and welcomed. Open political discussion, the defence of a political position, had no place in their experience.

The literature on clientelism and on patterns of exchange is illuminating of many Soviet practices. Goods (pay and services) were distributed among the elite according to a kinship system, i.e., through membership of a specific and exclusive group. For the rest of the population access to goods was open but controlled by the state. The result was a gigantic set of patron–client systems in which the littlest clients had nothing to bargain with except their livelihood. The state was the supreme patron, taking what it wished, but also providing a social welfare safety net. Society created elaborate networks as survival mechanisms in the absence of a market and given a shortage of goods.[5] Within such a framework,

---

[5] In such a society work and pay are not naturally linked in the individual's perception: employment is perceived as entry to a world of public goods. Pay is just another public good, existing independently of one's activities; the taking of bribes can be as 'appropriate' a form of reward as a regular salary. Work relations are governed by patron-like or

moves to reduce the state's welfare role would surely be viewed as the patron and provider abandoning his clients, even the pensioners who had toiled so hard in his service. Patron–client relations, one might predict, would form an obstacle to the creation of relations based on specific exchange (market-generated), and simultaneously hinder the formation of trade unions from below. They would make it very difficult to create a body of officials able to separate public and private interests. In their turn, the rulers, while advocating market measures, might be expected to continue to operate as patrons in their use and creation of networks of loyal supporters (they had, after all, no others).

They were operating in a society structured by vertical lines of command and without horizontal institutional connections. Unger has offered the term 'a disorganized society' to describe a situation in which 'the central government faces a society without stable collective instrumentalities of its own devising', and gives us post-colonial Africa as an example: societies in which old patterns were destroyed by the colonial experience and not replaced by any except more primitive ones based on village and family.[6] The similarity between a post-communist and a post colonial society lies in the destruction of earlier social relationships and, once the conquerors have departed, the emergence into the light of new social identities which had developed as a consequence of the system of rule. The difference lies in the degree of direct state intervention in the creation of social identities and institutions. In Russia, as a consequence of state action over the course of seventy years, older social institutions and structures were replaced by those devised and imposed from above. Some put down roots, others did not, but all the new social institutions and patterns of behaviour, whether they developed as their creators wished or not (and most did not), required for their existence a powerful all-embracing state. Without it they had no moorings. Soviet society was not so much a homogenized, atomized society as a society of state-

patriarchal considerations: the boss defends his collective against others in the claims on resources, which bring him status, power, and rewards and, at the margin, he has the ability to provide for the members of his workforce, who are heavily dependent upon him, in ways that in the short term make a difference to their lives. See S. Eisenstadt and L. Roniger, 'Patron–Client Relations as a Model of Structuring Social Exchange', *Comparative Studies in Society and History*, 22 (1980), pp. 42–77; Eisenstadt and R. Lemarchand (eds.), *Political Clientelism, Patronage, and Development* (London: Sage, 1981), chapters by Lemarchand, and by Tarkowski on a patron–client analysis of Polish society. The study by J. Chubb of party politics in Palermo and Naples (*Patronage, Power, and Politics in Southern Italy* (Cambridge University Press, 1982)) is suggestive of possible future developments in post-communist societies. On the phenomenon of networks, see E. Sik, 'Network Capital in Capitalist, Communist, and Post-Communist Societies', *International Journal of Urban and Regional Research*, 18 (1994), pp. 73–93.
[6] R. Unger, *Plasticity into Power: Comparative-Historical Studies on the Institutional Conditions of Economic and Military Success* (Cambridge University Press, 1987), pp. 81–5.

structured collectivities. It is this feature that makes it unique. It did not have the attributes of a civil society but it had characteristics we are only beginning to understand.[7] The state not only created the officially spon- sored organizations, its existence was also essential to those activities that emerged in the perestroika period and after – whether the new informal groups, second economy, or opposition groups. They could not be similar to (or even seen as embryonic) institutions of a civil society that had come into being in other countries in a quite different state/society environ- ment.[8] In such a context, the ending of state control would be as unset- tling for the informals as for the Komsomol. If the state went, they had to change: either wither away or refashion themselves into new institutions with an independent personality. And, in turn, we might surmise, it would not be easy for a state-dependent or a state-structured society to allow the state to extricate itself and emerge as an autonomous institution.

Perestroika and the re-emergence of political debate

By the early 1980s the seemingly all-powerful Soviet state was in deep trouble. Its military needs were swallowing up resources from an economy that was failing to expand; it had become overextended territorially and its weakened centre faced increasingly autonomous local elites. The concern to fund and supply a huge network of public goods was producing intolerable strain on the exchequer, an 'institutional scle- rosis' within government institutions and a blurring of public and private interests.[9] The attempt by the new, reform-minded general secretary, Mikhail Gorbachev, to reform the political and economic order through glasnost and perestroika resulted in its collapse. The details need not concern us, but the way in which our regional elites were drawn into the political struggle and the situation they faced when the USSR dis- appeared requires a brief discussion.

Once public debate was allowed, words long drained of meaning began to regain their strength. They began to represent real interests, to signify claims which could not be disregarded. Previously devalued, emptied of

[7] V. Zaslavskii, 'Rossiia na puti k rynku: gosudarstvenno-zavisimye rabotniki i populizm', *Polis.*, 5 (1991), pp. 65–79.

[8] I return to this question in chapter 9. An abbreviated version of 'Oppozitsiia i totalitarizm v SSSR', an interesting analysis by I. Kudriavtsev of the 'state-dependent' relationships of dissidents and informals appeared in *Reiting*, St Petersburg, 6 (1992), p. 4; an early article which posed the problem is V. Kostiushev, 'Obshchestvennye dvizeniia v post- katastrofnom obshchestve: protsessy sotsial'noi sub''ektivatsii', in A. Alekseev, V. Kostiushev, and E. Zdravomyslova (eds.), *Sotsiologiia obshchestvennykh dvizhenii: kon- tseptual'nye modeli* (St Petersburg, 1992), pp. 61–71.

[9] 'Institutional sclerosis' is from M. Olson, in M. Mann (ed.), *The Rise and Decline of the Nation State* (Oxford: Blackwell, 1990), p. 107.

content in order to serve whatever political whim the party leadership was indulging in, they began to assert themselves. But what words were chosen, and what was being said? Struggles for power, the clash of interests that emerge with regime breakdown, have to be verbalized – relations of domination and subordination, and of authority, have to be expressed in words – and the question then arises: what are the languages on offer? Which cultural constructs or symbols can be used? Speech, language, is a central element in modern politics. New rulers and their publics have to choose from what is available – they may then creatively embroider it – but they are operating within a particular ideas environment (with its inherited and imported elements) just as they are within a particular territorial and time environment. In Russia the environment was unusual in that a highly literate society had not engaged in public political discussion within living memory. The once-powerful languages of socialism, democracy, and national self-determination had been drained of content; the meaning of their words could not be contested, nor their claims subjected to public scrutiny. Now debate was invited. Not surprisingly it was sometimes chaotic and often confused; it had a variety and effervescence about it. Positions changed with remarkable rapidity. Ideas were looking for constituencies rather than, as is usually the case, developing together with a constituency. The intelligentsia had been discussing ideas in kitchens and out in the forests since the 1950s, but public discussion and the linking of ideas with collective activity in which the participants recognize the constituencies each represents did not exist.[10]

When in 1990 elections were held throughout the USSR for republican, regional, and local soviets, three topics dominated the political agenda: republican sovereignty and the future of the Union, democracy and party rule, and ownership and the market. National self-determination, democracy, and private ownership had become the key elements in the language of reform. While popular movements in some Union republics (the Baltic states, Moldova, and then in the Caucasus), linking calls for national independence with democratic rights, were persuading their elites to forswear their allegiance to the centre, within Russia opinion was deeply divided.[11] In Leningrad the democrats swept to

[10] In this important respect the situation was quite unlike that in 1917, and the difference is immediately apparent in the degree and sophistication of the political debate in 1917 compared with that in 1989–91.

[11] Although there were tussles in places, the ease with which the KGB and procuracy, despite being part of a Union structure, transferred their allegiance to the new republican governments in 1991 is an indication of how weak their commitment to the Union had become. In contrast, the armed forces, a truly Union organization, and sometimes referred to as the sixteenth republic, were thrown into confusion by the break-up of the USSR.

power, and in Tomsk they gained nearly half the seats in the city soviet and a substantial block at regional level, but, in our other four regions,[12] the political establishment won a substantial or at least a clear majority of seats. The political complexion of the deputies they returned to the Russian Congress was very similar, and not atypical of the Congress as a whole. They now took up these issues, and in particular that of sovereignty. But before looking at the Congress discussion, I ask why it was these words that had moved to the forefront of debate.

In Europe and Russia, at least since the eighteenth century, a shared language of protest has included demands for justice, freedom, rights to property and to the fruits of labour, equality, political rights, and the abolition of privileges. In the nineteenth and twentieth centuries these found expression in the powerful languages of democracy, national self-determination, and socialism. In the USSR the original language of socialism became emptied of content, transformed into a strange language of dogma and cliche in order to serve as a legitimizing tool for party rule. By the 1980s this had had two consequences. Its very emptiness allowed those who owed their positions of power to its unchallenged existence to feed into it words that better expressed their views of the world: Russian or Soviet patriotism, militarism, anti-intellectualism. At the same time the contrast between the emptiness and cynicism of the official ideology and the original socialist ideas meant that, within the party, there was always a minority of reformers in permanent ideological opposition. When, in 1987, Gorbachev began the movement for party reform, they were among those who responded. But there was no way socialist ideas could be used to dislodge the conservative apparatus. The notion of a class assault upon the directors and government in order to return the property into the hands of the workers had no place in Gorbachev's thinking nor, one should add, in the minds of most of the reformers. Gorbachev's socialist pluralism was anathema to those who wished to preserve communist party rule and too authoritarian for those pressing for the ousting of the apparatus. As this became apparent the constituency for socialist pluralism shrank and shrank. A handful of socialists continued to argue that state ownership was a travesty of social ownership but, by the 1980s, the disillusionment was such that claims that private ownership would produce results carried much more conviction. Socialism, in people's minds, had become identified with communist party rule. Just as in established liberal democracies many think of

[12] Although formally two – Tatarstan and Sakha-Yakutia – were autonomous republics, for stylistic reasons and where it makes no difference to the point at issue, I shall simply use the words 'regions' or 'localities'.

democracy as 'what we have', so in communist party states many considered socialism to be 'what exists here'.

The apparatus clung on, still mouthing the old slogans, but the socialist claims hardly reflected its interests and, with the end to its monopoly of power, its language evaporated. Patriotic elements would need to find another host. Communist party rule had worn away socialism's constituency while giving birth to the democrats, free-marketeers, and the nationalists. In the official ideology the identification of the system with socialism was always stronger than with democracy. An alternative bourgeois democracy existed and was parodied, whereas no other socialism was deemed conceivable. Hence, for those seeking an alternative, liberal bourgeois democracy offered a choice.[13]

At the beginning of the century, in Russia as in Europe, democracy had expressed the demand for equal rights, for the wresting of power away from the wealthy and privileged, for a government elected by the people.[14] It lived on through the Soviet period but as 'Soviet democracy', now no longer part of a language of protest but rather one of rule, and with a claim that, in contrast to 'bourgeois democracy', it was real democracy because it allowed no room for wealth and birth to determine outcomes. By the 1980s repressive and corrupt party rule had undermined the claim, and some began to seek explanations and theoretical alternatives. 'Democracy' resurfaced in the language of those critical of the system. The attractions of a system with freedom of speech and a democratically elected government became more and more marked. Some of the younger economists studied theories of free-market economies. Ideas of private ownership and the market as solutions to Soviet ills began to percolate. Democracy, now associated with private ownership, became a key word in the arsenal of those attacking apparat rule, and the 'democrats' emerged.

Democracy meant different things to different individuals and what it meant to those who voted for the 'democrats' in 1990 we shall never

---

[13] Poland is instructive here. Whereas in the 1950s and 1960s working-class protest had still been couched in the language of socialism (workers' councils, workers' control, reviving true socialism), by 1980 socialist ideas were too discredited to be able to work. National identification could, however, still serve, given Soviet domination of Polish affairs, and the existence of the Catholic Church could provide a much-needed symbol to a community in opposition. Solidarity could be reaffirmed through religion rather than through class interests. The workers could make their claim to be acting for the Polish people, and gather support from all sections of society. In a country such as Russia, however, it has proved immeasurably more difficult for workers to find a voice. Only the miners have done so and they have tended to speak of miners' and regional interests.

[14] It was also used to refer to a social constituency, the 'demokratia' or the urban lower orders, and it was interpreted differently by the Constitutional Democrats, the Bolsheviks, and the Anarchists.

know. In 1988, in a survey of urban school-leavers and students which asked what they understood by democracy, the answers included:

> The ability to use constitutional rights
> Complete freedom of elections
> Freedom of speech
> Participation by the people in administration from top to bottom
> Justice for all strata of society
> Equality in everything, no privileges
> Each is the independent owner of his land and answers for his labour
> Defending the correct path of social development
> Observing human rights
> The subordination of the minority to the majority[15]

A political analyst, writing in 1992, suggested:

> The whole country, all of us, pushing and shoving, are chasing after democracy but nobody knows what it is. Everyone asks each other: have we got democracy? After all we never lived under it . . . [but] most don't need an explanation. Democracy is something good, and if there is nothing good about our existence, then it's not democracy.

Four different concepts of democracy, he suggested, figured in popular discussion: the right to do everything that was previously forbidden, a passion for public speaking, the need to put outstanding, capable people in power, and the existence of a large pension ('which I have deserved').[16] A reform-minded Politburo member might describe it as 'popular control over the authorities', i.e. procedures for passing laws, and glasnost, and elections, and emphasize the importance of morality and conscience; a Moscow intellectual might view it as 'a means to guarantee a normal life, worthy of a person' and 'a way of building national character and individual personality'. The academic journals discussed the separation of powers.[17] A worker at a political meeting in 1989 argued that '"Democracy is equality" in Lenin's words'; a 1990 election leaflet claimed that 'Democracy is competence and responsibility.'[18] At the Russian Congress Yeltsin argued that 'the guaranteeing of real people's

[15] Survey by the Institute of Further Education, Leningrad, of the political knowledge of urban youth, unpublished.
[16] S. Soleivchik, 'Demokratiia pod voprosom', *Novoe vremia*, 30 (1992), p. 49.
[17] A. Yakovlev, *Mosk. nov.*, 7 January 1990, pp. 6–7; D. K., *Mosk. nov.*, 14 November 1990, p. 5; see the discussion 'Chto znachit byt´ demokratom segodnia?', *Polis.*, 4 (1991), pp. 47–61, where a telling comment comes from Iu. Boldyrev: 'Most of us democrats think of democracy *situativno* – as the democrats holding office – but the essence of democracy, in my view, is that it is dilettantes who make decisions' (pp. 51–2).
[18] Election folder, Elections Leningrad 1990, Archive on Social Movements, Institute of Sociology, RAN, St Petersburg.

power in Russia . . . [requires] that kind of sovereignty that will not mean the shifting of the power and privileges of the Union bureaucrats to their Russian counterparts'.[19]

For some, 'democracy' had become associated with a particular political position, one which involved support for competitive elections and a free press but also included advocacy of private ownership and republican rights. It had been appropriated by those who, at the very least, wished to hasten the reform process. Their election leaflets tended to attack the privileges and arbitrary power of the 'party bureaucratic nomenklatura' and the state monopoly of the economy. Certain new phrases characterized individuals as democrats: 'human rights' and 'private property' were two key ones. The electoral programme of the 'Democratic Elections 1990' bloc in Leningrad called for 'Freedom and Democracy! For well-being and social justice!' They called for human rights to take precedence over any group rights; a mechanism to defend individual rights and to help the weaker members of society; sovereignty of the RSFSR, national self-determination; free associations, churches for believers, measures against crime and to save the environment; clause 6 of the constitution, which confirmed the Communist Party's leading role, to be abolished; different property forms to be legalized, but social rights protected.[20]

The party apparatus, now compelled to compete for votes, had little to offer. It did not try to defend an alternative Soviet democracy. The recognition of competitive elections as a democratic procedure could not be denied – this was now official policy – but party officials did draw a distinction between properly organized democratic procedures (i.e. controlled from above) and 'meeting democracy', the noisy, uncontrolled public meetings beloved of the democrats. Nomenklatura candidates tended to ignore the most contentious issues or referred vaguely to the need to end 'monopoly in all spheres of life', while stressing their experience and achievements as 'managers'. A Leningrad party secretary was for 'competence, practical ability, social justice, and the future of Russia'.[21] It was the absence of the key reform words, rather than an

---

[19] *Sov. Ross.*, 25 May 1990, pp. 6–7.

[20] Election folder, Elections Leningrad 1990; *Nevskii kur'er*, 1 (1990), p. 7. Some made explicit claims for the connection between wealth and freedom: 'Our poverty, the empty shelves in the shops, and other misfortunes are the result of our UNFREEDOM! A free people, consisting of free citizens, is always able to feed and clothe itself and achieve a worthy form of existence' or 'The way to enough for everyone lies through the pursuit of individual interest.' More familiar language could make its appearance too: Filippov, in true Bolshevik fashion, exhorted 'Let's expropriate the wealth that belongs to all of us from the bureaucrats', while Konstantinov and Stabitskii claimed that their candidatures represented 'the union of the working class and the intelligentsia' and their opponents' 'the union of the party and economic apparatus'.

[21] Efimov, Election folder, Elections Leningrad 1990.

explicit counter-position that characterized an apparat programme, although suspicion of private property and a concern for the Union might well be voiced. From the head of a department of the history of the party came a call for a traditional economic policy, for 'Incomes – according to labour!' (but for freedom of speech and putting the question of a multi-party system to a referendum), all 'So as not to be ashamed of ourselves as a Great Power' and with the claim 'Without great Russia there will be no great indivisible union of free republics!'[22] And Nina Andreeva, shortly to lead the most Stalinist of the new communist parties, addressing an army meeting in February 1990, suggested that talk of Baltic secession was equivalent to advocating that California secede from the United States, and that only 'By gathering around great Russia will the indivisible union of free republics be renewed and strengthened! Support the unbreakable unity of army and people! Motherland or death! Are we not Russians like you?!'[23]

These concerns brought some communists together with the patriots, although the latter were as critical of unaccountable communist party rule as were the democrats. The patriots advanced the claim that they, and not the discredited party apparatus nor the western democrats, would bring a rebirth of Russia and of the Russian nation; they would halt the 'bazaarization and break-up of Russia; the plunder of Russia by the central ministries and agencies and also by the western "do-gooders"'.[24]

If democracy dominated the reform agenda in Russia, in several of the Union republics national self-determination came first. Everything in the Soviet context conspired to bring calls for national self-determination hurrying to the fore. National self-determination remains one of the powerful languages of liberation at the end of the twentieth century. It may be that we are witnessing the last flicker signifying the end of an era, but it is almost impossible, at present, for those demanding a redrawing of state boundaries or a new system of rule to escape its demands.[25] In Soviet doctrine, widely accepted, 'nation' had its basis in an ethnic group with a language and culture, a history and territory, and it was this nation which

[22] Fortunatova, Election folder, Elections Leningrad 1990.

[23] *Svoboda mnenii*, 7 (1990), n.p.

[24] Lysenko and Riverov, Election folder, Elections Leningrad 1990. But not all fell into one or other of these three groups. Up in Kronstadt a naval officer, from a working-class family ('one of us', his supporters scrawled on his posters), standing against a vice admiral, stated: 'I see Russia powerful and independent, an economically independent republic, whose people will join battle with the mafia, with crime, with the undeserved bonuses of the party and state bureaucrats': Alekseev, Election folder, Elections Leningrad 1990. A democrat? A patriot?

[25] Established states may be discussing new forms of supra-federalism, but state-builders are in thrall to national self-determination, just as they are to democracy and to freedom from foreign, imperial, colonial oppression. The only rival is an Islamic state.

had the right of self-determination in the form of a sovereign state. Despite the claims in the constitution that the sovereign socialist republics had the right of secession, and that the rights of all nationalities were safeguarded, the knowledge that Moscow took all important decisions and, most crucially, that any expression of national sentiment was viewed as anti-Soviet, made nationalism a natural candidate as a language of opposition. A system constructed largely on a national (ethnic) basis, a passport system based on nationality, and affirmative action for titular national groups had worked to produce 'populations defining themselves in terms of ethnicity'.[26] In the absence of other identifications (the emptiness of 'worker', the weakness of religion, the absence of political collectivities) and in the presence of ethnocratic elites looking for a constituency in order to defend their position against the centre, ethnicity filled the vacant place. At the same time the customary linking of national self-determination with sovereignty, and hence with ideas of *popular* sovereignty, meant that it could simultaneously serve as a call for democratic rights. The party, so clearly the bearer of power and authority, never laid claim to sovereignty: that lay with the people.

The 1990 debate over sovereignty

If with the 1990 elections a major step had been taken in the acquiring of democratic rights, the questions of communist party control of resources and of republican rights remained unresolved. These became key issues, addressed through a debate over sovereignty. Sovereignty had come on the agenda following the escalation of the demands from the Baltic republics for greater autonomy. By 1990 the Lithuanian republican party had broken away from the CPSU and the country had declared its independence. Its achievement would mean the end to the CPSU and to the Union. But when in Russia the democratic movement, anxious to push perestroika forward, took up the flag of sovereignty for the RSFSR, its members were operating with a rather different agenda. By the time the Russian Congress opened in May 1990 two opposing political camps

---

[26] The quote is from D. Dragunskii, 'Naviazannaia etnichnost'', *Polis.*, 5 (1993), p. 27. The literature on national identification is voluminous and often cited. For the post-Soviet period, see in particular: R. Suny, *The Revenge of the Past: Nationalism, Revolution, and the Collapse of the Soviet Union* (Stanford University Press, 1993); V. Zaslavsky (Zaslavskii), 'Nationalism and Democracy in Transition in Postcommunist Societies', *Daedalus*, 121 (1991), pp. 97–122; Dragunskii, 'Naviazannaia etnichnost'', pp. 24–30; V. Tishkov, 'Etnonatsionalizm i novaia Rossiia', *Svob. mysl'*, 4 (1992), pp. 21–4; and 'O prirode etnicheskogo konflikta', *Svob. mysl'*, 4 (1993), pp. 4–15; N. Petrov, 'Chto takoe polietnizm?', *Polis.*, 6 (1993), pp. 6–15; V. K. Volkov, 'Etnokratiia – nepredvidennyi fenomen posttotalitarnogo mira', *Polis.*, 2 (1993), pp. 40–8.

were clearly visible. One favoured party rule, a cautious programme of economic and political reform, and no concessions to Baltic independence. Despite Gorbachev's attempts to maintain a centrist position, it was clear that the Union authorities, which he headed, leaned to this side. (And within the Communist Party, in the Russian republic, the running was coming from those who considered the Gorbachev line too reformist.) The other, the democratic camp led by Boris Yeltsin, was anxious to push ahead with reform within the party, introduce a multi-party system, speed up economic reform, and renegotiate the terms of the Union treaty on the basis of a looser federation. Its members were not primarily concerned with independence for Russia. The linkage of Russia and the Union in terms of institutional control over resources and personnel meant, however, that Russian government control over RSFSR resources would entail the end of the Union in its present form and fatally undermine the party's lingering authority. A declaration of republican sovereignty would therefore strike a simultaneous blow at CPSU and Union rights, and enable a Russian government to pursue its own agenda. The issue of sovereignty and of the chairmanship dominated the Congress. Yeltsin narrowly won election to the chair; the declaration on sovereignty passed by a larger margin. Yet the debate was a bitter one. It revealed the different concerns of regional spokesmen, and allows us to see the context from which future conflict came. For this reason I look at it in a little detail.

Sovereignty, argued the democrats, would lie with all the peoples of the Russian republic. The declaration which finally passed did indeed state:

1. The RSFSR is a sovereign state, created by the peoples historically united within it.
2. Sovereignty of the RSFSR is the natural and necessary condition for the existence of the statehood of Russia [*Rossiia*],[27] which possesses a centuries-old history, culture and traditions.
3. The bearers of sovereignty and the source of state power in the RSFSR are its multinational people. The people exercise state power both directly and through representative institutions in accordance with the RSFSR Constitution.

Yet the subsequent clause proclaimed:

---

[27] In Russian *Rossiia* refers to the state of Russia; *rossiane*, or the adjective *rossiiskii*, to all its citizens or peoples who include dozens of different nationalities, for example the Chuvash, Tatars, and Jews as well as Russians. The adjective *russkii*, in contrast, refers only to ethnic Russians. When therefore a patriot talks of *russkii narod*, the Russian people, it is immediately clear that he is excluding all the other nationalities. Unfortunately, in translation, we have only the one term 'Russia' and 'Russian' (as though there was only one word for British and English). Where it is important to the meaning I have included *rossiiskii* or *russkii* in parentheses.

4. The state sovereignty of the RSFSR is proclaimed in the name of high ideals – the guaranteeing to each person of an inalienable right to a worthwhile life, to free development and the use of a native language, and to each people self-determination in national-state and national-cultural forms chosen by them.[28]

Some were aware that to include the principle of national self-determination was dangerous for Russia, a multiethnic federation. Regardless of whether one believed that ethnic identity was innate or constructed by Soviet and past experience, it was none the less real and accompanied by institutional structures. According to the census, forty-five nationalities lived within the borders of the RSFSR. The largest nationality, the Russians, whose members were spread throughout the territory, accounted for 82 per cent of the population.[29] Thirty-three of the smaller nationalities (and some were very small indeed) had their own national territory – either an autonomous republic or a district. The republics, twenty-one in all, had been created around a concentration of a national minority – the Tatars, Buriats, Komi – but, given the demographic dispersion of many of the ethnic minorities and population movement, only slightly more than half of the national minority populations lived in the territories that bore their name, and in only six of the territories did the titular nationality account for more than half the population. The six were the four republics of the North Caucasus, the Chuvash republic, and Tuva. Eleven autonomous districts, created on the same principle, existed within regions.[30] Only 14 per cent of the federation's population of

[28] *Sov. Ross.*, 14 June 1990, p. 1.

[29] The Russian population accounted for 85 per cent of the urban population, 71 per cent of the rural: V. Sheinis, 'Natsional'nye problemy i konstitutsionnaia reforma v Rossiiskoi Federatsii', *Polis.*, 3 (1993), p. 46.

[30] When the RSFSR gained its independence (and its new name: Russian Federation), twenty republics existed within its boundaries, but subsequently Ingushetia was created. Formally one autonomous region and ten autonomous districts existed but, for simplicity's sake and because they had the same rights, I shall refer to them all as autonomous districts. Only 26 per cent of the 5 million Tatars in Russia lived in the Tatar republic. This is an unusual example because the boundaries of the Tatar republic had been drawn up in such a way as to prevent too heavy a concentration of the Tatar population, but approximately two-thirds of Mordovians lived outside Mordova and nearly half the Chuvash outside the Chuvash republic. In most of the territories the largest single ethnic group was Russians (due to in-migration over the centuries), but Ukrainians, Belorussians, Armenians, and members of a different national minority could be present in substantial numbers. Four million Ukrainians lived in the Russian Federation: O. Glezer, et al., 'Sub''ekti federatsii: kakimi im byt'?', *Polis.*, 4 (1991), pp. 149–59. A. Salmin, 'Soiuz posle soiuza', *Polis.*, 1–2 (1992), p. 53 n., gives figures for different republics, as does I. Busygina, 'Regional'noe izmerenie politicheskogo krizisa v Rossii', *MEMO*, 5 (1994), pp. 5–17. Other authors give slightly different figures. For a detailed account in English, see G. Lapidus and E. Walker, 'Nationalism, Regionalism, and Federalism: Center–Periphery Relations in Post-Communist Russia', in Lapidus (ed.), *The New Russia: Troubled Transformation* (Boulder: Westview, 1995), pp. 79–113.

170 million lived in these national territories. But if the territories were short on population, the opposite was true as far as land and resources were concerned. Together they accounted for 76 per cent of the territory of the RSFSR, much of it in the inhospitable Far North, but home to oil, gas, coal, diamonds, and gold.

The great majority of the overwhelmingly Russian population lived in the fifty-seven regions, the more common administrative sub-unit. These bore some relation to those of the tsarist period, the *gubernii* (slightly less than half of which dated from the time of Catherine II), but essentially they, as the republics, had developed their profile and identity during the Soviet period. The regions tended to be based on a powerful city centre, itself often more closely linked to Moscow than to other towns within its own region.

The potential for conflict if sovereignty was to be based on national self-determination was surely clear. As a leading demographer would subsequently argue:

It is impossible to ignore the fact that Russia is a huge ethno-cultural conglomerate with regions of compact habitation of a number of ethnic groups, whose territory was defined by the Soviet regime as 'a national-state formation'. In political ideology and language the principles of 'socialist federalism' grounded exclusively on an ethnic basis are upheld. The inheritance of tsarist Russia and the Soviet regime includes a whole array of injustices and crimes against peoples, their culture and way of life. The Russians as the dominant ethnic group (both demographically, politically, and culturally), although they are less imbued with ethnic nationalism than the titular nationalities of the other former Union republics, nevertheless continue to be the most powerful competitors among the peoples of Russia.[31]

Yet the issue was largely side-stepped, and the explosive right to national self-determination included in the declaration. Why was this? There were several very different reasons. The first has already been mentioned. The debate, at the time, was inspired by a different agenda: the relationship with the Union and communist party rule. The declaration stated that the Congress,

expressing the will of the peoples of the RSFSR, proclaims state sovereignty of the Russian Soviet Federal Socialist Republic over all its territory and declares its determination to create a democratic legal state within a reconstituted Union of the SSR.

The crucial clause 5 read:

In order to secure political, economic, and legal guarantees of sovereignty for the RSFSR:

[31] Tishkov, 'Etnonatsionalizm', p. 22.

complete power will rest with the RSFSR in the deciding of all state and social questions, with the exception of those which have been voluntarily handed over by it to the Union of the SSR;

the Constitution of the RSFSR and the laws of the RSFSR are the supreme authority within the RSFSR; any Union SSR acts which contradict the sovereign rights of the RSFSR are invalidated by the Republic on its territory. Disagreements between the Republic and the Union are resolved in accordance with the procedure laid down in a Union treaty,

and the document declared that the people had the exclusive right of 'possession, use and distribution of the national riches of Russia'.

Nothing, it would seem, could be clearer. Yet the vote in favour included many who favoured the Union, opposed Lithuania's declaration of independence, and had no sympathy with a radical agenda.[32] To understand how this could be we need to realize, first, that 'sovereignty' was a word with a meaning that was far from clear – often there was simple confusion[33] – and, second, that almost no one was thinking in terms of *actual independent statehood* for the RSFSR. Even the small minority who were prepared to see the Baltic states leave the Union would have found the idea that within less than two years the USSR would or

---

[32] The Baltic leaderships had declared their unwillingness to sign a new Union treaty under the terms of which they would remain part of a federation. Most of the deputies to the Russian Congress considered the Lithuanian stance unacceptable: sovereignty should not entail leaving the Union. A minority of the more radical deputies recognized Lithuania's claim that, as an independent sovereign state, its leaving the Union was legitimate. The first draft of a resolution (with a two-thirds majority vote in favour) – which spoke of 'recognizing Lithuania's right of self-determination' but of the conviction 'that only within a renewed federation of the USSR is genuine sovereignty and the blossoming of our peoples possible' – brought objections from them that it was not sufficiently supportive of the Lithuanians. Tension rose appreciably over the issue. The final telegram sent to the Lithuanian parliament was slightly more positive. the Congress, it stated, understood the Lithuanian striving for sovereignty, given that the RSFSR was doing the same, and believed genuine sovereignty and renaissance were only possible on the basis of a new federal treaty: *Sov. Ross.*, 22 May 1990, pp. 4–5; 23 May 1990, p. 6.

[33] Rutskoi stated that he could never agree that, 'while Russia remains in the USSR, genuine sovereignty is impossible'. The aim behind sovereignty, for him, was one of renaissance: 'without spiritual renaissance neither real sovereignty nor economic progress is possible . . . sovereignty of a state and of a people is not only measured in rubles, and accounts, but in the dignity [*dostoinstvo*] of its people and, I would add, its spirituality'. A view of sovereignty which included Russia's having its own army was, he argued 'distinguished, to put it mildly, by its incompetence': *Sov. Ross.*, 23 May 1990, p. 1. Yeltsin produced the argument that sovereignty included devolving ownership of property downwards to the republic, and to the regional level. 'The scheme is the following: the most important, primary [holder of] sovereignty in Russia is the individual, his rights. Further – the enterprise, collective farm, state farm, any other organization – here there exists the strongest, primary sovereignty. And of course there's the sovereignty of the district soviet or of some other local soviet': *Sov. Ross.*, 25 May 1990, p. 6.

should break up into 'sovereign' states, with borders, armies, and independent state institutions quite inconceivable, and alien.[34] Although the image the words of clause 5 conjure up is of an independent state voluntarily agreeing to form a loose union or perhaps a confederation with others and handing over certain limited powers to a joint authority, the existing reality was of a central authority, still associated with a powerful Union-wide party apparatus, controlling the armed forces, most economic resources, and policy-making. Citizens were Soviet citizens, borders with the outside world were Soviet borders.

Because sovereignty was an acceptable, long-sanctioned word, yet one whose meaning was not agreed, a dialogue could be maintained, despite deep disagreements, and resolutions could be adopted which allowed for different interpretations. Sovereignty was variously taken to mean independence, greater autonomy for territorial units, cultural autonomy, the acquiring of republican resources, or the priority of state institutions over party. Some had long felt Russia's interests were ill served by being managed by Union institutions. If, from the vantage point of other republics, the Union institutions were effectively Russian, to some among the Russian intelligentsia and to some regional officials, Russia suffered by having no one to defend its interests (those of the dying Russian village, for example), or to advance the interests of its scientific and cultural community. It was part of popular wisdom, within Russia, that its resources were used to help the poorer Central Asian republics. Baburin from Omsk, who would become one of the leaders of the patriotic deputies, spoke of

Our priceless national riches – the Russian character, Russian extravagance, and the Russian soul – all were locked away. How can we regain our treasures? How can we bring back to life our former Russian glory? Only one magic weapon can prize from our shoulders the burden of our injuries and insults – and that is the gaining of sovereignty.[35]

For many republican politicians Russian control over its resources was a priority. A. V. Vlasov, chair of the Council of Ministers, argued that 'the statehood of Russia has been, as it were, dissolved in the Union structures'; the republic had suffered more than most from the centralized rule, its problems could only be solved with full economic and political sovereignty:

[34] A year later, in 1991, when the referendum was held, with the slightly ambiguous wording, 'Are you in favour of a renewed federation of Soviet Socialist Republics?' (which made it difficult for those who supported a federation but not necessarily of Soviet Socialist Republics), over 70 per cent of the three-quarters of the population of the RSFSR who voted were in favour; slightly more, one should add, than were in favour of establishing a Russian presidency; *Izv.*, 27 March 1991, p. 2.

[35] *Sov. Ross.*, 16 May 1990, p. 1.

We are in favour of the principle 'what is Russian must belong to those of Russia'. (Applause.) . . . Life has objectively brought us to the point where we must renew the Union federation. The key issue is the replacement of the tight administrative centralization by contractual, economic, and other ties between the republics and the centre, and between themselves, on a democratic voluntary basis . . . Only an autonomous, independent Russia, possessing the full panoply of power and sovereign rights, can become the guarantor of a strong voluntary Union of equal republics . . . it goes without saying that the situation in which Russia was excluded from participation in elaborating important foreign policy decisions must be radically changed.

But he shied away, as did almost everyone, from the question of defence.[36] If his position seemed dangerously close to spelling the end of the Union, others, such as V. Vorotnikov, were adamant that although sovereignty meant

the possession of all formal and real rights and possibilities of disposing, independently, of its material and spiritual values in the interests of its population, and choosing those forms of internal organization and foreign relations which in the main accord with its traditions, needs, and the wishes of its people,

as was Russia's right, in no way would it mean a weakening of the Union.[37] The occasional deputy tried to clarify the issue. 'The sovereignty of Russia within the Soviet Union – that's one notion [of sovereignty]; the sovereignty of Russia as a principle upon which one could advocate Russia's leaving the Soviet Union – that's altogether another.'[38] But clarification was not really in anyone's interest. It would have opened the lid to a Pandora's box of problems whereas ambiguity allowed agreement to be reached on paper. The heated disagreement over the wording of certain clauses was, however, evidence of strongly held positions. In 1990 the contentious issues could be glossed over; when independence came they could not.

A major fault-line running through the Congress was between those for whom the preservation of the Union was the key consideration and those who were prepared to countenance a rethinking of the existing territorial and political arrangements. Among the former were those who, rightly sensing danger, were wary of any declarations of sovereignty. The chair read out a telegram from a group of citizens calling upon the deputies, 'in these difficult days for the Motherland, to act together, show strength and responsibility, stop the demagogic splitters . . . defend and preserve the

---

[36] *Sov. Ross.*, 20 May 1990, p. 3. The decree specifying the basis for negotiations for a new Union treaty proposed that the Union retain control over the armed forces, KGB, civil aviation, communications, and energy (although the future of the KGB should be a matter for discussion): *Postanovlenie*, 23 June 1990, in *Sov. Ross.*, 24 June 1990, p. 1.

[37] *Sov. Ross.*, 23 May 1990, p. 2.   [38] *Sov. Ross.*, 25 May 1990, p. 7.

party and the country'.[39] For them, probably party veterans who had fought through the war, their country was the USSR. V. Shumeiko, an enterprise director from Krasnodar who would go on to higher things, criticized the way the issue of sovereignty was being rushed through, and read out a letter from a farm mechanic whose words, he suggested, the Congress would do well to bear in mind: 'Love Russia, value Russia, take care of Russia, preserve Russia! Without Russia we are without a roof. Neither our descendants, nor history, will ever forgive us if we allow the break-up of the Union.'[40] Note the unconscious identification of Russia with the Union. The Soviet Union was of course greater than Russia but, for almost all, regardless of whether they favoured sovereignty or not, Russia was inconceivable without Ukraine, Belorussia, the Caucasus – maybe the Baltic states could leave, maybe one could conceive of a time when the Central Asian republics would sever their ties – but Russia and some kind of Union were bound up together. This imperial identification had consequences. On the one hand it could bolster the conviction that the Union, as it was now, must be maintained; on the other, ironically enough, it allowed many to support the call for Russian sovereignty because for them this did not mean a Russia without Ukraine, or Belorussia, say. That idea defied the imagination, both politically and conceptually.

This perspective, a Russian perspective, dominated at the Congress and was another reason why the inclusion of the principle of national self-determination for the peoples of the Federation was not perceived as a threat. The idea of Russia itself breaking up was simply too far-fetched. The Tatar autonomous republic, it is true, was requesting Union republic status but the democrats could argue that the problem lay with a Union where federal ideas had been distorted by CPSU domination and excessive centralization. If states were sovereign and democratic (if the words were realized in truth), then a real Union could be achieved. Lithuania's stance could be explained by Union intransigence. The rights of the

---

[39] *Sov. Ross.*, 19 May 1990, p. 5. There were others too who sensed the danger that sovereignty posed to the Union and party rule. This was no time for divided loyalties, especially after the unofficial demonstration at the May Day parade in Red Square. G. Ziuganov, a leading Communist, recounted how, a war veteran, 'in a carefully ironed suit, with medals for work and for bravery on his breast', stood beside him with his eyes full of tears. 'The trade union committee had for the first time sent him an invitation to the celebrations in Red Square. Times might be hard but he had gone to join in the festivities and found himself in a political farce . . . he could not follow its logic but he understood perfectly that everything that was happening was cheap and contemptible': Ziuganov, interviewed in *Sov. Ross.*, 5 May 1990, p. 3 (a classic statement, containing all the ritual words to describe a member of the working class, and still granting the trade union a legitimate status as a benefactor).

[40] He also criticized as an absurd notion Yeltsin's suggestion that enterprises should have sovereignty: *Sov. Ross.*, 2 June 1990, p. 1.

different nationalities would be secure in a new democratic Russia. If this was an imperial perspective, and it was, the challenge to it from the smaller nationalities was weak.

For a start leaders of the autonomous republics did not speak with one voice. The key question facing them was whether they would be better served by a Russian republic than by the Union authorities. Control over their resources at present lay in Union hands. Was there any advantage in this passing to a Russian government? R. Abdulatipov, claiming to speak on behalf on many, declared that nothing would be gained from the break-up of the Union, and spoke in support of the autonomous republics acquiring present Union republic status.[41] The Tatar leadership had already formally applied for its republic to be upgraded to become the sixteenth Union republic. It was not anxious to see a declaration of sovereignty by the RSFSR that tied its hands. Stepanov, from Karelia, expressed his dismay at the amount of idle chatter; for him sovereignty meant that the rights and autonomy of the autonomous republics, regions, and autonomous districts in both Russia and other republics should be increased – but with the aim of 'preserving our Russian union and the Union of Soviet Socialist Republics formed in 1922, but on a new basis', and this required a sober approach, not a rush to change the existing constitution.[42]

Although Vlasov, among others, had insisted that sovereignty meant 'real independence' for the autonomous republics, which would then delegate some powers to the RSFSR authorities, the idea of secession had no place in his perception.[43] And, one might add, nor did it for many from the autonomous republics. M. Sabirov, chair of the Tatar Council of Ministers, reported to the Congress that, during a break in the tense discussions over the final wording, representatives of the autonomous republics had agreed to propose to their Supreme Soviets that they adopt points similar to those listed under clause 5, and a right of leaving the RSFSR. But if Tatarstan and Chechnya did think in these terms – and the issue would become a real one once Russia became an independent state

[41] *Sov. Ross.*, 25 May 1990, p. 8.
[42] *Sov. Ross.*, 22 May 1990, p. 1. The first secretary of the Evenki district party committee ended his plea for more help for the North with the claim, 'For us there is one motherland – the USSR.' The spokesman for the Gorno-Altai had a different concern – they wished to leave Altai krai, and have autonomous status within the RSFSR: *Sov. Ross.*, 22 May 1990, p. 7.
[43] 'I consider that the autonomous republics [within the RSFSR] are sovereign state-socialist states. They are subjects of the federation of the USSR ... it is most important that the sovereignty of the autonomous republics be given a concrete content in order that they are really independent, sovereign, and their relations with the union republics in which they lie should be decided by agreements and treaties within the framework of the constitution': *Sov. Ross.*, 20 May 1990, p. 3.

– the majority saw their future within the RSFSR. A representative from Yakutia suggested that throughout history peoples in need had turned to Russia and it had always helped. 'So it was, is now, and will be. (Applause.)' He hoped all would work together to make Russia great. But the peoples of the north needed particular help, and relationships needed to be rethought: 'The sovereignty of Russia will be total and complete if all the conditions are created for the free, independent development, within the RSFSR, of such peoples as Yakuts, Buriats, Kalmyki, Tatars, Bashkiri, and many, many others.'[44] There were occasional voices which suggested a less than harmonious future agenda. A student from Dagestan suggested that democratic renewal of the Union was only possible if the RSFSR first sorted out its own domestic problems: 'The central question is – what is today's RSFSR? In my view, being de jure a republic, de facto it remains an empire and, in its turn, is part of another empire.' Its component parts, including Dagestan, had not the slightest input into policy-making; laws and rights came from above; natural resources were sacrificed to Moscow's interests. But even he advocated sovereignty for Russia, and autonomy for its units.[45]

The spokesmen of the autonomous republics were outnumbered and overshadowed by representatives of the regions, often powerful people, responsible in most cases for a much larger population and industrial output. Their constitutional rights were, however, less than those of the leaders of the republics, some of whom were now talking of sovereignty and national self-determination. To many from the regions this seemed plainly perverse. Even those who did not place the gaining of greater regional autonomy at the head of their agenda had no desire to see the republics benefiting at their expense. A request from a Kabardino-Balkar deputy that more resources should remain with the republics, and the tax system on natural resources be altered to their benefit, was greeted with 'disturbance in the hall'.[46] The issue of the regions versus the republics, which would become highly contentious after 1991, was prefigured in the difficulty the two sides had in agreeing the wording for the declaration. As M. Tolstoi reported to the Congress, the feeling on the part of the regions that their interests were not being sufficiently recognized was causing the most dissension. Finally the contentious clause 9 was agreed as follows:

The Congress of People's Deputies of the RSFSR supports the need to broaden qualitatively the rights of the autonomous republics, the autonomous regions, the

---

[44] *Sov. Ross.*, 25 May 1990, p. 3.   [45] *Sov. Ross.*, 23 May 1990, p. 8.

[46] *Sov. Ross.*, 23 May 1990, p. 6. A statement by Vlasov that he was in favour of responding positively to requests from some of the autonomous districts that they acquire autonomous republic status also provoked 'disturbance in the hall' (*Sov. Ross.*, 22 May 1990, p. 5).

autonomous districts, and equally so those of the RSFSR regions. Concrete questions relating to the realization of these rights must be decided by RSFSR legislation on the national and administrative-territorial make-up of the Federation.

There was another reason for the disagreement too. For those who were part of the elite of the titular nationality in an autonomous republic, the world that mattered was their republic. But for those in the Russian regions the USSR was their state; their power and authority was bound up with the party, and hence the Union, and they were as suspicious of Moscow and its democratic intellectuals as they were jealous of the privileges of the republics. P. Gorbunov, chair of the Tambov soviet executive committee, emphasized the importance of maintaining the Union ('the dissolution of the Union is in the interest of those who wish to see our motherland without rights and weak'), and then turned his attention to the situation in the provinces:

In no way do I wish to oppose the Muscovites. After all, Russia has no existence without Moscow, but neither is Moscow all of Russia and nor do the Muscovites account for all the people of our republic. (Applause.) Real Russia is scattered in the little towns, settlements, villages, in the open spaces of Siberia, the Urals, the East European plain. But it is that Russia which is eternally poor . . . once upon a time a simple man from Kholmogor gave Russian science world-wide recognition. Today he would only be able to do that if he got a Moscow residence permit. Even such millionaire-cities as Leningrad, Kuibyshev, Sverdlovsk, and Rostov-on-Don are conscious of their economic and social deprivation. And how do towns such as Tambov feel?[47]

Russian independence: a new environment

The declaration's challenge to Union authority was unmistakable, and other republics followed suit. By 1991 six of the Union republics had claimed their independence, and others, including some of the autonomous republics in the RSFSR, had adopted declarations of sovereignty and announced their support for a confederation or a looser federation. A war of laws ensued as each claimed precedence for its legislation. The Union authorities still controlled the resources and were prepared on occasion to send in the troops, but the Gorbachev leadership found itself obliged to try to negotiate a new Union treaty, and opted for holding a Union-wide referendum on the desirability of maintaining a 'renewed' USSR. Meanwhile, within Russia, the Congress voted for holding a referendum on a presidential form of government, based on a popular vote. In the spring of 1991 the two referenda were held

---

[47] *Sov. Ross.*, 26 May 1990, p. 6. The reference is to M. Lomonsov, the father of Russian science, born in a village in northern Russia in 1711.

simultaneously. The majority of the RSFSR population, in a high turnout, voted for retaining the Union and for a president.[48] But when, in June 1991, Yeltsin resoundingly won the Russian presidential election, negotiations for a new Union treaty took on a new urgency. A document was finally agreed by nine of the fifteen republics, including Russia, but it did not resolve the crucial question of where final authority lay.[49] It was its proposed signing on 20 August that prompted the attempted putsch and, with its failure, Yeltsin and the Russian authorities emerged as the victors. Even before the formal dissolution of the USSR at the end of the year, they clearly felt able to dictate terms to the Union institutions, and Yeltsin banned the Communist Party. Yet the Russian government, unlike that in most of the republics, was not able to command the allegiance of key sections of the republican elite. In Russia there was no close-knit republican elite, bent on wresting the territory out of Moscow's grasp. With the end of the USSR federal agencies became Russian institutions without any overt conflict, as did most of the ministries, but the consequence was that the new Russian federal government consisted of large, cumbersome institutions, whose officials were accustomed to thinking in Union terms and of obeying party orders.

Within the Russian republic some remodelling had occurred in 1991 with the introduction of a presidency, popularly elected and separate from the Congress of People's Deputies. Under the original system Yeltsin, as chair of the Congress and its smaller Supreme Soviet, had worked with a praesidium of ministers and committee chairs to produce legislative proposals and to put them before the Soviet or Congress. With the creation of the presidency, the executive became quite separate from the legislature. The president proposed leading ministers to the Congress, but the Congress could reject them, as it could presidential legislative proposals. The potential for conflict between the executive and legislature was there. But, given that the Union ministries still controlled the bulk of resources, decisions taken by the Russian president, the government, or Congress were of limited importance. Those who were opposed to the reform programme did not look to the Russian Congress as the place to take issue with a reform-minded president: other, more powerful allies existed within the Union structures. With the ending of the Union the situation changed radically. Policy-making prerogatives now lay in the hands of a president, awarded extraordinary powers by the Congress, and his Council of Ministers acquired responsibility for a programme of action. In the absence of the Union, and under the new

---

[48] See n. 34 above.   [49] *Izv.*, 23 July 1991, p. 1.

separation of powers, not only the Russian president acquired a real importance. The Congress, and its Supreme Soviet, elected from among the deputies to sit in permanent session, became much more significant as a policy-maker and clearly had the potential to become the focus for those who opposed the reform process.

For the moment other issues occupied centre stage and the initiative lay with the president. At the start of 1992, in the face of an ever more acute food shortage, Yeltsin authorized price reforms, followed by the privatization programme. The nettle of economic reform had finally been grasped. The other key issue that faced the new Russian Federation was its own federal arrangements. Independence quickly brought to the fore the tensions already apparent at the 1990 Congress. The solution adopted was the signing, simultaneously, in March 1992 of three separate Federal Treaties (between the Russian Federation and the autonomous republics, the Russian Federation and the regions, and the Russian Federation and the autonomous districts). This, it was hoped, would hold the ring until a new constitution could be agreed upon. By now all the autonomous republics had adopted declarations of sovereignty and dropped the designation 'autonomous'. The new Russian Federation was a sovereign state, and its twenty republics were also sovereign states. Eighteen of the republics agreed to the wording 'within the Federation', but Tatarstan and Chechnya refused to sign the Treaty, claimed independence, and declared their willingness to sign a treaty on equal terms 'with the Federation'. Even for those who did sign, the question of how disputes between a republic and the federal authorities were to be decided – where ultimate authority lay – was left unclear.

How were the regional elites affected by these changes? Although the original RSFSR Constitution, with the appropriate amendments, still operated, and its key institutions, the soviets, remained in place, the dissolving of the party had major consequences. In the republics the republican party buro had been the key decision-maker, in the regions the obkom or the kraikom. Now they had gone. Executive authority now lay, not only in name, with the permanent administrative structures of the soviets: the Councils of Ministers in the republics, the soviet executive committees in the regions. Their officials had always wielded power, under the aegis of the party, but now they were expected to share this with the newly empowered soviets. Many of the republics chose to adopt a presidential system, while retaining their existing Supreme Soviets. For the Russian regions a new executive was introduced in the form of a chief administrator, appointed by the president but with the agreement of the regional soviet, and a president's representative was appointed to oversee the working of the new arrangements and to act as a link with the centre.[50] Not only institutional arrangements changed. The press became free of party control, as did all political activity.

For most of the local elites, still largely the pre-1990 party and soviet administrators who had supported the Union cause, the situation was highly disconcerting. While the unresolved conflict between the Russian and Union leaderships had continued, local authorities had largely been compelled to mark time. Some had taken advantage of the dispute to try to gain concessions from one side or other. Now, with Russia's acquiring control over Union resources and the banning of the Communist Party, the regional rulers found themselves looking upwards to a new, untried government in Moscow. Its ministers were talking of a market economy, of private property, and of local and individual rights. Suddenly a great deal became open for renegotiation, and the languages in which people were talking were those of sovereignty, democracy, and national self-determination. They had become the vehicle through which people voiced their protests against the existing order and staked out claims for a future redistribution of power. It was not irrelevant which words were used. Language plays a part in structuring a struggle for power, in creating opportunities and closing off other courses of action. Elites may advance or defend their interests, but they need languages to express and justify their actions, and some languages will lend themselves more easily to this than others. Elite behaviour, we might say, was itself a consequence of opting for sovereignty, democracy, and the market in a post-communist multiethnic environment. But it is equally important to realize that the public discussion had appeared very quickly; the words lacked organized communities behind them. 'Sovereignty', 'democracy', 'national rights', 'the market' – all held out the promise of a better future, but how they would serve to structure debate and help resolve the basic issues of community identity, political authority, representation, and citizens' rights remained to be seen.

In the following chapters I trace the reactions of our regional elites to the ending of party power, to the opportunities and the dangers. It may help, in following what is a complicated story, to start with a sense of the macro developments as they unfolded after 1991. Over the next years three issues dominated the agenda: the nature of the federation, the relationship between president and the Congress, often now referred to as the Parliament, and the direction of economic policy. They led to conflict and then deadlock at the centre. By December 1992, when the Seventh Congress met, both presidential powers and the reforms were coming

---

[50] For the details, see below, p. 123, n. 38.

under serious challenge from the Congress. A constitutional crisis occurred, and E. Gaidar lost the prime ministership. The reforms continued, under V. Chernomyrdin, but so did the conflict between president and Congress. Its smaller Supreme Soviet, under its speaker or chair, R. Khasbulatov, had developed into an institution jealous of its powers and a conduit for opposition to the reforms. In this environment attempts to frame a new constitution made little progress. Yeltsin attempted in April 1993 to force the agenda with a referendum on support for the president and his policies, and won. But renewed negotiations over a draft constitution, with republics and regions at loggerheads over their respective rights, brought increased tension during the summer. In September 1993 Yeltsin broke the deadlock by dissolving the Parliament; a defiant stance by some of its members ended in the violence of the October days and the storming of the White House.

Elections to a new federal assembly were announced for December, and a new presidential constitution was drawn up. While executive–legislative arrangements within the Federation's republics remained their affair, the Russian regions came under presidential scrutiny. The chief administrators received greater powers, the regional soviets were charged with producing charters for new regional assemblies and holding new elections; the lower soviets were dissolved by presidential decree. The elections of December 1993 saw the constitution pass, but the reform-minded democrats failed to win a majority in the assembly. If 1991–3 were years of institutional conflict, 1994 witnessed an uneasy peace under stronger executive rule.

We now turn to our regions, to see the way their politicians and people reacted and contributed to these developments. The story is a complex one. It has to be detailed if we are to account for similarities and differences, and provide any depth, but I have tried to keep it as straightforward as I can. To help the reader keep track, a listing of the political actors, by region, is included (as appendix 1, pp. 317–21), and I refer back, wherever possible, to earlier events. Let us begin with the republics of Sakha-Yakutia and Tatarstan.

2   Post-imperial politics: the national republics

Under the Soviet system autonomous republics had enjoyed neither the scope for decision-making nor the status of the Union republics. Their leaders were used to looking to Moscow for decisions. But the political turmoil of 1989–91 provided the opportunity to rethink the relationship with the imperial centre and, once the Union collapsed, there came the necessity to develop strategies towards both Moscow and their own populations. In renegotiating the relationship with Moscow, the republican leadership in Tatarstan and Sakha-Yakutia reacted very differently. The Tatar leadership adopted a high independence position in 1991 and maintained it until the spring of 1994. The Sakha leadership maintained a loyal position throughout. None the less, by the spring of 1994 their relations with the centre were very similar. They were both units within a federal state whose authorities controlled the armed forces, security services, and foreign relations. They had both gained greater control over their own resources, and over domestic policy within the republics. In both cases the original elite, drawn from the titular nationality, had pursued conservative economic policies. Its members had secured their political positions and control over the new institutions of government. Both had adopted presidential systems very similar to the Russian one and, by 1994, their legislatures were largely subservient to the executive. Although in constitutional terms the Tatar Supreme Soviet had greater powers than the new Sakha assembly, in practice their powers were little different. The two questions I want to explore here are, firstly, what prompted the different strategies towards Moscow? Secondly, what enabled the existing incumbents in the new environment of electoral choice to consolidate their position? The reasons for the similar outcomes are addressed in the conclusion. I begin with a profile of the two republics. Historically, geographically, and culturally they were very different places.

Kazan, the capital of Tatarstan, with its Kremlin, mosques, Russian churches, and medieval Tatar monuments, lies on the banks of the Volga, in the heart of the Russian Federation. During the thirteenth and fourteenth centuries the Tatars ruled much of the Russian lands, extending their conquests as far west as Kiev. By the fifteenth century the Russian princes were beginning to drive the Tatars back eastwards and, in 1552, during the reign of Ivan the Terrible, a Russian army took and sacked Kazan, then a city of 50,000. The Tatars now suffered the fate of their earlier subjects. Tatar lands were divided and, until the reign of Catherine the Great, the Islamic religion was suppressed. By the nineteenth century the Volga Tatars formed part of the population of several adjoining Russian provinces, one of which was Kazanskaia. Following the revolution and a short-lived attempt to create a larger Tatar republic, Kazanskaia became the nucleus of a Tatar autonomous republic within the RSFSR. The majority of Tatars, however, lived outside its borders.[1] Until 1989 the fifth largest nationality within the USSR (i.e. considerably more numerous than any of the Baltic peoples, the Georgians, and some of the Central Asian peoples), the five million Tatars occupy second place within the Russian Federation, accounting for a modest 3.5 per cent of its population. Tatar communities are scattered far and wide across the face of Russia. The neighbouring republic of Bashkortostan, and adjoining regions, have substantial Tatar minorities, and Tatar communities exist in Siberia and in Moscow. A distinct community, the Crimean Tatars, expelled from its homeland during the war, is now again to be found far to the south, in the Crimea.

The Tatar republic is roughly the size of England and Wales. In 1926 its population was 2.3 million, perhaps half Tatar, over 40 per cent Russian; by 1992 it had grown to 3.7 million, with very similar proportions. The main change had come in the shift from a largely rural to a heavily urban (74 per cent) population and, within the urban community, the Tatars had risen from a quarter to 42 per cent. In Kazan itself, a city of over 1 million by the end of the 1980s, Russians accounted for over half the population, the Tatars for just over 40 per cent. In the rural areas, inter-ethnic marriage is rare but in the towns roughly a third of families are mixed. The growth of the urban population has come from the influx of rural Tatar youth and the in-migration of young Russians in the postwar period. The discovery of oil brought expansion in the 1940s and 1950s (the republic has oil reserves to last for another thirty to forty years, and natural gas), followed by a decision to base huge automobile works and defence plants in the republic. The mid-1960s to the mid-1980s saw the creation of new towns on the basis of old agricultural settlements. The most striking example is Naberezhnye Chelny, built round the KamAZ truck and car plant, a company town that grew to half a million in the

[1] See chapter 1, n. 30.

1980s and which, between 1982 and 1988, was renamed Brezhnev. This was a period of extravagant construction of public buildings, characteristic of the end of empire. The central squares of the regional capitals were bulldozed. Huge ponderous white concrete and glass party and soviet buildings, a new house of political education, and a new theatre or opera house were built in the great empty spaces. The new towns, however, simply grew, haphazardly, around the plants.

Tatarstan is an exporter of oil (dependent for this upon the pipeline that links it via Russia to the west), of electro-energy, and of its trucks. Although the republic's economy is based upon agriculture, energy resources, and industry, and has a strong educational and cultural base in Kazan, the heavy concentration of defence industry made it a recipient of federal funding rather than a creditor republic. The nature of its resource base and industrial profile (it occupies eighth place in industrial production in the federation) and its strategic position make it important from the federal point of view, but at the same time its location and its dependence on the pipeline and federal support for its industries put cards in the hands of the centre.[2]

By the mid-1980s, as in the other autonomous republics, the political elite of Tatarstan was increasingly being replenished by members of the titular nationality. By 1989 more than half the posts of the regional nomenklatura were held by Tatars. In industry Russians were well represented at top levels but even here by 1989 Tatars accounted for 64 per cent of the directorate. In contrast to some of the other republics, Tatarstan had highly educated specialists of the titular nationality in most professions and its proximity to Moscow meant that ideas travelled fast.[3]

Sakha-Yakutia, the largest republic within the federation, covers a huge expanse of northern territory, far away from Moscow. This is permafrost country. Its great rivers, the Lena, Yana, Indirgurka, and Kolyma, frozen from October to May, loop their way northwards through the taiga and the tundra to the Arctic seas. In winter it is dark from four in the afternoon till eleven in the morning, and the temperature falls to −30 °C; in the short summer the sun shines day and night. Inhabited for centuries only by its wild life and the 'Little Peoples of the North', who hunted, trapped, and fished, the region and its forests became the homeland of the Sakha, a

[2] M. R. Mustafin and R. G. Khuzeev, *Vse o Tatarstane* (Kazan, 1992), pp. 8–97; Mustafin, *Novye tendentsii v rasselenii naseleniia Tatarii* (Kazan, 1990), p. 101; E. P. Busygin, *Etnodemograficheskie protsessy v kazanskom povolzh'e* (Kazan, 1991), pp. 48, 71; *Tatary i Tatarstan* (Kazan, 1993), p. 97; M. Zakiev, 'Nationalism and Democratism in Tatarstan: The Ethnonym of the People', in *Tatarstan Past and Present* (London: SOAS, 1992), pp. 1–14.

[3] D. Iskhakov, 'Sovremennoe tatarskoe natsional'noe dvizhenie: pod''em i krizis', *Tatarstan*, 8 (1993), p. 31.

people who came from the south, and followed the Lena northwards. In the eighteenth century Russian explorers and military expeditions appeared. They referred to the Sakha as the Yakuts, and named the future capital, the outpost on the Lena, Yakutsk. By the nineteenth century the huge territory had been incorporated into the Russian empire; by the beginning of the twentieth it was clear that this was the place to seek for precious metals and gems, including gold and diamonds.

With the creation of the USSR Yakutia became one of the autonomous republics within the Russian republic. In 1990 it was renamed Sakha. In 1926 its population included 236,000 Sakha, just over 30,000 Russians, and 14,400 Little Peoples of the North, approximately 280,000 in all. By 1959 the population was still fewer than half a million; by 1989 it had passed the one-million mark, but its composition had changed dramatically. Now more than half the population was Russian, the Sakha accounted for a third, other newcomers (Ukrainians in particular) another 15 per cent, and the Little Peoples were still fewer than 25,000.[4] Gold had long been mined, and in the Kolyma region prisoners had worked in the mines since the 1930s, but the discovery of a diamond pipe by a group of young Leningrad geologists in the early 1950s brought, for the next thirty years, hundreds of thousands of newcomers from all over the Union to Yakutia. New towns, initially of tents and wooden hostels, sprang up. There was Lensk, the trading post on the Lena, to which not merely provisions but everything for the new towns and mines, except timber, was shipped and then transported north up the one road, carved out of the frozen hills and taiga; Mirny, where the first diamond pipe was found and mined, and then, further north, Udachny; Chernyshevsk, where a new hydroelectric station was built on the Vilui river. Oil was found at Neriungri and a settlement of fewer than 10,000 grew to 117,000 in the space of a few years.

A population growth from half a million to just over a million in the space of thirty years is not large, but to understand the republic's demographic profile we need to add a different statistic. During 1959–89, the years of rapid growth, over 4 million came and found work in the republic; each year saw an influx of roughly 100,000 but a roughly equivalent outflow of population.[5] Those who came were the young, both specialists and the unskilled, recruited through *orgnabor* (the state system of labour recruitment), or demobilized from the army, and via the Komsomol. Some came to build socialism, others in search of the 'long ruble' (wages were high), others in search of adventure. A common pattern was to stay

---

[4] Iu. Danilov, *Tret'e izmerenie Yakutii* (Yakutsk, 1991), pp. 7–8; *Sots. Yak.*, 27 March 1990, p. 1.   [5] Danilov, *Tret'e izmerenie*, p. 5.

seven years or so, marry, start a family – and then move back to the softer climate and conditions of Ukraine or western Russia. But even those who stayed reckoned that when they reached their pension (and pensions would be high) they would move back home, to the town or village they had come from. The big companies reckoned this too and built settlements back in the west for their employees to retire to: they received an apartment there and the company took over the one they vacated. Hence the population was multilayered: the Sakha and other indigenous peoples, a thin stratum of those of all different nationalities who came and stayed at least until pension age, and a larger, shifting, short-term population. Roughly eighty different nationalities were represented by the end of the 1980s – from the Evenki to the Buriats, from Greeks to Germans, Chuvash to Estonians – and intermarriage was common.

By the end of the 1980s the pattern of the past thirty years was changing again. The inflow of population was slowing down, the outflow increasing. For the first time the census returns showed an increase in the Sakha share. No longer was youth coming, as it had done in the past; and the children of those who had come in the 1960s, stayed, and become the republic's specialists left for universities in western Russia and did not return. With the downturn in the economy in the early 1990s, the big companies no longer needed to recruit; on the contrary they began to shed labour, but they faced the problem that the skilled workforce was leaving, and the recruitment of specialists was proving more and more difficult.[6] In terms of wages and salaries the Far North had always been favoured. By the early 1990s the differentials had decreased, and, at a time of rapid inflation, the original rationale of coming to save money to spend back home had gone. Those who had stayed saw their savings wiped out. Real wages fell by 19 per cent in 1993, about the Russian average, and air-fares rose astronomically. Apart from the long river journey south (a week from Yakutsk to the railway junction at Ust-Kut, and that only in the short summer months), the aeroplane is the only link with the rest of Russia. By 1993, for most people, the price increases had made air journeys impossible and the republican air company was running into deeper and deeper debt.[7]

Yakutsk, the capital, had begun to develop as the republic grew in economic importance. The departments of the federal and republican min-

---

[6] By 1994 the government had drawn up a labour plan for Yakutalmaz, the diamond company, which stated that only local labour would be recruited: *Yak. ved.*, 8 (1994); also *Res. Sakha*, 27 April 1994, p. 3, on outflow; interviews with Yakutalmaz management representatives, Mirny, May 1993.

[7] *Res. Sakha*, 1 February 1994, p. 1: there was a 30 per cent drop in passengers and cargo in 1993.

istries were based there; the republic's higher education institutions (a pedagogical institute) and a branch of the Academy of Sciences were there. And, in keeping with the nationality policies of the Brezhnev period, the Sakha began increasingly to occupy places in the party and soviet elite. Industry and mining, however, remained the preserve of the newcomers. In 1994, for example, the management of the 375 large and middle-size industrial concerns in the republic was 57 per cent Russian, 16 per cent Ukrainian, and only 4.5 per cent Sakha. The Sakha and the Little Peoples remained primarily in the rural settlements, which had been converted into state farms.[8]

Renegotiating the imperial relationship

What might explain different strategies towards the federal centre? Types of leadership? In background, training, and professional careers the Sakha and Tatar elites were very similar. In Sakha it was nomenklatura representatives, including M. Nikolaev, the Sakha chair of the Supreme Soviet returned unopposed with a vote of 70 per cent, who won seats in the Russian Parliament in 1990. The republic Supreme Soviet too differed from its predecessors only in the falling away of the obligatory groups of workers, peasants, and women. Party officials made up the largest contingent, followed by soviet officials and industrial managers in roughly equal numbers; a small number of the intelligentsia, and a handful of agricultural managers, and cultural and police officials made up the rest.[9] Mikhail Nikolaev, born in 1937, a graduate of Omsk veterinary school, had returned to his native Sakha to Komsomol then party work. He had moved between posts as minister of agriculture and obkom secretary before becoming chair of the Supreme Soviet in 1989, a post to which he was re-elected. In 1991 he won the presidency, comfortably, with 77 per cent of the popular vote, although this time faced by an opponent, also a Sakha, an ex-party secretary with a more pro-market programme.[10]

Data on the political and industrial elite are few. I have referred to the Russian and Ukrainian dominance of the industrial directorate. The political elite, in contrast, was predominantly Sakha, although the

---

[8] *Res. Sakha*, 27 April 1994, p. 3. Complementary data on the republic can be found in M. Mandelshtam and V. Vinokurova, 'Nationalism, Interethnic Relations, and Federalism: The Case of the Sakha Republic (Yakutia)', *Europe–Asia Studies*, 48 (1996), pp. 101–20, an article which appeared after these chapters were written.

[9] *Sots. Yak.*, 3, 6, 7, 8, 10, 13, 20, 22 March 1990.

[10] *Res. Sakha*, 26 April 1990, p. 1; *Yak.*, 24 December 1991, p. 1. In the presidential election the turnout was 75 per cent. The Sakha adopted Russian names in the nineteenth century.

Russian presence was still strong at the highest levels. In early 1992, after the reorganization of the government under the presidency, four of the seven top posts were held by Sakha, three by Russians (Nikolaev's running mate in the presidential election had been a Russian, V. Shtyrov). Of the twenty-seven members of the republican government, slightly more than half were Sakha, but among the thirty-five regional and district administrators, 80 per cent were Sakha, Eveni, and Evenki. More than half the members of the government had not previously been in state administration (this is surprising) – the newcomers were from science, higher education, and 'non-traditional economic organizations' as well as from the directors' corpus. Seventy per cent of its members had been born in the republic, including a third of the Russians. Only three were women. In late 1993, when a new two-house assembly was elected, roughly 60 per cent of the deputies (many of them state officials) were Sakha, 25 per cent Russian.

More than half of the political elite of 1992 had been born into worker or peasant families, and had acquired an engineering or agricultural education; most had started their working lives in production, only 15 per cent as Komsomol or party workers. They were younger than their counterparts in 1984, and more technocratic in background.[11] These characteristics are reminiscent of the elite of an earlier generation in the industrial west of Russia. In terms of social background, education, and career patterns, the post-perestroika Sakha elite was similar to that earlier Soviet elite which rose to power after the industrialization campaigns. Unlike that earlier elite, however, it had much more scope for independent action.

Of the Sakha deputies to the Russian Parliament only Nikolaev made any mark. Most of them, including Nikolaev, associated themselves with the Sovereignty and Equality fraction and tended to vote against reform measures. Only V. Kolodeznikov, the Yakutalmaz Institute director, aligned himself with Democratic Russia. In general, they were among those deputies who, lacking any very clear orientation, reacted to developments, often indecisively.[12] None of them stood for re-election in 1993,

---

[11] Iu. Tarasov, 'Praviashchaia elita Yakutii: shtrikhi k portretu', *Polis.*, 2 (1993), pp. 171–3; for the 1993 assembly, which I shall come back to, see *Res. Sakha*, 18 December 1993, p. 1.

[12] Democratic Russia, or DemRossia, was an organization that came into existence in 1990, with the aim of bringing all the different democratic parties and groups together. Although it continued to exist until 1994, from the very beginning it was plagued by factional infighting, and the leadership, membership, and the organization's authority in the wider democratic community underwent continual change. For voting behaviour in the Russian Parliament, here and throughout, I rely on A. Sobianin and D. I´urev, *S´´ezd narodnykh deputatov RSFSR v zerkale poimennykh golosovanii* (Moscow, 1991); Sobianin and I´urev, *VI s´´ezd narodnykh deputatov Rossii: politicheskie itogi i perspektivy* (Moscow, 1992);

with the exception of Nikolaev himself who, in the space of three years, had not only established his personal control of the political structures in the republic but emerged as one of the more influential of the republican leaders at federal level. Diamonds doubtless helped, but Nikolaev proved himself an able politician too.

The president of Tatarstan, Mintimer Shaimiev, born in the republic in 1937, graduated, as did many of his party colleagues, from the Kazan Agricultural Institute. He had moved up to become minister of irrigation, then in the early 1980s to deputy chair and then chair of the Council of Ministers, before becoming first secretary of the republican party. His reputation was that of a technocrat, personally honest, and stingy (rather than using the president's plane, he had been known to cadge lifts off wealthy foreign visitors). The prime minister, M. Sabirov, had served as deputy chair of the Council of Ministers since 1983; before that he had held party secretaryships and industrial management posts. Farid Mukhametshin, the speaker of the Supreme Soviet, had come from being a deputy chair of the Council of Ministers. His career had started with the Komsomol, then included party work, government posts, including minister for trade, and more party work.[13] The odd man out among Shaimiev's top circle of ministers and advisers was his vice president, V. Likhachev, a lawyer, Russian by nationality. It had been clear to all that the post of vice president should be held by a Russian. The question was finding someone with whom Shaimiev could work, and who would work with him. Likhachev proved a good choice: educated, courteous, diplomatic, he had the task of promoting international links, and of presenting Tatarstan's image abroad, one which he executed with zeal. His was not a position of power but he was important to the Shaimiev leadership.[14]

In 1992, of Shaimiev's government of thirty ministers, chairs of state committees, and equivalent posts (for example, chair of the supreme court), twenty-six were Tatar, and seventeen had official party careers behind them (city or district first secretaryships, or spells at republic level); only one (the minister of health since 1989) had moved in from a non-nomenklatura post. Six of them had been in post since 1985 or earlier; the rest had moved up from deputy ministerial posts or from

Sobianin and I'urev, *Rasstanovka sil v korpuse narodnykh deputatov RF po itogam trekh dnei raboty vneocherednog VIII s''ezda (10–12 marta 1993 g.)* (Moscow, 1993). For fractions in the Parliament, see chapter 8, n. 37. I translate *fraktsiia* as 'fraction' rather than using the term 'faction' which in western politics usually refers to a group within a political party.

[13] See n. 15.

[14] For a good example of his role, see the article by him in *Nezav.*, 5 June 1993, p. 3; see the interview with him in *Tatarstan*, 2 (1993), pp. 3–9; interview, 5 June 1993, p. 3, and his interview in *Tatarstan*, 2 (1993), pp. 3–9; interviews with Likhachev, and with Tatar politicians, Naberezhnye Chelny and Kazan, September 1993.

district party secretaryships; two had been rectors of higher education institutes. Only two of them had been born outside Tatarstan; only one had not received a higher education in the republic: the agricultural institute, economics-finance institute, and law faculty of the university could each claim several graduates. The age cohorts divided roughly equally between those born in the late 1930s, during the war, and the last period of Stalin's rule. Only one was a woman.[15]

The president appointed the chief administrators of the towns and districts. Here the continuity with the old order was even more marked. Of the nineteen individuals in 1992, fifteen were Tatar (two Russian brothers, both born in the republic, featured among the others); most had been born in rural areas but among the six chief administrators in Kazan, three were from the city itself.[16] On average they were younger than the ministers, born either during the Second World War or in the period after it; all had been educated in the republic, several in the agricultural institute, and some in the veterinary institute. More than half had served as farm chairmen; only two had no party career behind them. Twelve of them had occupied the post of party secretary or chair of the soviet executive committee at the time of their appointment to chief administrator: in other words, they had stayed in post. Three of them had held the post of chair of the local soviet, and ten of the nineteen now combined the post of chief administrator with that post.

An analysis published in 1994, which examined the holders of ninety-six executive posts at republic and district level, confirmed this very strong Tatar and nomenklatura presence: 78 per cent were Tatars, 68 per cent had come from party or soviet work or, if one widened the category to include all posts previously on the nomenklatura list, 92 per cent had a nomenklatura background. Three-quarters came from rural backgrounds, and agricultural or veterinary training still characterized nearly half the younger incumbents.[17]

Although in Sakha there were more newcomers to government, in other respects the elite in the two republics was very similar. Nothing in their backgrounds would suggest they might adopt very different policy

[15] All the elite data for 1992 has been calculated from the biographical details provided in *Tatarstan*, 4, 6, 8, 9 (1993).

[16] The Social Democratic Party had assembled data for Kazan as of January 1992: of the 123 responsible administrators, 43 per cent were Tatar, 50 per cent Russian; of 512 directors of state enterprises, 45 per cent were Tatar, 49 per cent Russian; of the directors of 911 small enterprises and cooperatives, 40 per cent were Tatar, 53 per cent Russian. These percentages roughly matched the ethnic composition of the city. Data provided by the SD party, September 1993.

[17] M. Farukshin, 'Politicheskaia elita v Tatarstane: vyzovy vremeni i trudnosti adaptatsii', *Polis.*, 6 (1994), pp. 69–70.

stances towards Moscow. Perhaps, then, it was resources which provided their elites with very different bargaining strength? Tatarstan had oil but was dependent upon the federal pipeline to sell it abroad or to reach refineries; it had sizeable defence and industrial plants, including the giant KamAZ truck and car factory, but these required federal support. Geographically it was land-locked. Sakha, on the other hand, was the diamond mine of the federation, and home to gold and other precious metals. But it too needed federal assistance in marketing its diamonds and, as a northern republic, was dependent upon the federal network for food and supplies. Its vast potential wealth and opening to the Arctic seas made it of interest to long-term foreign investors. Of the two, Sakha looked to have the stronger hand to play. But a policy of confrontation and independence might result in too fast an exodus of the skilled Russians from the republic. The Sakha population was still largely rural. Unable to work its diamonds and gold, it might have to seek help from Japan, or the United States, hardly preferable to Moscow. Neither republic had an obvious advantage in terms of resources and strategic position.

In one respect, however, the two elites found themselves in very different situations. In Sakha there were a few voices calling for independence. They argued that the republic *could*, on a democratic basis and with a different economic policy, develop its resources. The leadership, they claimed, was too cautious, conservative, tied to old ways, too inclined to look to Moscow. But these were isolated voices, and meanwhile the local Russian diamond elite was prepared to join the Sakha elite in bargaining with Moscow for greater republican control over the industry. In contrast the Tatar elite was backed by a nationalist movement and locked on a course, one that was working because the Russian government was anxious to avoid confrontation. The Tatar leadership could opt for a referendum, given that nearly half the population of Tatarstan was ethnically Tatar, whereas in Sakha the Russians held a clear majority. The existence of sizeable communities of Tatars in neighbouring republics – Tiumen, Bashkortostan, not to mention in Moscow – was not to be ignored either. But by 1993 the nationalist movement, which played a crucial role in pushing a cautious leadership along a path of confrontation with Moscow, was ebbing. This, and not simply a tougher federal line and the worsening economic situation, is needed to explain the agreement to a treaty with Moscow in 1994. By then the Tatar leadership could accede to Moscow's demands without jeopardizing its own position. This would suggest that the agenda of the Tatar and Sakha elites was very similar, and that the critical factor in the different strategies was the presence or absence of a nationalist movement.

In order to explore their agenda we need to look at domestic policies, and the way in which they reacted to the new structural constraints of elections, and to a free press. These topics are addressed in the following chapter. Here I am concerned with negotiations with Moscow; and that requires us to begin with the relationship between the elite and the nationalist movements or groups.

The elite and the nationalists in Sakha

At no time was the republican leadership challenged or even pressured by a nationalist or democratic opposition. There were only two real players throughout: the political leadership, heavily Sakha, and based in Yakutsk, and the directorate of Yakutalmaz, the Russian-dominated diamond concern based in Mirny. Developments in Sakha were determined by negotiations between these two elite groups and the federal authorities in Moscow. The response from Moscow was influenced in part by the state of relations between president and Congress, in part by the actions of other regional players. Tatarstan's intransigence, for example, could work to Sakha's benefit as Moscow indicated the advantages that could be gained from moderation.

The story of the opposition can be told briefly. At the beginning of 1989 a small group of intellectuals of different nationalities set up a National Club to work for the independence of Yakutia. Based initially in Mirny, they attracted some supporters in Yakutsk. By independence they meant 'economic and political independence' within the USSR, the acquiring of Union republican status, the ending of 'colonial' rule. Their impact on the 1989 elections was minimal. Among those elected to the USSR Congress of Deputies, however, was one democrat who was active in creating a democratic Electors' Club at the time of the 1990 elections. The National Club, which subsequently registered itself as the Mirny People's Front, joined forces with it. In Mirny itself, which was the centre for democratic activity, the city authorities nervously acceded to a request to hold a meeting, on condition that no calls would be made to boycott the elections in any districts or indeed to support any particular candidates. And in Mirny, but only there, a group of democratic candidates did win election to the town soviet.[18]

In September 1990 its Supreme Soviet had declared Yakutia to be the sovereign republic of Sakha within the USSR and the RSFSR but, as of then, these words signified little.[19] By this time a division had appeared in

---

[18] The individual was O. Borodin, who joined Travkin's Democratic Party of Russia; see appendix 3 (pp. 324–6) for political parties. Details from Danilov and Zaleskaia in interviews, Mirny, May 1993; *Mirnyi rab.*, 1 March 1990, p. 1.

[19] *Yak.*, 25 September 1991, p. 1, refers to the date, and to the idea of a presidency being broached at that time.

the democratic ranks – between those grouped round the People's Front who favoured independence and others, mainly from the Electors' Club, who argued that democracy was more important than sovereignty. The division was largely but not entirely a Sakha–Russian one. It did, however, herald the split that was to come, a split that repeated itself in other republics, just as it had done in, for example, the Baltic states after independence. The reform movement attracted those of all nationalities, but once the issue became the form in which a republic should realize its independence those of the titular nationality and the sometimes numerically dominant Russian population 'saw' democracy differently. In Sakha in April 1991 they combined forces to hold a Congress of the Democratic Forces of Yakutia but this only brought the division out into the open, with the one side arguing that national self-determination was a democratic right and the other denying that it was essential.

At the time of the August putsch, the party press supported the GKChP. The putschists may well have had adherents among the conservative Sakha leadership. Only a month earlier, following Yeltsin's election to the presidency, the republican party committee had made its position clear: it would support his measures, while reserving the right to be critical; it favoured only small-scale privatization, and not of land, and it was against any attempts at 'desovietization by the organs of state power'.[20] But on 20 August the praesidium of the Sakha Supreme Soviet and the Council of Ministers telegrammed the RSFSR government that they saw no need for special measures and would continue to function normally, and on the 21st Nikolaev broadcast to this effect. These actions earned Nikolaev and the Supreme Soviet a place among the loyal supporters of Yeltsin and democracy. The party press was temporarily shut, then taken over, the republican committee and other party bodies faded away, and the Council of Ministers and city council began to squabble over the division of party property.[21]

Nikolaev, as chair of the Supreme Soviet, was in a position to capitalize on the situation. By the middle of October the Supreme Soviet had voted to introduce a presidency. The consequence was a final split in democratic ranks. Those who favoured national independence as an end goal were in favour of a presidency. They supported Nikolaev as the only realistic candidate because, they argued, a presidency was the first step towards a new constitution, elections, and independence. Their opponents were, for the same reasons, opposed to it, arguing that the clause which

[20] *Sots. Yak.*, 10 July 1991, p. 3.
[21] *Sots. Yak.*, then *Yak.*, 20–3 August 1991; 31 August 1991, p. 1: 'Upon his return from Moscow, M. Nikolaev resolved that the paper should make a fresh start as a people's paper. What joy!'; and for the transfer of party property to a children's hospital, 5, 20 September 1991, p. 1.

required the president to speak both Sakha and Russian was discriminatory and that Sakha claims for national self-determination were inappropriate in a republic where they constituted a minority of the population. Russian deputies in Mirny put the question of holding a referendum on Mirny's gaining the status of an autonomous Russian district or leaving the republic on the agenda of the town soviet, and got majority support but, following the presidential elections, the issue subsided.[22] Although several small political parties were formed, none of them, including the Sakha nationalist organizations, exerted any influence on the republic's relationship with Moscow. This remained a matter for the elite to decide. In Tatarstan it was very different.

The elite and the nationalists in Tatarstan

The concentration of intellectual ability in Kazan, and its relative nearness to Moscow, less than a two-hour flight away, meant that in the late 1980s democratization and republican rights quickly became issues. Tatar activists travelled to the Baltic states to print materials and draw lessons from the national independence movements. In several respects developments in Tatarstan resembled those in some of the smaller Union republics: the emergence of a national movement, joint action by nationals and members of other nationalities for democratic rights and greater republican autonomy, even independence. The outcomes, however, were very different. Whereas the Union republics gained their independence as a consequence of a coincidence of a popular movement, a split within the republican elite, and western support – and in some cases, where none of these factors were present, they gained independence by default as the USSR fell apart – no such fortuitous combination of factors blessed the Tatar independence movement. As time passed, the agendas of the Tatar nationalists and reformist Russians began to diverge; the elite was content with lesser gains; only Chechnya joined the call for independence, and there was no western interest. The nationalist movement waned. Negotiation with Moscow over the republic's resources came to be determined by elite interests – the Sakha scenario – but between 1988 and 1992 it was the nationalist movement which set the agenda.

By 1988, in both Kazan and Chelny, clubs of Communist Party members, both Tatars and Russians, had formed to support perestroika and party reform. In June 1988 the first Tatar organization appeared: an initiative group of twelve intellectuals was elected at a meeting at Kazan

---

[22] On the presidency: *Yak.*, 19 October 1991, p. 1; on the split: interviews with Danilov and Zaleskaia, May 1993.

university to work for the acquiring of Union republic status, for perestroika, for encouraging the use of the Tatar language, and the spiritual
rebirth of the Tatar people. Its brief included working with Tatar groups
in other parts of Russia. This was the origin of TOTs, the organization
which came to play the most important part in the movement for national
independence during 1988–92. Party members dominated its leadership
and, until 1993, its chair was M. Miliukov from the department of the
history of the CPSU of Kazan university, still a party member in August
1991. One of its founders was R. Khakimov, who subsequently became
President Shaimiev's political adviser. Some of the more radical nationalists would later claim that TOTs was a party creation and had always
worked with the nomenklatura.[23]

In February 1989 TOTs held its first congress, attended by delegates
from thirty-two towns, and by the summer it was officially registered as a
popular movement.[24] The party authorities were unenthusiastic. They
reacted negatively to a non-party association meddling in political
matters and, in particular, to its endeavour to establish extra-republican
links. Any attempts to create horizontal links that disturbed the vertical
regional parcelling of party and soviet administration always met with a
sharp, almost enraged, response from regional authorities. They, after all,
were responsible for their territory, a unit which was subordinate to
Moscow. The affairs of their neighbours were of no interest to them,
except as potential rivals for Moscow's favours. They had no experience
of working with the neighbouring authorities. Any movements, transactions, or dealings between regions or republics had always been organized
in Moscow. Within such a context, attempts to establish links, from
below, appeared as a direct threat to the established order.

However, during 1989 and early 1990, differences between the ruling
elite and the reformers, either the party clubs or Tatar organizations, or
between the reformers themselves did not dominate the relationships. All,

[23] For the history of Tatar groups in the Soviet period, see Iskhakov, 'Sovremennoe
tatarskoe', pp. 25–7; for TOTs, see Iskhakov, 'Neformal'nye ob''edineniia v sovremennom tatarskom obshchestve', in *Sovremennye natsional'nye protsessy v respublike Tatarstan*
(Kazan, 1992), pp. 5–52. For some early statements: *Vestnik NF*, 13 (1989); *Respublika*, 1
(1990), p. 3 (which has the TOTs declaration 'For the political and economic sovereignty
of the Republic; for the transformation of Tatarstan into a Union republic which would
guarantee the economic independence of the Republic and provide the possibility for the
all-round development of the people of Tatarstan'); then *Tatarstan*, 4 (1993), pp. 18–21,
interview with Marat Miliukov, September 1993; for the criticisms of party links, interviews with Sovereignty representatives and Agliullin, September 1993.

[24] On the origins, organization, and membership of associations and political parties in
Tatarstan, see Iskhakov, 'Neformal'nye ob''edineniia v sovremennom tatarskom obshchestve'; *Obshchestvenno-politicheskie dvizheniia i organizatsii v respublike Tatarstan* (Kazan,
1992); interviews with the activists, party leaders, September 1993.

at this time, shared a common aim: the acquisition of Union republic status. Fauzia Bairamova, the poet, who would later become a passionate supporter of independence, explained to 'our Russian comrades' that all that was meant by independence was Union republican status.[25] None of the nationalists conceived of anything else. Of all the peoples of the USSR, the Tatars could make the best claim to such a status. As a nationality they were much larger than most of those who had Union republic status. The difference was that the Tatar ASSR lay within Russia, and that more Tatars lived outside the republic than within it. The issue had come up at the time of the Stalin constitution, and again in the 1970s when the new Brezhnev constitution was drawn up. Perestroika, and in particular the moves to renegotiate the Union Treaty in the face of Baltic and then Moldovan demands for independence, provided the context for its revival. Union republic status would give the leadership greater status, and direct access to Union party and state authorities; the republic would acquire all those institutions that went with a Union republic; its leaders would be recognized as the peers of the Ukrainians, Georgians, or Uzbeks. Not surprisingly, the party nomenklatura pushed hard for the Union republic. For reformers of different persuasions it symbolized reform of the old rigid Union system; for the Tatar groups it was seen as a step forward to a new Tatarstan; and for many of the Russian population (as for their counterparts in the Baltic republics) one that would give the republic and its population greater control over its own resources.

The 1990 elections to the republican parliaments provided a powerful impetus to nationalist movements, but in Tatarstan the issue was confused by the electorate being part of the RSFSR, and being asked to vote for candidates to the Russian Congress. TOTs, renamed VTOTs in spring 1990, declared itself in favour of a boycott[26] but staged no serious campaign against the vote. The party elite was content to stand. Among those elected were three ministers, the chair and deputy chair (M. Sabirov and Iu. Voronin) of the Council of Ministers, and one city first party secretary. The 24-strong contingent contained both reformers (favouring the Social Democratic fraction), centrists, and the more conservative Sovereignty and Equality members; but, in general, the deputies from Tatarstan were of a centrist persuasion.[27] The Tatar Supreme Soviet was also a moderately conservative body, as regards both its Tatar and its Russian members.

---

[25] *Vestnik NF*, 13 (1989), p. 1.   [26] *Respublika*, 1 (1990), p. 1.

[27] Only one of the twenty-four, Iu. Voronin, joined the Communists, and there were no radical democrats among its members. Despite the demands of some of the nationalist organizations, the deputies continued to participate in the Russian Parliament, dividing their voices roughly equally in favour of and against reform policies. By the spring of 1993, however, at the VIII Congress, they had all swung behind the Supreme Soviet and against the president: Congress data, cited in n. 12.

By the summer, divisions within the republican political community were beginning to appear. The Russian declaration of sovereignty, and the beginning of the war of laws between the USSR and the RSFSR, made the acquisition of Union republic status seem a real possibility while at the same time whetting the appetite of the more militant nationalists. In the aftermath of the Russian Congress, the more radical members of VTOTs set up a national independence party, Ittifak, open to all but with the requirement of learning the Tatar language, and aiming at an independent Tatar state. The natural sympathies of the republic leadership were, however, with the USSR leadership, whom they viewed as old friends and colleagues, not with the democratic Russian leadership. They were quite willing to play on the conflict between the two but they were unenthusiastic about a declaration of sovereignty, a move that would be opposed by the Union leadership. In August 1990 Yeltsin, however, came to Kazan and made the famous statement, 'Take as much sovereignty as you can manage', and the Tatar associations demanded action. Shaimiev, chair of the Soviet, announced himself in favour of sovereignty but *within the RSFSR*. The Supreme Soviet found itself surrounded by a crowd of perhaps 30,000 protesters. Bairamova, now one of the Ittifak leaders, wrote an emotional public appeal to Shaimiev, demanding that he act like a real Tatar man and not a slave to Moscow, and went on hunger strike; VTOTs and Ittifak leaders met with Shaimiev and Sabirov and told them that, if Shaimiev's proposed declaration were adopted, 10,000 people would lie on the railway tracks to stop through transport, the Tiumen Tatars would cut off the oil supplies, and the Tatar workers at KamAZ would come out on strike. Shaimiev spent a sleepless night, then put a new declaration to the Supreme Soviet that made not a mention of the RSFSR. The forces in the Supreme Soviet were fairly evenly divided, but at 11 p.m. the resolution went through.[28]

By the autumn VTOTs had spawned a youth organization, and a group of the cultural intelligentsia had formed Sovereignty, a 'committee to defend and realize the sovereignty of Tatarstan', which began to produce its own newspaper, and whose congress sent notice to the Russian Supreme Soviet that it opposed deputies from Tatarstan working in the parliament of a neighbouring sovereign state.[29] Among the Russian community, offshoots of some of the new Moscow parties had appeared and, in September 1990, following the declaration of sovereignty many of

[28] Interviews with R. Mukhametdinov, A. Makhmutov, R. Iusupov, and others, September 1993; for useful chronicles of political developments in the republic for August 1990–May 1992, see *Tatarstan*, 7–8 (1992), pp. 13–18; and for June 1992–July 1993, 8 (1993), pp. 9–12. For more on the Tatar language, see pp. 84–5.

[29] *Suverenitet*, 3 (1993), pp. 13–16; 9 (1993), p. 2, has an article by R. Mukhametdinov, 'Tatarskii patriotizm', which outlines the group's aims; also interview with him, September 1993.

them grouped together as Consensus, an association to defend the position of Tatarstan within the RSFSR.[30] By the end of the year more than thirty political associations or parties had registered. But unlike the situation in some of the Union republics the political elite itself did not split nor did a section of it join forces with the nationalist movement. Its eyes remained focused on acquiring Union republic status and on Tatarstan's signing the Union treaty as a member equal to others. It is difficult to know how realistic the Tatar hopes were (in retrospect many felt that, had the Union not broken up, the republic would have achieved Union status, although this is surely debatable), but the events of August 1991 changed everything.

By this time Shaimiev, standing as the only candidate, had been elected as president of the republic. Elections had been held to coincide with those for the president of the RSFSR. Roughly 35 per cent of the electorate voted in the RSFSR election, giving Yeltsin slightly under 50 per cent of the vote; many more, 63 per cent, voted in the Tatar presidential election, and of them 71 per cent voted for Shaimiev.[31] VTOTs and Ittifak supported his candidacy, reckoning that no alternative Tatar figure was available, and that what was important was to have a Tatar president. In August Shaimiev and the republican leadership supported the GKChP. The reason is not difficult to see. It was not just that their nomenklatura sympathies were with the old order – as long as it provided for a Tatar Union republic and the rights and privileges that went with one – but that they were more likely to benefit from belonging to a USSR than to a Russian Federation. They backed the wrong side, as it happened, and Khasbulatov, linked with local activists from the Democratic Party of Russia, Russians who had supported Yeltsin, demanded that Shaimiev be brought to Moscow in a cage for his support of the plotters. The triumphant Yeltsin leadership, however, stayed its hand. It had no desire to inflame a situation in which emotions were already running high.

The nomenklatura was in a state of acute anxiety. Not only had they backed the wrong Moscow fraction (and the usual consequences of this were well known) but the party itself was now banned. Calls came from both reformers and nationalists for changes in the government. VTOTs announced the establishment of a national guard and called for a declaration of independence. The Chelny branch, even more radical, called for action against the authorities, and organized a sizeable demonstration (perhaps 5,000 people attended) in Kazan, calling for independence. The

---

[30] Interviews with I. Grachev and Iu. Rostovshchikov, September 1993; *Tatarstan*, 4 (1993), pp. 22–5.   [31] Election details, official document.

leadership hesitated, torn between fear of Moscow and of a popular movement. The Supreme Soviet became the target of the nationalists, now united behind the demand for a declaration of independence. Perhaps 50,000 people, in what was to be the largest meeting, with feelings running high, massed outside the Soviet; there were calls from some for its storming, and there were clashes with the police. The leadership was saved by Moscow's recognition that any action taken against the Tatar leadership could unite it with the nationalists, and by its own assessment of the nationalist movement. At the end of October the Supreme Soviet passed a declaration of independence, but softened the impact with the announcement that a referendum would be held, in the spring, on the issue.[32] From this moment on, however, the relationship between the Tatar and the Russian authorities became very strained.

The Moscow leadership, both president and Supreme Soviet, campaigned hard against the holding of the referendum on independence. The question to be put to the electorate was the following: 'Do you agree that the republic of Tatarstan is a sovereign state, a subject of international law, building its relations with the Russian Federation and other states on the basis of treaties between equal parties?' The Supreme Soviet of the Russian Federation turned to the Constitutional Court with the request that it consider the constitutionality not merely of this but also of the republic's earlier rulings on sovereignty. The court ruled that those points in the original declaration on sovereignty which gave precedence to Tatar laws were unconstitutional, as was the phrase in the referendum on the republic being a subject of international law.[33] The Tatar Supreme Soviet, where by this time a Tatarstan fraction – in support of independence – faced a People's Power fraction, anxious to keep Tatarstan within the Russian Federation, refused to change the wording. (The Russian parties, at the end of 1991, had combined in an association, the Movement for Democratic Reform, to urge voters to vote no in the referendum.) Shaimiev appealed for a vote in favour; Yeltsin stated that the Federation would not allow Tatarstan to leave. The procurator (clearly revealing, in the eyes of the nationalists, the extent of Moscow control of certain key institutions) issued an instruction that polling booths should be shut because of the illegality of the wording of the referendum. This was ignored.[34] According to one source, the directors of the large defence

[32] *Izv. Tat.*, 26 October 1991, p. 1; interviews with participants and VTOTs activists, September 1993.

[33] Decision of the Constitutional Court of 13 March 1992, in *Vech. Kaz.*, 16 March 1992, p. 1.

[34] And, following the referendum, Moscow could do little but accept his replacement by Shaimiev's proposed candidate, a local man: O. Fomenko, 'Tatarstan', in *Pol. monit.*, May 1992.

plants were summoned to a meeting in Moscow and warned that if their workers voted in favour they should not expect federal subsidies.[35] Whether true or not, the statement is revealing for its assumption of the director–labour force relationship as regards voting. The turnout was high – 82 per cent – and 61 per cent voted in favour, 37 per cent against. This translated into 50 per cent of the electorate in favour, 31 per cent against. In rural areas 75 per cent were in favour; in the towns 56 per cent; in Kazan itself the yes vote slipped to 47 per cent of those voting. Support was higher among the Tatar population but, as in the Baltic states, a proportion of the Russians voted in favour too.[36]

As in August 1990, and in October 1991, the tension subsided once the issue was decided. Although in this instance the demoralization of the Russian opposition may have been relevant, Russian fears of a new language or employment policy were not realized. Nothing changed visibly as a result of the referendum. It signified a symbolic victory. Many of those who had supported the national independence movement now reckoned that a compromise was the best policy. One founding member of TOTs wrote:

I swear before Allah I have dreamt all my life of the rebirth of the national statehood of the Tatar people. And now, when the aim is close to being achieved, I have to recognize that it is not so simple. The more I think about a new formula of statehood for Tatarstan, as an independent power, the clearer it seems that it must be of a super-national character.[37]

The radicals found this unacceptable. Dissatisfied with the moderation of the leadership, several of the Tatar associations (but not VTOTs) had announced the calling of an All-Tatar Assembly to elect a Milli Medzhlis, a supreme governing body for the Tatar people. This met in February 1992, with delegates from all over the former Soviet Union, and elected the Milli Medzhlis. The authorities refused, however, to register it as an institution and the Supreme Soviet ruled that its resolutions had no legal basis. It was clear that it lacked any real popular support. This saw the final split within the nationalist movement. VTOTs was accused by the radicals of having come to terms with the Shaimiev leadership and, indeed, Khakimov, one of the key individuals among the original group, became an adviser to the president.

The final battle to be fought involved the constitution, a document which would legalize the different declarations and establish the type of presidential rule to be adopted by the republic. Discussions continued

[35] Zakiev, 'Nationalism and Democratism', p. 12.
[36] Electoral data documents; also see *Vech. Kaz.*, 26 March 1992, p. 1, for some data.
[37] T. Bareev, *Mol. Tat.*, 21 February 1992, p. 7.

throughout the summer. The 'Muscovites' wanted agreements with Moscow to be signed before the constitution was agreed; the 'Tatarstan' fraction wanted the constitution as further ammunition in the negotiations with Moscow, and on this they won. A draft was brought before the Supreme Soviet in October 1992. The main parties involved were the fractions Tatarstan and Consensus, essentially the Tatar group against the Russian group. Shaimiev assumed the role of negotiator. The sections of the constitution dealing with the role of the Supreme Soviet and the president were agreed without too much difficulty. In most respects they were similar to those of the Russian constitution. They retained for the Supreme Soviet its rights to confirm ministerial appointments, and rights over the budget and legislation, and, after discussion, the presidential team gave way on the question of local administrators, whose appointment, it was agreed, should be confirmed by the local soviets.[38] Early re-election of the deputies or president was not envisaged. The three problem areas were language, citizenship, and the nature of the federal relationship.

Although there were those, for example Bairamova, arguing for Tatar as the one official language, here the Tatarstan fraction gave way and agreed that Tatar and Russian should have equal status. The citizenship issue was finally resolved with a complicated wording which stated that the republic had its own citizenship, based on its own laws; that citizens of Tatarstan also held citizenship of the Russian Federation; that dual citizenship could be held on the basis of agreements between Tatarstan and 'other states'; and that no one could be deprived of citizenship (statute 19). This was clearly a compromise, and one surely open to different interpretations. On the federal relationship, however, the two sides dug their heels in. Tatarstan proposed:

The republic of Tatarstan, a sovereign state, a subject of international law, realizes [the preservation of the unity of] its statehood in relation to the Russian Federation–Russia based on cooperation in the form of the joint execution of certain powers as laid down in treaties between equals [*ravnopravnye dogovory*].

Consensus proposed:

The republic of Tatarstan, being a subject of international law, realizes its state sovereignty without state delineation from the Russian Federation and changes to its [RF] territorial unity and borders.

The republic of Tatarstan builds its relations with the Russian Federation based on the constitution of the republic of Tatarstan, the constitution of the Russian Federation, the Treaty on the delimitation and mutual delegation of powers and

[38] A subsequent presidential decree allowed the chief administrator to hold simultaneously the post of chair of the soviet.

administrative responsibilities of the organs of state power of the republic of Tatarstan and the federal organs of the Russian Federation.

Grachev, leader of the Consensus group, argued that 'The fog of this constitution hides dictatorship and complete state separation from the Russian Federation. It can only be adopted if a deal is done between the president's team and the national-extremists.' Miliukov, of VTOTs, claimed that 'if the constitution is not accepted, the deputies must resign. There is nothing dearer than independence.'[39]

Moscow took the issue of the constitution seriously. Yarov and Rumiantsev, leading politicians in the Supreme Soviet, flew down to participate in the session. Rumiantsev was outspoken:

In essence the draft constitution is one of an independent state. If the deputies adopt it they will legally strengthen the state delineation of the republic of Tatarstan from the Russian Federation . . . The deputies of the republic and, incidentally, the electors too should understand that the relationship between the Russian Federation and a republic within the federation is one thing, and that with an independent state is something quite different . . . the federation will not send monies from its pension fund abroad or support foreign universities. And, of course, it is hardly likely that the Russian Federation will place orders for military equipment with the factories of 'a neighbouring state' and make multimilliard ruble grants for conversion.[40]

The message was clear, if hardly diplomatic. After three days of discussions the conciliation commission was no nearer agreement. Shaimiev proposed a new, compromise, version:

The republic of Tatarstan – a sovereign state, a subject of international law, is associated with the Russian Federation–Russia on the basis of the Treaty on the mutual delegation of powers and spheres of authority [*vedeniia*]. [41]

After further lengthy discussion, this (statute 61) was agreed by 174 votes in favour, 9 against, and 25 abstentions (the soviet had 249 members). And then the constitution as a whole was passed: 176 in favour, 1 against, and 9 abstentions, but some of those who were most opposed to the final version simply left the session before the final votes were cast.[42]

The radical nationalists were dissatisfied. Why, A. Makhmutov, the Sovereignty leader, was asking six months later, why was there 'an association' with the Russian Federation, and why should citizens of Tatarstan have Russian citizenship; the constitution could only be considered a

---

[39] Quotes from *Vech. Kaz.*, 26 October 1992, p. 1; draft clauses from *Izv. Tat.*, 6 November 1992, p. 1; on different positions, see also *Ross. gaz.*, 14 October 1992, p. 2; *Vech. Kaz.*, 28 October 1992, p. 1; *Izv. Tat.*, 30 October 1992, p. 1.
[40] *Vech. Kaz.*, 28 October 1992, p. 1.   [41] *Izv. Tat.*, 6 November 1992, p. 1.
[42] *Izv. Tat.*, 7, 10 November 1992, p. 1.

transitional one.[43] But by now the nationalist movement was not only badly split, but interest in politics had waned. The constitution had engaged the hearts and minds of the politicians but not the public; the nationalist movement had ebbed, and there were no stormy meetings around the Supreme Soviet. By the end of 1992 only 4 per cent of the population expressed any commitment to VTOTs.[44] The subsequent fate of the nationalist movement is a depressing and not uncommon one. With the appearance of a more radical fraction from Chelny, led by the young Z. Agliullin, a marginal individual, advocating violence if necessary, VTOTs split yet again. In the spring of 1993, at the III Congress, the threatening behaviour of Agliullin and his supporters persuaded the moderates to leave the hall, whereupon Agliullin was elected to the chair. A few months later, however, he was arrested and charged with, among other things, holding weapons. During his time in detention, the moderates staged a counterattack; at a second attempt they managed to call another congress, and formed a new collective leadership of five. By the autumn of 1993 the two rival fractions, which did not recognize each other, occupied different rooms in the same building. Agliullin advocated a nation-state, with one official language, Tatar; his rivals also wanted a nation-state, nuclear-free and demilitarized, and a more active promotion of the Tatar language but favoured leaving the two languages as official ones. Neither favoured an Islamic state. If Agliullin saw himself leading a small group, committed to direct action, the moderate leaders viewed VTOTs as a social organization, with a brief to link up Tatar communities and to work for the rebirth of the Tatar peoples in general. Perhaps, its supporters thought, it might evolve into a Tatar Party of Russia.[45]

In the spring of 1992 a group of Tatar intellectuals had founded a Republican Party of Tatarstan which claimed to represent both Russian and Tatar interests – without, however, having any Russian members – and favoured a state for both. By the autumn of 1993 one of its leaders, R. Iusupov, rector of the Pedagogical Institute, was claiming 3,000 members, and that the party, with the backing of its more radical associates – Ittifak, Sovereignty – would advance as the Tatar party, a real political force, in any forthcoming elections. Ittifak and Sovereignty, both of which wanted more action on the language issue, were highly critical of the Shaimiev leadership (whereas VTOTs maintained a cautious but not hostile attitude towards the president) and had no dealings with VTOTs. Sovereignty, by the autumn of 1993, was producing three bi-monthly

---

[43] *Tatarstan*, 3 (1993), p. 1.   [44] *Tatarstan*, 4 (1993), pp. 3–9.

[45] *Nezav.*, 15 June 1993, p. 2; *Nezavisimost'* (publication of Sovereignty, Kazan), 6 (1993), p. 1; *Izv.*, 15 July 1993, p. 2; *Mol. Tat.*, 35 (1993), p. 2; interviews with Agliullin and with the leaders of the moderate group, September 1993.

newspapers: *Independence* and *Kommersant,* both in Russian, and *Sovereignty,* in Russian and Tatar. The Ministry of Information had attempted, unsuccessfully, to close the latter for insulting the president. They were financed, it was claimed, by wealthy sponsors: a state-farm chairman, Tatars in Bashkiria, rich patriots. Some in the Tatar community, however, doubted that matters were so straightforward. It seemed unlikely that individual Tatars had the money to support these ventures; it was surprising how easily some of the most radical nationalists received favourable treatment that required official backing (foreign passports, trips abroad, permits and housing in Kazan). Might it not be that Moscow had an interest in encouraging an increase in ethnic tension, to be used as an argument against the Tatar leadership's ability to control the situation, if necessary?[46]

Negotiations with Moscow

Sakha style

It was the summer of 1991 before the republican authorities began to take advantage of the struggle between the Union and Russian leaderships to try to gain greater control over their own resources. The Russian Parliament had passed a decree in December 1990 which gave the republics greater autonomy. Of little practical significance, given Union control of key resources, it allowed the chair of the Sakha Council of Ministers to argue, in August 1991, that the decree and the failure of the USSR Supreme Soviet to meet its promises on budget allocations gave the republic the right to determine the percentage of profits it would pass on to the Union and to the RSFSR authorities. Moscow, he complained, claimed ownership of 85 per cent of the republic's productive assets and took all but 4 per cent of the profits.[47] This announcement followed what must have been an unfruitful visit a month earlier by Pavlov, the USSR prime minister.[48] By October Sakha had ceased to supply the Union authorities with gold and diamonds. By the end of the year Nikolaev had won the presidency and struck a new deal with the Russian government that included the republic retaining 10 per cent of the diamonds mined.[49]

Increasingly Nikolaev began to argue in the now-fashionable language of people's rights and to stress the wrongs suffered under the old system. Moscow not only seems but is a very long way away, eight time zones, an

[46] Interviews with Iusupov, Mukhametdinov, and Makhmutov, September 1993.
[47] *Sots. Yak.*, 10 August 1991, p. 1.   [48] *Sots. Yak.*, 19 July 1991, p. 1.
[49] *Yak.*, 19 October 1991, p. 1; 20 December 1991, p. 1.

eight-hour flight. Nevertheless, according to Nikolaev, it used to be that all key decisions affecting the republic were taken in Moscow. The republic, he suggested, was treated in a colonial fashion, as a supplier of raw materials, the profits from the diamond industry went almost entirely to Moscow, and Soviet policy towards the indigenous peoples was one of 'denationalization', of imposing a uniform lifestyle. On another occasion he referred to the old situation when 'we had to crawl on our knees in front of the Moscow bureaucrats', and 'to the destructive *diktaty* of the centre'.[50]

But in the spring of 1992 Sakha signed the Federal Treaty which, Nikolaev would argue repeatedly, established a true 'federation of nation-states'. The republic's new constitution, adopted by its Supreme Soviet in April 1992, provided for 'sovereignty, democracy, and a law-based state, all based on the right of the republic's people to national self-determination'. This, it was argued, did not contradict – on the contrary, it underpinned – the idea of federalism: 'In accordance with the principles of freedom and equal rights, on which the Federal Treaty is based, the republic of Sakha is a member of the federal state of the Russian Federation.'[51] The treaty, Nikolaev frequently stated, gave the republics the ownership of their own natural resources. 'For the first time it was directly stated that the republics, within Russia, are states. And raw materials, and the forests, the animal and plant world are the property of their peoples.' The slogan for all, he asserted, should be 'Enrich yourselves and enrich your republic!' In June 1993 Nikolaev was arguing that 'We understand our sovereignty as based on a treaty relationship with the federal organs.'[52]

Not surprisingly the draft constitution for the Russian Federation, produced in the summer of 1993, which proposed equal representation for republics and regions in the upper house, came in for strong criticism. The constitutional conference, Nikolaev argued, was trying to turn the clock back; the draft did not recognize that Russia was a federation of nation-states; in emphasizing unitarism it was riding roughshod over 'the peoples of Russia', interpreting democracy as the interests of the majority, regardless of the minority. The republic could not agree to it.[53] But even when at his most critical of federal developments Nikolaev continued to insist that Sakha's future lay within the Federation. There are boundaries, he suggested, across which one should not step, and raising the question of leaving the Federation was one of them; he regretted that

---

[50] *Sov. Ross.*, 8 December 1992, p. 3; *Res. Sakha*, 25 December 1993, pp. 1–2; *Nezav.*, 19 March 1993, p. 5; *Sots. Yak.*, 16 August 1991, p. 1.

[51] *Sov. Ross.*, 8 December 1992, p. 3.   [52] *Izv.*, 22 June 1993, p. 2.

[53] *Nezav.*, 30 June 1993, p. 2.

Tatarstan, in holding its referendum on independence, had crossed this boundary.[54]

Why the caution? Yeltsin, Nikolaev argued, had understood when he visited Sakha in June 1993 that the power of Russia would depend upon its having strong republics and territories. (Chernomyrdin, the Russian prime minister, when visiting Tomsk a few months earlier, had claimed exactly the opposite.) 'The wellbeing of Russia will to a large extent depend upon the wellbeing of Yakutia'; the republic was the only one which received no subsidy from the federal budget, and all would benefit if it received more economic autonomy. And on his visit Yeltsin, seeking to strengthen his support among the republican leaders, agreed that 'We should give the republics greater economic independence.'[55] However, and despite Nikolaev's claims that the republic took not a kopek from the federal budget, the republic could not do without the centre. A report on a long meeting between Nikolaev and Chernomyrdin in March 1994 sheds light both on the issues involved and on Chernomyrdin's style of government. First Nikolaev raised the matter of the creation of a federal fund for the socio-economic development of the republic. Although the fund had been long agreed in principle – its realization had first been delayed by the need to get the approval of the Ministry of Finance and of the Ministry of Economics – the project was now held up somewhere in the government. Chernomyrdin promised to try to expedite matters. Secondly, Nikolaev raised points relating to a presidential decree that were not being implemented: federal funding for housing in the Far North, for helping agriculture, and the unfreezing of foreign currency accounts held by the Foreign Trade Bank. Chernomyrdin ordered an assistant to look into these matters, with a view to resolving them, if possible. Thirdly, and more directly, Nikolaev asked for extra credits (300 mlrd r. for the quarter) in order to buy and stock the provisions needed for the coming year. (Most food and consumer goods, as well as primary materials, have to be imported during the short summer, and stored; the republic has therefore always operated on a credit basis, paying at the end of the year.) Chernomyrdin gave no direct answer but promised to look into it. Nikolaev proposed the creation of an International Bank for the Reconstruction of the Arctic; Chernomyrdin ordered the Ministry of Finance and the Central Bank to respond within a month. Nikolaev handed over a draft decree on the development of the Arctic regions; Chernomyrdin promised to consider it. Finally, Nikolaev raised the matter of a gas consortium involving the Russian Federation, Sakha, and

[54] *Ross. gaz.*, 8 September 1993, p. 4.
[55] *Izv.*, 22 June 1993, p. 2; *Nezav.*, 30 December 1992, p. 3; *Ross. gaz.*, 8 September 1993, p. 4.

South Korea which was to be discussed during his forthcoming visit to South Korea, and Chernomyrdin authorized him to act on behalf of the Russian Federation.[56]

It is notable that Nikolaev obtained only one unequivocal decision: on his right to act for the Russian Federation in South Korea. On all the others Chernomyrdin responded in a business-like fashion, but in each case this involved passing the matter on to another institution or merely promising to look into it. Republican representatives might no longer have to crawl on their knees in Moscow, but the federal bureaucracy could hold up decisions for months and, when it came to actually getting credits, the bureaucratic obstacles multiplied. 'Today', Nikolaev said in December 1992, 'we no longer have any pretensions towards Russia', but credits for the purchase of winter supplies were essential. This was still true in 1994.

The second issue that was central to negotiations with the centre was control of the diamond industry. The republic mined the diamonds but it lacked the expertise to rework them, or to trade them on the world market; it needed to recruit skilled specialists and to be able to retain its immigrant industrial population – its own labour force was, as yet, ill equipped for the task. The republican leadership succeeded in 1991 in renegotiating the terms under which it mined the diamonds, in particular, the percentage it retained for its own use. Privatization now magnified the issue of control. As might be expected where so many interests were involved, it proved extremely complex. In February 1992 Yeltsin signed an edict under which one huge corporation, with branches in Sakha and in Moscow, and within which the government would retain a controlling share, was to be created. It took over a year to set up. There were ministerial officials in Moscow who objected to the whole idea; then problems arose over ministerial representation (the Ministry of Finance, the state property committee, the state committee on precious metals, and the Ministry for Foreign Trade, as well as representatives of the Sakha government, were all to be included). A new presidential edict on corruption necessitated a redrafting of the rights of the Council of Advisers. Agreement on a name caused problems. Finally, however, AO Almazy-Rossii-Sakha came into existence as a share-holding company of a closed type, centred in Mirny, but with one of its two vice presidents based in Moscow to supervise the Moscow offices. It was granted the right to buy back a substantial proportion of the above-quota diamonds from the state committee on precious metals. Of its after-tax profits, 32 per cent went to the federal government, 32 per cent to the republican government, 8 per

---

[56] *Res. Sakha*, 22 March 1994, p. 1.

cent to the town of Mirny, and 28 per cent were distributed in dividends to the share-holders. Employees (40,000–45,000 in the Mirny region) were entitled to one share each. The company also set up an investment company in which these shares and vouchers could be invested.[57]

All were aware that the economic future of the company and the economy of the republic were closely intertwined. The importance of the diamond mines is evidenced by their providing 80–90 per cent of the tax revenue of the republican budget. Reporting on the economic situation at the beginning of 1994, the vice president of the republic (who had just attended the company's board of directors' meeting to hear the end-of-year totals) emphasized that, although they had managed to halt the fall in production, as an exporting republic the dollar–ruble exchange rate hurt them badly. He also drew attention to problems facing the republic's agricultural sector: it needed to be slimmed down, it could not be maintained out of the budget, but then the problem of the displaced labour would arise.[58] In February at a conference on labour resources for the diamond industry it was suggested that shortly the agricultural sector would have 30,000 unemployed and ways should be sought to bring them, gradually, into the industrial sector; work on the drilling sites could be a transitional stage. The unspoken problem lay in the rural unemployed being almost entirely Sakha, traditionally unwilling to move into industrial employment. Meanwhile the skilled were leaving – 31,800 left the republic during 1992–3.[59] The government issued a decree on 'The recruitment and retention of the labour force at the enterprises of AO Almazy-Rossii-Sakha during 1994', which specified that there should be no external recruitment (apart from specialists), and included a complete plan of the company's labour policy for the coming year.[60] The decree is witness to the close relationship between company and government, an aspect of domestic policy to which I shall return in the next chapter.

One prong in Nikolaev's strategy of increasing the republic's autonomy was to develop international links. He broached the idea of developing the polar sea route with the creation of a Northern Forum (an association of northern states with an Arctic interest), and acted as host to a meeting of its members in March 1994. Resolutions of good intent rather than actual programmes emerged but Nikolaev's status as an international player was enhanced. It was clear that the international community was interested in the Russian Far North and Nikolaev had become its spokesman.[61] By the spring of 1994 he was increasingly busy with foreign travel – to Japan,

[57] 'How goes it in the diamond kingdom?', *Mirnyi rab.*, 6 January 1993, p. 3; interviews with company officials, May 1993.   [58] *Res. Sakha*, 11 January 1994, p. 1.
[59] *Res. Sakha*, 18 February 1993, p. 1; 27 April 1993, p. 2.   [60] *Yak. ved.*, 8 (1994).
[61] *Nezav.*, 19 March 1993, p. 5; *Res. Sakha*, 3 February 1994, p. 1; 15 March 1994, p. 1.

where he signed various deals giving Japanese companies access to the republic, to Sweden, and to South Korea; the vice president meanwhile was accompanying the president of Almazy-Rossii-Sakha to Botswana.[62] Nikolaev, however, and presumably the management of the corporation were aware that their possession of precious stones and metals did not automatically ensure their economic independence. It was not just diamonds. An attempt to start manufacturing clothing, reliant upon the import of both materials and machinery, quickly found it could not compete with imported Chinese goods.[63] A gloomy assessment of the economic situation in early 1994 was given by A. Alekseev, leader of the republic's Communist Party, and, perhaps surprisingly, his conclusions were seconded by a new Analytic Centre attached to the presidency: given the general economic catastrophe that had overtaken the Russian Federation, any talk of Sakha's economic independence was absurd.[64]

In a rare admission, which revealed the key reason for remaining within the Russian Federation, Nikolaev admitted 'It is out of the question for us to part company. Even when faced by the most negative aspects of our relationship, only a madman could today countenance a break with Russia, risking the consequence of sliding into dependence upon some state or other [read Japan or the USA] . . . I am deeply convinced of the truth of the popular wisdom that says an old friend is better than two new ones.'[65] But at other times too the fighting talk of a newly independent leader who had thrown off colonial oppression gave way to that of a subordinate partner. Sakha, he suggested on one occasion, given its huge territory and poorly developed social infrastructure, should perhaps be given a special status within the federation: 'after all Finland and Poland had a particular status within the Russian empire'.[66]

The federal constitution

Whether it was part of a conscious strategy or, as some critics charged, an inability to shed their dependent status, members of the political elite showed a willingness to play their parts as befitted those from a second-ranking republic. The Baltic leaderships might begin to question the Union, or the Tatar leadership put forward demands for the status of a Union Republic, but not those in Sakha. Although in September 1993 the Sakha government and Supreme Soviet came out in favour of early elections of both the Russian Parliament and president, Nikolaev took a

---

[62] The Japanese visit was, however, authorized by the Russian Foreign Ministry: *Res. Sakha*, 29 March 1994, p. 1; 13 April 1994, p. 1.
[63] *Izv.*, 9 June 1993, p. 2.   [64] *Res. Sakha*, 1 March 1994, p. 1.
[65] *Ross. gaz.*, 8 September 1993, p. 4.   [66] *Izv.*, 22 June 1993, p. 2.

public stand on 4 October in support of Yeltsin, and the republican authorities put up no opposition. How did he react to the presidential constitution of December 1993 that removed the word 'sovereign' from the republics and emphasized the unitary aspects of rule? Does it not, asked an interviewer, reduce the rights of the republics to nil? Nikolaev was too much of a politician to agree to this. He suggested that, regardless of his view of certain clauses, now was no time for criticism. 'There's no need to dramatize the situation', he replied. The constitution had received majority support in the country, and 54 per cent of the republic's vote. 'The rights of the republics are not reduced, neither economically nor politically. In multifaceted Russia it is impossible to adopt the same approach to all – Sakha's problems are different from Samara's . . . for the past two years we haven't taken a kopek from the federal budget . . . but if the idea of empire is reanimated, Russia will fall apart . . . A sovereign Russia must guarantee the rebirth and the blossoming of the national republics which make up its body . . . but we must not fan national issues.'[67] For his support he received a glowing accolade from Yeltsin:

Take Yakutia, the republic of Sakha, and its president, Mikhail Efimovich Nikolaev. A native northerner, Sakha by nationality, by right he takes his place in the ranks of the leading politicians and statesmen of Russia. His talent has blossomed in the past two to three years. He is on a creative upward path; he has far from reached the limits of his ability. Mikhail Efimovich impresses me as a man of few words, by his thoughtfulness and his integrity. I know he has come under fire for endeavouring to act independently, including in raising the status of the Sakha republic.

However, President Nikolaev is a sober politician, a stubborn organizer, not inclined to opportunism and populism. Very carefully, but resolutely and cleverly he managed the stage of increasing the sovereignization of the republic. He managed, in a very short period of time, to bring the status of the republic into line with the demands of life, which allowed the transformation of a huge territory into a high-income region with a stable socio-economic situation . . . In all of this he has been governed not only by republican interests but also by those of Russia. I consider that one of his strongest features, and one which characterizes him as a mature politician.

And Nikolaev, although president of a sovereign state, replied that 'the republic of Sakha is tied to Russia with unbreakable bonds of genuine brotherly cooperation and centuries of friendship. We shall remain within the Russian Federation; we are selflessly interested in preserving and strengthening its unity.'[68]

These are revealing statements. The first point to note – and it is not important who wrote the statement, or whether Nikolaev's words were his

[67] *Res. Sakha*, 25 December 1993, pp. 1–2.   [68] Ibid.

own – is how the parties adopt the canons of ritual Soviet exchange. Yeltsin uses the opportunity, in praising Nikolaev, to indicate the kind of behaviour that is undesirable; we are led to understand that there are others who, alas, lack Nikolaev's virtues. With his description of Nikolaev's successful policies, he offers a clear statement of the federal position towards republican sovereignty – there is no mention of independence, rather of 'increasing the sovereignization' of the republic (republics, it would seem, can have more or less sovereignty) in accordance 'with the demands of life' (which must surely be open to negotiation), and the importance of federal interests is emphasized. Yeltsin does not need to mention Tatarstan for the message to be clear. Whether his praise of Nikolaev is politically motivated or simply reflects the natural language of the imperial ruler, Yeltsin manages to emphasize Nikolaev's junior status – he is learning, developing; Yeltsin holds out the promise of higher office, thus combining the offer of a reward for service with the reminder that more important posts exist than that of president of a republic. Nikolaev makes a ritual obeisance.

What have we here? Two ex-party secretaries engaged in dance steps so often executed by them both? But the situation was different now: they were engaged in a real conflict over power and resources. Moscow could no longer simply dictate policy to the republic while the republican leadership still wanted resources from the federal government. Unable to resolve their differences, they opt for second best – Nikolaev supports Yeltsin in return for the best deal he can get – and they hide their disagreements under the cloak of the old language. They could do this because there was no challenge to them from their respective intelligentsia, let alone any joining of forces between them. Yeltsin's critics in Russia were no supporters of national self-determination, and Nikolaev's opponents in Sakha were a few voices crying in the wind.

Negotiating Tatar-style

Immediately following the referendum on Tatarstan's independence in February 1992, the Tatar leadership had flown to Moscow for discussions. Resting their case on the referendum, they did not sign the Federal Treaty at the end of March. It was agreed between the two sides that relations between the Russian Federation and Tatarstan would be based upon a series of agreements or treaties covering economic issues, foreign relations, citizenship, etc. Progress was extremely slow, almost negligible until the spring of 1994, but it was in neither side's interest to demand decisions. Moscow was not prepared to accept Tatarstan as an independent state, and the Tatarstan leadership knew it, but nor did Moscow want a showdown. The Russian negotiating team was always changing or, according to the Tatars, putting off the meetings.

Under the terms of a provisional agreement, the republic retained 5 million tonnes of the 29–30 million tonnes of oil produced in 1992 (compared with 1 million in 1991), but the terms for 1993 still needed to be decided as well as crucial matters concerning the budget, citizenship, and conscription.[69] On 21 January 1993 the two presidents, Yeltsin and Shaimiev, each flanked by a high-level delegation, met for the first of what was announced to be a series of monthly meetings in order to agree the terms of the treaty between the two states. The Tatar delegation adopted a tough position, stating that if the agreement was not signed by April, Tatarstan would not participate in the forthcoming federal referendum on the constitution, and Yeltsin agreed that it should be.[70] Seven out of ten points were agreed at the January meeting, including the selling of the oil quota for hard currency, but they were not made public. The question of conscription and of Tatarstan's share of the former USSR debt were not resolved, and the February meeting was put off until mid-March. By now political developments at the centre had pushed any hope of an agreement by April off the agenda.[71] The non-signing had its advantages for the Tatar leadership. It could hold Moscow responsible for social and economic difficulties. More than that, it could delay adopting economic reforms and privatization on the grounds that its hands were tied until more important questions such as that of citizenship were decided. Shaimiev used this argument in December 1992.[72] And in the meantime it could try to ensure that 'its own people' occupied the posts that would give them claims to ownership when privatization came.

The question of the budget was very contentious. According to the federal authorities, and economists writing in the central press, in 1992 and 1993 Tatarstan failed to meet its obligations to the federal budget. The Tatarstan minister of finance hotly denied this, quoting figures to show that, in accordance with the temporary agreement in operation until the treaty be signed, Tatarstan had paid more into the federal budget than it had received for the pensions fund and higher education.[73] Sabirov, the Tatar prime minister, denied Moscow's claims and responded with counterthreats: the pipeline from the Tiumen oil fields ran through

[69] Interview with Tatarstan government representative.
[70] *Nezav.*, 23 January 1993, p. 2.
[71] *Nezav.*, 6 March 1993, p. 3; 25 February 1993, p. 1; 14 May 1993, p. 1. *Izv.*, 11 March 1992, p. 4, has a reasonable account of the different political positions within Tatarstan at this time.   [72] *Nezav.*, 22 December 1992, p. 1.
[73] *Mol. Tat.*, 33 (1993), p. 4, which includes references to the central press, and see, e.g., L. Smirniagin, in *Ross. vesti*, 26 June 1993, p. 2, linking this with a call for a territorial federation.

Tatarstan and could always be switched off, and train traffic halted.[74] Where the truth lay is difficult to ascertain. Figures given in the central press bore little relation to the official Tatarstan figures, and inflation played havoc with all figures during the course of 1992 and 1993. However, after the treaty had been signed in the spring of 1994, Sabirov caused a minor sensation by stating, in reply to a question from Bairamova, the radical poet, that the republic was receiving more from the federal budget than it paid in, and Shaimiev confirmed this: 'If it was not for the real help we receive from Russia it is possible that our situation would be significantly worse . . . from the federal budget we today receive for current expenditure [for the industrial enterprises] more than we pay back. Just for the spring sowing we have received favourable credits for more than 60 mlrd r. That's ten times more than our payments.'[75]

Although the leadership might bargain, hold up the payment of taxes, and play the nationalist card, it could not do without federal funding. It might have oil but, as a land-locked state, it could not refine and sell it abroad without the use of federal facilities; it needed federal funding to maintain its higher education institutions; and, most important, 20 per cent of its employed population worked in defence plants which, along with the giant KamAZ plant with a population of half a million dependent upon it, required federal subsidies for survival and, in the case of the defence plants, conversion to consumer production. During 1992 and 1993 the republic gained control, or ownership, of the majority of enterprises on its territory including KamAZ and Tatneft, the oil company.[76] This was a mixed blessing. Although in 1993 KamAZ and fifteen other large enterprises contributed 60 per cent of the republican budget, the republic authorities, in turn, now had to find substantial subsidies for most of them. Federal subsidies were sought in return for federal shares.[77] The hard-currency oil budget was quite separate: initially the Foreign Trade Bank in Moscow froze the Tatarstan account but by 1992 the republic had gained control over it, and transferred it to a Swiss bank. These items featured among the seven points in the treaty on which agreement was reached in the spring of 1993. But interested deputies

---

[74] *Ross. gaz.*, 22 September 1993, p. 3.

[75] I. Akhmetov, 'Tatarstan', *Pol. monit.*, May 1994.

[76] If, in 1987, 80 per cent of the industrial enterprises in the republic were administered by Union, and 18 per cent by RSFSR institutions, by 1994 the Tatar government was responsible for 65 per cent of the state property on the territory: Farukshin, 'Politicheskaia elita', p. 68. Without proper definitions of both 'privatized' and 'state' property, the statement leaves much unclear but, without doubt, the republican government had acquired control over substantial resources.

[77] Interviews with government spokesmen, September 1993; *Izv. Tat.*, 18 September 1993, p. 1.

gained access to the documentation only with extreme difficulty, and not before mid-summer. To their dismay they discovered that the wording on items concerning defence plants, oil, and the environment either contradicted points in the constitution or existing international agreements and, given their status of confidential state documents, no public discussion was permitted. Similar secrecy surrounded the agreement reached over Tatneft.[78]

By the summer of 1993 the leadership sought a high international profile, as befitted 'a subject of international law'. Trade agreements were signed, initially with Uzbekistan and Lithuania, and then with six of the other republics of the former USSR, and negotiations took place with the Crimea. Shaimiev visited the United States, Canada, Turkey (all in 1992), Hungary, and Greece (in 1993) to establish business contacts. Unesco and other international organizations were targeted: if they gave Tatarstan status as a member country, maybe diplomatic recognition would follow. There was talk of a union with Bashkortostan. But here the situation was complicated. Bashkortostan had a large Tatar population and fewer resources: it had no wish to become a junior partner or part of a future greater Tatarstan.[79]

Despite, however, all the foreign links and the leadership's bold talk, Moscow had the stronger hand. It could not enforce conscription (indeed, only 10 per cent reported for service in 1993), but it controlled the army, the police, and the KGB. (Some of the nationalists claimed that 30 per cent of the federal officer corps was Tatar but, even if this was true, no nationalist association or demands came from them.) Moscow could, if need be, enforce an economic blockade and seriously damage the republican economy. This might be true, agreed the nationalists, but it was also true that the Shaimiev leadership was timid, still scared of Moscow. Events at the centre, and the nationalist movement, had pushed them towards independence; they would not have chosen the path themselves. And indeed it is noticeable that Shaimiev's statements grew bolder or weaker depending on political developments at the centre. Yeltsin's appeal to the people of Russia on 20 March 1993, and the strengthening of central presidential power, had Shaimiev claiming: 'We shall live according to our constitution', followed by a confused statement that 'regardless of what happens in Moscow . . . we are in favour of the wholeness [tselostnost] of the Russian Federation'.[80]

---

[78] See concerns raised in *Mol. Tat.*, 30 (1993), p. 2; interviews with deputies, September 1993; *Izv. Tat.*, 24 September 1993, p. 1.

[79] *Nezav.*, 25 February 1993, p. 1; 2 March 1993, p. 1; *Tatary i Tatarstan*, p. 97; *Nezav.*, 5 June 1993, p. 3; Unesco funded conference in Naberezhnye Chelny, September 1993; interviews with politicians, including Likhachev, and journalists, September 1993.

[80] *Ross. gaz.*, 24 March 1993, p. 4.

Shaimiev, together with other republican leaders (apart from those from the Chuvash republic and Mordova), did not favour the holding of a federal referendum in the spring of 1993 – describing it as a destabilizing factor – and could not resist pointing out to the Russian public and their politicians that in Tatarstan there was a president, Parliament, and government, and yet they managed to work together. When, however, Yeltsin announced that a referendum would be held on 25 April, the Tatar leadership confirmed that polling booths would be open throughout its territory. Given that its citizens held Russian citizenship, they must be given the possibility of voting but, Shaimiev suggested, most would hold back: the memory of Moscow's insulting and offensive pressure at the time of the republic's own referendum the previous March was still too fresh in people's minds. The results confirmed his prediction: only 23 per cent turned out to vote.[81]

The federal constitution

Like his colleague Nikolaev in Sakha, Shaimiev saw nothing good in the constitutional drafts that appeared in the summer of 1993. Any attempt to give republics and regions equal status or rights produced the strongest reaction from him and Tatar spokesmen. In April he was arguing that 'a territorial unit can never become a republic';[82] this remained the Tatar position throughout. The format of and discussion at the constitutional conference dismayed the Tatar delegation, which departed for Kazan, leaving V. Likhachev, the vice president, to speak to Yeltsin.[83] The Tatar position on the draft constitutions was clear. The Federal Treaty, despite its inadequacies, had recognized that Russia was a multinational country, and that its peoples had the right of self-determination. It was on this basis that the republics had been given their privileged status. If now republics and regions were to be given the same status as administrative units, this signalled a step backwards, an infringement of the rights of its peoples. Under the Soviet regime, argued Khakimov, the notion of a Soviet people had been used to deny individual peoples their right of national self-determination; now a new term, 'the Russian people [*Rossiiskii narod*]', was being employed to the same end. The republics had become sovereign states. Was the intention that the regions too should move towards this? (Khakimov was, of course, well aware that some regions, notably Sverdlovsk, were contemplating such a course of

[81] *Izv.*, 11 February 1993, p. 1; 14 April 1993, p. 2; *Nezav.*, 13 March 1993, p. 1; 1 April 1993, pp. 1–3; 14 May 1993, p. 1.
[82] *Nezav.*, 1 April 1993, p. 3; see also 26 May 1993, pp. 1–3.
[83] *Ross. gaz.*, 16 July 1993, p. 3.

action.) The republics, he argued, should decide which powers they would delegate to the federal authorities; a federation should be constructed from below. It was then for the federal authorities to decide how much autonomy they would grant the regions. If the latter wanted independence, they should first claim sovereignty. Tatarstan, he concluded, and this was the official position, was linked to the Russian Federation only on the basis of clause 61 of its constitution which spoke of 'association'. Its independence as a state had been acquired by all the appropriate legal and democratic procedures but it had no wish to cut itself off from the federation.[84]

During the following months spokesmen for Tatarstan continued to insist that they were not the splitters; they wished for a constitution that took account of the interests of all the peoples of the federation. It was difficult to see how this could be achieved. If one accepted Khakimov's argument on self-determination, the Russians, whose representative institutions were the regional bodies, could be said to lack their own sovereign institutions; it could be argued that the regions should constitute one republic, and the federation then should be constructed by agreement between the new smaller number of units. Khakimov did not take the argument this far, for two reasons. Any suggestion that the Russian regions, which accounted for over 80 per cent of the population, should constitute one republic of equal weight at federal level was plainly absurd. But, from the point of view of the regions, his suggestion that the republics, but not the regions, should decide which powers they would delegate to the centre was equally unacceptable. Many of the regions had much larger populations than those of the republics, were strategically and economically important, and saw no reason why the accident of nationality and Soviet history should make them lesser partners in a federation. Republican leaders could, but did not, point out that the present arrangements ensured an overwhelming Russian dominance in the federal institutions, and this surely safeguarded the rights of the Russian people. Whom, it might be asked, were the federal authorities representing when they acted as co-signer of the Federal Treaties, if not the Russians?

What kind of a federation could have satisfied the Tatars? This was indeed difficult to answer, just as it was difficult to answer the question, 'Is Tatarstan part of Russia or not?' (The only conclusion on the status of

---

[84] *Nezav.*, 24 June 1993, p. 1. A few months earlier he had invited the readers of *Nezavisimaia gazeta* 'to compare, for example, the position of Greenland within the framework of a *unified* but democratic Denmark with the rights of the subjects of the Russian *Federation*. It's like heaven and earth . . . it only remains for sovereign Tatarstan to envy non-sovereign Greenland' (5 January 1993, p. 2; emphasis in original).

Tatarstan, a journalist remarked, that could be drawn from the answers of local politicians was that Tatarstan was to be found in the northern hemisphere, somewhere in the region of the 55th parallel.)[85] Statements made by Tatarstan spokesmen revealed the confusion. If Likhachev thought that perhaps what was needed was a special clause for Tatarstan in the new constitution, Shaimiev, criticizing the unitarian spirit of the constitutional drafts and suggesting that 'Russia has a long way to go before it becomes a genuine federation', was in favour of Tatarstan joining a true federation, while the chair of the Tatarstan Supreme Soviet advocated a confederation.[86] By early September, reacting to the ever louder calls from the regions that they be listened to, Shaimiev was blasting the federal authorities on the pages of the central press. The government, he argued, had no policy on the national question; if one was to emerge, 'the spirit of imperialist thinking must be swept out of the corridors of power in Moscow'; the federal authorities must realize that a union would be strong only if powers were delegated upwards from below:

The centre only thinks it administers but objectively it cannot because it has no levers with which to administer – neither a planned economy nor the centralized material-technical supply system . . . the regions, and primarily the republics, must be given the maximum freedom of action . . . and be represented in all the federal institutions.

What kind of a state was it, he asked, where many of its peoples still studied their own language as if it was a foreign one? The Russian leadership must decide: was Russia to be a mono-national or a multinational state. He understood the Cossacks' desire for the restoration of their long-suppressed rights but why should they, and not others, be allowed military formations? And all the talk of constructing a federation on a territorial basis was a nonsense: the peoples who had gained their sovereignty would not give it up.[87] Even the usually diplomatic Likhachev, reacting sharply to threats from B. Fedorov, the Russian minister of finance, that tax debtors might find themselves in trouble, mentioned a proposal to set up a union of the Volga regions to defend their common interests.[88]

Republics and regions fell largely silent in the aftermath of the bloodshed in the capital in October 1993. The centre had, for the time being, re-exerted its authority. The Tatar leadership toned down its vocal criticism of the federal authorities but continued to maintain that the federal

[85] *Izv.*, 11 March 1993, p. 4.
[86] *Ross. gaz.*, 16 July 1993, p. 3; *Izv. Tat.*, 7, 8 September 1993, p. 1.
[87] *Ross. gaz.*, 8 September 1993, p. 4. See pp. 84–5 for more on the Tatar language.
[88] *Izv.*, 22 September 1993, p. 2; *Izv. Tat.*, 21 September 1993, p. 2.

elections were of little relevance to Tatarstan. No candidates were forth-coming for the elections to the Council of the Federation in December. The nationalists, for the first time in alliance with the Communists, called for a boycott of any elections. The Tatarstan Supreme Soviet passed a resolution critical of the new draft constitution.[89] Although the polling booths were open, only 14 per cent of the electorate voted.[90] The results of the elections in the rest of Russia brought no joy to any of the political groupings, and in particular to neither the leadership nor the nationalists. A neo-conservative Russia, the chair of the Supreme Soviet remarked, was not good news for Tatarstan. A gentle reminder that Tatarstan was, after all, part of the Federation came the next day when the Supreme Court of the Russian Federation overturned a verdict of the Tatarstan Supreme Court.[91]

Thereafter matters moved fast. In January 1994 negotiations over the remaining points of the treaty between the Federation and Tatarstan were reopened and, on 15 February, the two presidents signed a treaty: 'On the delimitation of the spheres of authority and the mutual delegation of powers between the organs of state power of the Russian Federation and the organs of state power of the Republic of Tatarstan'.[92] Some hard bar-gaining had taken place but, without any doubt and, despite the state-ment that the signatories had been guided by the constitutions of the Russian Federation and Tatarstan, there was little in the treaty that accorded with the spirit of Tatarstan's recent claims to be an independent sovereign state. Tatarstan was referred to as a 'state', it is true, which 'par-ticipates in international and foreign trade relationships', but there was no mention of sovereignty. Further clauses made it quite clear that foreign relations, defence, and the legal system (including the procuracy) lay within the brief of the federal authorities. The wording chosen in the pre-amble to define the relationship between the republic and the Federation was that the republic was united (ob''edinena) with the Federation, a much stronger term than that of 'association' found in the republic's constitution.

A revealing statement by S. Shakhrai, RF minister for national affairs and regional politics, following the signing, suggested that the treaty left much unresolved. He began by claiming that during the past three years the laws of the Russian Federation had not applied to Tatarstan, but now

[89] Izv., 30 November 1993, p. 1. The Supreme Soviet also discussed possible changes to its own structure, could reach no agreement, and left the existing arrangements and the deputies' term of office unchanged (Izv., 8 December 1993, p. 2).

[90] One individual from Tatarstan did gain a seat in the Duma: I. Grachev, leader of the Consensus group, who went through on the Yabloko party list.

[91] Izv., 21 December 1993, p. 4; 22 December 1993, p. 5.

[92] Ross. gaz., 18 February 1994, p. 5.

they did. (The treaty, on the contrary, claimed to be guided by both the Russian constitution and the Tatar constitution, which did not recognize federal laws as relevant for the republic.) Shakhrai continued:

This treaty does not require ratification, so as not to give the illusion of its being an international legal document. *The two sides acted very wisely. Where there was disagreement, political discussion, we simply excluded the issues from the text of the treaty* [emphasis added].

In other words they had simply fudged the difficult questions.[93]

Yeltsin came to visit on 30 May 1994: 'Under the treaty', he declared, 'Tatarstan has taken for itself as many powers as it is able to manage. The remainder, those that remain the prerogative of the federal organs, satisfy us. This is the first treaty of such a kind and it's important that I see with my own eyes how it is being realized in practice.'[94] KamAZ got no more money – Yeltsin reminded the management that they had already had favourable credits of 140 mlrd and 50 mlrd r. – but the republican government was promised that certain projects (the bridge over the Kama, reconstruction of the airport) would be financed out of federal funding. Leaders of the parliamentary block which had so consistently championed keeping Tatarstan within the Federation, the 'federalists' as we might describe them, were not invited to meet with the president; neither did the nationalists mount any demonstrations.[95]

Why did the nationalist movements fail to mount any real challenge to the nomenklatura? In Sakha the small number of the Sakha intellectual or professional community without elite links, and the numerical dominance of the Slav population, made the weakness of the nationalist movement unsurprising. In Tatarstan it was rather different. Here there was a sizeable community. But, unlike the nationalist movements in the Baltic republics, the Tatar independence movement never had a clear idea of its aims. Iskhakov has argued that it began to die as early as the autumn of 1991 because the Tatar intellectuals were unable to work out a national idea (the consequence of their totalitarian heritage); initially ensnared by the idea of a Union republic, they floundered when national independence, whose attainment had seemed inconceivable, offered itself as the alternative.[96] Totalitarian heritage or not, they were in a much more difficult position than the Baltic or Georgian intellectuals. The Tatar republic did not correspond to a historic Tatar homeland and more

---

[93] He continued: 'Clause 73, however, is of principle importance; it states that in all areas where authority is not reserved for the Russian Federation, the subjects possess the full authority of statehood. This is a formula of sovereignty, albeit restricted' (*Ross. gaz.*, 18 February 1994, p. 1).   [94] *Izv.*, 1 June 1994, p. 1.
[95] Akhmetov, 'Tatarstan', May 1994.   [96] Iskhakov, 'Sovremennoe tatarskoe', p. 31.

Tatars lived outside than inside its borders. What should a national idea mean? The Tatar community itself was dispersed throughout Russia: what was the vision of those in Tatarstan? An independent republic? A greater Tatarstan?

It was also important that Tatar demands aroused no support from the west. Baltic independence quickly found its western champions, but the Tatars had almost none. But would support from outside have allowed the movement to maintain its momentum? It seems unlikely. Developments within the nationalist movement were in many ways similar to those of the democratic movement in Russia: unity in the face of a common enemy, a victory, then the appearance of very different agendas. A few of its leaders were siphoned off to join the government. Uncertainty and disagreements split its ranks. The partial fulfilment by the government of some of its demands rendered it largely impotent as a critic: how could it act against its own? Did it then simply fall apart following partial victory? But was it a victory or had the rulers simply stolen some of its clothes? Iskhakov has suggested that the very closed type of nomenklatura made it difficult for the nationalists to break in. I might put it rather differently: unlike in the Baltic states, no cracks appeared in the elite itself. Meanwhile criticism from Moscow allowed the elite to claim the national mantle and be seen as 'our leaders' by much of the population. The national movement was unable to offer any real alternative and became increasingly marginalized.

This would suggest that the success of a national independence movement in the late Soviet or post-Soviet environment will depend upon the tightness of the bonds among the nomenklatura. Unless the existing political elite splits, fragments, with a section identifying with the reform-minded nationalists, it is going to be extremely difficult for a popular movement to mount a serious challenge to its power. The existing elite, while still in control of the offices of state, and acquiring control of the economic resources, can claim a new legitimacy based on its role as national leader. Only serious cracks within the elite would allow that to become a matter for dispute.

Why did the Tatar leadership so readily abandon its former stance in the spring of 1994? One report had the federal team issuing a warning that the oil pipeline would be shut off if the Tatar delegation refused to sign the Treaty.[97] In some of his statements Shaimiev hinted that there had been little choice: to think of 'an isolated Tatarstan was senseless'.[98] The political situation had changed. But then how concerned had the

[97] E. Teague, 'Russia and Tatarstan Sign Power-Sharing Treaty', *RFE/RL Research Report*, 3, 8 April 1994, p. 20.   [98] *Ross. gaz.*, 12 February 1994, pp. 1–2.

leadership been with the issue of independence in the first place? In order to understand their concerns and actions, and those of the Sakha leadership, we need to look at them as rulers within their own republics. That is the subject of the following chapter.

3   Patronage politics: Tatarstan and Sakha

How might we explain the behaviour of the Tatar elite? Was it cowardly or cunning? Did it care about the rebirth of the Tatar people or merely that those who now held power should hold on to it and grow rich? The same questions, as we saw, were raised in Sakha. In both cases nationalist critics claimed that the rulers had betrayed the cause of independence, preferring an accommodation with Moscow and their own control of resources to furthering the interests of their people. The Tatar elite, claimed some, was almost entirely concerned with gaining the resources for themselves; they needed an independence strategy in order to pursue a policy (for example, issuing their own type of vouchers and holding back privatization for the time being) that would ensure this. They were content to use the national issue as ideological legitimation, if it served them. If not, they would abandon it, and strike deals with the Russians. Their concerns were all tactical; shifting with the wind was their strategy, whether it blew from Moscow or Chelny. They would use whatever appealed to the population at a particular moment, be it national independence or their ability to guarantee stability.

The signing of the treaty with Russia, according to these critics, proved the point. The nationalists, both the Milli Medzhlis (elected at the II All-Tatar Assembly which met a week later, chaired by Fauzia Bairamova, the poet) and VTOTs, came out against it. In their eyes the treaty was a betrayal, a tragedy, a step back to 1989.[1] By this time, it was argued, the presidential team had put its people into the positions which would control privatization. It had gained republican control of the majority of enterprises, and expanded state activity. No one denied that compared with the situation in 1991 the leadership's control over the republic's economic resources had increased dramatically. Sabirov, the prime minister, claimed that in the economic sphere (taxation, banking) they had achieved a good deal. The oil quota retained by the republic, from some accounts, was set to rise to a third of the total – whereas neighbouring

---

[1] N. Mukhariamov, 'Tatarstan', *Pol. monit.*, February 1994; *Izv.*, 10 March 1994, p. 1.

Bashkortostan kept only 14 per cent.[2] The government had developed links with foreign corporations – particularly in Turkey, Greece, and Hungary – where its members could rely upon relatives. The government had made itself responsible for distributing the profit it acquired in kind from enterprises, KamAZ trucks, for example. The hard-currency account (from oil) was managed by a special council under the president, and the Supreme Soviet was denied any access to it. Key decisions, such as the ownership of Tatneft, lay with the president.[3]

Similar kinds of charges were made against the Sakha leadership. Although one might expect to hear a Social Democrat claiming that a new ethnocracy, concerned primarily with defending its own interests, had come to power, a representative of the nationalist association Sakha Omuk could be heard arguing that statehood had brought no benefits to its native peoples; it was the in-comers who were benefiting from the greater economic independence, and none of the profits from the diamonds were being put into the agricultural sector.[4] The presidency very clearly had kept key decision-making powers and control of resources in its own hands. In both cases we observe the incumbent elite bringing federal resources under republican control, into the hands of the executive, and moving slowly on policies of privatization. Does this justify the accusations of the nationalists?

The leaders themselves did not engage in a rebuttal of charges such as these, which anyway rarely appeared on the pages of the republican press. In Sakha, Nikolaev, at least publicly, claimed that a great deal had been achieved. First the Federal Treaty had given the republic political statehood; then, in 1993, for the first time, the republic had 'really controlled its resources' and begun to establish foreign economic links.[5] Egorov, the Sakha deputy prime minister, suggested that the years 1992 and 1993 would, in retrospect, be seen as the period when state sovereignty and presidential rule were established, and the move towards economic independence and the introduction of market relations was begun.[6] For Shaimiev in Tatarstan it was difficult, given the volte-face on the treaty. He had to suggest, on the one hand, that they had had no option, on the other, to claim it as a victory. He hailed the treaty as 'a document that [witnesses to] a reformed Russia, the renewal of the federation on a democratic basis, the guarantee of the statehood of Tatarstan' and announced to a surprised Supreme Soviet that it would now be appropriate to hold

---

[2] Teague, 'Russia and Tatarstan', pp. 22–3, for brief details on the agreements; Mukhariamov, 'Tatarstan', February 1994.
[3] Interviews with activists and deputies, September 1993.
[4] *Res. Sakha*, 18 January 1994, p. 2; 5 February 1994, p. 1.
[5] *Res. Sakha*, 1 February 1994, p. 1.   [6] *Res. Sakha*, 22 January 1994, p. 1.

elections for seats in the Russian Council of the Federation and Duma. The apparatus, government, and press, which in December had gone into action to dissuade the electorate from turning out, mounted a major campaign, using all the traditional methods of propaganda, including signed statements of support from work collectives, to get the voters to the booths.[7] But Shaimiev, like Nikolaev, could always argue that gaining political control of the republic's resources had to be the first priority, that they were working for the long-term interests of their peoples, and that their nationalist critics were simply naive in their view that now was the time to claim independence from Russia.

Proving one or other of these claims is impossible, but one can ask what might count as evidence of commitment to the interests of a people. Regardless of whether one agrees with the claim or not, in the nationalist post-Soviet context it was assumed that a people's interests would be best served if their rulers were their own people:

'Your own' statehood, exercised over 'your own' territory (these ideas have taken root over dozens of years) continue to be viewed as the crucial, indeed as the only, way in which the welfare of a people can be improved and its way of life protected.[8]

Appointment of nationals to decision-making posts was certainly part of the new rulers' strategy but, argued the critics, in and of itself this meant little because of the type of appointments that were made. The individuals might be Tatar or Sakha but they were drawn from a particular in-group who still thought in nomenklatura ways. (Although those who argued thus implicitly undermined the argument that ethnicity determined behaviour, they still assumed that a Russian would pursue Russian interests. Hence they felt hamstrung: either they voted for a Tatar or for no one.) What else might count as evidence of a commitment to a nation? Language policy is often taken as a barometer. It was an emotive issue in Tatarstan. Compared with the Sakha the Tatar community had a rich literary and intellectual history to draw upon, and Tatar intellectuals and writers, to say nothing of generals, had played and continued to play a significant role in Russian culture. But that was part of the problem: it was *Russian* culture and statehood that they enriched. Stressing the historic contribution Tatars had made to Russia did nothing to advance the case for developing Tatar culture today. The Tatar intellectuals were well

---

[7] Substantial federal help, three times that of December, was also forthcoming: *Ross. gaz.*, 12 February 1994, pp. 1–2; *Izv.*, 9 February 1994, p. 2; Mukhariamov, 'Tatarstan', March 1994, p. 2. See also the argument by Farukshin, 'Politicheskaia elita', pp. 76–7, on propaganda, and on the face-saving clauses as part of the negotiation, and for his analysis which emphasizes the Tatar elite's defence of its corporate interests.

[8] Tishkov, 'Etnonatsionalizm', p. 23.

aware of the problems facing them. Tatar is a Turkic language, unrelated to Russian, but which has come to use the Cyrillic script, and to be used by rural communities. Many urban Tatars speak better Russian than Tatar. Shaimiev is a case in point. A survey of Tatar students in 1993 found that 65 per cent admitted to either using Tatar only for everyday conversation or not knowing it all, and three-quarters rarely or never read Tatar literature.[9] All sixteen institutions of higher education offered education in Russian. Tatar programmes occupied a four-hour slot on television. Two of the four main republican newspapers were in Tatar (and in 1993 had a circulation of 200,000, double that of their Russian counterparts – but Russians tended to read the central press).[10] What was needed, Tatars argued, was a major language programme.

Initiatives had come from within the community, rather than from the government. New Tatar gymnasia had been set up in Kazan; a new extra-mural national university, at which the faculty would teach for free in the evenings, was established in the autumn of 1993; five mosques were rebuilt and opened in Kazan. By the autumn of 1993 a new language law was under discussion. It provided for the introduction of official announcements and public names in both languages, and for a gradual move towards a dual use in public offices and institutions. Tatar was now to be offered in schools, and in kindergarten.[11] The drafters of the law were not optimistic. The main problem lay in finding resources for it, and on this score the legislation was silent. A book publishing programme was needed (before the October revolution 800 new Tatar titles were being published annually; by the 1990s the figure was only 150), but, in the existing economic climate, money was not forthcoming. One is led to conclude that a commitment to language development did not come high on the leadership's list of priorities and that, without such a commitment, there would soon be little left of the Tatar heritage.

In Sakha both Russian and Sakha were the official languages of the republic. In practice Russian was used, not only because the majority of the population did not know Sakha, but also because many of the

---

[9] Farukshin, 'Politicheskaia elita', p. 72.

[10] In 1990 sixteen republican newspapers and journals and forty-five city and district newspapers were published in the republic, employing 1,200 journalists (T. Minnibaev, *Politicheskaia kar'era provintsialov* (Kazan, 1991), p. 112) for a population of fewer than 4 million! These were all published and subsidized by the party and state budgets.

[11] Documents; discussions with politicians, September 1993. Under the existing arrangements, Russian, as the official federal language, received funding from the federal budget – hence Russians everywhere were catered for – whereas, in Tatarstan, was the responsibility of the republican authorities, and the Tatars in Moscow were no one's responsibility. In Tatar eyes this was quite inequitable. It meant, for example, that the quarter of a million Russians in Naberezhnye Chelny could receive an education in Russian, but the quarter of a million Tatars in Moscow had not a single Tatar school.

educated Sakha were themselves more fluent in Russian. In his public statements in the federal press Nikolaev sometimes raised the language issue, arguing that more must be done to reverse the 'denationalization policies' of the Soviet regime. He occasionally argued that state policies should give priority to the interests of 'the native peoples', including those of the Little Peoples of the North. But the responsibility for uniting all the peoples of the republic should lie with the Sakha, whose historic home-land it was, and whose ability to survive had demonstrated their poten-tial.[12] However, little was done in practical terms. Exemption from military service was obtained for the Little Peoples,[13] but in general the leadership's actions were remarkably Soviet. The Supreme Soviet resolved that an Assembly of the Peoples of the Republic should be called. The delegates would be elected or proposed by local authorities and by registered organizations.[14] The colourful assembly, delayed by the polit-ical events of late 1993, duly opened (given that the local soviets had been abolished, the choice of delegates presumably lay in the hands of work collectives, though this is unclear); the delegates listened to a long speech from the vice president on the demographic, political, and economic state of the republic, which included references to 'Russia – our common home – which we built together', and 'The might of Russia lies in the strength of its republics, and the might of the republics in the unity of Russia', and published an appeal to the republic's peoples to strengthen the ties of friendship existing between them.[15]

Patronage politics

The nationalism of these elites was then of a subdued kind: it seemed to consist of little except recruiting their own kind. How then to explain their actions? Were they, as some charged, simply motivated by their own greed for power and resources? Or were they just cautious, provincial, Soviet in their way of thinking? At the beginning of April 1994 *Vatanym Tatarstan*, the most authoritative of the Tatar-language papers, a govern-ment paper, and *Molodezh Tatarstan*, the most adventurous of the Russian language press, published a series of articles by R. Khakimov, the presi-dent's adviser, strongly critical of the leadership's overall policy. (Shaimiev himself was on holiday in Karlovy Vary.) The treaty, argued Khakimov, had traded legality for political expediency; in its subservience to Moscow the leadership had shown irresponsibility for the fate of the republic. The government was failing to tackle the pressing economic and

[12] *Izv.*, 22 June 1993, p. 2; *Sov. Ross.*, 8 December 1992, p. 3; *Ross. gaz.*, 8 September 1993, p. 4.   [13] *Res. Sakha*, 26 March 1993, p. 1.   [14] *Mirnyi rab.*, 5 June 1993, p. 1.
[15] *Res. Sakha*, 24 April 1993, p. 1; 27 April 1993, p. 3; 29 April 1993, p. 1.

domestic problems. Covering itself with an aura of 'the support of the people', the leadership was allowing the republic's economy to slip, its lack of concern for the scientific and cultural potential of the republic meant that the republic would simply suffer from the consequences of faulty federal policy. 'The republic has lost any dynamism . . . the government is the prisoner of a "regional" cast of mind . . . Life in the government is locked in a cast of STAGNATION.'[16]

These elites, I would suggest, reacted to the new environment by using those mechanisms of rule they knew and understood. This entailed their taking control of resources, administering them on behalf of the population, and benefiting as part of the process. They recruited their kind of people. In the search for a new legitimacy, they turned naturally to ethnicity but, at the same time, they used other familiar means to ensure that they remained in control. They behaved like the provincial Soviet rulers that they were and that, in the new environment, meant consolidating their role as patrons.

In an interesting study of the provincial nomenklatura, Minnibaev has suggested that among the factors that impelled individuals on party careers in the post-Stalin period was the desire, particularly among those from rural backgrounds, to escape from the countryside. They needed to find a protector and the party was the best option. Active talented individuals, he suggests, then moved to other things, the mediocre remained and practised laziness, the art of doing nothing; their education trained them simply to borrow (or steal) ideas, not to think creatively. For the provincial elite, he argues, clan-thinking was paramount, and any battle within the nomenklatura was a battle to the death because there was no other territory which would take the loser.[17] More research needs to be done on the consequences of the Brezhnev twin policies of affirmative action and the provincialization of the party apparatus but we can see how, while opening up prospects within the locality, they could make it more difficult to move to posts outside. Long gone were the days when party activists – and indeed professional people – moved round the

---

[16] Quoted by Mukhariamov, 'Tatarstan', April 1994. Nor did Khakimov refrain from a dig at Likhachev's extraordinarily busy timetable of foreign visits which, he suggested, gave the illusion of a government engaging in a foreign policy.

[17] Minnibaev, *Politicheskaia kar'era*. This is a tantalizing book by a talented scholar who died young. He attempts an analysis of the Tatar elite, based on 316 biographies, taking 1959 as his starting point, and tracing subsequent careers. He suggests that substantial turnover occurred between 1985 and 1990. Unfortunately his data are hard to interpret, and his analysis not always clear. The seizure and distribution of power and resources characterized, he argues, all political activities during 1989–90 and 'When passions cool, elections have been completed, and a new wave of *lumpen* activists come to power in the regions, then we, all of us – the authorities, and their opponents, and those in the background – are lit in a *lumpen* light' (p. 41).

country, from one post to another. Careers had to be made at home, and the costs of failure were high. Against this background we can see why members of the regional or republican elite, ethnocratic or not, were desperate to hold on to their positions: there was nowhere else for them to go. There were no openings in neighbouring Bashkortostan for people from Tatarstan, or in Irkutsk for those from Mirny, quite regardless of the difficulty of acquiring accommodation. The only place where there might be a job, if one had retained the right connections, was Moscow.

Whether this picture of an elite closing ranks is overdrawn or not, there were features of the environment that would encourage it, regardless of self-interest. With the disappearance of the party the existing system of personnel recruitment and political promotion collapsed. No new organizations appeared to fill the gap. There were no political parties, able to insist on their candidates being given posts. Whether he desired it or not, the president in a republic had a free hand. What could he rely upon except personal connections, and existing networks? Territorial groups, rather than families, had always been important in the Tatar nomenklatura, and these were there to be used. Movement out, change within the elite, might be expected either with a new leadership or where new job opportunities presented themselves, but for that economic reform would be necessary.

Both elites were very sceptical of market reforms and wary of the private sector. Little was done in Tatarstan to reform the republic's economy. The leadership prided itself on its 'soft approach to the market'. By this it meant controlling prices and moving very slowly on privatization. Sabirov, the Tatar prime minister, was an old colleague of Chernomyrdin, the Russian prime minister, from their Cheliabinsk days. Asked how he reacted to Chernomyrdin's disapproval of economic independence for the regions, he replied,

I agree with him when he says that we must not lose the leadership of the economic system. But the question is: how should we manage it? Why is the economy of Tatarstan in better shape than that of other regions? . . . It is because we retained control over the economy. We are moving towards the market, but not in a hurry, carefully analysing each step. We don't command the enterprises but we control them through economic levers.[18]

This meant through controlling prices, subsidizing agriculture (a third of the budget went on agriculture) and retail prices, and maintaining existing industrial production through federal grants and oil revenues. No real privatization occurred. In Naberezhnye Chelny, although the mayor referred to 2,000 new small enterprises whose taxes provided 30 per cent

[18] *Nezav.*, 25 February 1993, p. 3.

of the budget, republican policy still held in late 1993. The town had leased shops but, the mayor announced, he did not favour privatizing them. Prices were held down, with subsidies, and rationing was still being used in the summer. Shops which attempted to take advantage of demand and raise their prices were fined – as a bookshop learnt when it responded to a rush on Jules Verne by raising the price.[19]

It was not only in Chelny that the old order prevailed. A visitor from St Petersburg, returning to Nizhnekamsk after twenty years' absence, found the town as she remembered it: the word 'market' was only used in reference to the collective-farm market, the local press had not changed, the population was mobilized, as always, to go and bring in the harvest. The only difference was rationing for key products, now only a memory in St Petersburg.[20] Even in Kazan old ways died hard. The first item on the president's cabinet meeting agenda in September 1993 was the harvest. The city's chief administrator put the potato question first on his weekly press conference. He urged the population to hurry to get their supplies in, and reminded them that if they were intending to go out to purchase potatoes at collective farms they must get the appropriate forms from their local district administrations, and take them along in order to avoid problems with police checks; furthermore, 'townspeople who bring in potatoes, not from the collective farms, but from their relatives' plots, also need to get the appropriate papers from the local administration'. He asked people to behave in a proper fashion when gathering the potatoes – not simply to take all the big ones and leave the small ones in piles by the side – and emphasized that, thanks to the new Dutch technology, there should be plenty. A week later he provided an update on the potato news: the town had already laid in 32,580 tons, slightly above plan; he hoped people would not delay in purchasing their winter supplies because the town had no proper storage. Next week's press conference, he announced, would deal with beetroot.[21]

The soft approach had fully justified itself, claimed Shaimiev in early 1993. 'Reforms are not worth a farthing if people suffer from them.'[22] And indeed industrial production in the republic fell by only 12.7 per cent in 1992,[23] and in 1993 retail prices were still rising more slowly than

[19] *Chelny izv.*, 4 August 1993, pp. 1, 2.   [20] *Izv.*, 4 September 1993, p. 5.

[21] *Kaz. ved.*, 17, 22 September 1993, p. 1; *Res. Tat.*, 23 September 1993, p. 1. There were some changes. In Elabuga, the little country town where Shishkin grew up and painted his landscapes, and Marina Tsvetaeva committed suicide, there was a smart new private restaurant where the young chief administrator held a reception for conference delegates. Who would pay? The administration but, if it failed to honour the agreement, the young proprietor was prepared to pick up the tab.

[22] *Izv.*, 11 February 1993, p. 1; *Tatarstan*, 4 (1993), p. 5.

[23] *Nezav.*, 25 February 1993, p. 3.

average across Russia. To what extent the oil revenues were responsible it is difficult to say, but by 1994 troubles were looming. In the spring of 1994 Shaimiev began to speak of pushing ahead with privatization and of price liberalization. Although prices and inflation were still much lower than average for the federation (one of the planks in the leadership's claim that its policies benefited the people), industrial production in some branches had fallen by 30 per cent in the first quarter of 1994, and the general problem of indebtedness was acute. Oil production was down, and the oil workers threatening to strike. Even government spokesmen began to accept that the economy was in deep trouble.[24]

The Sakha economy too, in the spring of 1994, was in crisis but here the response was to urge strengthening state control. The Analytic Centre, attached to the presidency, suggested that such a process was already under way: a return to the 'socialist method of production' whereby 80 per cent of the profit was extracted from the producer by those officials who had adjusted to the new order. A complete return of the 'Soviet' economy, the analysts argued, was to be expected in the republic, whose northern conditions prevented rapid change, and where none of the preconditions for a market system – a free labour and capital market, and legal regulation – existed. Market tendencies, they predicted, would increase in Russia but the republic needed to take preventive measures to save its economy from collapse, preferably 'the administration of the whole economy by the regional authority'.[25]

Apart from an announcement in October 1992, in connection with the abolition of the rural soviets, that he favoured the privatization of land,[26] President Nikolaev never demonstrated any particular enthusiasm for economic reform. In the autumn of 1992 he was arguing for putting the national bank under the control of the president.[27] By the spring of 1994 little had occurred, and we can see that the peculiar conditions of the North – its traditional and poor agriculture, its combination of extractive industry, energy resources, and a transport system geared to the bringing in of supplies and the export of raw materials – were hardly conducive to the development of a flourishing private sector. The economic strategy favoured by Nikolaev was 'state-led development', state control of the key resources and developing industries. Just as the Russian state had managed industrial development towards the end of the nineteenth century, so would the Sakha develop their state. But they understood the North in a way that Moscow never had and never would.

But did such attitudes have anything to do with ethnicity? There were

---

[24] *Ross. gaz.*, 12 February 1994, pp. 1–2; *Izv.*, 10 June 1994, p. 2.
[25] *Res. Sakha*, 1 March 1994, p. 1.   [26] *Mirnyi rab.*, 28 October 1992, p. 1.   [27] Ibid.

plenty of Russian provincial politicians, equally sceptical of market reforms, who dragged their feet. And in both Sakha and Tatarstan there were long-established patterns of management and political rule that were shared by all in positions of authority. By way of example we look at Naberezhnye Chelny, home of KamAZ, and Mirny, the diamond capital.

The company towns

In mid-September 1993 Rafgat Altynbaev, mayor and chair of the Naberezhnye Chelny soviet, celebrated his 45th birthday. It coincided with an international conference, held in the KamAZ conference hall. The forecourt was crowded with the latest models of the big KamAZ trucks and with Tatar nationalists demanding an end to imperialist oppression. The happy coincidence of the mayor's birthday provided an opportunity for President Shaimiev, through the person of the vice president, Likhachev, to award him with an honorary award for his work as mayor, and for Altynbaev to speak of the bright and beautiful future that lay before Tatarstan under the wise leadership of Shaimiev. The following day Altynbaev chaired a session attended by mayors of the new towns, attending the conference. All received presents, and refreshments covered the tables, but the young administrator from Elabuga did not forget the host and, in honour of his birthday, presented him with a large painting.[28]

Altynbaev could not, however, claim to be the most important person in the town. That was Nikolai Bekh, the director of the KamAZ plant. He did not attend the conference in person but sent one of his deputy directors to represent KamAZ. Chelny is, after all, a company town. What did this mean under the old system? It meant that a decision was taken in Moscow, in the late 1960s, to make a small rural town of 38,000, on the Kama river, but with no railway or air links, the site for the USSR's major truck and automobile works. Decisions, plans, financing, and key personnel questions were all taken in Moscow, at All-Union level. The republican authorities were not involved. This was a Union, not a republican, town. Between 1970 and 1979 300,000 came – from outside and from the neighbouring villages – living in tents or hostels, and working either in the motor works or for the company's construction enterprises and its energy complex. By 1990 the town's population was 524,000. The

---

[28] The discussion of Naberezhnye Chelny is based on attendance at the conference, the papers presented at it, and interviews with the participants; all statistics, where not otherwise referenced, are from R. Altynbaev, 'Politicheskie, ekonomicheskie, i sotsial'nye kharakteristiki g. Naberezhnye Chelny', Unesco conference, 'The Culture of Young Towns', September 1993, Naberezhnye Chelny, and the paper by S. Dybrin and Iu. Platonov, 'Naberezhnye Chelny v zerkale obshchestvennogo soznaniia ego zhitelei'.

average age was twenty-seven, and the Tatar population was beginning to rise in percentage terms as in-migration now came almost entirely from the local rural population. By 1989 the Tatars accounted for 41 per cent to the Russians' 49 per cent. The most dissatisfied group within the population was rural youth, whose low level of skill and recent arrival put them in the most disadvantageous position as regards work and housing. It was from among this group that the radical nationalists came and drew support.[29]

The town consisted of the plant – a town in itself – and then mile after mile of huge apartment blocks, spread along wide streets. There was no town centre. KamAZ employed 150,000 in the motor-works in 1993 and provided employment for most of the townspeople. Clinics, leisure, culture, the media – all belonged to the company. It owned and ran the trams. Gas, electricity, water, housing – all were its responsibility. Its output, perhaps 150,000 motor vehicles a year, accounted for 83 per cent of the town's industry (and 20 per cent of the republic's). The town had almost no light industry. Ninety percent of products and consumer goods were brought in from outside. Under the old system the town received central allocations of food and consumer durables. The soviet had played little part in its life but the party committee had had an important role. It had resources, and responsibilities for cadre appointments, and for the media, education, and culture. Although key managerial appointments were made in Moscow, party opinion was consulted. Rais Belaev, the first secretary from 1969 to 1985, sometimes referred to as the father of Naberezhnye Chelny – small, energetic, authoritative – worked with the KamAZ leadership to build the town. It was still his town. He arrived from Kazan, where he had moved to become rector of the Institute of Culture, for the international conference. Although he had not featured in the programme, he was immediately included among the dignitaries on the podium, and given an opportunity to speak at the opening session. Altynbaev, who began his career as a Komsomol official at the KamAZ energy construction plant, is one of his proteges. He became a district party secretary under Belaev and then, after his departure, was promoted

[29] A study of the KamAZ plant in 1990 found that the majority of Tatars and Russians viewed ethnic relations within the work collective to be normal but the further the questions moved away from the immediate environment the more the respondents tended to view relations between the two groups as unstable or with apprehension. Yet at the end of 1992, 64 per cent of Chelny respondents reckoned the political situation to be normal, and there was no difference between the Russian and Tatar replies. For the KamAZ and Chelny data, see Ya. Garipov, 'Sotsial´no-etnicheskaia struktura rabotnikov i mezhnatsional´nye otnosheniia na KamAZe', *Sovremennye natsional´nye protsessy*, pp. 70–4; Dybrin and Platonov, 'Naberezhnye Chelny v zerkale obshchestvennogo soznaniia ego zhitelei'.

to second secretary of the town party committee. In 1990 he became chair of the soviet executive committee, and in 1991 the new mayor. In 1992, by mutual agreement, the chair of the soviet resigned and Altynbaev combined the two posts. How different, I asked Belaev, is Altynbaev's job from yours? Is he less powerful? The answer was yes, although he considered Altynbaev his direct successor. Altynbaev has less influence over appointments in KamAZ. He cannot simply command. 'For example, if we decided to build a railway, we built it; Altynbaev would have to raise the money from taxes. We worked with force and enthusiasm, and interfered in everything. Now it's no longer one system: KamAZ and town and party.'[30]

Altynbaev restructured the town government – abolishing district soviets, and introducing a new system of prefects responsible to the mayor – and set up a town duma or advisory council to discuss policy proposals before bringing them before the Soviet. In it we see the town elite. It had twenty-seven members, fourteen Tatar, and thirteen Russian. They divided as follows:

Mayor	Tatar
Deputy mayor	Tatar
Deputy mayor	Tatar
Deputy mayor	Tatar
Deputy mayor	Tatar
Deputy mayor	Tatar
Deputy mayor	Tatar
Deputy mayor	Russian
Deputy mayor	Russian
Vice chair, city soviet	Tatar
Chair, control commission	Tatar
Head, internal affairs	Russian
Head, security services	Tatar
Procurator	Tatar
Chair, natural resources	Tatar
Chair, apprentice schools	Tatar
Chair, veterans' association	Russian
General director, KamAZ	Russian
Deputy director, KamAZ	Russian
Deputy director, KamAZ	Russian
Deputy director, KamAZ	Russian
Deputy director, KamAZ	Russian

---

[30] Interview, Naberezhnye Chelny, September 1993.

Deputy director, KamAZ	Russian
Director, machine-tools plant	Russian
Director, paper factory	Russian
President, corporation	Russian
Manager, industrial-construction bank	Tatar

We see very clearly the division between the political elite, now heavily Tatar, and the company management, still wholly Russian. The security forces are shared.[31]

In 1990 KamAZ became a share-holding company, no longer a Union enterprise. This affected its relationship with the republican authorities, which obtained shares in the company and became vitally interested in its fortunes, both for the taxes it paid to the republic and because of the potential human crisis if it could not maintain production. Quite apart from the fire in the engine-shop in April 1993 which destroyed the complex, KamAZ still had to prove its competitiveness in the new market economy. By 1993 its management was becoming aware of just how costly its services were. The trams were the first item to be off-loaded onto the town budget. In the spring of 1994 the company decided to begin selling the housing to its employees. The town authorities had no wish to take on the housing (the plant built it all), the clinics, and sports facilities, and, for the time being, the company still accepted responsibility for child benefits and funeral costs.[32] Here we see the source of future conflict. The more profitable KamAZ tried to be, the more difficult would become the task of the town authorities. Unemployment was still low (60 per cent of the unemployed were women and youth) but particularly threatening in a company town. In the autumn of 1993, 70,000 people were in severe need, but 70 per cent were dissatisfied with their housing. The ecological situation – water and air pollution – was causing substantial concern and as many as a third claimed readiness to participate in actions of protest on this score. The crime rate had trebled in the past four years.

The scope for policy-making by the town authorities was very limited. They had introduced Tatar into the schools, and opened the first Tatar gymnasium, but they still faced a system of double-shift schooling for lack of buildings. KamAZ still dominated. It could take decisions affecting its facilities and services, without regard to the town authorities; it could, when it wished, exert pressure upon them. The media was controlled by the company. The party paper had passed to the soviet, but then the company had stepped in to finance it. Criticism of the company had no place here.

[31] *Chelny izv.*, 14 May 1992, p. 2.   [32] *Chelny izv.*, 4 September 1993, p. 1.

Mirny, the diamond town in Sakha, had much in common with Chelny. Here the giant diamond corporation found itself facing a number of problems as it emerged from the chrysalis of Moscow control. It was not just that, in the spring of 1993, it was as much a victim of the debt problem as other large concerns throughout the country – it was owed 15 mlrd r. by Goskomdrag (the state committee for precious metals and gems) and was two months behind in paying its workforce. There was also the question of its future in a competitive industry. The diamond world was a closely knit one, and the sale of diamonds was controlled by De Beers. The Soviet government had worked with De Beers; matters were no different now.[33] Throughout its existence the company had simply mined the diamonds and done the simplest of reworking, regardless of costs. It now found itself operating in a competitive world, and one which revealed how labour intensive and expensive its mining operations were. To move to diamond cutting, a highly skilled and traditional profession, would take years, even if it was decided that it was a sensible long-term strategy. Furthermore the company still lacked experience in trading diamonds and gold on the world market.[34]

Almazy-Rossii-Sakha or Yakutalmaz, as it was still referred to, owned not only the mines, the huge brown blue craters, around which the towns had grown up, but the towns themselves. In Mirny the housing, shops, warehouses, even the schools and hospital, not to mention the research institute, football club, and cinema all belonged to the company. The consequences of the ending of party rule and the economic crisis were to cast even those institutions which previously had been supported from the state budget (the hospital, the schools) or by the party (the newspaper) on the mercy of the company. It saw itself, for the time being at least, as having little option but to pick up the tab. The price was that the soviet should simply accept the dictates of the company. Some argued that little had changed with the disappearance of the party – the company had always ruled the town, but before it had been through the party – others suggested that the party had sometimes acted as a check and, through its responsibility for cadres, had provided a mechanism whereby new blood came in from outside. In any event the difference was marginal. The redundant party officials were found jobs within the company, and life in Mirny continued much as before. In his election campaign Nikolaev had stated that, if elected president, he would appoint chief administrators only with soviet agreement, but none was sought for the appointment of Kirillin (a company choice) in Mirny. In his turn Kirillin

[33] See the long article, largely critical of the 'exploitative' relationship, in *Ross. gaz.*, 3 July 1993, p. 5.
[34] *Res. Sakha*, 11 January 1994, p. 1; interviews with company officials, May 1993.

appointed one of the deputy directors of the hydro-electric station to act as the chief administrator of its settlement, Chernyshevsk.[35]

Privatization remained a dead letter in Mirny. The managing director was not *against* the shops privatizing themselves, but the company owned all the warehouses and supplies. Individuals need not, of course, have put their shares and vouchers into the corporation's investment company – but there was nowhere else to put them. The company devised different arrangements both to use its hard-currency earnings and to hold out incentives to its labour force. One was to issue dollar cheques as bonuses, which could be spent in the company stores on imported consumer goods. Another was the 'ear-marked cheque' system. These were bonds, which the employee was entitled to buy, cheaply, one per family member, and which could be traded in, after two years, for a car at the Togliatti car works in Saratov. The car had to be collected. There were misunder-standings and disagreements, and a court case on the legality of the arrangement which the company won, but the cheques began to be traded, and some with large families made a substantial amount of money.

A difference with the old days was the existence of a few individuals – but they were a few – who were prepared to criticize company actions. Even *Mirnyi rabochii*, the party paper now owned by the company, occa-sionally published a critical piece (and was notified of the ensuing dis-pleasure in high circles). The distribution of housing, such an article claimed, suggested a less-than-proper attitude on the part of certain company officials.[36] But the dependence of almost all on the company for their livelihood made criticism very difficult. This extended to the top. L. Safronov, the managing director, only needed to pronounce on the type of housing he thought appropriate for the town, or the size of school he favoured, and the decisions followed. The new trade union chairman stated that he agreed in general with the managing director's view on the undesirability of strikes, and that the union's main task was to create a good atmosphere within the work collective.

In Mirny a by-election to a seat in the republic Supreme Soviet was held in September 1993. There was one candidate, Safronov, vice presi-dent and managing director of Almazy-Rossii-Sakha, whom the town soviet had elected to honorary citizenship earlier in the year.[37] And, of the 60 per cent who turned out to vote (a very high figure for a by-election), 98 per cent approved his candidature. He stood again in December for a seat in the new upper chamber, and won with 75 per cent of the vote. No candidate polled more. Why, asked the journalist who reported the result,

[35] Interviews with deputies and activists, May 1993; *Mirnyi rab.*, 16 October 1992, p. 1.
[36] The offending piece appeared on 10 October 1992, p. 2.
[37] *Mirnyi rab.*, 16 January 1993, p. 1.

why should this be? On no account could it be explained by his having served for twenty years as a deputy, or by his being vice president and managing director of the company – on the contrary:

By his *intelligentnost*, goodness, and approachability, Lev Alekseevich is the very opposite of the stereotype that many have of a high-level leader as a mannequin on a pedestal . . . this is a person who really knows his job, is principled, just in his dealings with people, someone who constantly and effectively pays attention to the needs of the working people.

Recently the relatives of a family of seven children, orphaned by the death of their mother, had written to him:

On the very same day that the letter arrived on his desk the appropriate departments received a clear instruction: provide all that is necessary as humanitarian aid for the unfortunate family, free. And soon the furniture arrived in the Anikanov house – for the bedroom, the living room, and kitchen. Now they have proper bedding, a sewing machine, and to the great joy of the little ones, a television. In a word, the management of the company did not abandon the orphans in their hour of sorrow, but spent nearly three mln r. on them, and responsible individuals in the share-holding company now keep a constant eye on the children's welfare.

Those who know Lev Alekseevich, continued the journalist, could quote many such cases:

Given that the diamond-mining industry is the town's basic employer and much depends on how well the company operates, it is clear that most of the population of town and district rely upon the leadership of Almazy-Rossii-Sakha and in particular upon its vice president, the general manager. Not all the 40,000 who live here can know him personally – although on the street he is always being acknowledged . . . but when someone feels he needs his advice or help, they usually try to catch him rather than signing up for an appointment. Of course most of the time Safronov is in his office; from the very first moment of the working day, he is working at a high tempo: telephone calls from the different company departments, from different regions of Russia, plans, meetings – there are a mass of key decisions to be taken. It is difficult to take up a request, sort out a housing matter, under such conditions, so Lev Alekseevich tries to deal with those early in the morning. Of course he could say that he is too busy, or limit them to his appointment hours – but it is far more important that each and every one has the right to come and be listened to, and the director has an obligation to take a decision on the crux of the matter.[38]

This accolade is pure Soviet. It follows the format, perfected over the years, for writing about leaders. Note the attributes – principled, just, caring for the working people – and the use of a family example. The leader responds – immediately, effectively, and responsibly. The leader is

[38] *Res. Sakha*, 30 December 1993, pp. 1–2.

one of the people; he is to be found walking the street, like any ordinary person. Note the use of his name and patronymic when this is being stressed, his surname when he is in his office. His humanity is matched by his effective work-style: the reader is given the picture of a leader who is at work on time, and begins straightaway. There is nothing of the bureaucrat about him; on the contrary, he makes time *before* a hectic working day in order to deal with petitions and requests for advice, and then he decides, no hesitating, fobbing off.

Its appearance at the end of 1993 makes it hard to believe that it is not satire or, to put it differently, in a St Petersburg paper, it could only have been satire. In 1989, in Leningrad, the democratic 'Elections-89' group produced the following leaflet for the electors of the Nevskii district where Iu. Solov´ev, the first secretary of the party, and Politburo member, was standing unopposed:

A great celebration is approaching for the electors of the Nevskii district! It is for you to elect as your USSR people's deputy the first secretary of the Leningrad obkom, Iurii F. Solov´ev. Have no doubt – he is a stagnant [*zastoinyi*, punning on *dostoinyi*, worthy] figure.

How our city has blossomed under his leadership! The people's standard of living rises ever upwards; that disturbing phenomenon of shortages disappears into the past, the housing problem is almost solved; crime, alcoholism, and drug-abuse are almost non-existent. The water which we drink, and the air which we breathe, become cleaner with each passing day . . . The crush on city transport is lessening, the streets and squares of Leningrad are becoming ever cleaner.

We thank Iurii F. Solov´ev for his closeness to the people. Who of us has not met comrade Iurii F. Solov´ev in the shops, on city transport, in the municipal canteens? Bureaucrats tremble when they catch sight of the first secretary but honest employees rejoice! We could go on forever about the services performed by Iurii Filippovich but we shall simply remark upon his fatherly care for his electors.

Dear comrade electors of the Nevskii district! You do not have to worry about choosing between several candidates! Elections for Iurii Filippovich – they are a real celebration![39]

And the voters responded by voting him out, just. But then Leningrad was not a company town.

Gradually the Sakha leadership had begun to move towards greater direct involvement in management of the diamond corporation. Traditionally dominated by Russians, the board now included Sakha members. In 1993 its president V. Rudakov was a Russian, as was Safronov; the other vice president, A. Kirillin, a Sakha whose brother was a member of the board, was in charge of the Moscow office. But Russian- or Sakha-dominated, the company still faced a decision: was it going to continue its existence as a *company town* (and that required a prior deci-

---

[39] *Sever-zapad*, 7 (1989), p. 25.

sion on whether Mirny or any of the diamond settlements had long-term futures as *towns* or whether they should be conceived of as drilling-sites with a short-term population – a question that neither federal authorities nor company directors had ever addressed) or was it going to shed its responsibilities and become a *company*?

Institutional arrangements and ruling practices

If company towns lend themselves to paternalist government, at republican level there was scope for creativity. How then did the elites react to the opportunity to restructure their ruling arrangements? Ways of ruling, it would seem, die hard, regardless of new constitutional rules. From Tatarstan we have the examples of Shaimiev's practice of keeping decision-making within a small group, refusing to divulge materials to the Supreme Soviet, and favouring direct appointment of chief administrators without soviet approval. Politics, he argued, depends above all on leaders of state; it is they who 'formulate the aims and principles of policy, take the decisions, influence the state of public opinion'.[40] The Tatar leadership ignored the moves of some other republican leaders to redesign their constitutional arrangements following the October clashes in the capital. Developments in Moscow, they argued, did not affect them because they were an independent state and, even after signing the treaty, they decided to leave the republican institutions as they were. In Sakha, in contrast, Nikolaev took the opportunity of the developments in Moscow to strengthen his position within the republic. The new constitution and Nikolaev's attitude towards the legislature are revealing about his views on an appropriate system of rule.

Nikolaev coupled his support for Yeltsin with a proposal that the republic Supreme Soviet dissolve itself to make way for a new two-chamber assembly. A few days later the Supreme Soviet met and, over-riding a protest from six of its members that at first they should vote on the proposed changes to the constitution, finished its business in an hour. It accepted a packet of proposals from the president that included a (very confused) conception of a two-chamber assembly, elections on 12 December, and the right of the president to act as he thought fit until the assembly was elected. It contented itself with ruling that 'the constitution of the Republic Sakha and the laws of the republic operate in so far that they do not contradict these decisions'. It then dissolved itself.[41]

One of the deputies was quite open about the options available to them. In answer to the criticism that no one had paid any attention to the constitution, he replied, 'Well, what could we do under the circum-

---

[40] *Izv. Tat.*, 7 September 1993, p. 1.
[41] *Res. Sakha*, 23, 25, 28 September 1993, p. 1; 5, 9, 13 October 1993, p. 1.

stances? Either firmly defend our constitution and come under pressure from the centre, and without any doubt economic sanctions would have been applied which, in our northern conditions, would have affected the lives of ordinary people. Or, taking the revolutionary developments into account, dissolve the Supreme Soviet and elect a new representative organ democratically. I think that the republic took the right tactical move. Politics, not legality, was given priority.'[42]

Before the new assembly opened, E. Egorov, one of the deputy chairs of the government, discussing the need to introduce changes into the constitution, argued that

It is clear that in one republic, in one state, the power of the people is one and indivisible. Therefore the so-called 'principle of the separation of powers' seems to me irrational. From the legal point of view it is incorrect to talk of legislative power, executive power, and legal power. In fact the issue is one of dividing the branches and functions of one tree of state power, of the legislative, executive, and legal organs . . . of course they have their specific tasks . . . and, in this sense, they are not subordinate to one another. But according to the constitution . . . 'the source of state power in the republic is its people, consisting of the citizens of the republic of all nationalities' . . . and therefore the popularly elected president of the republic must head this indivisible state power and coordinate the activity of all its highest organs.[43]

And indeed as Il Tumen, the assembly, opened, Nikolaev was busy issuing edicts on its structure and organization. Under the previous arrangements the president appointed the members of the government, and either he or the vice president chaired the meetings depending upon how busy he was.[44] This did not change. He moved to appoint someone from the presidential office to head the new assembly's apparatus. An objection to this was outvoted. The upper house elected a former raikom secretary, recently the president's representative at the constitutional conference, as its chair, and Egorov, from the government, as one of the deputy chairs. The lower house elected the president's adviser on constitutional and international law as its chair, and a former deputy minister as deputy chair. Nikolaev then suggested to the assembly that some of its members had not yet realized that the assembly was not the Supreme Soviet:

The deputies have a worthy task, one that answers to the demands and possibilities that exist today – *it is to perfect the legislation from the point of view of its form, but not its political content* [emphasis added], and not to seek confrontation in this respect with the presidential structures.

[42] *Res. Sakha*, 15 January 1994, p. 1.   [43] *Res. Sakha*, 22 January 1994, p. 1.
[44] *Mirnyi rab.*, 2 June 1993, p. 1.

The assembly was not always docile. In mid-April, to the consternation of the chairs of both chambers, the upper house voted to discuss the draft law on local government, presidential edicts which infringed points in the constitution, and the problem of the delay in the payment of wages and salaries. In vain the first deputy chair of the government insisted that the government had all these matters under control. Nikolaev reacted two days later by announcing that he was very opposed to the deputies' calling themselves 'people's deputies' and trying to assume functions of control; he wished to have a closed meeting with them. When the police and then representatives of the president's administration tried to evict the journalists, the deputies came to their aid. In reply to the president's representative saying to the journalists, 'We didn't invite you', the deputies responded with 'Nor did *we*, as it happens, invite *you*.' The journalists stayed.[45] Although on this occasion Nikolaev gave way, his view of the assembly's function was clear: it was to create a legal base for economic activity, an environment which would allow the executive to operate with maximum efficiency. Parties should work together.[46] He raised the question, still to be decided, of the structure and functions of local authorities. Over a year earlier, in the autumn of 1992, the soviets in rural areas had been dissolved and the rural administrators appointed by and made responsible to the president.[47] He now declared himself to be in favour of all local authorities

having rights only on non-political matters, local economic and social issues. They should be representatives of the state where general state matters are concerned. This will allow, firstly, us to preserve the stability of the state; secondly, it will give the population autonomy in deciding local issues; and, thirdly, it will get rid of the struggle for leadership between legislative and executive organs.[48]

There was still no local government law by April, and the president had authorized his local appointees to act on their own authority until such a law appeared.[49]

---

[45] The point of dispute was who should decide on the wording on the powers of the assembly: Nikolaev favoured a referendum; the deputies argued that according to the present constitution the people expressed its will through its deputies, a referendum would take time, and it had not been considered necessary in October to ask the people regarding the dissolution of the Supreme Soviet. Nikolaev gave ground: *Res. Sakha*, 13, 15, 16, 20, 21 April 1994, p. 1.

[46] The chair of the parliamentary commission responsible for links with social and political organizations saw his task to be one of encouraging parties to work together fruitfully with other organizations. To this end he called a meeting for their leaders, deputies, and entrepreneurs. Only two democratic leaders and two deputies turned up; the entrepreneurs came in the hope of lobbying the deputies: *Res. Sakha*, 15 February 1994, p. 1.

[47] *Mirnyi rab.*, 28 October 1992, p. 1.

[48] *Res. Sakha*, 25, 26, 27 January 1994, p. 1; 1 February 1994, p. 1.

[49] *Res. Sakha*, 7 April 1994, p. 1.

For Nikolaev then the role of the legislature was to assist the executive. The idea of shared but equal powers had no place in his perception. But then why should it? It was too alien a concept and, one might add, very difficult to conceive of in a state-run economy. What if a parliamentary form had been adopted, one in which the executive is chosen from the legislature? Would this have allowed for greater legislative control? The question of the relevance of the type of constitutional structures is one we shall return to after looking at our other regions. Here I simply note that both Nikolaev and Shaimiev considered it important for the executive to play the dominant role. The difference was that Shaimiev moved to organize a presidential party to ensure support from the legislature, while Nikolaev had no need to. This brings us to the relationship with the electorate.

Electoral legitimacy

If challenged, both Nikolaev and Shaimiev could argue that they enjoyed the support of the electorate. In Sakha there were elections in December 1993 both for the Russian federal assembly and for the new republic assembly. In Tatarstan, in contrast, the great majority of the electorate abstained from voting in the federal elections in December (no candidates stood for the Council of the Federation), but then, after the signing of the treaty, turned out in substantial numbers in March 1994 to elect representatives to both the Duma and the Council of the Federation. The republic Supreme Soviet remained in place.

In Sakha a consistent feature of voting behaviour was high turnout and the election of those already in positions of authority.[50] Choice in any meaningful sense did not exist. Political parties were insignificant. In 1991 activists from the People's Front, mostly Sakha, had set up a Republican Party, and for a short while could claim over 1,000 members; a national independence association, Sakha Omuk, was created. Some of the Russian and Ukrainian democrats formed a Democratic Party Yakutia, others a Social Democratic Party, but neither were branches of the Moscow parties of the same name. Moscow was just too far away. In 1993 they still existed in name, now joined by two revived communist parties, but in little else. The hope of Iu. Danilov, one of the organizers of

---

[50] The one exception to this was in 1990 in Mirny when the Yakutalmaz candidate nominated by the Mirny party committee lost to a journalist. In another constituency, Botkinov, the leading democratic activist, came ahead of both the mine director from Udachny and the deputy chair of the Council of Ministers, but in the run-off he lost to the director of the Yakutalmaz Institute: *Mirnyi rab.*, 4 January 1990, p. 1; 13 March 1990, p. 1.

the Republicans, that in a future election his party and the communists would engage in battle for the seats, was not realized. In the December 1993 elections, with a 64 per cent turnout, the minister of education romped home to win the Duma seat against weak opposition from three government officials and the chair of the trade union of the river fleet. Nikolaev and the chief administrator of Neriungri comfortably won the two seats to the Council of the Federation, defeating a young trade union student leader.[51]

Although two-thirds of those who went to the polls voted for none of the parties on the party list, the party preferences – taken together with voting in the April referendum – suggest that ethnicity may have played a role. In the April referendum, although Yeltsin received 70 per cent support from the republic as a whole, there were substantial differences between high levels in the Russian towns, and low ones in the Sakha rural areas; in the latter, Yeltsin scored even less well than did his policies. This was not, therefore, simply a rural vote against price rises.[52] In December the party votes were very similar one to another: Zhirinovskii's Liberal Democratic Party gained 12.8 per cent of the vote, Russia's Choice 11.0 per cent, Shakhrai's Unity and Accord 10.5 per cent, the Women of Russia 9.4 per cent, the Agrarian Party 8.3 per cent, the Communist Party 7.8 per cent, and Yabloko 5.9 per cent. But in the Russian towns the vote for Zhirinovskii went as high as 23 per cent.[53] Either the Russian electorate was behaving inconsistently: for the president's policies in April, and for Zhirinovskii in December, or it was trying to express and emphasize its Russianness – but without more data we cannot tell. How did Ukrainians vote, one wonders?

Elections were held simultaneously for the new two-house republican assembly. Although here a handful of individuals associated with one or other political organization did win (A. Alekseev from the Communists, and V. Nikolaev, vice president of Sakha Omuk), none of the parties put forward candidates. The assembly, roughly 60 per cent Sakha and 25 per cent Russian, was dominated by state officials and the mining and construction directors. They divided up the lion's share of the seats

---

[51] *Res. Sakha*, 10, 16, 18, 19 November 1993, p. 1.

[52] For the Mirny region, see *Mirnyi rab.*, 8 May 1993, p. 1. Mirny and Chernyshevsk voted 85 per cent and 82 per cent for Yeltsin and approximately 10 per cent less for his policies, whereas the smaller rural areas (85–100 per cent turnout) voted 30–40 per cent for Yeltsin, and 40–50 per cent for his policies. In the June 1991 election for the Russian presidency (the electorate had previously voted in favour of the Union treaty, and in favour of a Russian presidency), the turnout was over 75 per cent but Yeltsin's lead over Ryzhkov (45 per cent to 25 per cent) was much less marked than in the democratic regions, much more similar to that in conservative Krasnodar.

[53] *Res. Sakha*, 16 December 1993, p. 1. See appendix 3 (pp. 324–6) for details on the December 1993 election procedures, and the party list.

roughly equally. The remainder fell to half a dozen representatives of science, education, and health, a few from law and order, and two workers. Although two deputies were from the banking sector, and another two from firms, it was clear that in Sakha, unlike in St Petersburg or Perm for example, new business and commercial interests had made few inroads into the monopolized republican economy.[54] The nationalist and democratic opposition had faded away; parties had failed to put down roots. An elite retained office and seemed able to control electoral outcomes, whether its members were Russian industrialists or Sakha politicians. What was responsible for this, and was it the same in Tatarstan?

Here too political parties enjoyed little support. A series of opinion polls indicated that, by December 1992, with the exception of the Communist Party (27 per cent support in August 1991, 7 per cent in November 1992), no party or movement could claim anything but minimal support and even that was declining (VTOTs 4 per cent, the Democratic Party of Russia slightly less). Two-thirds of the electorate sympathized with none.[55] Within the Supreme Soviet itself the two main fractions lost members once the constitution passed. By the autumn of 1993 the number of Tatarstan supporters had dropped from 105 to 40–5, Consensus from 90 to 40–5, a further 40–5 adopted no particular position, and 100 stood by or had been bought by the president.[56] The only factor that united the Russian activists was defence of the integrity of the Russian Federation. By the autumn of 1993 a new bloc of parties or groups (thirteen or fourteen in all), based on the Supreme Soviet Consensus group and chaired informally by I. Grachev, its leader, existed to promote the ideas of an independent Tatarstan within the Russian Federation, equal rights, and economic reform. With the December election it splintered into small groups.[57]

A new party, a presidential party, had emerged, however. Named Unity and Progress, with its constitution drawn up by twenty-six deputies and members of the government, including Khakimov, the president's adviser, it looked to the chief administrators and collective-farm chairmen as its organizers. In it we see one type of executive response to the existence of elections: create a party based on the executive and its candidates will

---

[54] *Res. Sakha*, 18 December 1993, p. 1.
[55] *Tatarstan na pereskreste mnenii* (Kazan, 1993), pp. 45–51; *Tatarstan*, 4 (1993), pp. 3–9. An autumn by-election in Kazan saw a 35 per cent turnout: *Izv. Tat.*, 22 September 1993, p. 1.   [56] Interviews with deputies and journalists, September 1993.
[57] The most active of the political parties were the People's Party of Free Russia, the Democratic Party of Russia, and the Social Democrats, but their membership was tiny – in double figures. The Communist Party had re-emerged in December 1991, under the leadership of A. Salii, a retired army officer from the Kuban, and claimed a membership of 5,000 by 1993 but its political influence was minimal.

create a loyal legislature. The only private paper that made a regular appearance in Kazan (although already warned that its satirical treatment of the president could lead to its closure) dubbed the new party Unity of the Nomenklatura and Progressive Paralysis.[58] Was this so? 'We shall support the president as long as the people support him' was the evasive reply of its organizers but its constitution specified support for present government policies. Understandably it played no part in the December elections, given Shaimiev's favouring abstention from these 'Russian elections'. The nationalists too advocated a boycott, and only 14 per cent of the electorate turned out to vote. The low turnout can be plausibly explained by a combination of support for the government's position, lack of interest, and realization on the part of Russian Federation supporters that turnout would be too low to reach the minimum required.

How, though, do we explain the volte-face by the electorate three months later? Now the government was urging the people to vote for representatives to the Russian Parliament. The nationalists were effectively silenced. As in December they favoured a boycott but whereas then the nationalist paper *Sovereignty* had appeared and been widely distributed in Kazan it now experienced publication difficulties. (So where *had* its financing and patronage come from earlier?) This time the Communists decided to participate, and the Republican Party, led by Iusupov, came out in support of the president.[59] Neither played any significant role. The election developed into an unequal contest between the president's Unity and Progress coalition and Grachev's Consensus, now regrouped as Equal Rights and Legality (RiZ) and supported by both Gaidar and Yavlinskii. The presidential team, claiming that its policies benefited the republic's population, had control of the republican media, the television, and the administrative apparatus. RiZ had few resources of any kind. Although Grachev might criticize the secrecy in which the treaty had been drawn up, and the contradictions between its clauses and those of the constitution, RiZ's potential voters were those who had favoured Tatarstan's remaining within the federation. They would hardly oppose the treaty. RiZ criticized the conservative domestic policies of the Shaimiev leadership and its nomenklatura-style administration but, even so, it could not hope for the votes of Tatar democrats who shared these views.[60]

Shaimiev and F. Mukhametshin, the speaker of the Supreme Soviet, were joined by the deputy speaker in the contest for the two places in the

[58] Interviews with representatives of the new party, September 1993; *Tatarstan*, 3 (1993), pp. 17–21; *Kaz. tel.*, 57–8 (1993), p. 3; *Kaz. tel.*, 55–6 (1993), p. 7; notes from Free Russia party conference, Social Democratic Party meeting.
[59] *Izv.*, 19 February 1994, p. 1; 10 March 1994, p. 1.
[60] Mukhariamov, 'Tatarstan', February, March 1994.

Council of the Federation. Grachev's candidacy was disallowed by the republic and federal electoral commissions. The five Duma seats attracted a spread of candidates, both those committed to one or other bloc (or to the Communist Party) and independents. In the rural areas 86 per cent of the electorate turned out, in the towns 39 per cent – in all a respectable 58 per cent. Mukhametshin obtained 74 per cent, and Shaimiev a handsome 91 per cent of the vote (and 83 per cent even in Kazan). The town/country difference was noticeable: support for Shaimiev from the electorate as a whole (i.e. as a percentage of those on the electoral rolls) came out at just under 40 per cent in the towns, and just over 80 per cent in the countryside.

The five Duma seats were won by the chair of a town soviet, a Unity and Progress candidate; by O. Morozov, an energetic young ex-obkom secretary, now working in Moscow but writing regularly for the republic press (he defeated, among others, Iu. Voronin, the former deputy chair of the Council of Ministers); two independents, both Tatars, one an entrepreneur, the other the director of an orphanage, who went through in Chelny and in Nizhnekamsk; and, in the remaining urban constituency, V. Mikhailov, a deputy from the Consensus group and RiZ candidate, who narrowly defeated the well-known ex-party secretary, the one-time father of KamAZ, R. Belaev. Neither the Communists nor the occasional patriotic figure made any real showing.[61]

In the absence of data on how different groups within the population voted, I can only offer hypotheses on the electorate's behaviour. How important was the ethnic factor? Theoretically, given the rural–Tatar correlation, it is possible that the rural/urban difference in support for Shaimiev was almost entirely an ethnic vote. Surveys suggest that support for the leadership was consistently higher among the Tatar population than among the Russian (and other nationalities) but they do not control for the rural–Tatar correlation, nor do they provide evidence of their reliability.[62] The rural factor may have had an independent importance. A

[61] Mukhariamov, 'Tatarstan', March 1994. If one takes the electorate as whole, Shaimiev got 52 per cent of the vote, Mukhametshin 42 per cent: Farukshin, 'Politicheskaia elita', p. 74.

[62] A survey in late summer of 1992 on trust (*doverie*) in leading politicians reported that, whereas 58 per cent responded that they did, rather than did not, trust Shaimiev, the Tatar response was 66 per cent, the Russian 50 per cent; peasants 70 per cent, workers 57 per cent; the figure fell below 50 per cent among the Kazan respondents. For the surveys (and other responses towards immigration, and the nationality of one's elected representative), for what they are worth: *Tatarstan na perekrestke*, pp. 82, 86–96; *Tatarstan*, 11–12 (1992), pp. 13–17; *Sovremennye mezhnatsional'nye protsessy v TSSR* (Kazan, 1991); *Sovremennye natsional'nye protsessy*. Farukshin, 'Politicheskaia elita', p. 71, refers to a survey (on trust in the leaders) taken at six-monthly intervals from 1992; the percentages are consistently much lower, although the relativities are the same. On Chelny, see Dybrin and Platonov, 'Naberezhnye Chelny'.

survey in Chelny in 1993 suggested a more positive attitude towards the political leadership among the Tatar respondents, but a high rating from both. The ethnic factor surely played a role, but how significant a one we cannot tell.

How can the high turnout in the predominantly Tatar rural areas best be explained? (Was it as high in the Russian villages?) It could represent a willingness to follow 'our leaders' regardless of the issue, or a recognition that they had got the best deal they could. How can we tell which of these was the more relevant? Shaimiev certainly did not assume he could count on unthinking loyalty: he mounted a major campaign. Whether he was right in his assumptions is a different matter. Some other data could suggest that the electorate was relieved to see the relation with Russia sorted out. According to a survey in the summer of 1992, at least 60 per cent of the population still supported the idea of remaining within the Federation; although the percentage was much higher among the Russian population (81 per cent) than the Tatar (47 per cent), only just over a third of Tatars, and slightly fewer than a third of the village population, were in favour of 'full independence'. Yet a few months earlier, we should remember, 75 per cent of the voters in the rural areas had said yes to the referendum on sovereignty, announced as a referendum on independence. What should we conclude? That the survey was unrepresentative of the voters, or that attitudes had changed since the spring? Or that, at least for a sizeable part of the population, neither answering surveys nor voting signified stating a political position? Such activities may mean one thing to activists (or the urban population), another to those in the country.

It is tempting to suggest that two different patterns of behaviour coexisted. One was what we can call ritual voting behaviour, characterized by 'it doesn't make any difference', 'elections are just one of things that the bosses seem to think are important, like meetings, so we had better go along with them'. Voting is doing what is expected of one; ritual participation in a collective activity. If the leader happens to be of one's ethnic group, and deference to him is expected, this view of voting will be reinforced. From such a perspective, the behaviour of some of the democrats – the talking, criticism, opposition – is difficult to understand: they appear as badly behaved children who simply fuss the bosses and to no purpose. The leadership's volte-face on the treaty merely confirmed the view that government policy is decided on the basis of criteria known only to the leaders. It is not for the voter to have a view or presume to influence policy. The second type of behaviour is what one can call preference voting behaviour, involving the idea of making a choice, possibly expressing a political position. This became possible after competitive elections were introduced in 1989 and it was adopted, with avidity, by some sections of the community. For this to work the voter must either be offered a meaningful choice or be socialized into accepting that voting may require choosing between the better of two evils. In the post-Soviet environment, I would suggest, very different types of voter existed. But the more important point is that we need to know how voters perceive their actions when they cast votes before we can explain *why* they voted in one way or another.

What can we conclude? In both cases elites proved adept at gaining control over republican resources, although their strategies towards the centre varied depending on the extent of pressure from below. They sought as much autonomy and control over local resources as possible, both to retain power and to run the republics in what they considered the appropriate way. This, by and large, was the old way. New constitutional rules on the separation of powers and democratic electoral procedures not only failed to dislodge the incumbents but also allowed them to secure their position as patrons. The new procedures were irrelevant in the company towns, and freedom of the press meant little where the government or the companies provided the finance. At republican level the presidents succeeded in creating a strong executive presence, and marginalizing the legislature. The only political parties or opposition to make any impression drew their support from national concerns, but faded as these issues became the preserve of the republic and federal authorities. Developing a new legitimacy was not difficult for these national elites – the more awkward Moscow was, the more this worked to their advantage – especially at a time when claims for ethnicity and nationhood were high on the agenda.[63]

How important, though, was their being ethnocratic elites for their behaviour and the type of politics that emerged? Was it as much a matter of political conservatism as of ethnic concerns? Perhaps developments in those regions where ethnic relations were not an issue, and those which moved ahead with privatization, can shed light on this. Maybe there conflicts within the elite would produce competitive politics, and political parties would put down roots? But first we turn to a region where ethnicity was a divisive issue and rule lay in Russian hands.

---

[63] Volkov, 'Etnokratiia', sees ethnocracy as 'a mutant' which grew in the incubator of the authoritarian-bureaucratic system, 'the social-political monster'. He stresses the environment of a *lumpenization* of society, a substantial new nomenklatura, a shadowy second economy, and a national intelligentsia. See also N. Petrov, 'Chto takoe polietnizm?', p. 6, on the 168 territorial-ethnic boundary disputes in former USSR by the end of 1991, accentuated by new elites wanting territory and property.

4   The conservative borderlands: Krasnodar krai

The suddenness of the break-up of the USSR – the disintegration of Soviet space – left many bewildered, confronted with questions that were wholly new. To what country did the Ukrainian in Sakha belong? Or the Greek from Georgia, long settled in the Urals? The Siberian, with Chuvash and Tatar grandparents? The answer for ethnic Russians was not straightforward either. Although the map of the Soviet Union lay in political pieces, in strategic, economic, and demographic terms it was still sewn together. The economic infrastructure was still Union-designed and Moscow-centred, and 25 million Russians lived in the near-abroad, the surrounding, now independent states. The Russian Federation was a great power with responsibility for nuclear weapons and with large and very expensive armed forces, but many of these were stationed outside its new borders. Russia's strategic interests remained to be defined. But did this not require an agreement on what Russia was? The concept of 'the Russian state' had no one clear meaning. Its imperial (expansionist) and national prerevolutionary existence had been followed by an 'international' period, then a 'renationalization' in the form of the USSR with its Soviet people, giving it a layered meaning.[1] It was not even as though the new Russian Federation's boundaries were clearly defined. Within the USSR, republican boundaries were not always demarcated. 'Where', asked Il'in, writing after the break-up, 'is Russia's border with Afghanistan? Does it pass along the Tadzhik–Afghan border? Does it continue into the Orenburg or Sheremetova regions? Does a border between Russia and Tadzhikistan exist? . . . A fear of borders is an obstacle to creating territorial sovereignty. Both our politicians and the man in the street perceive the creating of borders (delimitation) as dividing people, breaking up an economic space, and so on.'[2]

---

[1] A. Zubov and A. Salmin, 'Soiuznyi dogovor i mekhanizm vyrabotki novogo natsional'no-gosudarstvennogo ustroistva SSSR', *Polis.*, 1 (1991), pp. 42–57.
[2] M. Il'in, 'Sobiranie i razdelenie suvereniteta', *Polis.*, 5 (1993), p. 147. In the USSR only 30 per cent of Union republic boundaries existed as frontiers in 1991: Glezer, et al., 'Sub''ekti federatsii', p. 155.

Despite the scorn subsequently heaped upon the claims that a Soviet people existed, while Soviet rule existed so did a Soviet identity which linked rulers and ruled. It had a clear territorial referent – the USSR – with tightly closed borders; it included a Soviet way of life, of which communist party rule was an integral part, and Soviet patterns of behaviour. It is not important whether individuals approved of or objected to these features, rather that all recognized they were part of being a Soviet citizen and that they distinguished one from a foreigner. Other components of Soviet identity included belonging to a great power and, for many, a belief that the Soviet system provided its citizens with a superior welfare service. Diligenskii has suggested that for some the feeling that they belonged to a moral community of socialism, of an international socialist world whose values were superior to those of capitalism, provided compensation for living under a repressive regime.[3] Finally, the 'other' or 'others' were clear: the capitalist world on the one hand, provoking either scorn or admiration and sometimes a mixture of both, and the Third World whose existence underscored Soviet superiority both materially and culturally.

With the collapse of the USSR and the end of communist party rule, all this was blown away. The Russian Federation not only lacked clear and undisputed borders, but those which existed leaked like a sieve: goods and precious metals drained away, refugees and Chinese traders streamed in. One million Chinese, it was claimed by 1993, had come into Siberia on their motorbikes to sell their goods or to settle.[4] Western films, reporting, and advertising flooded the television screens and video shops. Russian shoppers spent more in Stockholm than did either the Americans or the Japanese. In place of communist party rule, politicians and institutions came and went. The old Soviet way of life suffered rude shocks as prices rocketed, services were privatized, and law and order broke down. Was Russia any longer a great power? Its welfare achievements now appeared to have been primitive, and the international socialist community all but disappeared.

The Soviet Union was not only a centrally planned, communist party state; it was also the last of the great modern empires. As such it fostered identifications, both imperial and anti-imperialist, and in the process of disintegration many of its smaller nationalities saw themselves escaping from colonial rule. For them it was much easier to create an identity for

---

[3] G. Diligenskii, 'Dinamika i struktirovanie politicheskikh orientatsii v sovremennoi Rossii', in T. Zaslavskaia and L. Arutiunian (eds.), *Kuda idet Rossiia?* (Moscow, 1994), pp. 70–1.

[4] This was a figure which appeared in the press and acquired the status of truth, although based on no evidence and reckoned by specialists to be greatly inflated.

themselves: Moscow and the Russians were still there. But for the
Russians? As the old Soviet identification dissolved (it could not be sus-
tained as the structures maintaining it fell away), imperial perceptions –
ways of thinking, patterns of behaviour associated with running a huge
territory from a politically and culturally dominant centre – persisted.
Central structures identified with and occupied by those of the dominant
nationality continued to exist, and there was little to compel a rethinking
on the part of the intellectual elite. The situation in which Russian intellectuals found themselves was very different from that of their British or
French counterparts when they had lost an empire. The Russian intelligentsia had been simultaneously part of the imperialist centre and 'prisoners in their own land',[5] imperialists and colonized at one and the same
time. The challenge facing them, as they gained their freedom, was to
address the question of self-identity for the peoples of a post-imperial,
multiethnic community. It was an extraordinarily difficult task, and they
were not in good shape to undertake it.

Their imperialist past, which had never been subject to scrutiny, made
them insensitive to claims for equality from national minorities (and all
too often racist), while their new-found freedom led to a paramount
concern with 'recreating traditions' for their own nation. In engaging in
this exercise the intelligentsia was simultaneously trying to recreate its
own identity as the voice of the people. Here was a double self-absorption:
in itself, as the thinking part of the nation, and in the nation itself. But it
proved difficult to recreate the nation. Attempts to make the peasantry or
Church serve as the guardian of Russia's values simply could not be sus-
tained, any more than those to make the tsarist past emerge as a golden
age.[6] Nor did the Russian Federation as a state have a cultural content –
what was Russia without the Crimea and the Caucasus? Hardly surprisingly, once independence was a reality the issue of Russian identity began
to dominate discussion. Was Russia to be understood in geopolitical
terms or as a cultural space? The latter, argued some, because only on
that basis could one build a state, but that would mean losing territory.[7]
But then how should one understand the cultural space? Narrowly, in
terms of ethnic Russian-speakers, or in terms of Russia and all its peoples
– the imperial dimension? Or was the present a new phase in the history of
Russia? Tsymburskii suggested that Moscow had returned to its huge

---

[5] The expression is E. Said's, in his *Culture and Imperialism* (London: Chatto and Windus,
   1993), referring to colonial peoples. See further discussion, pp. 151–2 below.
[6] I am thinking of Govorukhin's documentary films here, and how he increasingly came to
   dwell on distressing aspects of the present.
[7] Iu. Shreider, 'Rossiia v mire XXI v.', *Polis.*, 2 (1993), p. 36.

island status surrounded by the 'rivers' of Eastern Europe, Central Asia, and the Caucasus; it was moving out of a west-central period in Russian history, and into one in which Siberia was coming forward to rival Moscow.[8] Dragunskii summed up the problem as follows:

> The polyethnicity of Russia [*Rossiia*], the fuzziness of its borders (for example, in the North Caucasus), the underdevelopment of the institutions of national sovereignty (domestic and foreign, for example, citizenship), the lack of sovereign traditions of a national state, Russian [*russkii*] sub-ethnic self-identity (for example, Cossacks, Siberian), and, finally, the existence of 26 million compatriots living outside the borders of today's Russia – all of this makes Russian nationalism either quite problematic, or quite specific.[9]

The specificity, he argued, lay in a viable Russian nationalism necessarily including 'an imperial component' which then contradicted the idea of Russia for the Russians (i.e. *russkie*). The democratic intelligentsia struggled with the dilemma and largely dodged it, disavowing the blatant Russian nationalism of the patriots but providing no answer in its place. Their concern with individual rights led to their neglecting the question of group political identity. 'Democracy' was no help here: it could not answer the question of *who* was to be included in the political community.[10]

The Russian intelligentsia's self-involvement led to a lack of interest in both the outside world (except as a place to visit) and the national minorities in the federation. The consequence was that the imperialist past attracted little attention, and discussions with national minorities continued to be handled by federal and local Russian representatives, whether conservative or democratic, in an insensitive way.[11] As a result members of the national minorities felt that nothing had changed. The democrats in the republics, both nationals and Russians who began by making common cause against the nomenklatura, found themselves at loggerheads. As we saw in Tatarstan and Sakha, the field was left open for the local elite to determine the terms of the debate. In the Russian regions, especially those far inland where the Russian population maintained its previous dominance, the issue could be avoided. But in the borderlands, with war close at hand, the anxiety induced by the new order was height-

---

[8] V. Tsymburskii, 'Ostrov Rossii', *Polis.*, 5 (1993), pp. 6–23.

[9] Dragunskii, 'Naviazannaia etnichnost'', p. 29. See the distinction between *rossiane* and *russkie* referred to on p. 28 above, n. 27, and a recent discussion: M. Beissinger, 'The Persisting Ambiguity of Empire', *Post-Soviet Affairs*, 11 (1995), pp. 149–84, and R. Suny, 'Ambiguous Categories: States, Empires, and Nations', pp. 185–96 in the same issue.

[10] 'The fact is that one cannot decide from *within* democratic theory what constitutes a proper unit for the democratic process. Like the majority principle, the democratic process *presupposes* a unit': R. Dahl, *Democracy, Liberty, and Equality* (Oslo: Norwegian University Press, 1986), p. 122.   [11] As we saw in the case of Tatarstan.

ened by a feeling of territorial insecurity, and here the issue of the identity of the political community came to the fore. This brings us to Krasnodar.

Krasnodar krai lies to the far south of Russia.[12] It is a border region of sharply contrasting territory and peoples. This was the area into which Ukrainian and Russian Cossacks moved in the eighteenth century, joining the Cherkess, Armenians and Greeks, who had long farmed the rich land in scattered settlements. In the middle of the nineteenth century, as the Russian empire pushed southwards towards Turkey, and the British and French displayed their interest in the region, the territory became a battleground in the war for the Caucasus. With the Russian victory in 1864, the greater part of the Cherkess were deported or fled to Turkey, and Russia gained the Black Sea coast and the mountains. In the Soviet period Krasnodar krai took shape as an administrative region. Its flat black earth lands, the Kuban, stretched north and east into the neighbouring Rostov region and Stavropol krai. In the south the land, rising sharply, embraced the mountainous region of the North Caucasus whose forests, alpine pastures, and snow-clad mountains are home to deer, mountain goats, bear, and bison. In the south-west its border was the Black Sea coast and Abkhazia, an autonomous republic within the neighbouring republic of Georgia. The Crimean peninsula, now a republic within Ukraine, was a stone's throw away.

The krai has always been home to very different peoples. During the Soviet period the territory with the heaviest concentration of the Adygei, part of the Cherkessian people, was granted the status of an autonomous region. Even here, however, the population was predominantly Russian and, in the post-Second World War boom, as industry and shipping came to the Black Sea ports, and the regional capital, Krasnodar, developed machine-building and a furniture industry, the Russian population strengthened its dominant position in the krai. In 1989 the population was four and a half million, five million including that of the Adygei autonomous region. Of the four and half, four million were Russian, 180,000 Ukrainians, and 170,000 Armenians. Adygei, Greek, German, Belorussian, and Tatar communities all existed. In the autonomous region, 100,000 Adygei shared the territory with nearly 300,000 Russians.[13] In the major towns, and in some rural areas, the different ethnic groups are intermingled but there are rural districts, old settlements, heavily dominated by one ethnic group, be it Armenian, Adygei, or Russian. Nearly half the population live in rural settlements.

---

[12] 'Krai' is the name given to *border* regions in Russia, as opposed to 'oblast', regions with no external border.

[13] M. Savva, *Mezhnatsional'nye otnosheniia: teoriia, praktika, i problemy Kubani* (Krasnodar, 1993), p. 31.

The krai is one of Russia's richer regions, a producer of agricultural goods, and home to holiday-makers from far and wide. The Black Sea coast is lined with resorts, sanatoria, and children's holiday camps. Sochi has an international reputation. Novorossiisk has become a major commercial port. Unlike many Russian regions with one dominant city linking it to Moscow, it has several, each with their own resources to draw upon. Although a border region, Krasnodar hardly felt like one in the Soviet period. There were no border posts between it and Georgia. The Crimea might have been allocated to Ukraine in the Khrushchev period but it seemed like another part of Russia. Krasnodar had no international airport. The only foreigners were the western tourists who flew to Sochi or whose cruises made it a point of call. In military terms Sevastopol, in the neighbouring Crimea, was home to the Black Sea fleet, not Novorossiisk with its merchant fleet and cement industry. The krai was part of the *Union* and in the referendum in March 1991 the population voted four to one for its renewal.[14] With the break-up of the USSR all that changed. Not only did Ukraine and Georgia become foreign countries but fighting broke out between Georgia and Abkhazia, between Armenia and Azerbaijan in the not far distant Nagorno-Karabakh, and, even nearer home, in the hills of Ossetia and Ingushetia. Krasnodar's southern border became, in effect, the edge of several battle zones.[15] In the environment of heady uncertainty and emphasis on national self-determination that accompanied the break-up of the USSR, the Adygei autonomous region, with its population of 400,000, predominantly Slav, was redefined as the Adygei republic and, under the new Federal Treaty, acquired greater rights than those of the krai within whose territory it lay. Border checkpoints were set up on the main roads into the republic.[16]

[14] *Kras. izv.*, 20 March 1991, p. 1. This compares with a vote of six to four in the regions of Tomsk, Perm, and Leningrad. The krai voted by only three to two for electing a Russian president and in the election itself gave Yeltsin a low 46 per cent of the vote, Ryzhkov 24 per cent, and Zhirinovskii 13 per cent. Again the contrast with our other regions, and with the average for the RF as a whole, is marked.

[15] By the spring of 1994, according to the regional head of the Federal Counterintelligence Service, its closeness to the battle zones, and its own Cossack formations, had attracted the attention of representatives of the security forces of several interested states, including those of the near-abroad: *Izv.*, 26 April 1994, pp. 1–2 (and on migration, extortion, etc.).

[16] In 1989 a group of the local Adygei intelligentsia created a Khas´e or assembly, and from this came the movement which called for the creation of the Adygei republic. In May 1991 a Committee of the Forty was formed; it then organized two congresses of the Adygei people: interviews with leading members of the Committee, March 1994. The republic adopted a presidential form of government and elected A. Dzharimov, a former kraikom secretary responsible for agriculture, as president: Law on the Presidency of the Adygei Republic, 25 March 1992, *Sbornik zakonodatel'nykh aktov respubliki Adygeia*, 1 (Maikop, 1993), pp. 133–6.

Elite reactions to perestroika and August 1991

In Krasnodar krai we observe a conservative community, predominantly Russian, anxious to retain its control of the territory. It was ruled by a conservative pro-communist political elite, but one which had already shown its distaste for developments in Moscow. How then did it react to being told that it must henceforth play by different rules? And what kind of politics resulted? We begin with the elite's reaction to reform.

During perestroika the krai was considered a stronghold of conservatism. It was no surprise when the Russian Communist Party, established in 1990 by those who wished to halt the perestroika drift to social democracy, elected a delegate from Krasnodar, I. Polozkov, as its first secretary. In contrast to Leningrad and Tomsk, also under conservative party leaderships, in Krasnodar no Democratic Platform emerged within the party to challenge the conservatives.

There was little democratic activity among the population. In 1988 and 1989 groups had appeared, protesting first against the use of pesticides, and then expanding their activities to include the saving of monuments, the revival of history, and the publication of banned prerevolutionary authors. Cossack organizations began to form and Adygei intellectuals in Maikop called a Khas'e or assembly. In the spring of 1990 Memorial held a public thirty-minute meeting (the meeting had not been authorized but neither had the city authorities forbidden it) in memory of those repressed and of the victims of famine.[17] There was no linking up between these very different and small-scale activities. A Democratic Movement of the Kuban, the creation of a small group of democratic activists, attempted to intervene in the 1990 elections. Its request to hold a meeting was turned down by V. Samoilenko, chairman of the Krasnodar city soviet executive committee, who proposed a round-table instead. *Sovetskaia Kuban*, the party paper, contrasted its 'Moscow-inspired' (i.e. alien to the Kuban) activities unfavourably with those of the Communist Party. Whereas, the editorial argued, the party saw democracy in terms of deep structural changes and was adopting concrete measures to achieve them, these so-called democrats favoured meetings because this allowed them to make empty promises, but the people would indicate which kind of democracy they preferred.[18]

Sovetskaia Kuban was not disappointed. The elections produced a largely conservative group of thirty deputies to represent the krai in the Russian Parliament: it included five party secretaries in addition to

---

[17] St Petersburg, Social Movements Archive, Krasnodar collection: *Tribuna*, 2 (1988); Memorial documents.   [18] *Sov. Kub.*, 23 February 1990, p. 1.

Polozkov, nine factory and farm directors, and three leading Soviet officials. One of those elected was V. Shumeiko, not a native of the krai, but general director of the big ZIP machine-construction plant, someone who would go on to higher things while continuing to exert influence in the politics of the region.[19] The maverick among the victors was V. Diakonov, head of a construction trust who, in the mid-1980s, despite opposition from the local apparatus and ministry, had gained permission from the Central Committee first to lease out sections and then to transform the trust into a successful share-holding venture, Kubansantekhuniversalmontazh. He quickly made a name for himself as one of the few democrats from the south and, with two allies among the Krasnodar contingent, become a strong supporter of economic reform and the Yeltsin leadership. The encouragement of private ownership was the key plank in his programme.[20]

At the time of the attempted August putsch, the krai soviet, which was equally conservative in composition, was chaired by N. Kondratenko, who had previously headed its executive committee.[21] Kondratenko had pursued a vigorous defence of the krai's interests, arguing with the Russian government for a review of the system of agricultural deliveries and, in the meantime, reducing the krai's contribution to the quota – this at a time when the shortage of food in the major northern cities was particularly acute. Kondratenko had little time for the Gorbachev leadership and even less for the Yeltsin democrats. As soviet chair he did not mince his words:

Calling themselves, this time, democrats, and taking advantage of the problems they themselves have artificially created, these antisoviet thieves [*kuroshchupy*] have set themselves the task of replacing perestroika with an order completely alien to us, just as their fathers and grandfathers did when they replaced and discredited socialism with a Trotskyist model of society . . . we must recognize that these forces are well organized, and quickly regroup. Now that they have in effect broken up the Union, they are redoubling their efforts in relation to Russia which,

[19] See the newspaper interview with several of the deputies in *Sov. Ross.*, 11 May 1990, p. 3.
[20] Interviews with Diakonov and Zhdanovskii, March 1994. *Kras. izv.*, 12 March 1991, p. 1, has a letter of support for Yeltsin from three RSFSR deputies and four from the kraisoviet.
[21] The reader should remember that the krai or oblast soviet outranked the city soviets within the region, just as the obkom or kraikom (the party committees) stood above the gorkoms or city party committees. In 1991 the krai first party secretary was A. Maslov; the chair of the krai soviet executive committee was N. Gorovoi. Three years later Maslov was deputy general director of the committee for foreign links in the krai administration, and Gorovoi had become first deputy director of Alkol, a commercial firm attached to the larger concern, Kubanvinprom; Kondratenko was director of a glass factory but, more importantly, one of the krai's two elected representatives in the Council of the Federation. See below, pp. 126–7, for details on elite movement.

throughout the century, has existed like a bone in the throat of international Zionism aiming at world rule.[22]

Relations between the krai leadership and the Yeltsin government were, as can be imagined, strained. On 19 August Kondratenko came out openly in support of the GKChP. The praesidium of the soviet and its executive committee made an appeal for calm; the buro of the krai party committee followed suit.[23] Diakonov and a handful of deputies from the krai and city soviets organized a committee to defend the constitutional order in Russia, and planned a meeting for the 22nd. A dozen activists were all that they could muster. Samoilenko, now chair of the city soviet, refused to authorize their access to television. By the 21st the tide was beginning to turn and more came to the committee's headquarters but Kondratenko held firm, insisting that Soviet power still prevailed, and, during a heated exchange with Diakonov, declared that, if necessary, he would deploy machine-guns on the roof tops to defend the people from the Gorbachev–Yeltsin–Zionist–masonic clique. On 22 August the tables were turned. Diakonov was appointed first as the president's representative in the krai and then, by a decree of 24 August, became the first chief administrator to be appointed in Russia. On 23 August Kondratenko was released from the chair of the soviet by a decision of the Supreme Soviet of the RSFSR, signed by its deputy chair, R. Khasbulatov.[24] The minister of agriculture, G. Krulik, and Shumeiko flew down from Moscow to 'introduce' Diakonov to a meeting of key individuals in the krai, and to express the desire of the Russian government that the disagreement between the krai and the central authorities over agricultural procurements be ended. A few days later the soviet met, attended by Diakonov and Teterin. After discussion the praesidium resigned en bloc, and a new chairman, A. Zhdanovskii, lecturer in archaeology at the university, one of the few democratic deputies, was elected. The soviet then rescinded its earlier decision restricting the export of agricultural products from the krai, and adopted a Russian government instruction on procedures for the selling of grain either from or within Russia.[25]

---

[22] Excerpt from a speech at the krai soviet, April 1991, republished by the journal *Kuban*, July–August 1993, as an end paper, under the heading 'Today the representatives of Zionokratia play their games under the label of democrats'.

[23] *Sov. Kub.*, 22 August 1991, p. 1.

[24] V. N. Teterin, an RF deputy, lecturer in a military training school, was appointed as the president's representative: interview with Diakonov, March 1994; decree of the president of the RSFSR, no. 75, 'O nekotorykh voprosakh deiatel'nosti ispolnitel'noi vlasti v RSFSR', 22 August 1991, *Ross. gaz.*, 27 August 1991, p. 3; *Sov. Kub.*, 27 March 1991, p. 1. [25] Instruction of 31 July 1991; *Vol. Kub.*, 30 August 1991, p. 1.

Here then direct intervention from Moscow removed the old guard from power and put new people in their place. In and of itself such action by a victorious but not yet secure political leadership was not uniquely Soviet. The way the personnel change was orchestrated and the reaction of the parties involved was, however, conducted according to the proper canons of Soviet behaviour. (But then what other canons existed?) In place of the general secretary, flying down from Moscow to introduce a new first secretary to the local elite, Shumeiko and a key minister came. The soviet's conservative majority obediently voted in a democratic chair, and reversed its previous policy. The praesidium did resign – overt political opposition to the winning side always brought the risk of dismissal – but for lesser individuals it was quite appropriate – indeed, it was expected – that they should change their position if the line changed. Two years later, following the October days and the president's victory, the soviet found itself caught wrong-footed again. On 22 September 1993 the little soviet[26] had declared the presidential decree dissolving the Parliament to be illegal; a week later the soviet as a whole had voted to halt all federal acts or instructions issued after 8 p.m. on 21 September.[27] When it was all over the soviet grudgingly met (at first it could not muster a quorum) and, in compliance with a request from the chief administrator and the procurator, the deputies recognized that their September decisions, in particular their view that the decree, no. 1400 of 21 September, was illegal, had been incorrect.[28] We note that all participated in these conventions, both democratic victors and vanquished.

The question of what constituted appropriate codes of political behaviour would not be decided by changing the formal rules or procedures. As we saw in Sakha and Tatarstan, long-established conventions did not disappear overnight. An interesting question is *which* conventions persisted, and how they influenced political practice under the new rules. Did the introduction of competitive elections, the separation of powers, and free speech encourage, work against, or have no effect whatsoever on particular conventions? The example of the Krasnodar soviet suggests that, in this case at least, a new canon of deputy behaviour – public disagreement with government policy – had already appeared but that, once the authoritative decision was taken, old codes of party/soviet behaviour reasserted themselves. In the old days an authoritative decision was an instruction

[26] By this time the large unwieldy soviets had elected small bodies from among their members to work full-time on soviet affairs; see p. 254 below.

[27] It had further called for an authoritative gathering of representatives of the subjects of the Federation to find a political way of solving the crisis and the holding of elections for both Parliament and president before the end of the year, and stated its support for the declaration of representatives of subjects of the Federation of 26 September: *Kub. nov.*, 23 September 1993, p. 1; 1 October 1993, p. 1.   [28] *Kub. nov.*, 14 October 1993, p. 1.

from the highest party body. Was it now one from the Soviet president? This was the point at issue between Union and Russian authorities in 1990–1. The failure of the putsch handed undisputed authority to Yeltsin – for the time being – and the soviet reacted accordingly. But by 1993 the issue had been reopened with the challenge from the Congress. Where did authority lie? Both president and Congress claimed they spoke for the people. Was it then 'the people'? In a situation in which the source of authority is contested or unclear, the demonstration of power will resolve the problem for those who can offer no other reason for opposing those who can wield sanctions. This was the reaction of the Krasnodar soviet.[29]

The actions of the editorial board of *Sovetskaia Kuban* in August 1991 provide another example of Soviet conventions at work. Like many other regional party papers it initially made no mention of Yeltsin's statements or announcements from the Russian Parliament. By 24 August it needed to justify its actions and safeguard its own future. Yeltsin's decrees appeared, and a statement from Diakonov, the newly appointed chief administrator:

It is necessary to introduce order in the means of mass communication. In all like-lihood we shall have to shut *Sovetskaia Kuban* which aided the activity of the GKChP. Its only future, it seems to me, is nationalization, a change of name, and its operation as a free democratic publication, not as an organ of the kraikom of the CPSU.

Is such an accusation justified, the editor asked. The paper was not an organ of the kraikom, but a general 'social-political publication', and as such it had a responsibility to publish the official information it received; it had no other during the August days:

A paper is a medium for reflecting views, attitudes, and for providing the informa-tion which it receives. Therefore we, quickly and openly, made public the

---

[29] Following the referendum of April 1993 when a majority voted in favour of re-elections to the Congress of People's Deputics, Nikolai Travkin, leader of the Democratic Party of Russia, resigned his mandate, arguing that the deputies should accept the popular verdict. A few respected his action, others thought it a populist strategy, but most consid-ered it simply an unnecessary gesture. The question of when resignation, either by a politician responsible for a policy that has failed, or by one who finds himself or herself at odds with ruling policy, is considered appropriate is one of convention. In the Russian context the convention of individual ministerial or official responsibility is lacking. At the time of the Budionovsk massacre in June 1995, when Chechens held inmates and members of the local population hostage in a hospital, it took nearly two weeks for the *president* to decide which ministers should proffer their resignations. In October 1993 the bungling of the closure of the Parliament, and its subsequent storming, brought never a hint of presidential mismanagement, or recognition of responsibility for the outcome. Responsibility is decided by the superior, not by the individual himself or herself. On the other hand resignations on grounds of principle by E. Panfilova, the minister for social security, by E. Gaidar, and also by B. Fedorov, minister of economics, in 1994 suggested that a new convention could emerge.

information that was available to us. We were concerned to preserve law and order in the krai.

It claimed to have acted within the law. Therefore, concluded the editor, there was no way the paper could be considered to have acted anti-constitutionally. Despite the disclaimer regarding the relationship between paper and kraikom, an announcement at the bottom of the page notified the readership that the kraikom had resigned its rights as founder of the paper and handed them over to the collective, and three days later the editors admitted that from January the paper had been owned by the kraikom and the newspaper collective.[30]

Diakonov ordered the temporary closure of the paper, but its collective was ready with a new name, and the following day, with his agreement, *Vol'naia Kuban*, 'an independent mass paper', appeared. It recognized:

With deep regret, during the tragic days of the coup the editorial collective was guided only by the official information received from TASS. The TASS information, as subsequently became clear, was false, particularly on the day of the coup. The editorial board acted in the old way, in a stereotyped fashion, showed no initiative, and did not use other channels of information which provided the decrees of the president of the RSFSR, B. N. Yeltsin, his appeal to the citizens of Russia, the decree of the Council of Ministers of the RSFSR, in which the actions of the GKChP were characterized as an unconstitutional state coup. The editors of the paper *did not find their feet in a complicated political situation* [emphasis added], did not unreservedly support the position of the lawful Russian leadership, and, by publishing the documents of the GKChP, disoriented the readership. Such behaviour brings little credit to either the leadership or the paper's editorial collective.

Henceforth, the editorial claimed, the paper would be independent, acting within the law.[31] It is notable that the behaviour of the editorial board was in good party tradition (and, we might add, Diakonov was abetting it). The line changed; the subordinates moved with it. The mistake, as its editors saw it, was that the paper had not supported the winner, the now lawful government. How this squared with a promise of future independence is difficult to see. The granting of freedom of speech did not in itself tell editorial boards how they should behave and, as will become apparent, the combination of new rules, political views, and conventions on press practice had interesting consequences.

Two styles of leadership

As I observed politics in Krasnodar I had a feeling that I was seeing a Soviet politics that I knew, now being played out on an open stage. It was

[30] *Sov. Kub.*, 24, 27 August 1991, p. 1.   [31] *Vol. Kub.*, 29 August 1991, p. 1.

as though the lights had gone on. The ending of communist party rule allowed its conventions to operate publicly. In this sense the post-communist environment gives us a double bonus: the opportunity to see a new politics in action and to revisit and better understand the Soviet past. In Diakonov we see a Khrushchev-type figure, energetic, impulsive, domineering, authoritarian. The ability of such a political individual to survive in the Krasnodar environment, let alone effect serious change, was, however, far more limited than Khrushchev's. Khrushchev had a party machine behind him that he could use, as long as he could retain the support of his close colleagues, and he had all the weight and authority of the General Secretaryship. A new obkom first secretary came into office with a ready-made power base, a network of clients and supporters from which he could draw, and Moscow's blessing. Diakonov lacked a power base: all he had was Moscow, and that was far away. His supporters were few, and they were people of no standing. Would the convention of 'all power lies with No. 1' be enough to allow him to effect reforms, and thus build up a following? Would this subsequently return him to office under the new rules of competitive elections? His situation was similar to that of the Yeltsin government, but Yeltsin owed his authority to a countrywide election whereas Diakonov had been appointed by *Moscow* and, in Kondratenko, there was a ready candidate for the role of local hero.

According to Diakonov three options faced him: either to work in alliance with the existing party–state nomenklatura, in which case reform would stand still; or to strike a deal with the mafia and stay in power forever; or to reckon his time was limited and attempt to introduce changes to property relations that would outlast him. He opted for the third and lasted for fifteen months. He was one of the few democratic appointees or elected administrators who tried the radical strategy of dispensing with the nomenklatura. His first moves were to confiscate all party property, earmark certain key buildings such as the party clinic, hospital, and garage for a new mother- and child-care centre, and to set up a commission under the new deputy chief administrator, N. Egorov, to distribute it. This was not unusually radical but he then announced a plan to abolish the existing executive structures and form a small regional administration of twenty to twenty-five individuals. The employees were given two months' notice.[32] He closed the departments responsible for provisions and trade, and suggested that a trading association of businessmen would regulate trade. The consequence was that the bread supply fell by half and his opponents organized a demonstration 'Democrats – where has the flour gone?' The only solution was to reopen the original

---

[32] *Vol. Kub.*, 11 September 1991, p. 1.

departments, and the bread supply miraculously reappeared. His achievements, in his eyes, were the 18,000 private farm households that existed as of 1994, and the beginnings of a market economy in the industrial sphere.[33]

It is natural for an ousted politician to reckon the odds were always against him. Zhdanovskii too, the democratic ex-chair of the soviet, argued in the spring of 1994 that although the democrats had made mistakes they never had a fighting chance against the nomenklatura. In this case, though, had it been a matter for the local elite, neither would have featured as candidates; if elections had been to decide the issue, the combination of a conservative electorate, increasing unhappiness over the influx of refugees, and a democratic Moscow government that appeared to ignore the krai's problems could hardly have kept them in power. Without doubt Diakonov was inept as an administrator. Egorov, who resigned from the administration, criticized him for a wholly arbitrary style of leadership, for ignoring proposals from the personnel commission he had set up, and appointing instead quite inappropriate people to administrative posts in the krai. We need not accept Egorov's word for it: he had good reason to distance himself from an unpopular administration, and his criticism was oddly reminiscent of an earlier, more famous, but similarly cautious, Soviet politician who had replaced a reformer. But Diakonov's early supporters and the democrats in the soviet and administration found him, to say the least, erratic.[34]

An example of Diakonov's short-sightedness was his reaction to the Cossacks. In the summer of 1992 relations between Diakonov and the soviets, at all levels, worsened following his appointment of local administrators from among little-known farmers or entrepreneurs, often without soviet support. The krai soviet voted by a two-thirds majority to request Diakonov's removal. Egorov came out openly against the administration's reforms, and opinion polls reflected a high degree of discontent among the population with the administration's inability to tackle the issues of corruption, crime, and the cost of living.[35] The main Cossack organization did not stand idly by but had its members participate in the picketing of local administrations. Diakonov's response was to ally himself with the breakaway and more militant Cossack splinter group and to register its charter, thus excluding any possibility of dialogue with the more impor-

[33] Interview with Diakonov, March 1994. The figure on farmers is from the Kuban association of farmers, *Kub. kur'er*, 10 November 1993, p. 1. Diakonov himself gave a much higher figure.
[34] For Egorov: *Kub. nov.*, 11 December 1992, p. 1; for appointments, and the commission, see *Kub. kur'er*, 15 January 1992, p. 1; 28 March 1992, p. 1.
[35] *Ross. gaz.*, 24 July 1992, p. 2.

tant organization, and confirming his image as an extremist. There still were those who came out in support of Diakonov. At the end of August *Kubanskii kur'er* carried an open letter to the president from the Democratic Forum asking for his support in the face of attempts by the former party nomenklatura and the 'ultraconservative soviet' to oust Diakonov; the forum saw no hope for reform until the 'Bolshevik' soviets were abolished under a new constitution, and a lustration law passed. The signatories demanded no compromise with the party nomenklatura and mentioned the unfortunate example of Yeltsin's appointment of Samoilenko, the previous chair of the executive committee, as mayor of the city of Krasnodar. The example of Samoilenko was, however, not well chosen: *Krasnodarskie izvestia* (Samoilenko's mouthpiece) had already pointed out that Yeltsin had only appointed him after receiving a document, with Diakonov's signature, supporting the appointment.[36] The conflict dragged on throughout the autumn until, at the end of November, Yeltsin dismissed Diakonov. *Kubanskii kur'er*, the paper that Diakonov had supported as the administration's paper, wrote the kindest epitaph:

Yesterday Yeltsin removed Diakonov, the last romantic of reform; inexperienced, impatient, far too honest, he divided the world between 'ours' and 'theirs'. He offended friends, and made neutrals into enemies by his attacks . . . he lost any sense of direction, entered into battle for battle's sake, and handed over the daily work to others . . . the leadership of the krai fell apart, confrontation between the administration and the soviet produced stalemate.[37]

Under the procedures in effect at the end of 1992 the chief administrator of a region could either be appointed by the president, on the basis of a recommendation put before him by its soviet, or be elected in a region-wide contest.[38] The Krasnodar soviet was divided over which strategy to

[36] *Kub. kur'er*, 29 August 1992, p. 1; *Kras. izv.*, 27 August 1992, p. 1.
[37] 28 November 1992, p. 1. In the autumn of 1993 a new congress of the 'democratic-patriotic forces', sponsored by Diakonov, resolved 'To turn to the president of the Russian Federation, B. N. Yeltsin, with a request for *the political rehabilitation* [emphasis added] of the former chief administrator of Krasnodar krai, V. N. Diakonov, on the grounds that the decision expressing lack of confidence in him was taken without popular agreement and under pressure from the pro-communist soviet': *Kub. nov.*, 13 November 1993, p. 1. Even if Diakonov simply wanted presidential backing in the forthcoming election, the form of the request suggested the perception of a political world still peopled by insiders and outsiders. Kondratenko's supporters were talking the same language: his removal from office in August 1991 was now described as 'an error' because, a year later, the decision based on his 'as it were' support for the putsch had been recognized as incorrect and annulled: *Kub. nov.*, 7 December 1993, p. 2.
[38] Ruling of the Supreme Soviet RSFSR 'On the organization of executive authority in the period of radical economic reform', 1 November 1991, *Ross. gaz.*, 5 November 1991, p. 1; decree of the president of the RF, no. 239, 'On the procedure for appointing chief administrators', 26 November 1991.

adopt, as were key contenders. Kondratenko, far and away the most popular politician in the krai, had competed in a by-election for a seat in the Russian Parliament in November 1992. Although the low turnout (37 per cent) left the seat empty, none of his opponents, who included such well-known figures as Borovoi, Kalugin, and Kasatonov as well as local figures, got more than 7 per cent of the vote while he picked up a cool 64 per cent.[39] He would surely win an open election, something that the Yeltsin leadership would hardly welcome. The main Cossack organization, not surprisingly, called for a popular election: 'At the moment the need is sharply felt for a clever, thoughtful patriotically inclined leader of the krai, someone who understands its economy, problems, and traditions.'[40] Not surprisingly, Egorov, Diakonov's ex-deputy and the candidate with the largest following in the little soviet, thought otherwise. He favoured the little soviet's recommending three candidates to Yeltsin: there was no need, he argued, to call a meeting of the whole soviet given that more than half its members had been consulted and were in favour of a little soviet decision; personally he would prefer an election but 'different political groups are already now knocking on doors in the Kremlin'. The three candidates, proposed by the little soviet, were Egorov himself, Kondratenko, and Poliakov, a construction engineer. Poliakov had been associated with the creation of a disastrous artificial sea for rice-growing near Krasnodar, and then promoted to the first secretaryship of the Sochi city party committee. Nearly a hundred dissatisfied deputies, however, insisted that the matter be put before the soviet. As this met, news came that Shumeiko had confirmed, over the telephone, that of the three candidates the president wished to appoint Egorov. The Kondratenko bloc agreed to drop their demand for an election and by a vote of 167 to 15 Egorov's appointment was accepted.[41]

Who was Egorov? In August 1991, when appointed as Diakonov's deputy, he claimed that his democratic outlook had been evidenced in his efforts to free the economy, that he had long parted company with the Communist Party and its ideology – but that neither he nor others should be required to prove this; it was sufficient to be a decent person.[42] A collective-farm chairman who had risen to head the krai's agricultural administration, he had been chosen by Diakonov as deputy because he favoured the introduction of commercial structures in agriculture. He had achieved certain successes in this area, against opposition, and now claimed to be 'for privatization both of land and in agriculture generally'. The black economy must be forced out into the open, and the Kuban

---

[39] Borovoi was a successful businessman; Kalugin, an ex-KGB, USSR deputy from the krai; and Kasatonov, an admiral of the Black Sea fleet: *Kub. nov.*, 18 November 1992, p. 1; *Ross. gaz.*, 17 November 1992, p. 2.   [40] *Kub. nov.*, 23 December 1992, p. 1.
[41] *Kub. kur'er*, 24, 25 December 1992, p. 1.   [42] *Vol. Kub.*, 29 August 1991, p. 1.

peasants should become the richest people in the region.[43] At the time of
the crisis in October 1993 when, as did most chief administrators, he supported the president, he saw enquiries as to his political views to be
unhelpful. This is no time, he said, for conflicts, rather 'we should be
working, working and, yet again, working'.[44] Egorov represents a particular political type, one that has emerged in the post-communist environment, often succeeding a radical reformer: technocratic, pragmatic,
avoiding a commitment to any 'political' views, often colourless. Such
individuals pride themselves on being centrists, administrators, practical.
The prime example is Chernomyrdin, the prime minister who succeeded
Gaidar: a past master at bureaucratic, business-like management and the
art of making statements which say nothing at all.[45] Some of them are
capable administrators, others less good. There is little evidence that
Egorov had any outstanding qualities. He was a heavy drinker, a machine-
politician, schooled in the ways of building support and using a position,
and he had learnt to bargain with Moscow. But he managed to use his
position to hold his own within the krai establishment, then to gain
appointment to minister for nationality affairs, and to ensure that his successor in the krai was one of his people.

With Egorov in charge direct confrontation with the soviet, and with
district figures, ceased. His appointments came from among members of
the local establishment.[46] His commitment to private ownership and economic reform appeared to wane once in office or rather, to be fair, to find
its expression within the limits of the kind of privatization allowed for by
the legislation. The big state and collective farms became share-holding
companies, but individual family farming hardly expanded, and privatization of industrial and trade assets took place under the aegis of the

[43] Ibid.   [44] *Kub. nov.*, 8 October 1993, p. 1.

[45] Shortly after being appointed as prime minister, Chernomyrdin was the guest on the live
television programme *No Barriers* on which the guest is quizzed by a panel of journalists.
(Chernomyrdin had insisted the programme be made in advance, and that he authorize
its showing; the vetted version was shown as though it were live.) One journalist asked
him what he saw as the most important task to be achieved before the end of the year. 'A
good question', he replied, and picking his words carefully, emphasizing the importance
of the reply, suggested that 'the most important task is to finish the year . . . and we should
all work together, be together, in this important matter of finishing, completing 1992
successfully . . . and then 1993 will begin . . . we should embark on the tasks of 1993, seriously, purposefully'. Like Egorov, Chernomyrdin's favourite admonition is to stress that
'we should be working, getting on with the real business at hand . . . not politicking'. What
it is that 'we' should be doing, and why, remains unspecified.

[46] A return to normalcy, 'trust in cadres' one is tempted to say, after the arbitrary interventionist personnel policy of Diakonov. But were we really back in the Brezhnev era? Not
altogether. Now an ousted ex-administrator might complain publicly that he should have
been offered the job as head of the state insurance company, and that the new administrator's offer of 'a broker's office, official transport, good salary' was not good enough: *Kub.
nov.*, 30 October 1993, p. 1. Note that the winner and loser both expected the loser to be
provided with an appropriate job.

original party–state nomenklatura. Any idea of the private ownership of land was forgotten. Egorov oversaw the process of the redistribution of property within the krai, and the conservative nomenklatura seemed to experience little difficulty in acquiring ownership of the assets.

I cannot offer a social and political profile of the Krasnodar political elite under Egorov similar to that for the Tatar or Sakha elite but, from looking at the career moves of the original nomenklatura, we can say something on the degree and kind of regrouping that took place. For our four Russian regions I have taken the regional and (capital) city party committees, elected in 1988, whose membership constitutes a good approximation of the pre-1991 regional elite. I identified the posts their members occupied at the time. I then traced the career moves of these individuals, and their occupation of leading posts in the regional and city administration in 1993/4. The findings, I hypothesized, would shed light on the degree of elite continuity and point to new areas of activity that might support a future elite.[47]

A substantial group within the regional and city party committees consisted of 'honorary' worker, peasant, and employee members whose jobs did not come under the nomenklatura. These I excluded from the analysis.[48] Of the 349 members of the Krasnodar kraikom and gorkom, slightly fewer than a third fell into this category. The remainder I divided between party apparatus, soviet and government officials (including military, and law and order), and professionals (industrial and farm directorate, cultural and academic leaders). For Krasnodar, data on the subsequent careers of the industrial directors and secretaries of primary party committees are poor; for the other categories something can be said with confidence. Those in charge of educational establishments or cultural institutions remained in post, with the occasional promotion, as did those in the military and law-and-order agencies. Nearly half of those in soviet administration retained their jobs; a third moved out into business and commerce (this included their remaining in charge of the now-privatized government concerns, or offshoots of them, for example, the chairman of Krasnodaragropromstroi headed the share-company

---

[47] Structures, and the power and authority of different offices, were changing too fast for it to make sense to choose any set of *offices* in 1993–4 as constituting the elite. See appendix 2, pp. 322–3, for details on the elite study. Additional data on the administration in Krasnodar is from A. Andreev, et al., *Politicheskaia stsena Kubani: kto est´ kto* (Krasnodar, 1994). O. Kryshtanovskaia, Institute of Sociology, RAN, Moscow, led a field-work team in 1994 to collect data on the krai elite which should be very illuminating.

[48] The question of their future careers is an interesting but separate one. They are the most difficult to trace but, from the St Petersburg data that I have, it looks as though they remained at their previous jobs – no privileges, no penalties – an indication perhaps of just how fictitious their membership of the committees had become by 1988.

Kubanagropromstroi; the director of the krai Vehicle Servicing Centre became the director of a company, Kuban-Lada). Here there were some demotions. What was the fate of the members of the party apparatus whose jobs had disappeared? Maslov, the ex-first secretary, as we have already noted, had moved to a key post in the krai administration.[49] Roughly a quarter of krai, city, and district secretaries moved into the administration, and approximately half into business or banking, usually as directors. Among the apparatus there was a minority who suffered a serious demotion to a much lower status job in industry or secondary education.

We would need additional data to know whether, in the fallout that followed the banning of the party and Diakonov's rule, some fractions within the apparatus won out over others and whether this affected personnel movement. In Krasnodar everyone talks of politics in terms of clans. Samoilenko, the mayor, for example, was said to make any decisions that affected property in the city of Krasnodar, together with its mafia. Novorossiisk was run by a different clan. Sochi too had its own people. Kondratenko, now director of a tobacco factory, was said to wield enormous influence even before he won a seat on the Council of the Federation in 1993. All assumed that he would become the leader of the krai at some future date. Egorov could control the rural administration, and the small towns; he had supporters among some of the defence industry directorate.

The data are sketchy. At best they support the hypothesis that in Krasnodar a conservative elite remained largely in place. The ending of party rule resulted in a struggle within it over the division of the spoils, one that was encouraged both by the existence of different 'bases' (Krasnodar city, Sochi, Novorossiisk, the rural sector), and by the presence of strong personalities. Whoever held the post of chief administrator had powerful instruments at his disposal: the distribution of federal subsidies (credits to agriculture, for example, could be lodged with banks of the administration's choosing), the issuing of licences for export, allowing trade deals with other parts of the country, and of course appointments. As Diakonov's example showed, it was necessary to build up one's supporters without offending other powerful interests too much. And it was vital to have people in post who could influence the outcome of an election, especially given opponents such as Kondratenko.[50]

---

[49] See p. 116, n. 21.
[50] Under Egorov's successor, E. Kharitonov (who, from a rural background, had worked his way up to town party secretary, then to administrator of a rural district), it seems as though out in the districts a new generation of rural and industrial managers began to move into government administration: Andreev, *Politicheskaia stsena Kubani*.

An important part of the chief administrator's job was negotiating with Moscow over the budget and for federal funds. Although Krasnodar krai was a net donor to the federal budget, it still needed credits at particular times of the year. Regional authorities took advantage of the conflict between president and Congress to play one off against the other in order to get financial concessions. Although there was strong political support in the krai soviet for the Supreme Soviet in October 1993, its members still recognized that Egorov's loyalty to the president had its uses. If there were concessions to be won from the president, it was important to have a chief administrator who could extract them and, at the end of October, Egorov was in Moscow concluding a credit deal with the government for 105 mlrd r. for the agro-industrial complex.[51] In this respect he took his job seriously. When, in March 1994, Yeltsin took a short holiday at the presidential villa near Sochi, Egorov was there to meet him at the military airport. It was a time-honoured practice that the general secretary, when holidaying, was met and seen off by the regional first secretary. Egorov took advantage of Yeltsin's holiday stay to discuss various pressing matters with him and obtained the president's promise of a decree that would make visas obligatory for those visiting from the near-abroad, and the granting of special border status to the krai.[52] The personal connection bore fruit when a few months later he replaced Shakhrai as RF minister for nationality affairs, took an active role in deciding policy towards Chechnya, and subsequently became head of the president's administration.

His qualifications for the post of minister were those of having preserved the peace in a region bordering on the Caucasus; and indeed the issue which had come to dominate the political agenda in the krai was that of immigration and ethnic tension. It was an issue that was largely absent from our other regions (with the exception of Tatarstan in 1991–2) and developments in Krasnodar allow us to see the painful and complex problems that faced the border regions, and the reactions of sections of the population and of the elite to them.

The issue of immigration

If the break-up of the Union produced new states, it did not simultaneously produce clear definitions of citizenship. What were the rights of

---

[51] *Kub. nov.*, 29 October 1993, p. 1.
[52] *Komsomolets Kubani*, 24, 26 March 1994, p. 1. He also got a decision on the much-disputed future of the city of Anape: it would remain a children's resort and not be developed as a port. The only incident that marred an otherwise highly successful strategy on Egorov's part was that he was late in arriving to see the president off, ordered his chauffeur to drive at speed onto the airfield, and crashed into a cow.

those millions of individuals who, belonging to one nationality, now found themselves in an independent state which claimed to represent the people of a different nationality? Twenty-five million Russians, millions of Ukrainians, and tens of thousands of other nationalities now found themselves in this situation. Krasnodar krai, as we saw, had its share of Armenians and Ukrainians, many of whose families had lived there for as long as could be remembered, longer than many Russians. Were they to take Ukrainian or Armenian citizenship? To allay anxieties, the Russian government ruled that any former citizen of the USSR had the right to take Russian citizenship if the application was made before 7 February 1995.[53] With its southern climate, rich land, fruits, and vegetables, the krai had always attracted population, particularly from the North. During 1980–3 its population (including the Adygei region) had increased, through immigration, by approximately 77,000; during 1984–7 the number went up to 120,000. Since 1989 it had become a place of refuge for people of all nationalities fleeing from battle zones or forcibly evicted. They came in their thousands, some to join relatives, some temporarily, some in the hope of settling permanently. By the autumn of 1993 the krai (excluding the Adygei republic) was second only to South Ossetia as an immigration zone, receiving up to 10,000 people a month.[54]

Although within the krai, and the Adygei republic, there were remarkably few instances of ethnic violence, its patchwork of ethnic groups, the general rise in ethnic assertiveness, and the reality of outright war in the neighbouring Caucasus made it a potentially dangerous area. The threat of violence came from sections of the host community, angered by what they perceived as the intrusion of unwelcome foreigners. Who, though, were the foreigners in such a long-settled, ethnically mixed region? To the Adygei, tracing their origins back to the Thracians, the Russians were the newcomers, but the Adygei had no wish to engage in confrontation with a vastly superior power. And, although there were exceptions, the Russian community recognized the Adygei right to its homeland – or to that part of it so designated by Soviet power. It was a different matter when it came to the Armenian settlements, now swollen by the influx of refugees.

The situation was complicated by the krai being a region of Cossack settlement. The rediscovery of Cossack roots that took place in the general atmosphere of reappropriating the past and the search for new identities resulted in assertive nationalist organizations, demanding

[53] RSFSR law no. 1948-1 'On RSFSR citizenship', 28 November 1991, in *Vedomosti s"ezda narodnykh deputatov RF i Verkhovnogo Soveta RF*, 6 (1992), pp. 308–20; *Ross. gaz.*, 20 March 1992, pp. 4–6.
[54] *Reshenie Krasnodarskogo kraevogo soveta narodnykh deputatov XXI sozyva: 9 sessiia, 5–7 avgusta 1992* (Krasnodar, 1992), p. 94; Savva, *Mezhnatsional'nye otnosheniia*, p. 34.

territory and autonomy, and *claiming* wide popular support. It is important to stress that none of those involved – federal authorities, regional authorities, the Cossacks, or representatives of the different nationalities – had any clear idea of popular attitudes or what the results of their actions might be. It is important too to recognize that, at any time when the future is so uncertain, short-term considerations will dominate. The authorities felt nervous of their ability to control the situation and considered that federal measures were essential to help them to do so. They meant by this the limiting of immigration, at the very least. The federal authorities' unhelpful attitude only confirmed their and the population's belief that the Yeltsin government was either incapable of doing anything or not interested in its Russian population. This, in its turn, was reflected in the election results in 1993 and 1994. But let us begin with the Cossacks.

The Cossacks

The Cossacks were settlers of Russian and Ukrainian origin who, as the empire pushed outwards in the eighteenth and nineteenth centuries, had been granted a large measure of self-government in return for their military services. They had developed into fiercely independent communities with their own rules governing land use, compulsory military service in their own regiments, and elected atamans or chiefs. Following the revolution their independent stance brought them into conflict with the Bolsheviks, and their communities were broken up and their members brought under Soviet rule. In 1988 and 1989 the first Cossack organizations appeared. In Krasnodar V. P. Gromov, a lecturer in the history faculty of the university, formed a club with his students to study Russian military history and from this came the first Cossack organization in the krai. By 1990, from different beginnings, Cossack organizations had sprung up in different parts of the country. In June a founding meeting in Moscow created the Cossack Union, elected the ataman and an administration, and began to agitate for the rehabilitation of the Cossacks as a repressed people, for their rights as 'a nation', and for the granting of their traditional social, cultural, and political rights. Cossack dress and military uniform reappeared, Cossack rallies swore allegiance to the motherland, and priests blessed their endeavours.

By the autumn of 1990 there were forty-three Cossack organizations in the krai, united under a council, the Kubanskaia Kazach´ia Rada (KKR), with Gromov as the elected ataman. But by October 1992, when the Rada attempted to hold a united congress and 182 local associations existed, the movement had irrevocably split into several different organizations. Ideological and political differences (pro- or anti-market, support or opposition to Diakonov) and personal rivalries all played a part.[55] In these respects the Cossack movement was no different from the other socio-political movements – the democratic movement, the patriots, TOTs – that grew rapidly, then split and fractured. Henceforth there would be two main Cossack organizations in the krai: the former KKR, now renamed the Vsekubanskoe kazach'e voisko or VKV, still led by Gromov and much the larger; and the breakaway Kubanskoe kazach'e voisko, the KKV, under its ataman E. Nagai, and associated with Diakonov. According to Gromov, the KKV could only boast 150 members in the spring of 1994, whereas his organization had 367 Cossack societies and, as of October 1993, 15,000 members.[56] What was the VKV programme and how much had been achieved by 1994? The Cossacks, it claimed, were a specific nation descended from Russians, Ukrainians, and the people of the mountains, constituting 'a nation within the Russian nation'; they had a right to the Cossack lands of 1917, including those which now lay within the Adygei republic; only with the return of Cossack lands to the jurisdiction of local Cossack authorities, the banning of the buying and selling of land, the observance of the Orthodox faith, the creation of Cossack border regiments, and Cossack self-government would the nation be reborn.[57] Their spokesmen were evasive when queried on how these aims were compatible with the rights of other nationalities (which they claimed would not be infringed) and on how their demands for the management of Cossack lands and self-government could be reconciled with federal laws. Their charter, adopted in 1992, claimed a special role for the Cossacks in the government of the krai: the VKV should have the right to 'participate in forming the organs of state power and administration . . . to participate in working out the decisions of the organs of state power and administration'; permanent commissions for Cossack affairs should be attached to the soviets, and deputy chief administrators should be appointed by the chief administrator on the recommendation of the Cossack organizations; Cossack representatives should be included in the commissions and committees on land reform, property, and privatization.[58]

[55] A. Andreev and E. Panasiuk, 'Kazach'e dvizhenie', *Polis.*, 3 (1993), 57–61; for few more details, see Andreev's 'Kazach'e dvizhenie: tendentsii i perspektivy', *Segodnia*, 12 February 1994, p. 10; interview with Gromov, March 1994.
[56] Interview, March 1994; *Kub. kur'er*, 24 March 1994, p. 1; see above, pp. 122–3 for the relationship with Diakonov.
[57] Interview with Gromov, March 1994; *Kub. kaz. ved.*, 4 (1991), pp. 15–16. The main difference with Nagai's group was that the latter favoured private ownership of land.
[58] 'Concept of a regional complex programme for the rebirth of the Cossacks', *Kaz. vesti*, 14 (July 1993), p. 3, together with the charter of the VKV, adopted at the III Congress in October 1992; see in particular statutes 3 and 8; *Kaz. vesti*, 21 (September 1993), p. 2.

In August 1993 Egorov gave official authorization to the charter and, according to *Kazach'i vesti*, 'the little soviet of the Krasnodar soviet after an unforgivable delay at last accepted the "Concept of a regional complex programme for the rebirth of the Cossacks"'. The chair of the soviet, however, stated that the soviet had recognized neither.[59] By the spring of 1994 the VKV could point to one tangible achievement. The krai authorities had agreed to unarmed Cossack participation in police patrols for special assignments (two Cossacks to one policeman), and 170 such patrols were in existence. The Cossacks gave this publicity ('in the railway station no. 1 fifty foreign citizens from the near-abroad, who lacked residence permits and other appropriate permits, were detained and fined. Knuckledusters, a picklock, and a dagger were confiscated from them'), claiming that the result was a decrease in crime.[60] The krai authorities clearly were anxious not to offend the Cossacks but neither were they about to implement Cossack demands, either as regards land or self-government.[61]

The federal authorities were similarly unenthusiastic but their response to Cossack demands was strongly influenced by short-term political considerations. In the legislation relating to the Cossacks we see an example of the way in which the conflict between the two branches of government was beginning to drive the policy process. In June 1992 a presidential decree 'On measures to realize the Russian Federation law "On the rehabilitation of repressed peoples" in relation to the Cossacks' gave the Cossacks the right, in principle, to re-establish their traditional forms of self-government, land use, and military government service; such arrangements should not infringe the rights of others, and should be registered with the local or republican authorities and, in the case of military service, be agreed with the Ministry of Defence. The decree obliged the government, together with the Cossack organizations, to prepare the detailed legislation by 1 January 1993. The Supreme Soviet responded by supporting and elaborating the decree, and proposed that the government should bring the proposals forward by 1 November 1992.[62]

---

[59] Information from *Kaz. vesti*, 21 (September 1993), p. 1; 18 (August 1993), p. 1; interview with Zhdanovskii, March 1994.

[60] *Kaz. vesti*, 14 (July 1993), p. 1; *Kras. izv.*, 24 March 1994, p. 3.

[61] When, for example, Erin, the minister for internal affairs, came from Moscow at the end of March 1994 to discuss ways of halting the crime wave with the regional authorities, the VKV was invited to participate. On the other hand, the Cossack congress noted that, although the krai authorities were responding to the Cossack documents, 'experience suggests, regrettably, that it is most probable that they will not be realized in practice', particularly the clauses on land without which 'the rebirth of the Cossacks is unthinkable': *Kub. nov.*, 8 October 1993, p. 1.

[62] *Vedomosti s''ezda narodnykh deputatov RF i Verkhovnogo Soveta RF*, 25 (1992), statute 1429; *Vedomosti*, 30 (1992), statute 1805.

According to Krasnodar politicians, the original presidential decree was drawn up with the authorization of Skokov, secretary of the Security Council, after he had been lobbied by Cossack spokesmen. There was no prior consultation with the relevant local authorities. When those in Krasnodar, Rostov, and Stavropol got wind of the decree, they flew to Moscow and managed to persuade Skokov of the need for certain changes. They were still not happy with the final version, envisaging serious problems if such rights were realized. From the president's point of view the decree would bring him Cossack support, while handing the near-impossible task of producing appropriate legislation over to the government. The Supreme Soviet in turn felt obliged to be seen to be more pro-Cossack than the president.

Nothing had happened by November 1992, or by January 1993. Then, in March 1993, a new presidential decree proposed that Cossack units should serve as border troops under the control of the Ministry of State Security and the Ministry of Defence.[63] Could the forthcoming referendum have had anything to do with this? It seems that it was drawn up by Shakhrai, minister for nationality affairs, and the local authorities only learnt of it on publication. This time the Supreme Soviet, by now locked in battle with the president, halted the decree, claiming to be working on the implementation of the earlier proposals – but again nothing materialized.[64]

In the spring of 1994 the government finally addressed the decrees of 1992 and 1993. A ruling of 22 April approved the basic principles of the conception of state policy towards the Cossacks. It requested the Ministry for Nationality Affairs to produce, by 1 June, a programme to realize the principles, including arrangements for holding a Cossack assembly before 1 October, and a law to put before the Duma; the Defence and Foreign Ministries, by 1 July, were to work out regulations covering Cossack military service. Shakhrai was to be responsible for seeing that all these measures were carried out. These proposals were discussed in the Security Council and, indeed, it is probably the Cossacks' military claims that were of most concern and interest to the authorities. On the one hand, as the principles stated: 'The specifics of creating Cossack detachments in which, periodically, the entire male population of call-up age serve, will allow for a substantial increase in the call-up cohort and go a long way towards solving the problem of making up the

[63] 'O reformirovanii voennykh struktur, pogranichnykh, i vnutrennykh voisk na territorii Severo-Kavkazskogo regiona RF i gosudarstvennoi podderzhke kazachestv', decree no. 341, *Ross. gaz.*, 23 March 1993, p. 3.
[64] *Kaz. vesti*, 17 (August 1993), p. 1; interview with Zhdanovskii, March 1994.

detachments'; on the other, there was no desire to grant military formations or Cossack communities any real autonomy. By the spring of 1994 only one military unit had been authorized, and that was within the ranks of the regular army.[65] On paper, however, the Cossacks had won considerable concessions. Their leaders had succeeded in persuading politicians, particularly at the centre, that they were a force to be reckoned with.

Were they, though? Assessment by local politicians varied. Some considered that Cossack activity peaked in late 1992 to mid-summer 1993. A Cossack spokesman suggested that financial difficulties in the spring of 1994 were affecting the publication of *Kazach'i vesti*. The leadership talked of growing support (according to Gromov, 30 per cent of the krai population supported Cossack aims in 1994); others tended to see popular support as highly contingent upon changes in the socio-economic environment. A survey carried out in August 1992 (800 respondents, six towns, eight rural settlements) suggested that perhaps 20 per cent of the population identified themselves as Cossacks but, of these, 72 per cent favoured *private* ownership of land compared with 59 per cent of the non-Cossacks. As regards self-government, 40 per cent of the Cossacks were in favour, 31 per cent opposed, 29 per cent unsure; 43 per cent of the Cossacks (and 23 per cent of non-Cossacks) favoured auxiliary Cossack detachments to help maintain law and order. Although the leadership laid great stress on the Orthodox Church as a crucial element in Cossack life, religious affiliation did not distinguish Cossacks from non-Cossacks; they did give more weight to the importance of order, social welfare, and the maintenance of the unity of Russia. Other surveys in rural districts in the summer of 1992 suggested that there was little recognition of Cossack households as different, and little support for their programme, but conflicts between different atamans featured as part of local elite politics. The authors concluded: 'The number of Cossacks in a

---

[65] 'O kontseptsii gosudarstvennoi politiki po otnosheniiu k kazachestvu', *Ross. gaz.*, 13 May 1994, p. 4 (also for the principles, which referred to the Cossacks as 'a specific part of the *Rossiiskii* [emphasis added] people' who had developed their own way of life). The principles accepted the need to revive Cossack formations in the army and as border troops, based on the principle of universal military service, and as part of a reserve, but within and subordinate to the regular army command. The right of Cossack communities to elect an ataman was recognized but it was stated that these could only be 'merged' with the local government structures where the community had a Cossack majority, and could not replace them. A Main Administration for Cossack Affairs, chaired by the supreme ataman, who would be appointed by the president on the recommendation of the All-Russian Cossack Assembly, should be set up under the government. State land funds should be set up under regional administrations which would ensure that land was not privatized and would allocate it to Cossack communities for distribution.

given village or district cannot be finely established – it depends upon the situation. If the economic and political situation worsens, there will be many because being a Cossack now is a form of social protest rather than an ethnic statement.' In answer to a question on numbers of Cossacks, the ataman of the Tempiurskii district replied: 'Two hundred or two thousand – it depends on the situation. If national relations worsen there will be lots of Cossacks.'[66]

The ability of the Cossacks to exert political influence took two forms. On the one hand there was a core group who could be mobilized to make public protests and threats. In June 1992 a Cossack picket of a police station in Krasnodar demanded the expatriation of all Caucasian immigrants; in late 1992 and early 1993 there were incidents of violence in the Polytechnic Institute hostels when unauthorized Cossack patrols entered the buildings to 'maintain order'.[67] In March 1994 Cossacks were picketing the Adygei Supreme Soviet at the time of the language law, and in June 1994 Cossack pickets barricaded the regional administration in Rostov for six days until they achieved some minor concessions on credit for agriculture.[68] On the other hand, and more worrying for the authorities, the Cossacks could provide a means through which otherwise unfocused popular grievances might express themselves in organized, perhaps violent, action. In April 1994 a group from the Black Sea coast districts turned to Egorov, and to the head of the internal affairs department, and to the atamans of the leading Cossack organizations with a letter, in which they stated that

Our patience is exhausted and we resolutely declare: so as to prevent a national explosion in our districts, measures must be taken immediately to expel those who, arriving in the Kuban, stir up trouble, sow national enmity, and turn the Kubantsy into hostages . . . If decisive action is not undertaken on your part, we shall stand by our right to raise the people to act as social judges against the Caucasians who destroy our traditions and way of life.[69]

---

[66] Andreev and Panasiuk, 'Kazach´e dvizhenie', provides data from the first survey; A. A. Khagurov and A. Kh. Tleuzh, *Agrarnaia reforma na Kubani problemy i perspektivy* (Moscow, 1993), pp. 41–5.

[67] Savva, *Mezhnatsional'nye otnosheniia*, p. 35. At the time of the Polytechnic incidents Gromov publicly made a complaint that a soviet spokesman had referred to those involved in the criminal behaviour as Cossacks; this, he suggested, was to attribute criminal behaviour to millions of Cossacks and might incite hatred towards the Cossacks and hence provoke a reaction from them towards members of the soviets. Zhdanovskii, the soviet chair, in reply, denied that there had been any implication that the behaviour of the three Cossacks, members of Gromov's organization, was typical of Cossacks, and suggested that it was he, Gromov, who was raising the temperature: *Kub. nov.*, 12, 22 December 1992, p. 1.   [68] Author's notes from demonstration; *Izv.*, 9 June 1994, p. 2.

[69] *Izv.*, 8 April 1994, p. 2.

The Cossacks varied their target depending on the circumstances: as the refugees arrived the Armenians replaced the Turks.[70] In October 1993 a decision by Egorov to cancel the direct flights between Armenia and Krasnodar brought a protest from the Armenian community; this in turn brought a protest from the Krasnodar Cossacks: 'Who are they to be speaking against the interests of the krai? We support doing everything possible to stop the robbery of the Kuban, and to that end [we favour] closing the frontiers with a solid lock against citizens from the near-abroad.'[71] During the 1993 election campaign one of the candidates, G. Len, an advocate by profession but since 1992 associated with the VKV as a Cossack judge, published long and inflammatory articles on 'the Armenian question' in *Kubanskii kur'er*. He began by suggesting that it was estimated that Armenia would lose 5 per cent of its population in migration during the coming winter, and asked where they would go. Moscow was under curfew. He quoted figures for the Armenian percentage among the immigrants, and estimates of accompanying relatives, and produced facsimiles of documents suggesting a policy of settling Armenian refugees from Baku in Russian regions. Any accusation of nationalism he strongly denied; together with his childhood Armenian friends he simply wished to defend his land from an influx of refugees. If, however, they came with a map of Greater Armenia, which included Krasnodar and Rostov, 'they should know that in the Kuban are those who will stand in their way'. The paper published a long rejoinder by one Sarukhanova (subsequently described as an 'Armenian activist'), who queried Len's account of individual cases, and argued that there were indeed cases of homeless elderly refugees from Stepankiert joining their families in Krasnodar. It then devoted a whole page to outraged readers' responses, and a reply from Len himself. One reader begged the paper not to publish any more 'poisonous Russophobic articles' of the type written

[70] In November 1991 five Meskhetian Turkish houses were burnt out in a pogrom in the Krymskii district. Since 1989 approximately 5,500 Meskhetian Turks had arrived from Georgia, buying the houses vacated by departing Crimean Tatars, but objections from the local inhabitants resulted in the authorities' denying the in-comers residence permits and hence ownership rights; a special ruling from the chief administrator disqualified those without residence permits from registering marriages; their insecure legal status encouraged local employers to employ them on short-term contracts and then dismiss them while they were still ineligible for welfare, social security benefits, etc.; informally the authorities offered the Turks ownership rights if they agreed to sell and depart. Local Cossacks were demanding that all post-1985 in-comers should be deported to their homelands.

[71] *Kub. kur'er*, 21 October 1993, p. 1. This is not to imply that Russian refugees or immigrants could be assured of a welcome. In some parts of Russia they found themselves equally subject to harassment and discrimination. It is difficult to tell the extent to which they fared better in the south simply because there was another target for local discontent.

by the 'fifth columnist' Armenian activist. Another bewailed the fate of Moscow, which no Russian could any longer consider his capital city; Lermontov 'would be horrified to see the Sodom and Gomorrah created by the countless hordes of aliens':

we must act, support Russians, who care about Russian matters, so that those born in other states don't occupy leading posts on Russian land . . . they are strong not because of their own strength and not, of course, because truth is on their side, but because of Russian inactivity, and all of them, when it is needed, plead helplessness, beg to be defended by Russian weapons.

Two sentences in particular in Sarukhanova's letter had touched a nerve. In describing the old people's flight from Stepankiert, she had written of Russian tanks surrounding a village and the inhabitants being told to gather a few belongings and leave. She was implying, wrote the astounded respondents, that the Russian army was in some way responsible for their having to leave. Even worse, she quoted an elderly Armenian as saying, 'although my daughter-in-law is Russian, she is kind and good'. With this phrase, his groundless Armenian prejudices and those of Sarukhanova were revealed: how could he say 'although . . .' when it was an established truth that Russians by nature are kind and good!

Len, in his reply, was quite unrestrained. The local Russian population had not reacted when the immigrants bought land, permits, and shops but when they 'used their excess sexual energies against local girls and boys' – he cited the rape and murder of a fourteen-year-old girl – 'when a guest overturns his host's table and spits him in the face, tries to rape his wife and daughter, it is the duty of any man with an ounce of masculine self-respect to drive that type of scoundrel out of his house . . . We Russians are a Great Nation. Why should we be crowded in our own home by those who are hardly superior to us intellectually, are no more industrious, and do not shine as fighters?' He then produced documents, ostensibly from the Armenian Catholicus, advocating a resettlement policy in southern Russia, which he suggested, although he could not vouch for their validity, were interesting nevertheless. The problem, as Len saw it, was that the Russians were disunited: whereas 'they advance in a united force, we are divided between democrats and communists, supporters of Travkin and Zhirinovskii', and therefore could not become masters in their own land. 'There is no proper owner in the Kuban!'[72]

According to local officials, many were put off by the Cossacks'

[72] 23 October 1993, p. 1; 20 November 1993, p. 2. The documents were subsequently declared to be forgeries. The Catholicus registered a strong protest, and both the krai administration and soviet criticized the paper for its irresponsible behaviour, but only after the election: *Kub. nov.*, 15 December 1993, p. 1.

aggressive stance and slogans (and Len came a poor third in his electoral district). There was a tendency for the organizations to attract, at least in the large towns, 'lumpen personalities' with criminal records. The murder of two Kurds by nine drunken Cossacks was a case in point. The VKV attempted to clean up its organization, and to devise a new ideology but, despite the talk of unity, was plagued by splits between the atamans. However, a sudden worsening of the situation as regards immigration from the southern countries could make them the spokesmen for a political wave of protest, and with elections approaching the politicians trod carefully. Few were prepared to align themselves wholly with the Cossacks, but all the leading newspapers carried quite extensive and favourable reporting on the Cossack organizations.

The Adygei republic

Within such a context one might imagine that the newly created Adygei republic would have provided a focus for discontent, yet at elite level relations were remarkably amiable and at popular level quietly restrained. Decision-making lay in the hands of an elite inherited from the Soviet period, still coming to terms with the unexpected windfall of greater autonomy and the possibility of raising the status of and openings for the Adygei.[73] The gradual acquisition of property and office by those of the titular nationality, and the passage of the language law marked the first years of its rule. In Maikop, the capital, at the time of the debate on the language law, the Cossacks were demonstrating and, among some of the deputies, there were fears that trouble might erupt. Rumours had been circulated that the law would require knowledge of Adygei for employment and for entry to higher education, and that all court proceedings would be in Adygei. Yet no incidents occurred and neighbouring Krasnodar remained unaware that a language law had even been

---

[73] The newly elected president, A. Dzharimov, was a kraikom party secretary responsible for agriculture. Among the deputies there were newcomers, but few in the executive. Of the eleven ministers in 1994 most were Adygei, but they did not include the posts of internal affairs, or finance. The Committee of the Forty had argued for an election law that would give the Adygei half the seats in the new Supreme Soviet. Although it failed to achieve this, the outcome of the elections (held between December 1991 to March 1992) was forty-five Adygei, fifty-five Russian and other nationalities – or near parity; in the smaller permanent Khas'e (elected in October 1993) Adygeis occupied twenty-three of the forty-five seats: interviews with Adygei deputies, March 1994; *Vol. Kub.*, 30 March 1994, pp. 1–2, carries an interview with A. Tleuzh, the chair of the Supreme Soviet. In December 1993 Dzharimov and the mayor of Maikop, M. Chernichenko, won the two seats to the Council of the Federation; the Duma seat was won by the chair of the government, V. Lednev: *Kub. nov.*, 15 December 1993, p. 1.

passed.[74] The law attempted to raise the status of the Adygei language, to encourage its use, while implicitly recognizing the privileged position of Russian in a republic where fewer than a quarter of the population was Adygei and where, even for them, the usual language of communication was Russian. Such a law, one might have thought, would pose no threat to the Russian population. Was this the reason that a long article in *Vol'naia Kuban*, devoted to an interview with Tleuzh, the chair of the Adygei parliament, on the eve of the second reading contained no reference to the law?[75] Was that information of no interest to the Krasnodar reader – or had *Vol'naia Kuban* decided, in good Soviet fashion, that it would be best simply not to mention it?

How do we explain either elite relations or those between the local populations? Dzharimov, the Adygei president, and Egorov went back a long way, and were used to working together. The two different elites were not disputing control over the same resources. The Adygeis were still startled by their good luck and prepared to tread cautiously. Some among the local Russian population were less than happy. As residents of the republic, they now felt that their future was threatened, and that neither the krai authorities, whose responsibility they no longer were, nor the Russian government were at all concerned. But neither did they sympathize with Cossack demands. Who then would represent their interests? In December 1993 only Zhirinovskii of the leading politicians spoke to their concerns.

Policy towards immigration

In September 1993 Egorov, speaking to the krai soviet, gave the number of officially registered immigrants as 135,000 and estimated the number of unofficial immigrants at four or five for each officially registered individual. This gave a figure of 540,000–675,000 or approximately 13 per cent of the population. He suggested that approximately 27 per cent of the immigrants were Armenians (compared with their 4 per cent share of the krai's population) and that, given they tended to move to join fellow

---

[74] The law proposed that from 1998 both Adygei and Russian should be used at all official meetings and in all official documents. From the year 2003 both should be used in all state institutions; in schools instruction in the first four classes should be in the native language (Russian, Adygei, Armenian, or Turkmen, depending upon the community), and all would take Russian language and literature; from the fifth class instruction would be in Russian, but Adygei language, literature, and history would be offered as a special subject: 'O iazykakh narodov respubliki Adygeia', *Sov. Adygeia*, 1 April 1994, p. 1. Even the Adygei community in Krasnodar itself was little involved. A meeting of the Krasnodar Khas'e, a week earlier, had not discussed it: author's notes from meeting, 24 March 1994.

[75] *Vol. Kub.*, 30 March 1994, pp. 1–2.

countrymen, 'the historically evolved balance between different national groups will be upset in certain regions' – in particular in the Black Sea region nearest to Abkhazia.[76] Following the appearance of Len's articles, in which these figures were used, the administration publicly confirmed the total figures and provided further information: of the 135,000, residence permits had been issued to 100,000 people, and 36,000 had been found work. Of the 40,000 who had claimed refugee status, 13,500 had been granted it; of these 80 per cent were Russian, 3 per cent Ukrainian, 9 per cent Armenian.[77] And of those arriving in recent months (at a rate of roughly 10,000 a month), 89 per cent were Russians and only 6 per cent Armenians.[78]

There were two issues here. First, regardless of the real figures, in the perception of at least sections of the dominant Slav population the immigrants were overwhelmingly 'Caucasian' or Armenian, and they were disliked. It was they, it was popularly believed, who sent house prices up and were responsible for the rise in crime; Georgian criminals preferred operating out of Krasnodar because it was an easier environment than Tbilisi. From the administration's point of view the influx of immigrants put an intolerable strain upon already overstretched resources, as well as providing the potential for ethnic disturbances. Egorov referred to the inability of the krai to cope with health care, the drain on the pensions' fund, the increase in mafia dealings in selling land to foreigners, and the role of the middlemen, trading to and fro across the borders.[79] By the autumn of 1993 the krai soviet was registering deep concern that

the multinational immigrant influx is creating a serious threat to the socio-political stability of the krai: the prices of property are escalating far faster than the Russian average, property ownership is becoming stratified on an ethnic basis and creating preconditions for interethnic conflicts. During the past three months the authorities have been obliged to use force in order to prevent conflicts of a nationalist nature in the towns of Anape, Krymsk, and the rural settlement of Trudobelikovesk . . . in each case the cause of the disturbance was the discontent of the local population with the mass in-migration of those who are not Russian citizens.[80]

---

[76] Only slightly more than 3 per cent of the immigrants, he suggested, either had other than Russian citizenship or no citizenship: *Kub. nov.*, 30 September 1993, p. 1. See also *Vash vybor*, 2 (1993), pp. 14–19, for a series of short articles on the situation in the krai and excerpts from the soviet's decisions.

[77] *Kub. nov.*, 2 November 1993, p. 1. They came from: Georgia 60 per cent, Chechnya 18 per cent, Tadzhikistan 10 per cent (*Kub. nov.*, 19 November 1993, pp. 1–2). *Ross. gaz.*, 11 September 1993, p. 3, adds 9 per cent from Azerbaijan.

[78] *Kub. nov.*, 2 November 1993, p. 1.

[79] Speech to the krai soviet, 30 September 1993. See also Savva, *Mezhnatsional'nye otnosheniia.*

[80] *Reshenie Krasnodarskogo kraevogo soveta*, 28 September 1993, protocol no. 15, item 5.

The references here were to Armenian immigration to the already large Armenian communities on the Black Sea coast. Given the absence of data on actual incidents, or even survey material, it is impossible to say to what extent ethnic tension was dangerously high, to what extent the authorities considered it posed a real danger, and to what extent it was a useful argument to deploy when trying to get action from the federal authorities to slow down immigration. We can guess, but only guess, that the authorities' interest in limiting immigration was accompanied by the dislike, felt by many in the soviet and administration, for 'the Caucasians' and their fear of the Cossacks' ability to play upon popular feelings.

The krai had long practised a restrictive policy on residence but in August 1992 the soviet voted to adopt a 'Programme to stabilize inter-ethnic relations in Krasnodar krai' which introduced even stricter measures. The krai, it noted, with its

relatively high ethnic mosaic . . . [where] the developing processes of ethnic renaissance are taking place against a background of a structural crisis (economic, social, political, and ecological) . . . lies in a zone of interethnic conflict. Each worsening of interethnic relations in the neighbouring sovereign republics and regions of the Russian Federation brings in its train a wave of migrants to the krai. This is a long-term phenomenon and requires the taking of measures both by the krai and by the republican authorities.[81]

While all decisions would be based on the principle of equal rights for the krai's different nationalities ('the programme does not foresee priorities of any kind for any one of the ethnic communities of Krasnodar krai'), a distinction would be made between residents and newcomers. The government should not, as in the past, practise harsh control of inter-ethnic processes, but a policy which would allow the different communities to live without conflict. The new rulings gave the administration the right to establish, annually, district quotas for immigrants. Those entitled to residence permits – close relatives, demobilized or retired members of the armed forces originally resident in the krai, students, specialists with specific work contracts – were listed in detail. Penalties for breaking the law (fines) were specified. For non-Russian citizens, illegally resident, a system of deportation should be devised; the establishment of a firm international border with Georgia, and visa requirements, were priorities.

The soviet drew the attention of the president, the Supreme Soviet, and the government to the consequences of the absence of an established border between Russia and the now-independent states of the Caucasus – immigration, the export from the krai of food and consumer goods, an increase in criminalization – and asked the federal authorities to consider:

---

[81] *Reshenie*, 5–7 August 1992, no. 73. Further details are also from this source.

(a) awarding the krai the status of a border zone with the accompanying legal controls for regulating migration,
(b) excluding the krai from the list of regions which should accept refugees, with the exception of those with close relatives in the krai, and
(c) working out, together with the krai authorities, by 1 January 1993, a statute to regulate migration.[82]

A year later the only point to which the federal authorities had responded was the one on excluding the krai from the list of refugee-receiving regions. This had helped, but only a little. Not only had the influx of immigrants continued but, the authorities feared, the new federal law ending the residence-permit (*propiska*) system would result in an uncontrollable situation. Egorov argued there was a real threat 'of losing economic and political sovereignty in the Russian south'.[83] The soviet resolved to tighten up the categories of relatives eligible for residence permits and to dispute the legality of the new law which, it argued, 'infringes the constitutional rights of the inhabitants of Krasnodar krai, does not accord with the points in the [Federal] Treaty which specify the delimitation of federal and regional jurisdiction in particular areas';[84] it made a formal legislative proposal to both the Supreme Soviet and the president that the new law should only come into effect in the krai on 7 February 1995, i.e. the date by which any citizen of the former USSR wishing Russian citizenship had to register. The law, it argued, would place the krai 'on the edge of a social catastrophe':

its introduction will mean for the border zone of the Kuban a worsening of the situation, in criminal and epidemic terms, the destruction of the historically evolved numerical balance of different national groups, the growth of national tension. All of this will inevitably reflect upon the stability of the Russian Federation as a unitary state.

The soviet repeated its request for the status of a border region whose authorities had the right to introduce their own residence regulations.[85]

The Supreme Soviet had no time to reply before its dissolution but the

---

[82] *Obrashchenie: prilozhenie*, protocol no. 9, item 13.
[83] *Kub. nov.*, 30 September 1993, p. 1.
[84] In September 1993, reported in *Kub. nov.*, 21 October 1993, p. 1.
[85] *Reshenie*, 28 September 1993, protocol no. 15, items 6, 15–21; *Obrashchenie*, protocol no. 15, items 5, 6–8, 9–11. The law 'On the right of the citizens of the Russian Federation to freedom of movement, choice of place of being or residence within the Russian Federation' of 25 June 1993 (*Vedomosti s''ezda*, 32 (1993), pp. 2078–81) was to come into force on 1 October 1993 but the October crisis delayed the government's working out of the new registration procedures until the summer of 1995. Some regional authorities adopted, in the meantime, their own procedures which, for example in the case of Moscow, included very high registration fees, and were subsequently declared unconstitutional by the Constitutional Court: *Ross. gaz.*, 17 April 1996, pp. 4–5.

president's legislative commission suggested that a presidential decree was being prepared to delay the implementation of the law and, if this did not solve the problem, then the Krasnodar initiative would be considered. A few days later an edict was issued which, in accordance with the law on the Russian Federation border, specified the Black Sea coast area as a border zone and strengthened border police and customs points.[86] In his election campaign Egorov claimed: 'Although we can't prevent the entry of refugees into our territory, we are moving in that direction: forbidding their entry or deporting them. Such measures are essential or the living standards of the 5 million population of the Kuban will drop sharply';[87] and, as noted earlier, in March 1994 he obtained the president's undertaking that the krai would have special status.

The electoral battle

Unlike the election campaign in many parts of the country, Krasnodar's 1993 race was bitterly fought. It was not between parties but between candidates put forward by the different 'clans', now a visible feature of the political landscape. The combination of a conservative and unsettled community, a small democratic opposition, and powerful individuals with organized backing, all bitterly opposed to one another, made for a sharply contested election in December 1993 and again the following autumn when the local elections were finally held. In both cases turnout was comparatively high. December revealed a divided elite, unsure how to conduct its electoral affairs, and a disoriented population; by the autumn of 1994 three very different types of political organization had appeared as contenders for votes.

If in Tatarstan and in Sakha the administration could at least control who stood in opposition to the president, this was not so in Krasnodar. The key prizes in December were the two seats in the Council of the Federation. The three leading contenders were Egorov, Kondratenko, the popular hero, and Samoilenko, mayor of Krasnodar. They were joined by the general director of an oil company, the president of a wine-producing corporation, and the rebel Diakonov. Although Diakonov failed to emerge as a serious threat, the electoral commission attempted to exclude him on the grounds of the falsification of signatures. He successfully challenged the decision and the krai commission was overruled by the central commission.[88] The krai commission chairman, Iu. Lapkin, was outraged. Perhaps it was true that there had been irregularities in all

---

[86] *Kub. nov.*, 21, 26 October 1993, p. 1.   [87] *Kub. nov.*, 10 December 1993, p. 2.
[88] *Izv.*, 24 November 1993, p. 4; *Ross. gaz.*, 1 December 1993, p. 2.

the candidates' returns, he declared, but none on the scale of Diakonov's; his candidature was an insult to the others and he was 'convinced that the majority of the residents of the Kuban are dismayed by V. N. Diakonov's attempt to get into the new Russian Parliament by false and deceitful means'.[89] Either Egorov's desire to exclude Diakonov was based on a real anxiety that he might prove, after all, to have a following or it reflected an old Soviet attitude: since he had been defeated, he could have no political future.

Egorov could not prevent *Kubanskii kur'er* from reporting Diakonov's attempt to form a new electoral bloc to 'save' the krai. A meeting on 4 October advocated a constitution with a proper division of powers, a new executive structure in the Kuban, elections for both branches of power at krai level, and a law disallowing members of the original party apparatus from holding positions in the state structures.[90] The paper also reported a congress of the 'democratic-political forces' of the Kuban on 6 November to which all the above and more (Memorial, Russia's Choice, Union of Small and Middle-Sized Business) were invited, and which was attended by leading democrats from Moscow as well as 'fiery' Cossack spokesmen.[91] The only other paper to mention the congress was *Kubanskie novosti*, but its report included an official announcement from the administration accusing Diakonov of falsehoods and suggesting he should not attempt a comeback to politics.[92] Thereafter none of the press mentioned Diakonov's campaign or that of any of the democratic parties. *Vol'naia Kuban* took pleasure in reporting that Diakonov, 'the ex-guber- nator of the Kuban, the ex-people's deputy, and the ex-leader of "all the democratic forces of the krai"' had at last paid a court fine of 2 million r. in a libel case brought by Egorov.[93] The head of the television station lost his job as a consequence of allowing Diakonov to appear. Egorov requested a letter of resignation from the misguided editor in return for which, he was told, he would stay on in another capacity. But, once he had written the letter, he was notified that he would never work in local televi- sion again.[94] The only paper to report his resignation (and without giving

[89] *Kub. nov.*, 7 December 1993, p. 1.
[90] The meeting was attended by representatives of the entrepreneurs, Social Democrats, Democratic Party of Russia, the Christian Democrats, Party of Economic Freedom, New Generation, the farmers, Nagai's Cossack organization and the Cossack Association of Russia, the Slav Union, and the president's representative: *Kub. kur'er*, 6, 9 October 1993, p. 1.   [91] *Kub. kur'er*, 6, 10 November 1993, p. 1.
[92] *Kub. nov.*, 11, 13 November 1993, p. 1. It also published a letter from S. Shipunova, the patriotic Krasnodar correspondent of *Sov. Ross.* objecting to his (mis)use of her name in his television appearance: 11 December 1993, p. 1.
[93] *Vol. Kub.*, 29 October 1993, p. 1.
[94] Interviews with journalists and political activists, March 1994.

the reason) was *Kubanskii kur'er*, and indeed, it was only from the *Kur'er*, with its somewhat scandalous reputation, and only until mid-November that the public could get some sense of anti-establishment opposition in the krai.

The spectrum of the press in Krasnodar and its election reporting is revealing of press fortunes in the post-communist environment and of Krasnodar politics. *Vol'naia Kuban*, the former party paper, had no difficulty surviving as an independent paper, owned by the collective, and still under the same editor. The ex-party paper, in any of the regions, had an advantage over others: it was the best known, with the largest circulation; it had an experienced collective, good offices, and often the printing press. It could pick up advertising more easily. It might not be exciting (but then it never had been) but it was the paper people had read for years. These papers survived whereas some of the new ones, funded by the soviets, began to struggle; sometimes the administration stepped in to help out. The new independent papers found it more and more difficult to be commercially viable. People were not buying papers much anyway. All had to rely on commercial sponsorship, and those with a small readership lived from hand to mouth. The occasional 'scandalous' paper appeared, trying to attract a readership. In Krasnodar this was the *Kur'er*, originally the administration's new paper. Here, given the different political groups with resources, the press was more varied than in most places, but it was predominantly of a left-patriotic cast.

Vol'naia Kuban was strongly left-patriotic. It hardly reported the December election campaign and, by the spring, was supporting a new organization, Fatherland, grouped around Kondratenko. An editorial greeted its appearance enthusiastically, quoting from the founding documents:

We appeal . . . to all who feel themselves the inheritors of this land, each clod of which is soaked in the blood of our fathers and grandfathers, who defended the honour and independence of Russia . . . [to stop] the irresponsible rulers, the uncontrolled bureaucrats who have become all powerful . . . and under the cover of words which we all hold dear, such as freedom, are turning Russia into a rubbish dump for the industrial and radioactive waste of the West.[95]

Kubanskie novosti, the soviet paper, of a centrist-patriotic bent, initially referred to some of the party meetings – although it disapproved of parties as divisive[96] – but then concentrated its attention on its favoured candidates. These were almost entirely either non-party or of the patriotic-

[95] *Vol. Kub.*, 24 March 1994, p. 1.
[96] *Kub. nov.*, 28 October 1993, 1; 13, 16, 17 November 1993, p. 1.

communist orientation.[97] The only two party programmes presented to its readers, and this on the day before the elections, were those of the Communist Party and of Charity and Dignity. The candidate who received the most enthusiastic coverage, including full-page spreads of his diary of the October days in the White House, was S. Glotov, a young lecturer in the military school and an ex-Russian Federation deputy, who had established a high profile for himself in the krai as a conservative, patriotic deputy. As he was a military man, he suggested, it would be inappropriate for him to belong to a political party but his sympathies were left-patriotic and he supported Kondratenko for a seat on the Council of the Federation, and subsequently led the new organization, Fatherland.[98] *Krasnodarskie izvestia* supported Samoilenko's candidacy.

The only democratic publication, a weekly, *Iug*, failed to appear, for financial reasons, between June and December 1993. This left the *Kur'er*. In mid-November it was suddenly faced by demands to meet outstanding debts and then, inexplicably, by enormous increases in the bill for paper. It ceased publication for ten days, then reappeared, declaring that despite these attempts to put it out of circulation, it had friends and would carry on. Was it because it was the only voice not crying hosanna to Egorov, it asked? First it had received a complaint from the procuracy that although it did, from time to time, correctly mention the leading figures of today – Egorov and Shumeiko – it had carried advertisements for the sale of medals; then an objection had been made to its appeal to the president, in the summer, to dissolve the soviets and rule by decree but, lo and behold, the political situation had changed. Could the attempts to silence it, the paper asked, be because it was committed 'always to speak the truth and to give all the possibility to express their views?'[99] A week later a bomb wrecked the editorial office, killing one young office worker and wounding another. The paper continued, no longer criticizing anyone, and reporting electors' meetings with Kondratenko and Samoilenko. The bombers were not found.

To suggest that all could find a place in its pages was, however, an exaggeration. Originally a paper that had supported Diakonov, it gradu-

---

[97] The three exceptions were V. Onopriev (one of more reform-minded of the ex-RF deputies), who did not hesitate to state that 'The former party nomenklatura, which shifted from party into soviet armchairs, and from soviet into administration seats, carefully hid and still hides the truth about the ecological catastrophe in the Kuban', but he finished with an attack on political parties, *per se*, which 'in their struggle for power fan the flames of national and religious feelings'; only 'people with scientific achievements to their credit . . . can bring common sense and agreement' (8 December 1993, p. 2). The other two were N. Zakharova, the leader of what remained of the Democratic Party of Russia (4 December 1993, p. 2), and V. Gritsman, one of the Russia's Choice candidates.
[98] *Kub. nov.*, 17 November 1993, p. 3; 9 December 1993, p. 3.
[99] *Kub. kur'er*, 20, 25 November 1993, p. 1.

ally moved closer to Zhirinovskii's LDP. The head of the regional LDP,
V. Serdiukov, was a leading member of its editorial board. Radical-patri-
otic would perhaps best describe it. It regularly published articles by Len,
the Cossack lawyer. But its political line was quite unstable, reflecting the
widespread feeling that the present order was a scandal, but also revealing
the absence of a political position from which to attack it. In early October
the *Kur'er* came out against the Supreme Soviet, against Egorov and
Zhdanovskii, the krai soviet chair, for attempting to find a common language, and against Gromov, the Cossack leader, for threatening to introduce order if the political authorities could not resolve their conflict. Its
reporting of political activities in October and early November concentrated on Russia's Choice (a founding meeting was held in its offices on
2 October) and initially it gave coverage to Diakonov. It reported ironically on the activities of former Komsomol officials, now working for the
soviet, who were trying to attract candidates to join Shakhrai's party.
They revealed their past by their use of 'comrade' and their attempts to
enlist sportsmen in their cause. A long interview with Zhirinovskii
appeared early in the campaign but his party got no special treatment; the
editorial on the eve of the election suggested that Gaidar (representing
the class of comprador traders) would win, a period of stalemate would
follow as his policies would be blocked by his opponents, and 'then the
hour of the patriotic forces will strike, otherwise Russia will not
survive'.[100]

None of the parties, except the Communist Party, had anything
approaching an organization in the krai. Diakonov attempted to rally the
democrats around Russia's Choice, and had the support of Nagai's
Cossacks. Members of the administration set up an organization to
canvass for Shakhrai's Unity and Accord (PRES). Gromov's organization
(which was opposed to Cossacks being members of political parties),
after a meeting with Shakhrai, himself of Cossack background, also
agreed to put its support behind PRES. But although the administration
of the Union of Cossacks (Moscow) spoke of the need to organize for the
elections, and, although the Cossack Academy published a ten-point list
of desirable candidate qualities (never having been a member of the party
nomenklatura; not a state official; honest; preferably orthodox and
Cossack; and so on), the VKV did not field many candidates nor did it
campaign particularly actively.[101] Without doubt the Cossacks' preferred
candidate was Kondratenko, who shared their anti-semitic views. During

[100] *Kub. kur'er*, 2, 3, 8, 13 October 1993, p. 1; 22 October 1993, p. 2; 11 December 1993, p.
1.
[101] *Kub. nov.*, 2 October 1993, p. 1; 11 November 1993, p. 1; interviews with deputies and
administration officials, March 1994.

the summer of 1993 *Kazach'i vesti* featured the Protocols of Zion as a regular topic. Its view of the current Russian leadership ('a corrupt mafia government', in the words of one of its spokesmen) was demonstrated by its drawing comparisons between items from the presidential project for a new constitution (for example, on the right to declare a state of war or appoint ministers) with points from the Protocols.[102] In December Kondratenko took up the anti-Zionist theme at election meetings: just as in 1917 the Bolsheviks had opened the way for Zionism, so were the democrats of today ruining and selling off Russia; this was not anti-semitism, but an explanation to the working Jew of the essence of Zionism; not all Jews were Zionists, just as not all Germans were fascists.[103] The patriotic literary journal, *Kuban*, originally an organ of the regional Writers' Union, now sponsored by the Russian Writers' Union, and with leading local Cossacks on its editorial board, featured Kondratenko as 'Our Leader' in its July–August 1993 issue:

In keeping with our Russian maximalism we declare that we have no leader. There is no one to lead the people in the creation of real people's power. And certainly, look at the Yeltsin spokesmen, listen to their twisted and cynical speeches – and to today's district-regional maw, aided by the poisonous democratic lackeys and untalented soiled timeservers of the Alexander Zhdanovskii type . . .

But we don't need to seek a leader. He exists. He is Nikolai Kondratenko, a political leader and a practical leader in the very highest sense of the word. One of the first in the Kuban courageously to stand up in defence of the motherland and the people, he was slandered and removed from his post as chair of the krai soviet. And he was one of the first to be called by the people of the Kuban to service – in the name of the real Russia of the people which it is time to tear out of the hands of the occupiers and traitors, those very people incidentally whom he named as early as April 1991.[104]

Kubanskie novosti gave him a more statesmanlike image: he had spent four days in the White House in September and had supported the Congress resolutions, but he had spoken in favour of the Congress dissolving itself and leaving the Supreme Soviet in place. He had not favoured Rutskoi's call to arms. Kondratenko himself claimed that the political parties amounted to no more than political intrigues, but his sympathies lay with Govorukhin, the patriotic film director, the Agrarian Party, the veterans, and some Communist fractions. He was interested, first and foremost, in the saving of Russia – whether socialist or capitalist was of secondary importance to its being free and independent. 'Not confrontation but only unity, regardless of Russians' political convictions, can realize that

---

[102] *Kaz. vesti*, 15–16 (July 1993), p. 8.   [103] *Kub. kur'er*, 7 December 1993, p. 1.
[104] *Kuban*, July–August 1993, frontispiece. The excerpt from Kondratenko's speech in April 1991, quoted on pp. 116–17 above, appeared as the end paper.

aim.'[105] He was not a conservative, he argued. Towards the end of Brezhnev's period of office, he had disagreed with his policies; at one of the last Congresses he had wanted to cross out Brezhnev's name but, he reminded the reader, as there was no private voting booth, he would have to have done it in public view; even if he could have done it privately, what would have been the point – how many others would have done likewise?[106] Career politicians everywhere may reason like this but do they say so, publicly, and unselfconsciously?

Egorov, in contrast, was not prone to political statements. His campaign resonated with stability, centrism, and saving the krai from immigration, but less aggressively than Kondratenko. More effort went into making use of the administration's apparatus (enterprises and institutes received forms from their local administrations for signatures in support of his candidature),[107] and getting the backing of the directors of the huge agro-industrial amalgamated firms, and of the farms. He campaigned strongly and successfully in the rural areas, whereas Kondratenko did better in the towns. Samoilenko – deeply involved in business deals, the only Russian to speak Adygei, 'a crafty politician, with a large clan'[108] – aimed at the city population.

The turnout in the krai was 57 per cent, and just over the 50 per cent of those participating cast their votes in favour of the constitution.[109] The two seats for the Council of Federation were won by Kondratenko, the easy winner, with Egorov a clear second. Diakonov came a poor third, and Samoilenko fourth. The shock came in the voting for the party list for the Duma: Zhirinovskii's LDP picked up 25 per cent of the vote (with no campaigning), the Communist Party – not unexpectedly – 16 per cent; Russia's Choice received 12 per cent; and Yabloko 9 per cent. The Women of Russia came fifth, then the Agrarian Party.[110]

As in most places there was no correlation between the votes cast for parties and that for their representatives fighting the six seats under the plurality system. (And, shortly after the election, 40 per cent of those polled in a survey in Krasnodar could not remember whom they had voted for.)[111] Directors of now-privatized industrial, commercial, and

---

[105] *Kub. nov.*, 7 December 1993, p. 2.   [106] *Kub. kur'er*, 7 December 1993, p. 1.

[107] *Kub. kur'er*, 20 November 1993, p. 1.

[108] Quote from interview with journalist, March 1994.

[109] The press did not give the turnout figure; it and other figures are taken or calculated from the unpublished official election returns. *Kub. kur'er* gave a slightly higher preliminary figure on 16 December 1993, p. 1; *Kub. nov.*, which had opposed the constitution, provided the result on 21 December 1993, p. 1.

[110] Some considered that Diakonov's identification with Russia's Choice had been damaging to it, but the combined democratic vote does not look low.

[111] Interview with Zhdanovskii, March 1994.

agricultural enterprises figured largely among the candidates; they were joined by a few journalists, military officers, and the occasional academic and administrator. The successful candidates included Dolgopolov, a retired army officer and the only successful Cossack candidate, who won comfortably, and a non-party entrepreneur, with a quasi-criminal past, supported by Egorov. Glotov, the left-patriotic military instructor, romped home in the central Krasnodar district, followed by the Russia's Choice candidate, a television journalist (a woman), as a poor second, and Len, the Cossack lawyer came third. In this district, however, if one excluded the two rural wards, Yabloko came out first on the party vote. The Novorossiisk seat was won, perhaps surprisingly, by a left-patriotic director of an educational centre (another woman), beating the deputy director of the big shipping company and the city administrator, a Russia's Choice candidate, into second and third place. More predictably, one of the rural districts returned the chairman of an agricultural enterprise, backed by the Agrarian Party, as an easy winner; here the LDP candidate (the only one fighting a seat), the editor of the *Kur'er*, came third. The Black Sea district was won fairly comfortably by a democratic journalist, Boiko, defeating the Communist candidate, a cosmonaut. He was joined in the Duma by one Russia's Choice candidate who had gone through on the party list. They found, however, that they had much in common with Dolgopolov, the Cossack: the only real disagreement was over the privatization of land. Relations with Glotov, whose room in the hotel was next to Boiko's, were strained: Glotov either failed to greet them or managed it only through clenched teeth.[112]

The politics may have been dirty but they were real. In November the soviet had drawn up a constitution for its successor, the future regional assembly, which gave it considerable powers, and had voted for the holding of elections in March 1994. However, in early January, Egorov summoned ten of the most compliant members of the little soviet and persuaded them to resign. He then dissolved the soviet as no longer quorate and set up a committee to take over its property. He did not consult with or notify the chair, Zhdanovskii, but subsequently offered him a post in the administration. The elections were put off until the autumn. The original kraikom building now housed the chief administrator's office, and the administration itself now occupied both the main building of the original executive committee and the soviet offices. It had a staff of a little over 1,000, somewhat fewer (Zhdanovskii estimated)

---

[112] *Iug*, 2 (1994), p. 2; *Kub. nov.*, 22 March 1994, p. 3. Most of the Krasnodar deputies joined Baburin's small Russian Way fraction in the Duma and, in consequence, remained outside the registered fractions.

than the original party and soviet executive committee apparatus combined.[113]

Thinking forward to the regional elections, Egorov built his political bloc on the basis of institutional power. 'A Rich Kuban – A Rich Russia' was based on the administration, with the involvement of bankers, part of the old industrial elite, and those farm chairmen loyal to Egorov. The bloc had no clear ideology – as we saw, Egorov avoided any political commitment – describing itself as centrist, pragmatic, and, of course, defending the interests of the Kuban. In it we see an example of the post-communist phenomenon of 'the party of power': based on the holding of office which gives its occupants control over jobs, property, and access to wealth. In a national republic it can claim to be representing 'its people'; in a region it lacks even this substitute for a political ideology. Hence we find its spokesmen emphasizing its ability to deliver 'stability', 'effective government', and their skills as administrators. If it is led by an individual who can also attract a popular following, it is probably invincible because it can control the electorate through pressure from local administrators, manipulation, and money, and the lack of an alternative. The threat to it comes if there is a competitor, either ideological or personal. In Krasnodar, and here the krai was unusual, there was one, combining ideological appeal and personality. In Kondratenko it had a popular leader, and a conservative pro-communist public had no difficulty in marrying its opposition to western liberalism with patriotism. In a border region experiencing immigration, patriotism carried great appeal and the democrats had no weapons with which they could counter.

This brings us back to the question of fashioning an identity for the political community that suddenly found itself described as the Russian Federation. How did one citizen of the federation recognize another, and who were the 'outsiders'? The democrats' programme did not speak to this. Their eyes were focused on something rather different: how to create a democratic political system and a property-owning public. Liberal democracy, with its emphasis on the individual, blots out considerations of class, ethnicity, gender, and 'prioritizes the featureless' liberal individual.[114] Not only is this not helpful for nation-building but the implication

---

[113] For the constitution, *Reshenie Krasnodarskogo kraevogo soveta XXI sozyva*, seventeenth session, 10 November 1993; for the dissolution of the soviet, *Kub. nov.*, 12 January 1994, p. 1; interviews with members of the little soviet, March 1994. Zhdanovskii initially refused a post in the administration, but accepted the directorship of the civil service training college (the successor to the old higher party school) and by the autumn was acting deputy chief administrator (under the new chief administrator). The attraction of returning to a lectureship in archaeology in the university paled in comparison.

[114] A. Norton, *Reflections on Political Identity* (Baltimore: Johns Hopkins University Press, 1988), p. 129.

for self-identification ('who are we?') was: a second-rate copy of the West. This was hardly attractive. The policies of privatization and the commercialization of the means of communication had consequences (shops dominated by high-priced western goods, and a television bombardment of western advertising, violent and pornographic western films) which underscored the association of the government and the West, while recreating a new, more visible but familiar divide between 'them' and 'us'. Not surprisingly, even those convinced that the way to a better future lay in this direction grew uneasy. The structures necessary to support democratic practices – electoral procedures, political parties, an independent judiciary – did not exist; society was not composed of independent, liberal-minded individuals. The intelligentsia discovered, to its dismay, that psychologically it was more state-dependent than the entrepreneurial nomenklatura and, even more disturbing, there seemed to be no special political role for the intelligentsia in a democratic society.[115]

Who then was 'the other' in relation to whom the ordinary citizen in Krasnodar could define himself or herself? It had to be 'the West', allied with 'the Moscow politicians' and 'the democrats' who were trying to foist an alien identity upon the people. The use by all, including Diakonov, of the epithet 'patriot' has to be placed in this context. The feeling among Russians, in those communities where they found themselves either challenged by national minorities with new rights or faced with an influx of immigrants, was that they had been betrayed by the political leaders. Hence the appeal of a Kondratenko or, for those who would not vote for an ex-nomenklatura figure, of Zhirinovskii.

Fatherland's appeal to its fellow countrymen spoke to those

in whom conscience has not been extinguished, those who have not reconciled themselves to the reform that has been thrust upon us, aimed not at raising up the country but at finally destroying the foundations of Russia . . . we did not believe the conscientious patriots who, two years ago, warned us 'the Fatherland is in danger, the country is being turned into a supplier of raw materials'. Stupefied by the propaganda machine, we let the destruction of the country take place, the annihilation of industry, the catastrophic treatment of agriculture . . . while we still have something to save of the country, before all our children have become the victims of immoral shadowy moneybags, before all are thrown out of the factory gates and forced to stand in the rows of traders of 'snikers' and 'baunti', we must unite.[116]

[115] I return to this problem, from a different perspective, at the end of chapter 9. See V. Pastukhov, '"Novye russkie": poiavlenie ideologii', *Polis.*, 3 (1993), pp. 22–3; also Iu. Levada, 'Problema intelligentsii v sovremennoi Rossii', in Zaslavskaia and Arutiunian, *Kuda idet Rossiia?*, pp. 208–13.
[116] *Kub. nov.*, 22 March 1994, p. 3. And we should not think that this resonated only among Russians; there were those among the Adygei who responded too.

After the first conference of the new patriotic bloc, aimed at 'the consolidation of all patriotically inclined citizens, regardless of their political views and convictions', a number of organizations expressed their desire to join. They included the Association of Large Families, Russian Community, Slav Union (Sochi), the club Truth, the krai committee of the Communist Party, the United Workers' Front, the krai committee of women Cossacks, Democratic Party of Russia, and the district councils of veterans. Glotov became chair of its council. Its aims, he suggested, were simple: to win a majority in the new legislative assembly, take the chair, and then move on to decide the question of elections for chief administrator, 'the outcome of which I consider to be already decided . . . If an individual received the support of nearly two million Kubantsy in an election (as did N. Kondratenko), it is obvious who people wish to see in charge of the krai administration.'[117]

There were fifty seats in the assembly, to be contested in seven districts. A total of 278 candidates competed, slightly over half of whom were sponsored by an electoral bloc or party as opposed to standing as independents. Fatherland put forward thirty-eight candidates; the Liberal Democratic Party, which had come into existence after its December victory, attracting money and activists, put up thirty-six; and Kuban, led by E. Kharitonov, the new chief administrator, fielded twenty-nine. The Communist Party also, separately, fielded ten candidates; Yabloko six, and the others two or three each.[118] Almost 40 per cent of the electorate turned out to vote, high for a local election. The three key blocs picked up sixteen, ten, and nine seats respectively, and with the addition of sympathetic independents the final distribution of 'forces' in the assembly gave Fatherland twenty-three to twenty-four seats, Kuban fifteen to sixteen, and the LDP nine to ten. Fatherland failed to get its hoped-for majority, but no democrat voices remained, and the Samoilenko clan was shut out. (Samoilenko, who had been dismissed as city administrator by a presidential order on the eve of the elections, failed to win election to either the krai assembly or the city duma.) Among the new deputies farm chairmen and members of the administration dominated; they were joined by seven

---

[117] Quoted in Andreev, et al., *Politicheskaia stsena Kubani*, p. 6. Where not stated otherwise, details on political groupings are taken from here.
[118] A new procedure, or, if one likes, an old one, was adopted under which several deputies represented a single district. The democrats split between Gaidar's party, Yabloko, the Party of Economic Freedom, and Diakonov's Union for the Renaissance of the Kuban, also styled a 'progressive patriotic party'. Gromov spoke of the Cossacks putting forward candidates, yet when the time came they mounted no challenge. Is it that Gromov reckoned his Cossack supporters were more likely to vote for Kondratenko or for an LDP candidate than for a Cossack candidate? This seems quite probable, and suggests that the Cossack organizations could not play an independent political role.

lawyers, four head teachers and doctors, two journalists, three atamans, and two LDP workers.[119]

What light do developments in Krasnodar shed on the type of political relationships that emerge in an unsettled, conservative post-communist community, one where different bases for power existed? The introduction of new institutional rules – a separation of powers, a free press – seemed, at least in the short run, to bring different clans out in the open, and to encourage machine-politics. Privatization, in a lawless environment, both underpinned this and made the carving up of 'territory' even more important. As those in charge sought to retain their control over resources, the administration itself emerged as a political actor and entered the electoral arena. Very different types of organizations emerged to compete for the electorate's vote: the 'party of the administration' (and I observed this too in Tatarstan), a patriotic bloc grouped round a leader, Kondratenko, and the one organized political party, the Communist Party. The LDP appeared as a *consequence* of a protest vote against an unpopular, 'western' government that had ignored its people's rights.[120] Its subsequent successes in the local elections (not repeated anywhere else in Russia) suggested the existence of at least a minority as patriotic as the followers of Kondratenko but unwilling to support candidates from the old nomenklatura. They could easily shift their allegiance to another leader. In Krasnodar, as in Tatarstan and Sakha, the new political parties failed to put down roots, and a socio-political movement, such as the Cossacks, seemed to suffer from many of the same weaknesses as the Tatar national movement.

Politics in Krasnodar was highly competitive, and the press expressed a variety of views. It was ideological politics and power politics, but of a particular kind. The aim was to defeat one's opponents and then – as the people's representative – rule on their behalf. There were few democratic voices and they could make little headway (even had they any answers to the krai's problems), but, even so, the ideological dislike they engendered among the conservative elite resulted in their being shut out wherever

---

[119] Details are from information presented to the federal Duma by Glotov, chair of the Duma sub-committee on federal affairs. The procedure also allowed for the compiling of a list of 'reserve deputies' (twenty-two in all), presumably the runners-up. One of the results of having large electoral districts (and no residence qualification) was that more than a third of those elected came from Krasnodar itself. (In the Krasnodar city duma the LDP emerged as the largest fraction, with ten out of the twenty-seven places, but in Sochi, a bloc called Democratic Russia won nine of the twenty-six.)

[120] Without more data, we can only hypothesize on the different constituencies which made up the LDP vote. Did the refugees vote? Tishkov, 'O prirode', p. 8, has suggested that Russian refugees from republics, who had unthinkingly taken their cultural dominance for granted and then found themselves as migrants experiencing anti-Russian feeling and loss of status, could provide a basis for Russian nationalism.

possible. It remained for the clans to fight it out and two main contenders emerged: the more pragmatic, managerial, party of the administration and the more ideological, nationalist, movement round Kondratenko. Is it too fanciful to ask whether we were witnessing the last struggle within the Communist Party between the 'administrators' and the 'ideologists', the battle that had continued in different guises since 1921?[121] When Kondratenko won, perhaps his victory rather than Diakonov's in 1991 would, in retrospect, signify the beginning of a new order?

[121] For the battle, see D. Priestland, 'Ideological Conflict Within the Bolshevik Party, 1917–1939', DPhil. thesis, University of Oxford, 1991. Egorov, who had been promoted from minister to head the president's administration, a post he did not hold for long, returned to the krai in 1996 to compete in the elections for chief administrator. He came second to Kondratenko but fewer than 50 per cent of the electorate turned out to vote, invalidating the election. The krai assembly voted to change the electoral rules, retroactively, to allow Kondratenko's election, but this was declared unconstitutional. A second election was held and Kondratenko was the easy winner. He appointed Gromov, the Cossack, as his deputy.

5   Regional variations: Perm and Tomsk

In Perm and Tomsk, far inland in the centre of Russia, nationality and ethnicity rarely featured as political issues. Occasionally conflicts flared up over and between the market traders from the south, but these were tranquil regions, far from battle zones. Their regional capitals were both centres of the defence industry, closed to foreigners until 1989; both were university and scientific centres. Tomsk has been a place of transit or residence for political exiles throughout its history; Perm was known for its prisons for both criminals and politicals. Politically, though, they were very different. The Permiaki pride themselves on their moderation. Here a centrist party elite eschewed conflict, and perestroika brought little public politics. In contrast, E. Ligachev, summoned from Tomsk to join the Politburo, left behind him a conservative apparatus and reform-communists. Here the apparatus was publicly challenged in 1989 and 1990, and the democrats emerged as a force in the soviets. In Tomsk, in August 1991, both local authorities and part of the public came out against the putsch; in Perm the authorities dithered and the population stood aside.

Here then were two regions which began their lives as subjects of the Russian Federation with very different political profiles. Both had the same new institutional structures, both were subject to the same rules on political organization and the press, and in both cases their elites were charged with the implementation of a new policy of economic reform and privatization. How did they react – both to the new policies and the new structural arrangements, and to the conflict in Moscow? And how similar or different were their political complexions three years later? These are the questions I explore in this chapter and the next. I begin with a brief background on the two regions, and the developments which produced the very different political environments in which the new rules were to operate. I have tried to keep the detail to a minimum but some readers may struggle to keep track of the political actors. If the account becomes difficult to follow, I advise moving to the chapter's conclusion and treating that as the introduction to the more important chapter 6.

Perm oblast lies in the Urals, the mountain range that divides European Russia from Siberia and the Far East, but there are no mountains here, just gentle undulating hills, forests of silver birch and pine, and the flat river plain of the huge Kama river which winds its way westward to join the Volga at Kazan. To the east is Ekaterinburg, historically the centre of the Urals region. Its nineteenth-century brick buildings and few remaining ornate wooden merchants' houses are grander than anything in Perm, and the white party buildings, where Yeltsin ruled, and the nomenklatura blocks of flats are larger and more spacious than those in Perm. But Perm has an older university, and an opera house built under the sponsorship of Diagelev's grandfather. In the late nineteenth century, metal-working factories, surrounded by worker settlements, appeared on the outskirts of the city. In the Soviet period the huge plants turned out shells and aircraft, nearly 5 per cent of Russia's military production, and their worker settlements became part of the city. For a short while Perm was renamed Molotov but, with his fall from power in 1957, reverted to its original name.

The population of Perm city was just over a million in 1989. The total oblast population was three million – of whom 200,000 were Tatars or Bashkirs. To the south the oblast border is with Bashkortostan, and Kazan is not far away. In the north of the oblast, where the land grows poorer, lies the Komi-Permiak autonomous district, whose population of perhaps 125,000 is linguistically related to their northern neighbours in the Komi republic. In the north too were prison settlements and camps, while the notorious camp no. 36 for politicals was located to the east.[1] The region has resources of timber, a little oil and gold, and mineral fertilizer, the sources of employment in the towns of Berezniki, Kungur, and Solikamsk respectively. Three-quarters of the population live in urban settlements but a third is still employed in a not very flourishing agricultural sector. The winters are long and hard. The standard of living in the oblast is about average for Russia. It receives no subsidy from the federal budget.[2]

---

[1] The adjacent camp no. 35 was for less serious offenders. This camp complex, the only one of the Gulag camps being restored, has been given the status of a museum; Perm Memorial, which spearheads the project, is seeking funding to assist with the restoration, museum, and educational activities.

[2] For data on Perm, where not otherwise referenced, and a more detailed account of developments between 1988 and 1991, see M. McAuley, 'Politics, Economics, and Elite Realignment in Russia: A Regional Perspective', *Soviet Economy*, 8 (1992), pp. 46–88. For comparative analysis of the economic and budget profiles of the regions and republics, see O. Dmitrieva, *Regional'naia ekonomicheskaia diagnostika* (St Petersburg, 1992).

Tomsk oblast, larger in territory than Perm, twice as far from Moscow, is part of west Siberia. Originally a Tatar settlement on the banks of the Tom, still home to perhaps 20,000 Tatars, Tomsk claims its birthdate as a Russian city from 1608. First a military outpost, then a place of exile or transit for those being sent further west – the Decembrists and Bakunin both passed through – it is now a heavily Russian city. It received its last exiles, the families of the enemies of the people who had been sentenced or executed, in the 1930s and 1940s. In 1993, 30,000 could claim the identity cards which would give them, as victims of repression, health care and transport privileges. The city and oblast are also home to small communities of very many nationalities, including Germans, Balts and Central Asians, as well as the Little Peoples of the North. The Balts are leaving, and the overall birth-rate is falling. The population, by the beginning of the 1990s, was hovering around the one-million mark, with nearly half concentrated in Tomsk itself.[3]

The Siberian regions lie between the Urals to the west and Sakha to the east, stretching from the Arctic seas in the north down to the border with Mongolia in the south. They are the site of most of Russia's mineral and energy wealth (perhaps the richest site in the world). Some are richer in resources than others – Tiumen with its oil and gas, Kemerovo with its coal fields – but Tomsk is relatively poor. Apart from Tomsk-7, a top security defence city, there are no other large towns. A third of the population lives in scattered rural settlements, a quarter of which have no transport links with Tomsk. There is oil-drilling in the northern districts. Timber and woodworking, chemical products, and the defence industry are the main employers. In Tomsk itself 85,000 are occupied in higher education and research; 12 per cent of the population are students, many of whom traditionally came from other republics, in particular from Central Asia.[4]

The complaint of the Siberian regions is that they have traditionally been treated as a colony by Moscow: their resources are exploited, and their populations live worse than those of many of the western regions. Certainly, in terms of housing and all amenities apart from health care, Tomsk oblast is far below average for the Russian republic. In Tomsk 20 per cent of the housing lacks sewerage and piped water; in the worst district more than half of the school-age children are chronically sick. The

---

[3] *Tom. vestnik*, 5–6 (1991), p. 8 (this weekly newspaper appeared sometimes with a number, sometimes with a date; hence the different types of reference in the notes); *Kr. znamia*, 12 March 1990, p. 5; *Nar. trib.*, 16 February 1991, p. 3.

[4] Oblast administration development programme, November 1992; interviews with university administrators, March 1993.

river is badly polluted (chemical waste from Kemerovo) and drinking water has to be boiled.[5]

Contrasting reactions to perestroika and the putsch

The Permiaki looked askance at the crusading conservatism of their fellow countrymen in Krasnodar and the radical reformism of the Leningraders. This was as true of the party elite, centred in Perm, closely integrated with the industrial, cultural, and academic establishment, and fanning out through the region, as it was of the wider population. By the 1980s it was rare for an outsider to move in, just as it was rare for the young to leave. A handful went each year to Moscow and Leningrad to study, but most of those returned to the jobs already earmarked for them. As far as the Permiaki were concerned, party and non-party alike, perestroika was something happening in Moscow and of little relevance to everyday life in Perm. The national television networks were presenting more critical programmes, and parts of the central press were beginning to talk another language, but this did not change the way things were run in Perm. A little informal activity surfaced. In 1989 the party leadership, accustomed for years to following instructions from above (if leasing was the new policy, a little leasing campaign followed; if reducing alcoholism was the target, so be it), reacted in the traditional way to the wind of change blowing from the top. It organized a new-style election for the USSR Congress of People's Deputies with two candidates for each seat. To its consternation E. Chernyshev, the first secretary, was narrowly beaten and other nomenklatura figures lost to little-known candidates.[6]

[5] Tomsk, according to a deputy, 'exported' 15 million tons of oil and 8 million cubic metres of timber to Moscow in 1991, worth US$ 2 mlrd, but its budget was a paltry 1.5 mlrd r.: V. Perov, 'Sibirskii paradoks', *Narodnyi deputat*, 3 (1992), pp. 51–3. Oblast admin. programme; *Nar. trib.*, 26 March 1991, p. 6; 6 July 1991; *Gorod. gaz.*, 26 December 1991, p. 4; *Tom. vestnik*, 26 December 1991; author's notes from city soviet meeting, 10 March 1993. This is not to imply that all the housing in Perm has sewerage and piped water; throughout the city water must be boiled.

[6] In February 1990 an Electors' Club of reform-minded party, non-party, and social democratic activists organized an open-air meeting which became more and more critical of the CPSU. Banners proclaimed 'Partokratia – the source of our sorrows', 'Soviets – without apparat functionaries', and 'Citizens' Action – the alternative to the apparatus'. Chernyshev and Petrov, the chair of the soviet executive committee, faced hostile whistles, calls for their resignation, and found themselves unable to speak, while other party and soviet officials hid behind them. A spontaneous vote went in favour of the resignation of both the obkom and the executive committee. 'Honestly speaking', Chernyshev later told a journalist, 'I found myself in a situation of that kind for the first time in my life. I faced a hail of shouts and boos, and felt to the full a storm of emotions that had got out of hand.' However, the obkom resolved that no resignations were called for. Further details, and references, are given in McAuley, 'Politics, Economics', pp. 62–5.

In 1990 Chernyshev was one of the few party secretaries to stand for election, both to the Russian Parliament and to the oblast soviet. He narrowly lost the parliamentary seat, but won a place at regional level. Party officials did not do well at regional level but the final results both for the RSFSR seats and for the oblast soviet showed the establishment still firmly in place. Of the twenty-one deputies to the Russian Parliament there were two party secretaries, four oblast and city executive committee chairs, two officials of the Ministry of Internal Affairs, the editor of the Komsomol newspaper (the only woman), the directors of the three largest industrial associations, and three other enterprise directors. The few democrats contesting these seats made no headway.

Unlike their counterparts from Leningrad, Tomsk, or Krasnodar, no Perm deputies shone in the Russian Parliament or played a leading role in local politics. True to tradition, they tended to adopt centre positions and were loathe to express their views on contentious issues. When issues broke, *Zvezda*, the party paper, had difficulty in establishing contact with them, let alone extracting an opinion from them. Only one of them stood for re-election in December 1993.[7] The oblast soviet was also a largely conservative body. A quarter of the deputies were industrial managers; party and soviet officials made up another quarter; then came doctors, industrial workers, and those in higher education. There were very few Yeltsin supporters among them, rather more who saw themselves as champions of regional rights. A group which called for 'All power to the soviets!' and included V. Gorbunov, a gorkom secretary, claimed that

The process of rebirth has to begin with each republic, each region . . . Today the central institutions are in no fit state to influence matters at the grass-roots. We see our problems better than they do . . . Our slogans are: unprofitable enterprises should be leased or sold with the aim of altering their profile to produce mass consumption goods! Give the green light to cooperatives producing goods, ideas, services, projects! All decisions by the soviet executive committee must be taken in public view.

And one of the group's members, E. Sapiro, an economist, argued that the idea of 'the deputy waiting in the corridor to catch a minister by his jacket and beg him to do something for the region is profanation of the idea of parliamentarianism and legislative power'.[8]

Although the closely knit elite had suffered some shocks in the elections, this did not affect the close relationship between the party buro and the soviet executive committee. The soviet elected as chair R. Shvabskii, a

---

[7] This was Belorusov, who had stayed to defend the White House in October 1993.
[8] *Vech. Perm'*, 26 January 1990, p. 1; 24 February 1990, p. 2.

classic apparatus figure, originally a turner from Solikamsk, who had risen through the Komsomol to management posts in the car industry, and then to city soviet and party work. V. Petrov, who had easily won the seat in a rural constituency, was re-elected as chair of its executive committee. The few democrats were restricted to voicing criticisms: the 'partokratia', they claimed, still had things sewn up and the soviet was powerless. The city soviet had a larger democratic contingent (38 out of 200 in 1990) but this could not affect the election of its leaders. When the chair resigned in early 1991, the soviet struggled for six months to find a replacement. Finally it elected V. Khlebnikov, a middle-of-the-road economic administrator; the chair of its executive committee was a raikom secretary, V. Fil.[9]

If in Krasnodar the party was united in its opposition to reform, and in Leningrad reformers within the party were locked in battle with the conservatives, in Perm everything was more muted. The conservatives were not so conservative and the reformers not so radical. By 1991 Perm was home to Travkin's Democratic Party of Russia with 200 members, a Social Democratic Party with perhaps half as many, and small Christian Democrat, Cadet, and Green organizations. The soviet allocated them three rooms in a basement. The Union referendum of March 1991, and then the Russian presidential election of June, provided foci for their activity but they were reliant upon Moscow for literature, and never managed to produce more than flysheets. Nor did they receive any support from a democratic movement within the party. Although the developing rift within the CPSU between conservatives and reformers could not but produce dissension within the Perm party, there was no open challenge to the largely conservative leadership. In a compact community anyone who stepped out of line lost all access to the media, all part in the debate (there was no thriving counterculture as in Leningrad); but, at the same time, the party leadership needed the services and talents of the professional intelligentsia. It was prepared to sponsor new reform-oriented publications: a new soviet newspaper, *Permskie novosti*, clearly modelling itself on *Moscow News*, and a new obkom weekly, *Positsia*, with a young reformer as editor. Nevertheless, holding the party together was becoming increasingly difficult. The presidential election revealed the divisions. The obkom buro was in favour of N. Ryzhkov, the USSR prime minister, but was unable to prevent officials in the city party committee openly supporting V. Bakatin, the more liberal-minded minister of inter-

---

[9] The only democrat on its little soviet was Potapov, of the Christian Democrats, who moved to the far right during the next two years.

nal affairs.[10] Chernyshev continued to argue that the danger of the party splitting must be avoided but, by the summer of 1991, the activists saw it as inevitable. They would, however, wait for it to happen rather than engaging in the process themselves.

During the critical August days the only action came from the democrats in the city soviet, who organized a small meeting; they managed to get a quorum together by the evening of the 19th and passed a resolution against the GKChP. In contrast Shvabskii and M. Bystriantsev, who had replaced Petrov as chair of the oblast soviet executive committee,[11] announced that no comment was called for from the oblast soviet, and all should observe calm. On the evening of the 20th, however, the praesidium shifted ground and passed a resolution in support of Yeltsin. *Zvezda*, the party paper, published the GKChP proclamations but also a short announcement that informal sources in Moscow had reported objections by Yeltsin and Khasbulatov.[12] The obkom buro met both on the 19th (without Chernyshev, who was in Moscow) and on the 20th (upon his return), and strongly supported the GKChP, but made no announcement at all. The regional KGB ignored the request for information from its superior, the Russian ministry, which was supporting Yeltsin.[13]

With the Yeltsin victory, the few democrats tried to push home their advantage. On 29 August they organized 'A city meeting of representatives from among the deputies, from work collectives, political parties, and social organizations' in the political enlightenment centre, adjoining the obkom building, where they had already been active sealing offices. The first item on the agenda, 'Conclusions and Lessons to Be Drawn from the Events of 19–21 August', occupied most of the meeting. Criticisms were directed against the regional authorities, party and soviet, and the resolution, signed by the chair of the city soviet, Khlebnikov, criticized both Shvabskii and Bystriantsev personally. The meeting also resolved to propose to Yeltsin that S. Kharif, the democratic director of a cement factory, be appointed to head the oblast administration.[14] Meanwhile everyone was scrambling to absolve themselves of responsibility and to pin the blame on others. The gorkom passed a vote

---

[10] In the April referenda on the renewal of the Soviet Union and a Russian presidency, the Permiaki had voted in favour, in an unremarkable way. When it came to the presidential election itself, they turned out to give Yeltsin, who had spent part of his youth in the oblast, a handsome majority: 80 per cent in Perm city, 71 per cent in the oblast (McAuley, 'Politics, Economics', p. 58).

[11] He had moved to a top job in the Moscow consortium Kama-Granit: *Perm. nov.*, 16 February 1991, p. 1. See pp. 178–80 for further career moves.

[12] *Zvezda*, 20, 22 August 1991, p. 1.

[13] Where not otherwise footnoted, developments after August 1991 are based on interviews with participants, March 1993 and May 1994.   [14] *Zvezda*, 30 August 1991, p. 1.

of no confidence in the party leadership at city, oblast, and central level. The obkom buro now came out against the GKChP, and justified its silence with the claim that Chernyshev had been unable to get any proper information from the Central Committee. *Zvezda* and Vokhmianin, the KGB chief, insisted that they had been behaving properly, even bravely, throughout, and the paper cast the blame on the buro for its lack of leadership. The praesidium of the oblast soviet recognized that its reaction to the GKChP had been inadequate but tried to deflect the blame on to *Zvezda* and *Vechernyi Perm*.[15] *Zvezda* felt badly threatened. The editor offered to resign but asked for the continuation of the paper on an independent basis and – perhaps to demonstrate its new convictions, perhaps to point the finger back at the buro – the paper began to publish copies of telegrams received by the obkom from the Central Committee during the August days. The soviet agreed to allow the paper to continue, as an independent, and to subsidize it.[16]

The way in which the authorities resolved these awkward matters demonstrated the Perm approach to conflicts: muffle them, smooth them over wherever possible. Chernyshev simply absented himself and went mushroom picking. The oblast soviet responded to Yeltsin's suspension of the party by agreeing to a request from the obkom buro for temporary accommodation and for help in finding jobs for its employees. The union of cultural workers announced that since all party officials belonged to its union it would continue to defend their interests; it had set up a commission to help them find work. Perhaps 1,000 individuals were involved and by mid-September approximately eighty had registered with the Perm labour exchange.[17] The oblast soviet delayed discussion of the August events until 3 October. Shvabskii defended the praesidium's actions on the grounds that it had lacked information, and stressed that he had been anxious not to destabilize the situation. A secret ballot on a motion to censure his actions did not get majority support. Chernyshev resolved the awkward problem of his continued membership of the soviet by

[15] *Zvezda*, 23, 24, 30 August 1991, p. 1. *Permskie novosti*, the soviet paper, but only a weekly, had been saved from having to take a position and was only too happy to discomfit its rivals. The city soviet moved to close the bank account of the publishing house, *Zvezda*, which controlled the printing press where all local publications were printed, but this brought an angry reaction from *Zvezda* itself – 'what are we guilty of? . . . In no way could we be compared with the miners, we did not engage in political games' – and a threat of a strike, which brought the reopening of the account. This kind of action was too extreme for Perm: 28 August 1991, p. 1.

[16] *Zvezda*, 30, 31 August 1991, p. 1; 6, 12 September 1991, p. 1.

[17] Under the redundancy clause of the labour code they were entitled to two months' pay, and could then register as unemployed and receive a further two months' pay (the sums would, however, it was stated, be repaid from party funds): *Zvezda*, 27 August 1991, p. 3; 4 September 1991, p. 1; 13 September 1991, p. 2.

resigning. He then departed for Moscow where he was given a job by A. Volskii, an ex-nomenklatura figure who headed a powerful industrial lobby, and moved back into his old office in the Central Committee building. The soviet contented itself with a resolution criticizing the oblast leadership and Shvabskii for irresoluteness. The KGB chief remained in post. For the moment no heads rolled. It was clear that some shake-up of personnel would take place, but why rush it?

If, however, valuable resources were involved, the authorities could move fast enough. The oblast soviet executive committee quickly acted to requisition all the party property in the city, as well as in the oblast, and ignored the city soviet's complaint that this was illegal. The praesidium of the oblast soviet resolved that the regional bank should, for the time being, be responsible for all party funds and that the chair of the executive committee should prepare an inventory of its property. Sapiro, the economist deputy, who was appointed to head a soviet commission to oversee its distribution, suggested that city and district representatives should participate in the decisions. He gave approximate figures for the value of certain properties, but thereafter public discussion of the party's assets faded away.[18] The oblast soviet remained in the draughty house of soviets while the administration took over the better-built party building. It provided the president's representative with an office, allocated a few rooms for the social organizations, political parties, and a shared office for the Tatar centre and the Komi–Permiaki club, and began to rent out those at the rear of the building to commercial structures. The adjoining political enlightenment centre became the cultural centre. The city authorities had to be satisfied with the city party offices, to the rear of their own. A gesture was made – the party hotel became a children's hospital – but all other party assets remained in the hands of the oblast authorities.

The key questions were who was to be the president's representative and who the chief administrator. In early September Yeltsin had appointed S. Kaliagin (a democratic USSR deputy, a skilled worker with higher education from the Sverdlov aircraft factory) as his representative, and one of his first tasks was to find appropriate candidates for chief administrator. His and the democrats' first choice, agreed with difficulty,

---

[18] In January 1991 the buro had set up a commercial firm, Ekocentre, with two rooms in the party building, and a working capital of 6 mln r.; individual buro members bought shares, and dividends were paid according to the intellectual investment of the share-holder (the first secretary's was rated higher than that of a department head). Ekocentre rented out party property, including the party hotel, Viktoria, which was supplied by the state network. The buro also set up a commercial car rental firm, charging foreign business-people hard currency, from the party car pool: *Zvezda*, 28, 30 August 1991, p. 1; 5, 7 September 1991, p. 1; see *Perm. nov.*, 7, 14 September 1991, p. 3; 21 November 1991, p. 3, for continued conflict over the garage, once under soviet jurisdiction.

was Kharif, the enterprise director.[19] Although he did not have majority support from the soviet, the democrats were confident that Kharif would be appointed. However, following a visit by V. Makharadze, inspector general and the president's plenipotentiary, in early December, Kharif was passed over in favour of the lacklustre Boris Kuznetsov, from the Kama Shipping Company. The soviet dutifully voted 102 to 32 in favour of his appointment.[20] Kuznetsov appointed two first deputies: E. Sapiro, the economist, and G. Igumnov, a long-term soviet administrator. B. Gorbunov, the former gorkom secretary, was given the key post of chair of the state committee for the management of property (i.e. privatization).

In November Shvabskii resigned the soviet chair but it took until January to elect his replacement. By then the democrats had lost whatever initiative they had. The little soviet at regional level was dominated by conservatives. Bystriantsev, the ex-executive committee chair (authoritarian, conservative, but an able politician) stood for the post, opposed by the democrats' candidate, V. Zelenkin, from the aviation institute. When neither obtained the required majority Sapiro, chairing the meeting, suggested that both should withdraw. Zelenkin agreed, but Bystriantsev remained, now facing a weaker opponent and, to the democrats' dismay, obtained the required majority. At city level the soviet elected Fil, ex-raikom secretary and head of the executive committee, to the new post of mayor. In the democrats' eyes, the conservative revanche was complete, but at least they had a new chief administrator.[21]

When Ligachev, the first secretary, moved from Tomsk to Moscow in 1983, he left behind a conservative party apparatus and an intellectual community looking for change. In Tomsk, as in Perm, the initiative came from students and young faculty but in Tomsk their activities snowballed into a democratic movement for reform. Their willingness to stand their ground against the hostile reaction from the party leadership encouraged the taking of sides, and soon the conservatives found themselves facing a challenge from within the party. The activities of those pushing for change during the years 1987 to 1991 deserve an account in their own right. Here I concentrate on those that made Tomsk different from Perm.[22]

[19] *Zvezda*, 24 November 1991, p. 1.
[20] O. Podvintsev, 'Report on Developments in the Perm Region, 1991–1994', ms.
[21] *Zvezda*, 29 January 1992, p. 1. V. Zotin, the democratic candidate, came third in the city vote: Podvintsev, 'Report'.
[22] I. Tarusina, a student and member of the Iskra group (see p. 166 below), acted as unofficial secretary, collected materials on the informals' activities and wrote her diploma work on the topic. The following account is based upon her materials, the press of the period, and literature in the St Petersburg Social Movements Archive, and the Archive of the Institute of Humanities and Political Research, Moscow.

In May 1988 a group based on the university resolved to call themselves the Union to Work for Revolutionary Perestroika, SSRP, to draw up a charter, and to hold open meetings to discuss ways to democratize the CPSU and to transform society in a progressive direction.[23] The response of the secretary of the university party committee was to propose that any who were party members be expelled. In June the SSRP succeeded, despite pressure from the authorities, in holding the first open political meeting the city had witnessed, in the sports stadium. Loyal party supporters were drafted in to boo the democrats and both sides claimed victory.[24] The group struggled to survive during the summer. In the autumn it began to host meetings in the university, attended by the city party secretary, V. Ketov. A branch of Memorial was founded, although not registered by the soviet executive committee. In December the gorkom allowed the first meeting of a political discussion club whose co-chairs included two from SSRP and N. Krechetova, the ideological secretary of the gorkom. The club also elected a committee to work on the forthcoming elections and, from early 1989, the elections for the USSR Congress occupied the political activists' attention.

The results revealed the same anti-nomenklatura mood as in Leningrad and Perm. The first secretary, V. Zorkal'tsev, who ran unopposed, received support from only 36 per cent of the voters and went down. The director of a poultry factory whose illegal actions had been publicized by SSRP lost to a hospital head doctor. In one district where the democrats had queried, to no avail, the electoral commission's choice of candidates, both candidates received heavy 'no' votes, thus forcing a new election. Although several democratic activists put themselves forward, the committee successfully concentrated its efforts on S. Sulakshin, a physicist from one of the research institutes, and former secretary of its party committee. In another district where there was a second election, N. Belous, a gas-electrician, defeated V. Kress, a rural raikom secretary.[25] Sulakshin, a dynamic figure who joined the Inter-

---

[23] V. Tirskii, a lecturer, who subsequently moved out to try and organize peasant cooperatives, was the leader of the SSRP, several of whose members came from a discussion group which called itself Iskra. It originated in a ballroom-dancing club and focused on reading Marxist classics, including Stalin, on living a healthy life, and on the fate of the Siberian rivers. Individuals from this group were active in setting up Memorial, ecological groups, and the elections club, and in producing literature.

[24] The only journalist who wrote of the content of the discussion, S. Suchkova in *Molodoi Leninets*, was sacked from her job: *Vestnik SSRP*, 1 (1988); see Tirskii, in *Nar. trib.*, 18 May 1991, p. 7, who gives a slightly different version.

[25] As in Leningrad, the party paper, *Krasnoe znamia*, inadvertently gave publicity to the opposition by criticizing the 'social committee on elections' and Sulakshin. In April it changed tactics and gave him the right of reply: *Kr. znamia*, 8 February 1989; 14, 28, 30 March 1989; 9, 16, 18, 19 April 1989; 23 May 1989.

Regional Group of deputies in the USSR Congress, became the unofficial leader of the democratic movement in Tomsk with the backing of a People's Deputy Club. In contrast to Perm, the youthful activists gained encouragement both from individuals, such as Sulakshin, publicly taking up the democratic cause, and from the existence of local figures well known for having suffered repression in the Brezhnev period, and now speaking out. The most important of these was V. Fast, a dissident mathematics lecturer, who led Memorial.

In the autumn of 1989 many of the original activists came together to found the Tomsk People's Movement. During the following few months this existed as an umbrella organization (and published a news-sheet), bringing together both the Committee of Electors and Sibir, an ecological organization. Its stated aim was to 'strive for people's power in all spheres of social life, for the introduction of radical economic reforms, for the development of an ecological movement; to defend the interests of Tomsk oblast, the Siberian region, and the Russian Federation'.[26] By this time the split in the party could not be glossed over. At the beginning of December the reformers set up a party club, which became the home for Democratic Platform supporters. Although the occasional non-party candidate did come to the fore in Tomsk, in the main the political struggle was within the party. The candidates supported by the People's Movement in large measure overlapped with those chosen to attend the Democratic Platform conference,[27] and by February 1990 they had captured the initiative. A meeting held in support of the democratic candidates in the forthcoming elections attracted several thousands, and the obkom recognized, under pressure from the reformers, that some organizational changes were necessary.[28]

There were seven RSFSR seats in contention in 1990. Although Zorkal'tsev, the first secretary, won his in the second round, the People's Movement could claim four victories, including the defeat of R. Popadeikin, the chair of the oblast soviet executive committee. Following the local elections, the democrats, with the support of the centre block, could outnumber the conservatives in the city soviet, but at

---

[26] *Tom. tribuna*, 4 (1989), p. 1.
[27] *Tom. tribuna*, 3, 4 (1990). The Democratic Platform was the reform wing of the CPSU which attempted, during 1990 and the early part of 1991, to transform the party as a whole into a more democratic organization. In Tomsk it claimed approximately 3,000 members by April: *Kr. znamia*, 10 April 1990, p. 2. A visit by Ligachev at the beginning of December was not a success. For him to enter the university, a corridor had to be cleared through pickets demanding his resignation and holding signs 'Welcome to the *prorab* [playing on Voznesenskii's use of the word in a poem] of "Tomsk socialism".'
[28] The reorganization involved merging the obkom and gorkom: *Kr. znamia*, 28 February 1990, p. 1; *Tom. tribuna*, 6 (1990), p. 2.

oblast level they were in a much weaker position.[29] Here Kress, the raikom secretary, was elected as its chair, and Popadeikin (106 votes to 47) re-elected to head the executive committee. At city level however, a compromise was reached: A. Cherkasskii, a skilled worker, a moderate democrat who agreed to stand when he learnt that the management lobby would oppose his election, was elected to the chair of the city soviet with G. Sapiro, another democrat, as his deputy, while V. Gonchar, the previous executive committee chair, retained his post.[30]

From the summer of 1990 until August 1991 the original party apparatus and the new democrats engaged in a struggle for position. The political environment was much more similar to that in Leningrad than that in Perm: the two camps were clearly visible. A branch of the conservative United Workers Front (OFT) had appeared in April and sent five delegates to the Leningrad-initiative conference. Sulakshin had organized a conference of all democratic deputies in the province, which was attended by 150 people, and created a new organization, Democratic Tomsk.[31] The city soviet published and repealed a soviet ruling of 1987 that awarded extra living space to the party, soviet, legal, and academic elite; the obkom kept a low profile but began to branch out into commercial activities (a bank, a publishing house, and work on a new hotel).[32] In the autumn of 1990 the democrats in the oblast soviet took advantage of a scandal to force Popadeikin, chair of the executive committee, to resign and elected a young director of a cooperative, A. Kushelevskii, in his place. The scandal involved a draft agreement that had been drawn up and submitted to the praesidium of the Supreme Soviet, for 'The creation of a stock-holding commercial timber-working company "Siberian Forest"', whose partners were to be Tomsk executive committee, Moscow city executive committee, the Russian–Finnish joint enterprise Khepos, the Russian–British joint enterprise Rouvin-Toko, and 'other Soviet and foreign firms and banks'. It was to be responsible for the felling, reworking, and sale of timber from districts where fire damage had occurred, and for reforestation; it would receive tax privileges for an initial two years, 200 mln r. credit from Gosbank, and 20 mln hard-currency r. credit. Although several clauses gave rise to considerable concern, the scandal was primarily over Popadeikin's 'for-

[29] *Kr. znamia*, 6, 10, 27, 30 March 1990; 7 April 1990; 11 May 1990, p. 3. For the city, see *Tom. vestnik*, 21 June 1990, p. 4.

[30] *Kr. znamia*, 17 April 1990, p. 3; 24 April 1990, p. 1; 19 May 1990, p. 1; see *Tom. vestnik*, 5 June 1990, p. 3, for interviews with Cherkasskii and Gonchar.

[31] The obkom did not distribute the OFT conference materials but reimbursed the delegates' travelling expenses: *Tom. vestnik* 5–6 (1990), p. 7; 10 July 1990, p. 4.

[32] *Tom. vestnik*, 4 (1990), p. 7; 5 (1990), 7; 9 (1990), p. 3.

getting' to put it before the soviet, whose approval was hardly likely to be forthcoming.[33]

Although now in a stronger position, the democrats soon revealed their weakness as prospective policy-makers. Without doubt the existence of hostile officials, obkom activities, and the stalemate in Moscow created an inauspicious environment, but also a democratic movement that had coalesced very rapidly in opposition to a conservative apparatus began to break apart. The Union referendum and Russian presidential election brought a closing of the ranks, but the absence of an agreed agenda and personal differences were wreaking havoc.[34] The most damaging split was within the oblast soviet between a group called Action (Deistvie), and from whose ranks Kushelevskii had come, and Democratic Tomsk, aligned with Democratic Russia,[35] who looked to Sulakshin as leader. The initial disagreement was over the new privatization committee, proposed by Action. The Sulakshin democrats argued that the committee would be exempt from soviet control and would have too much independent executive power. They were supported by the Communists, who objected that it was a second executive structure. The city soviet also came out against, arguing that certain clauses in the proposal were in contradiction with the legislation. In July 1991, Action recognized that certain clauses needed to be redrafted (for example, the committee was to have been responsible for managing the new commercial structures which would replace the original branch administrations in the food and catering network), but by this time Kushelevskii's critics had become even more vociferous. DemRossia charged Kushelevskii with incompetence, with relying on old party apparatchiki, with commercialization of

---

[33] *Tom. vestnik*, 29 October 1990; *Nar. tribuna*, 20 September 1990, p. 4. Popadeikin left to join the board of directors of a bank in Kemerovo.

[34] The KGB still reported to the obkom, and in the spring of 1991 Kushelevskii was accused of consulting with the new first secretary, Pomorov, on important decisions: *Nar. tribuna*, 20 April 1991. The Union referendum produced the following results:

	The renewal of the USSR (%)		An elected Russian presidency (%)	
	For	Against	For	Against
Tomsk city	52	45	78	19
Tomsk oblast	64	33	75	23

Source: Nar. tribuna, 6 April 1991, 4.

There was a 72 per cent turnout for the presidential election in June; Yeltsin polled 61 per cent of the votes in the oblast as a whole, Ryzhkov 15 per cent, and Zhirinovskii 7 per cent – a fairly average result.   [35] For more on Democratic Russia, see chapter 2, n. 12.

soviet executive structures, corruption, and undemocratic practices. His supporters replied that none of Kushelevskii's new appointments had come from the nomenklatura, that the charges of incompetence were exaggerated, and that no evidence of corruption existed.[36]

It is difficult to know to what extent the conflict between the two groups was one between different political types (and involved personal ambitions) rather than over policy differences. The Sulakshin democrats tended to be young, active party reformers who had proved themselves as able organizers and publicists; the Action group were a much more mixed set of 'non-political' individuals.[37] In the spring of 1991, Sulakshin, complaining of incompetence by the executive committee, had raised the idea of combining its chair with that of the soviet in order to strengthen decision-making. This was the time when, throughout the country, complaints were being made of ineffective soviets, and ideas were circulating on electing mayors or regional gubernators.[38] As USSR deputy, and leader of the Tomsk Democrats, Sulakshin had no wish to see Kushelevskii step into such a post. He was anxious to counter any moves by Kushelevskii to raise his standing either with the population or in the president's eyes. This is where the issue of the Siberian Accord came in.

A permanent complaint of the Siberian regions was the refusal of Moscow to recognize their right to their own resources, whereas the republics of the federation, at least formally, had such a right. The Siberian Accord was an attempt to join forces to defend their interests.[39] The fortunes of the Accord during 1991 and 1994 is a topic I can only touch on in passing, but the interaction with developments in Tomsk is of concern to us. At the end of 1990 representatives of seven regions, including Tomsk, Irkutsk, Omsk, and Novosibirsk, had met in Kemerovo to discuss ways of allaying the effects of the breakdown of the original supply

---

[36] *Nar. tribuna*, 2 July 1991, pp. 1–3; 13 July 1991, p. 4.

[37] This is based on the author's personal observation and notes from attending meetings of the Deistvie group and of DemRossia, March 1993. See a brief comment by N. Pogodaev, 'Tomsk', *Pol. monit.*, August 1993, on the party background of the new generation of activists. But both 'sides' had members who could not be categorized in this way.

[38] *Nar. tribuna*, 20, 23 April 1991.

[39] See J. Hughes, 'Regionalism in Russia: The Rise and Fall of Siberian Agreement', *Europe–Asia Studies*, 46 (1994), pp. 1133–61. Since I completed the typescript, my attention has been drawn to J. Andrews and K. Stoner-Weiss, 'Regionalism and Reform in Provincial Russia', *Post-Soviet Affairs*, 11 (1995), pp. 384–98. Although this is a study of popular attitudes rather than elite behaviour in four regions (Nizhninovgorod, Saratov, Tiumen, Yaroslavl), and I do not have comparable data, I find the suggestion that regionalist sentiment goes with support for economic reform puzzling, but perhaps this merely

and distribution system, and of ensuring a rational distribution of Siberian products between regions.[40] In July a second meeting was held in Novosibirsk, which Yeltsin attended.[41] On this occasion the question of creating a Siberian republic was raised, but the more important issue was the gaining of concessions over resources. Yeltsin signed a document which gave the members greater rights over the retention of a certain (small) percentage of their natural resources for their own use, and the right to sell 25 per cent at free prices. Given that power still lay in Union hands this was more of a gesture than anything else. Tomsk also got a promise of 150 mln r. for a new investment fund to support its intellectual potential. Kushelevskii argued that

Most important of all the 'Siberian Accord' today felt its own strength. The consolidation took place on the basis of the economic interests of Siberia. Tomsk, Irkutsk, and Krasnoiarsk played the first violins. Others, feeling that it might take off, joined in. For example, Tiumen, hearing of the free prices for 25 per cent of the raw materials, asked to join.

Did Yeltsin ask for political support in return, he was asked. Kushelevskii suggested that politics is more subtle than that, and that this was an economic agreement but

If the centre pursues a correct policy towards Siberia, it is unlikely that any political tensions will arise. On the other hand [sic]. It is possible that if the conditions that were agreed are not met, [the agreement] will turn into something different. Autonomy for example, or a republic.[42]

Kushelevskii could also claim that he had won advantageous deals for the region in negotiations with Silaev, the Russian prime minister, on timber prices and oil licences.[43] His successes were seen as a threat by Sulakshin, who insisted that it was he who had played a key part in getting the oil licences. By mid-July the two sides were engaging in accusations and counteraccusations. Kress, the soviet chair, tried to act as a moderator but, on the eve of the August putsch, by a fourteen to four vote, the praesidium of the soviet requested Kushelevskii's resignation and asked

underscores the need for more regional studies.
[40] The population of Siberia in 1990 was put at 24.4 million: *Tom. vestnik*, 32 (1993), p. 3. The huge territory is very poorly integrated, exporting goods while importing similar ones, and divided by bureaucratic boundaries. See *Tom. vestnik*, 37 (1993), p. 1, on the beginnings of the Accord; *Ross. gaz.*, 4 March 1994, p. 3, refers incorrectly to the first meeting as being in Novosibirsk.
[41] The new Accord included seventeen members: two krais (Altai, Krasnoiarsk), the four republics (Altai, Buriatia, Tuva, Khakasia), seven regions (Irkutsk, Kemerovo, Novosibirsk, Omsk, Tomsk, Tiumen, and Chita), and six autonomous districts.
[42] See *Nar. tribuna*, 6 July 1991, p. 4, for interview with Kushelevskii.

Kress to combine, temporarily, the posts of chair of the soviet and of its executive committee.[44]

The leaders of the oblast and city soviet reacted quickly against the GKChP. They made a joint announcement that no emergency rulings were necessary, the KGB and police were in control, RSFSR laws took precedence, and television would carry Russian government announcements. The heads of the KGB and the police and the garrison commander all worked closely with the soviet authorities. The police chief called all his staff together, told them that they would obey Russian ministry rulings, and that, if anyone felt unable to do so, he should notify the chief and stay at home; no one did. A large meeting was held on the 21st at which both Sulakshin and Kushelevskii spoke. *Narodnaia tribuna*, the soviet paper, had carried a short announcement on the GKChP proclamations on 20 August but had given the majority of space to Yeltsin's statement.[45] The party authorities reacted differently. *Krasnoe znamia*, the party paper, carried only the GKChP announcements on the 20th. On the 21st it published a statement from the buro to the effect that it basically was in support of the GKChP attempts 'to stabilize the situation' but it wished for a constitutional outcome, and for the Central Committee to be summoned; it agreed that no special measures were necessary in Tomsk. It then published Yeltsin's statement, the GKChP announcement, and the soviets' statement. On the 22nd A. Pomorov, the first secretary, called for calm and for attention to be concentrated on bringing in the harvest; the large meeting was not mentioned. Subsequently individual members of the buro justified their support or their wait-and-see attitude either on political grounds or, in the case of Pomorov, with the often-used argument that he could not get proper information out of the Central Committee. Twelve members of the obkom, including Kress, resigned in protest at the buro's actions but the obkom as a whole voted, by eighty-four to twenty-nine, in support of its buro's behaviour.[46]

Sulakshin was appointed as president's representative. The contentious question of chief administrator then came to the fore. Different groups lobbied different members of the president's administration: Kushelevskii was one candidate, while DemRossia proposed V. Bauer, a moderate democrat, dean in the physical education institute.[47] The choice, however, fell on Kress.

[43] *Nar. tribuna*, 2 July 1991, pp. 1–3.
[44] *Nar. tribuna*, 16, 18 July 1991, p. 1; 8, 10, 13, 15, 17 August 1991, p. 1; *TM ekspress*, 33 (1991), p. 6.   [45] *Nar. tribuna*, 20, 21, 22, 23, 24 August 1991, p. 1.
[46] *Nar. tribuna*, 27 August 1991, p. 1; 30 August 1991, pp. 1–3.
[47] *Komsom. pravda*, 11 October 1991, p. 3, carries an account of the bitter and undignified squabbling between the different groups.

At the beginning of 1992 the political configuration of the elites in Perm and in Tomsk, and the extent of public political activity, was very different. In Perm a centrist elite, used to working together, and a largely conservative oblast and city soviet found themselves with a chief administrator and a president's representative who were both outsiders to regional administration and imposed from on high. The new chief administrator was someone without strong party or soviet connections, but no radical. The president's representative was an upright individual but with little experience of politics and lacking the support of a strong democratic movement. In Tomsk the rulers, split between democrats and conservatives, already had a year's experience of open and divisive politics. Here the chief administrator was a centrist party secretary, previously elected by the oblast soviet as its chair, while the president's representative had a high profile as a democrat; in the oblast soviet the conservatives had the edge; the city soviet was evenly balanced. An active democratic movement, an ideologically committed Communist Party minority, and a lively press existed. The situation in Tomsk looked, in consequence, much more evenly balanced than in Perm.

6   Consensus versus pluralist politics

In Perm, despite the appointment of an outsider as chief administrator and the new separation of powers, the soviet and administration succeeded, after a brief period of tension, in working amicably together. Those who ruled Perm strove to recreate the old collegial atmosphere of decision-making and to cast the chief administrator in the role of chairing a united policy-making elite. They were remarkably successful. Divisive issues were kept off the agenda. After a slow start, and in response to pressure from Moscow, the tempo of privatization quickened but with a minimum of controversy. Even in the late summer of 1993, when conflict at the centre was forcing those below to take sides, and individuals were beginning to think of the forthcoming elections, disagreements within the regional elite were smoothed over. It might have been different if Kuznetsov, the chief administrator, had had the forceful personality of Diakonov from Krasnodar and the backing of a democratic movement. As it was, by 1994 both Kuznetsov and Kaliagin, the mildly spoken president's representative, although still in post, had been relegated to the sidelines. Kuznetsov had failed to win a seat to the newly created Council of the Federation in Moscow, while Kaliagin, fearful of confrontation and conflict, and long ignored by the power structures, had gradually moved to a centrist position, and earned the scorn of the remaining democrats.[1] Was it then personalities and the lack of pressure from below that determined policy and kept the establishment in place? If so, we would expect both reactions and outcomes to be very different in Tomsk.

Here indeed there was far more conflict, institutional and personal, and far greater reaction to and interaction with developments in Moscow. Tomsk continued to have a more politicized public and press than Perm. 'Agreeing to disagree' characterized its politics. Privatization proved to be very divisive. But in December 1993 Kress, the chief administrator, won a seat to the Council of the Federation, and the executive recaptured

---

[1] See interviews with him in *Zvezda*, 17 March 1992 and 20 January 1993; interviews with Kaliagin, with DemRossia activists, including Zotov, and with journalists, March 1993 and May 1994.

control. The democrats, with the exception of Sulakshin, went down to defeat, and the pluralist politics that had existed since 1990 faded away. By 1994 the political profiles of Perm and Tomsk looked very similar: not patronage politics, not clan warfare, but semi-corporatist politics. Political divisions and political activism were not the decisive factor after all or, if they were, they had unexpected consequences.

Let us begin with Perm and look at the way the elite regrouped and adapted the new institutional arrangements and policies to its liking, yet found itself engaged in the beginnings of a new kind of competitive politics. We then turn to Tomsk to observe how its pluralist politics became caught up in, and then a casualty of, conflicts at federal level. In the final section, I trace the fortunes of the press as a prelude to looking at the ways in which the two sets of political actors approached the electorate in 1993 and 1994, and the public's response.

Perm: consensus politics

A stable elite regroups

For years regional elites had been aware of their place in a hierarchical chain of command, stemming from Moscow, and of their responsibilities as regional administrators. They had to ensure that economic targets were met, primarily in agriculture, and to work together with the directors in the military-industrial sector. They had to maintain social and political order, and to oversee culture and education. Feeding the population was their responsibility, along with administering social welfare. They delivered the taxes to Moscow and were allocated a budget in return. But now the new federal government was advocating the privatization of trade, business, agriculture, and municipal services. It was arguing for independent initiative in all spheres and seeking to cut back on state control, but without damage to living standards. The rulers in Perm found some parts of the programme easier to adjust to than others. They were by nature adjusters, used to following the policy line from above, but they were also used to certain ways of working, imbued with an administrative culture with its characteristics of control and guidance. The result was a particular interpretation of the new policies that still left the local authorities very much involved in all spheres of activity.

In 1990 the chair of the regional soviet executive committee, under the direction of the obkom buro of which he was a member, had been responsible for personnel appointments, the law and order agencies, general socio-economic development, relations with other oblasts, and civil defence. Six deputy chairs had had the following responsibilities:

1 Economic reform, economy, ecology
2 Agriculture
3 Construction, including housing
4 Transport
5 Welfare, culture, sport, health
6 Local services, industrial relations, conversion, local energy supplies, political rehabilitation

Under the new order, Kuznetsov as chief administrator took direct responsibility for personnel appointments, relations with the soviet, representing the region, and dealings with Moscow. Party control of appointments and the nomenklatura system had vanished with the party, yet, I suggested, this seemed to present no problem to those in charge of the executive. They simply resorted to using their existing networks (Shaimiev in Tatarstan), or combining new with old (Egorov in Krasnodar) in the time-honoured way. Kuznetsov had little to draw on and was new to regional administration. He appointed G. Igumnov, an experienced soviet administrator, as one first deputy, E. Sapiro as the other; he retained three of the deputy chairs of the soviet executive committee in post, moved another to a different department in the administration, and brought in Gorbunov, from the city party, to head the property committee. All remained in post until 1994. As we saw, Bystriantsev, a former soviet executive committee chair, was elected chair of the soviet. The heads of other key institutions remained in post: the KGB chief, Vokhmanian, despite his action in August 1991, and Fedorov, police chief and RF deputy. There was a change of procurator after the incumbent, Lumpov, pulled a gun on a taxi driver. Stepankov, the Russian procurator general at the time, himself from Perm, came to effect a discreet changeover and to ensure that his previous colleague got a reasonable job – as a legal consultant in a bank.[2]

When, in the spring of 1994, Sapiro moved to chair the new regional assembly, there was a slight reorganization of personnel and structure in the administration. Igumnov remained as the sole first deputy administrator, and one more was appointed. Their responsibilities were divided; Igumnov became responsible for:

1 Economic development, external economic relations, law-and-order agencies, supplies for the population, taxation

The five deputy administrators oversaw:

2 Agriculture, including land reform
3 Construction and transport

---

[2] Data on oblast and city structures and personnel provided by the administration; interviews with Igumnov, Sapiro, and Gorbunov, June 1990, and with Igumnov, Sapiro, and journalists, May 1993.

4 Property and privatization
5 Welfare, culture, sport, youth, religion, sociological surveys
6 Conversion, ecology, labour, press and media, information, social
   organizations, rehabilitation, civil defence

It is notable that, with the party's going, the administration had picked up relations with Moscow (that now took more time) and general oversight of regional affairs. New tasks appeared – most notably privatization and foreign economic relations – and others, such as taxation and law and order, became more important. Dealing with the soviet was different, as was dealing with the oblast towns. Time spent on construction and transport was cut, but not much else. What did this mean in terms of staff? In 1991 the executive committee had 1,117 employees; by 1993 the administration had 1,198; by 1994 it had reduced this to 1,010.[3] Even this slight reduction is perhaps surprising, given the disappearance of the party apparatus. Should we draw the conclusion that the party as an administrative structure had been superfluous, or did party functions just disappear?

Party secretaries tended to argue that the party's 'state' functions (by which they meant economic management) were already shrinking and where necessary, for example transport, were taken over by the administration. It was in the sphere of ideology and culture that, in their view, the party's going left a hole. A legitimizing ideology is necessary to any state, argued one, and Yeltsin's attempts to provide one were not succeeding. That the administration should take on the responsibility for helping and overseeing the means of mass communication, religion, culture, and social organizations was seen as not only appropriate but necessary. Not surprisingly, therefore, we see that it was ideology and culture that had been added to the administration's brief. In 1994 one new deputy administrator was appointed, and he took on responsibility for these areas. He was Sergeev, an ex-party secretary who had just completed a spell as mayor of one of the oblast towns.[4] According to some commentators, the appointments made in Perm in the early months of 1994 suggested the bringing back of reliable but second-rank party officials to senior posts, while business interests were beginning to move

---

[3] Although regional administrations could adopt a structure of their choosing (within budget constraints), the need to deal with Moscow, particularly over finances, meant that there was a tendency for the region to copy any structures that appeared at central level, and thus the vertical relationship was reaffirmed. The size of the city administration, in contrast to the regional, nearly doubled during the period, from roughly 200 to 400 employees, as it took on responsibility for land, for agricultural foodstuffs, and more social welfare services.

[4] Interview with Sergeev, March 1994. On Sergeev's appointment, see *Zvezda*, 26 April 1994, p. 1. The department responsible for religion was headed by an ex-raikom secretary, who was about to retire and be replaced by a former party instructor.

their people in at a lower level. The official style began to change – away from the greater informality of the early 1990s – to the bland, formal politeness that characterized the end of party rule, and dress became again neater and more uniform.[5]

What can we learn from looking at the career moves of those elected to the obkom and Perm gorkom in 1988?[6] Of a total of 298 members and candidates, 'honorary' individuals accounted for 138, and a further 16 had either retired or died. The data, which are largely complete, suggest even greater stability than in Krasnodar, a very similar move into business and administration by the party apparatus and by some from soviet posts. There was very little demotion in Perm. Of the twenty-two who worked in education, culture, and health care (institute directors, university professors, health administration), we know the positions of nineteen in 1993. Three had made a career move upwards, one down, and the remainder had stayed in the same post. Of those in industrial and farm management, twenty-nine in all, we know the position of twenty-three. Here there was a little more mobility. Four had moved up within the enterprise, three to new jobs: one to Moscow, one to a bank, and one to the oblast administration. The picture overall is one of an industrial and cultural elite that was remarkably stable, not to say immobile, during these years of change.

There were forty individuals holding nomenklatura posts in soviet administration and federal agencies, of whom the fates of thirty-three could be established. Here there was, indeed, more movement. Fifteen were still in the same posts; eighteen had moved to new jobs. How many of those could be deemed a demotion? A few cases were clear (chief editor to editor of the commercial section of the same paper, a deputy chair of the soviet executive committee to the deputy manager of a construction department of an enterprise, a procurator to a legal consultant in a clinic), but in the great majority of cases the individuals had at the very least moved sideways, and probably to more lucrative employment. For example: the deputy chair of the city soviet executive committee had become the deputy director of the trading house Sadko; the chair of a raion executive committee was now the director of a factory. The deputy head of the KGB had become an assistant to one of the deputy chief administrators. The chair of the city soviet executive committee was now

---

[5] Interviews with journalists and political activists, March 1994. Certainly the change in atmosphere could be felt in the administration building. In Tomsk, in 1993, the newly elected city administrator, Konovalov, on being asked his response to Chernomyrdin's ruling that jeans should not be worn by government officials, and that trousers were inappropriate for women, replied that he would think about it but that he favoured the idea of insisting on skirts for women: *Tom. vestnik*, 27 (1993), pp. 4–5.

[6] See appendix 2, pp. 322–3.

running the railways; the head of the regional Gossnab was director of the share-holding company Permglavsnab. There is no sense here of heads rolling after the attempted putsch of 1991.

What though of the sixty-nine party officials? We can trace all but three of these. One of the eleven primary party secretaries was from a state farm and he became its deputy manager; the others were all in industry. One became a deputy district administrator; one moved to manage an enterprise in Minsk; one had become a shop superintendent; the others had all moved to leading management positions in their enterprises. The twenty-one raikom secretaries are perhaps the most interesting because they were the young up-and-coming administrators. Two had moved to posts in higher education; the remainder split between enterprise management (eight became factory directors, one went to head a state farm and another a collective farm) and state administration (head of the regional administration of meat and milk products, head of a district tax inspectorate, head of the labour agency in the regional administration, district administrator, director of Permagropromdorstroi, deputy manager of the railways). They did not move to new commercial enterprises.

This leaves thirty-one from the obkom and gorkom apparatus, including the first secretaries of the Komsomol.

Obkom

First secretary	Head, Licensing-Export Department, Ministry of Economics, Moscow
Second secretary	Head, department, Ministry of Defence, Moscow
Secretary	Director, metallurgical plant
Secretary	Head, department in Institute for Further Education
Secretary	Director, Fowl Trust
Department head	In a firm in Moscow
Department head	Director, Russo-Indian joint venture, then joined Fowl Trust
Department head	Agricultural department of administration
Chairman, Party Control	Deputy director, Cultural Centre
First secretary, Komsomol	Head, financial department of Velta
Administrator	Administration of the ballet

Gorkoms
Perm

First secretary	Deputy chairman, Perm Scientific Centre of Management, Academy of Sciences

Second secretary	Chairman, property committee

Other towns

First secretary	Town mayor
First secretary	Deputy chief, administration
First secretary	Chairman, Regional Association of Small Businesses
First secretary	President, AO Komiperles
First secretary	Director, Fund Interfund
First secretary	District administrator
First secretary	Chairman, Regional Association of Joint-Venture Companies
First secretary	Director, mine
First secretary	Director, energy plant
First secretary	Deputy director, metal-working plant
Secretary	Deputy director, construction, Velta
Department head	Director, Cultural Centre
Chairman, Party Control	Deputy director, Permkhlebprom
First secretary, Komsomol	Marketing engineer, Morion

Government and industry had opened their doors and found them jobs. A few moved into the new commercial world (as did a few from soviet administration), and of course the enterprises that they had taken over were in the process of being privatized, but it was the younger, the more junior, particularly Komsomol officials, who were the more active in developing new enterprises. Government lay in the hands of a regrouped party/soviet elite, joined by a few newcomers from industry (Kuznetsov) or academic circles (Sapiro), but this in itself represented no great change in the pattern of elite recruitment.

Regardless of whether the personnel were largely the same or not, a chief administrator had to find a common language with the soviet. If, previously, key decisions were taken by the obkom buro, then elaborated by the soviet executive committee voting as a collegial organ, the soviet had simply passed them. Now the administration operated on the principle of *edinonachalie* or one-man management. Decisions of the chief administrator were binding on institutions and individuals, but he had to work out a relationship with a soviet that had acquired substantial powers. Although the regional administration moved into the obkom offices –

Kuznetsov and his deputies took over the offices of the party secretaries – the chief administrator did not have the power of his predecessor. His control over personnel extended no further than the administration; he needed the agreement of the soviet and its leadership in order to get major decisions, like the budget, for example, passed. Kuznetsov, not an individual with a personal or 'party' following, found himself facing an experienced local politician, Bystriantsev, and a largely conservative soviet. He reacted by appointing as his key deputies individuals who themselves had experience and connections within the original soviet and party elite; he gave them considerable scope for action, and adopted a collegial form of policy-making. All of this encouraged the development of workable relations with Bystriantsev and the soviet. Both administrators and deputies agreed that by the second half of 1992 the soviet and administration, after a tense start, began to see each other as partners rather than rivals. In Sapiro's view this was because Kuznetsov and Bystriantsev knew how to compromise. Others considered that the smoothness of the relationship was ensured by Bystriantsev 'buying off' the little soviet of sixteen, and a tacit agreement between him and Kuznetsov to work in tandem. The little soviet rarely queried proposals brought to it by Bystriantsev. Romankova, the only deputy who tried, got nowhere, and the procurator who was a regular attendee upheld Bystriantsev's decisions. The consequence was that the small democratic contingent in the larger soviet became demoralized, and its members began to busy themselves with other things.[7]

The cosy relationship was sometimes highlighted. *Zvezda* published details of the illegal awarding of private cars by the administration to a number of officials at oblast and district level. The little soviet set up a commission to investigate; when it reported, confirming the misallocation, Bystriantsev suggested passing the matter to the mandate commission, the little soviet agreed, and the documentation never reached the commission.[8] Somewhat similarly, the chairman of the commission on legality, shot in the leg by a patrol when trying to cross a bridge illegally (possibly drunk), had his affair buried in the mandate commission. Kuznetsov himself was allocated a four-room apartment in the original party apartment block, breaking all the rules, but despite protests from the city soviet (to the procurator and president), no action was taken.[9] Both the procuracy and the security services took up the themes of

---

[7] *Zvezda*, 11 March 1993, p. 1, for Sapiro; interviews with deputies and journalists, May 1993.   [8] *Zvezda*, 4 March 1992, p. 1.

[9] *Zvezda*, 4 July 1992, p. 1. In the spring of 1993 the city soviet had had two further appeals to the procurator turned down: *Zvezda*, 26 March 1993, p. 1.

'economic crime' and 'official position/corruption' but there was little evidence of charges, let alone convictions, being brought against state officials.[10]

Renegotiating a hierarchy

In the summer of 1993 *Zvezda* asked Kuznetsov and Bystriantsev what Perm oblast had gained since the declaration of Russian sovereignty. Kuznetsov suggested greater independence, but then turned to the tasks that lay ahead: social support for the needy (although the help being given to half a million people was already an achievement), the need to develop market relations, entrepreneurship, and family farms, to ensure better food provision, to improve environmental health, and to combat crime. Bystriantsev stressed the achievements: the oblast had gained rights over its land and resources, and the right to engage in international economic relations; the soviet had acquired legislative rights in relation to resources and privatization, its greater control over the budget, and responsibility for social welfare. But, he added, not all the rights underwritten in the Russian declaration of sovereignty and in the Federal Treaty had yet been realized.[11] The answers reveal both the centrality of the issue of regional control of resources, and the authors' perception of their responsibilities as wide ranging. Let us take these in turn.

In Perm, gaining economic independence had been one of the planks in the programme put forward by Sapiro and Gorbunov in 1990. They were now in a position to push for it. Administration and soviet worked together to gain concessions from Moscow. Under the original regulations only 10 per cent of taxes raised remained with the regional authorities; by 1993 pressure from the regions had increased this to 30 per cent,

[10] *Zvezda*, 10 July 1992, p. 1; 15 July 1992; 4 September 1992, p. 1. Kaliagin, the president's representative, stood aloof, on the grounds that corruption and official misdemeanour was the business of the chief administrator. In another case, *Zvezda*, 10 February 1993, p. 1, reported the selling of surplus sugar to members and officials of oblast and city soviets and administration for 30 r. per 10 kg (much less than the market price) – which produced an embarrassed but angry reaction (someone had spilt the beans). Perhaps the most interesting case involved Fil, the mayor of Perm, who, under the influence of drink, and without documents but with a gas pistol, had driven his car into a large pothole off the road; he had resisted arrest, used insulting language, and, according to one version, attempted to use his gas pistol. The police, however, had behaved little better: Fil had received a blow in the face and had not been subjected to an alcohol test, no proper documentation had been made, and the affair had been hushed up. At the commission of the city council investigating the matter, Fil claimed that since no charges had been brought against him, he had nothing to answer to: *Zvezda*, 30 September 1993, p. 1; 7 October 1993, p. 1. There were no repercussions, and he went on to win re-election.
[11] *Zvezda*, 11 June 1993, p. 1.

and further concessions had been made on their share of VAT and export tax. In return, however, and from a local perspective quite unfairly, the federal authorities were shifting the burden of a number of services down to the region. Health, secondary and technical education, geological work, support for village communities, and the environment were now a cost on the regional budget. Furthermore, the federal authorities' control over funding for key areas, higher education, for example, enabled them to put the squeeze on a recalcitrant region that attempted to hold back taxes.[12] Despite Bystriantsev's claims, regional officials felt that not only did Moscow still control far too much but that, even where federal authorities had made agreements, they did not keep to them. A prohibition on exporting without federal agreement had meant that in 1992 Perm could not sell its mineral fertilizer abroad at a time when the market in Russia had collapsed because the farms had become too poor. Igumnov went to South Africa and Nigeria to sign contracts in the hope that once a deal was made, the central authorities would grant permission. Throughout 1993 the regional authorities complained repeatedly of the centre's failure to provide promised credits or budget allocations. During the visit by A. Soskovets, chair of the committee on metallurgy and a deputy prime minister, Kuznetsov brought up the 'continuation of ministerial and agency *diktaty*', the discrimination against the oblast in its foreign economic relations, and the need for new centre–regional relations.[13]

Regional representatives sighed over the time that had to be spent in Moscow, either bargaining with ministries or doing deals with politicians. The conflict at the centre probably aggravated this age-old practice. In April 1993 Bystriantsev headed a delegation to the Ministry of Finance and returned with the happy announcement that they had got the regional budget allocation for the second quarter more than doubled. Kuznetsov and Bystriantsev went together to try and do a deal on foreign currency earnings with Prime Minister Chernomyrdin.[14] If a federal leader came, he would be presented with a package of requests. For Makharadze's visit in 1992, the administration prepared requests for funds for conversion, four business plans for technical conversion, one for a French joint venture for producing tractors, and also proposals for changing tax regulations for entrepreneurs.

If, in December 1992, at the time of the crisis in relations between president and Parliament, and again in March 1993, administration and

---

[12] For example, Udmurtia and Cheliabinsk; interviews with Igumnov and Sapiro, March 1993.   [13] *Zvezda*, 7, 24 July 1993, p. 1.

[14] *Zvezda*, 27 March 1993, p. 1; 20 February 1993, p. 1.

soviet could suggest that conflicts in Moscow did not affect them,[15] by the summer it was becoming increasingly difficult to sit on the fence. Kuznetsov supported the president's draft constitution; the soviet favoured a compromise between the president's and the Supreme Soviet's drafts. The regional soviet's reaction to developments at the constitutional conference, called in the summer of 1993 to produce a new constitution, was typically Perm behaviour. Its two representatives, Bystriantsev and a pro-communist deputy, V. Zelenin, were among those who walked out in protest over 'the scandal' when Khasbulatov, chair of the Supreme Soviet, was forcibly denied a hearing at the opening session. They returned to Perm to seek approval from the soviet for their action but the little soviet was not convinced that such an outspoken support for the Supreme Soviet was desirable, and they returned to Moscow.[16] Once the constitution appeared, the little soviet wavered, decided not to take up a position on it, and instead to support the idea of ratification being the responsibility of the Congress of Deputies.[17]

By the autumn of 1993 it was almost impossible for regional administrations and soviets to be seen to be working together, even if they were: their mentors at the centre were demanding loyalty from their subordinates. This had certain advantages. Soviets sided with Khasbulatov, administrators with president and government: the region got gifts from both. How real was the disagreement in Perm is difficult to judge. The practice and inclination of the Perm politicians was to agree, to present a united front to Moscow and to their population. We observe them striving to maintain this, and largely succeeding. The taking of sides in the Moscow conflict was done because it was required from on high. But

---

[15] In December 1992 the soviet passed a cautious resolution, requesting president and Congress to find a compromise. The only reaction to the appointment of Chernomyrdin as prime minister came from Sapiro, who referred to him as an experienced administrator but hardly an advocate of economic reform. Kuznetsov was in Moscow and thus spared the need to comment. Kuznetsov's response to Yeltsin's appeal to the people in March 1993 was to shut the administration building, and give everyone a day's holiday, so as to make any demonstrations in front of it pointless. He came out in support of Yeltsin, as he would henceforth on each occasion. He urged all to vote in support of the president. At the same time, however, he emphasized that at oblast level the executive and legislative branches would continue to work together in a productive way. The little council resolved 'to demand of the Supreme Soviet and the president' that they find an 'agreed solution to regulate the conflict'; it opposed any attempt to remove the president from power or to dissolve the soviets, measures which would 'lead to a rift in society and the collapse of the state': *Zvezda*, 23 March 1993, p. 1.

[16] *Zvezda*, 28 May 1993, p. 1; 2, 3, 8, 9, 10, 19 June 1993, p. 1.

[17] Kuznetsov came out in support and, somewhat surprisingly, gave cautious approval to the idea of a Urals republic, stating however that Perm was in no hurry to join. The regional soviet was in favour of the region's acquiring the status of the autonomous republics. There was no major disagreement here: *Zvezda*, 7 July 1993, p. 1; see 30 July 1993, p. 1, for a variety of views; 7 August 1993, p. 1.

some issues were less easy to resolve. Kuznetsov and the soviet could not agree over their relative powers in the discussions over the new regional charter. Neither side wished to give away rights to the other. The soviet insisted that it should have control of key financial and property decisions, at present falling within the administration's jurisdiction. Sapiro, while still in the administration, argued that, although unfortunately there were cases of bribe-taking by administrators, it was not clear that deputies would be any more honest, and that it was important for professionals to be in control.[18] But if there were those defending an institutional separation of powers, others, even if not consciously, looked back to traditional ways of doing things. Cherepanov, the deputy chair of the soviet, favoured a joint organ, made up of key members of the administration and soviet, which would take decisions 'of principle' and decide contentious issues.[19]

By mid-September relations between Kuznetsov and the oblast soviet were worsening. Bystriantsev called a meeting of regional representatives before the soviet opened for its autumn session. He announced that, of the 102 mlrd r. paid to the federal authorities since January, the oblast had received back only 21 mlrd r. instead of the appropriate 91.5 mlrd r., and the meeting voted in favour of the oblast withholding any further taxes. Kuznetsov responded by citing quite different figures which suggested that, on the contrary, federal allocations exceeded Perm's contribution. He stated that the oblast would continue to work with the government.[20] The soviet passed a vote of censure on the administration's performance, and came out in support of the Supreme Soviet's policy line.[21] But Yeltsin's dissolution of the Parliament put them in a quandary. The little soviet put a resolution before the full soviet which criticized Yeltsin's edict of 21 September dissolving the Parliament. It received sixty-four votes for, twenty-nine against, and seven abstentions – but the soviet was one short of a quorum, and the resolution did not therefore pass.[22] The soviet had managed not to commit itself either way. The events of October 3–4, when confrontation between president and Parliament ended in bloodshed on the streets of Moscow, were sufficiently frightening to bring the local elite together again, at least publicly. Bystriantsev initially favoured dissolving the soviet but Kuznetsov maintained a diplomatic silence, leaving it to Igumnov to suggest that at least the little soviet should resign:

[18] *Zvezda*, 11 March 1993, pp. 1–2. Did he still argue this once he became chair of the assembly?   [19] *Zvezda*, 11 March 1993, p. 1.   [20] *Zvezda*, 7, 15 September 1993, p. 1.
[21] *Zvezda*, 16, 17 September 1993, p. 1.
[22] *Zvezda*, 23, 24 September 1993, p. 1; Podvintsev, 'Report'. Two Perm deputies, Belousov and Chetin, stayed in the White House to defend it, but this received little publicity. *Zvezda*, 25 February 1994, p. 1, mentioned it.

it was inappropriate, he said, to have deputies in post who had opposed the president and the government. The soviet, after discussion, decided by a large majority that it should continue its existence but that it should re-elect the little soviet. The consequence was an even more conformist body than the previous one. Igumnov stated, quite candidly, that since the soviet could no longer query administration decisions, the administration had no objection.[23] The little soviet voted for the holding of elections to a new regional assembly of forty deputies on 20 March 1994 and, together with the administration, produced a new temporary constitution for the region. The assembly retained control over the budget, the right to issue normative acts (and, if queried by the administration, these could be passed on a second reading by a two-thirds majority) and to exercise control over budget expenditure and property distribution; it had no control over administrative appointments or decision-making. A compromise had been reached.[24]

If regional-level disagreements were somewhat contrived, those between the oblast and city were not. The issue which caused most conflict in Perm was over the distribution of property and over budget allocations between oblast and city. This should not surprise us. The system that had been inherited was one of vertical chains of command with each level in the hierarchy defending itself before its superior and imposing its demands upon its subordinates. When control by the centre began to weaken, each level in the hierarchy sought to acquire resources and rights; it was from those above and below that institutions needed to defend themselves in the first instance. This involved negotiation within a recognized framework. It might be tough but it had its conventions. Vertical conflict, if we can call it that, caused no psychological discomfort, whereas horizontal conflict, between equals, brought acute distress: there were no mechanisms or conventional means for solving it. Conflict between a superior and subordinate could (and would) finally be decided by the superior imposing its will. Horizontal conflicts, whether at regional level or at the centre, were seen as battles for superiority: hence the difficulty of resolving them and the bitterness with which they were fought.

An early example of oblast–city conflict was the dispute over party property, one which the oblast won without difficulty. Essentially it was the same as regards taxation and privatization: the weapons that could be used by a town against regional authorities, or by district against town

---

[23] *Zvezda*, 9, 13, 14, 15, 16, 20 October 1993, p. 1.
[24] *Zvezda*, 30 November 1993, p. 1; 2, 28 December 1993, p. 1.

councils, were very limited. Yeltsin may have talked at the Russian Congress in 1990 of sovereignty beginning with the primary units, and satires were written on districts in St Petersburg setting up customs' borders and controlling their own airspace, but district or town control over resources remained minimal.[25] Taxes were paid by the region to the federal government, which then allocated funds to the regional authority, which it then distributed between itself, the towns, and country districts. Towns were aggrieved that they subsidized the country villages. A city such as Perm with a third of the oblast population considered it quite unjust that it received only 25 per cent of the regional budget and was expected to be responsible for such expensive items as transport. The oblast authorities controlled all the lucrative foreign earnings and, given their control over property, the profits from privatization. They also operated what was called an 'extra-budget fund' (*vnebiudzhetnyi fond*) – made up of 'outside' earnings and largely in the gift of the administration. Perm city officials claimed that in 1993 this equalled the city budget in size. The oblast towns began to delay their tax payments and, in 1993, the city took the oblast to court, claiming that its distribution of the budget was illegal. This was an unusual step, indicative of the strength of feeling in the city council and, even more unusually, both the oblast court and the Supreme Court decided in the city's favour.[26] Simultaneously the council took advantage of the conflict in Moscow to send a delegation to Khasbulatov, speaker of the Supreme Soviet (who was looking for supporters among town soviets). They returned with a promise of approximately 10 mln r. for social welfare schemes (the sum was not large, but what is significant is that Khasbulatov could promise it).[27]

As regards property and privatization, the oblast called the tune. According to Gorbunov, his committee decided which branches should be privatized, and then the city soviet drew up a list of those items which should be considered its property. City politicians suggested that the oblast administration simply crossed out those it wished to retain, or acted independently. For example, for most of 1992 the two sides disputed 'ownership' of the wholesale administration of food supplies (responsible for the warehouses and provisions). Given that the city was responsible for shops and services, the question was of particular importance to it. In December 1992, when the city finally gained control, it dis-

---

[25] A village in the Adygei republic, celebrating April Fools' Day, staged a humorous 'declaration of independence', in which it appointed a council of ministers, and produced its own currency, number plates, vodka, and flag.

[26] *Zvezda*, 7 July 1993, p. 1; 26 August 1993, p. 1; 30 March 1993, p. 1; *Izv.*, 1 June 1993, p. 1; interviews with city and oblast officials, June 1990 and May 1993.

[27] *Zvezda*, 3 August 1993, p. 1. Promises were not necessarily guarantees and, in this case, the soviet did not receive the money.

covered that some departments and buildings had already been rented out or commercialized by the oblast administration; often they had been leased by their former managers, who had the right to buy out the lease at a future date. From the city's point of view 1991 was a year in which the original oblast nomenklatura divided among themselves the profitable municipal property, and left the city with the task of privatizing the shops and services in 1992.[28] This brings us to the key plank in the government's programme: privatization.

Privatization

The ruling establishment in Perm, after initial hesitation, had no difficulty in going along with privatization. It certainly did not include itself in the small league of passionate privatizers (St Petersburg or Nizhninovgorod) but nor did its sympathies lie with its conservative neighbours in Kazan. As always it would conduct itself with moderation. Commercial activities were not alien to the original party establishment, as we saw with the example of Ekocentre and the car pool, and ideas for profitable activities were being floated around before 1991.[29] Privatization was, however, politically sensitive, hugely lucrative, and difficult to monitor. Not surprisingly, throughout 1992 and 1993, very different claims, accounts, and accusations were being made by interested parties. DemRossia, in 1992, accused the authorities of dragging their feet and were gratified when Makharadze lambasted the administration, on his visit in October, for discrediting privatization by moving too slowly and not providing employees with information. By 1993 criticism from the democrats

---

[28] Interviews with oblast and city officials.

[29] See McAuley, 'Politics, Economics', p. 75, for an excerpt from a discussion paper issued by the Perm obkom for party activists, in which the author advocated the local authority's identifying the most profitable local activity and setting up a corporation to run it:

> a management council should be created, the chairman of which would always be appointed by the chairman of the praesidium of the city soviet, and whose permanent members with voting rights would be the directors of local enterprises, the leaders of the financial institutions, each of whom should have a packet of shares to the value of 0.5 mln r., plus the first and second secretaries of the gorkom, the first secretary of the Komsomol, the deputy chairman of the praesidium of the city economic council, and certain others with an advisory voice, i.e. the chief economic consultant, chief legal consultant, chairman of the STK [council of labour collective], city procurator, head of police, and editor of the local paper . . . The corporation should carry out its entrepreneurial activity and own a construction firm to allow it to carry out housing construction for the city soviet (and make a profit).

> The author then moved on to propose a complex in Krasnokamsk consisting of a disco, a casino (profits to the local police and courts), and 'laundromats to help those who lived on fourth and fifth floors and had no running water . . . a bank to finance small entrepreneurs, the Komsomol to set up corporations' (Perm obkom, 1991, doc. 10).

tended to concentrate on the administration's misuse of money made from privatization.[30] Kaliagin, the president's representative, in contrast, tended to suggest that everything was proceeding smoothly.[31] According to Gorbunov, in May 1993, privatization was going better in the oblast than in the surrounding regions, and, by October, he was striking a high note. Privatization had gone well. A third of the vouchers had been invested compared with 19 per cent for Russia as a whole. All that remained was to tidy up the procedures – set up a bankruptcy service, expand the anti-monopoly committee and the tax authorities, the arbitration service, and the economic-security agency. He announced that 12 October would be Privatization Day and marked by an open meeting in the house of culture.[32] By February 1994 he was announcing that 75 per cent of the region's output came from non-state enterprises, that 89 per cent of the vouchers had been invested, and, as further evidence of market forces working, that 20 per cent of shops had changed hands since privatization.[33]

Banks, trading companies, a stock exchange based on an initiative from a graduate student but set up by the administration, investment companies created by directors of the leading firms – all these became features of city activities in 1993. Who was managing these new concerns? Some came from the original party establishment, continuing a process that had started before 1991. In May 1990 the obkom, in conjunction with Ekocentre, had set up the West Urals Foreign Economic Relations Association, headed by Kuzhma, formerly deputy head of the obkom defence department, and aide to Chernyshev, the first secretary. This institution survived August 1991 and continued to have its offices in the back of the regional administration building. The plaques on the original obkom front entrance now read Oblast Administration and Property Administration. Those on the back entrance announced the West Urals Foreign Economic Association, Peace Foundation, a sporting concern, and insurance companies. All major foreign deals were handled by the West Urals Association. Kuzhma was also a director of the new West Urals Bank, a commercial bank that came into existence after the original state bank had been closed (after trouble with the tax inspectorate in early 1994). Petrov, the former chair of the regional soviet executive committee, who had left for Moscow to join the new Consortium Kama-Granat,

---

[30] DemRossia leaflet; see also *Perm. nov.*, 18 June 1992, p. 1; *Zvezda*, 30 October 1992, p. 1; *Zvezda*, 26 June 1993, pp. 1–2.   [31] *Zvezda*, 20 January 1993, p. 1.

[32] The federal authorities, including A. Chubais, chair of the property committee and a deputy prime minister, mounted a similar celebratory campaign around privatization. In retrospect, I suspect, privatization may be seen as the last *Soviet* campaign, conducted with all the appropriate propaganda, exaggeration, and pressure from above.

[33] *Zvezda*, 26 May 1993, p. 1; 2 February 1994, p. 1.

became a director of the bank, Unity, that handled the regional administration's account. Other party and soviet officials moved, as we saw, into
business. They were joined by young ex-Komsomol officials. The most
successful company in town was EKS Ltd, founded by an energetic group
of ex-Komsomol officials, the key figure among whom had a sporting
background. They opened three or four large shops in different parts of
the city. Called 'One Hundred Metres', the shops offered a limited range
of high-quality foreign cars, footwear, clothes, furniture, electrical equipment, and cosmetics at western prices. When the first shop opened, on
Komsomol Street, there was a charge for entry – and people paid just to
come and look – by April 1994 most were still looking, but a few were
buying. Others from the Komsomol moved into construction and
banking, and there were enterprising individuals with other, rather different, networks.[34]

These important developments produced both a new private sector
and a quasi-government/quasi-private sector, ventures partly owned by
the local authorities, partly private; privatized concerns which received
state funding; private concerns which managed government contracts;
and, until new legislation was introduced, the acquiring of ownership
rights to newly privatized ventures by government officials. Meanwhile
the huge defence plants, which came under the federal authorities, and
were the major employers, continued to operate outside the oblast
administration's control. In theory the administration could require them
to observe environmental standards and could rule on their land use but,
as in Naberezhnye Chelny, local authorities could not afford to antago-
nize employers who provided 80 per cent of the kindergarten places,
sports complexes, and housing, and were used to subsidizing schools and
hospitals. City and regional authorities were as interested as the enterprises themselves in obtaining federal subsidies to keep the plants going
and foreign funding for conversion. The Sverdlov aircraft factory,
renamed Permskie Motory, obtained permission from the federal property committee in 1993 to move ahead with privatization, and began to

---

[34] A well-known figure was V. Neliubin, director of Uralskii Meridian, a young sports champion from a poor family, who built up his company with seventy young sportsmen and ex-
criminals from his and neighbouring courtyards. He began with a furniture factory,
moved into construction, and then into retail trade, acquiring a reputation for using
strong-arm measures if debts were not paid on time: *Zvezda*, 9 April 1993, pp. 1–2. The
mafia, he argued, was something different. The extent to which racketeers and organized
crime had infiltrated and controlled business in Perm is not a question I can answer.
F. Varese, 'Is Sicily the Future of Russia? Private Protection and the Rise of the Russian
Mafia', *Archives européenes de sociologie*, 35 (1994), pp. 224–58, offers an interesting
thesis, which he has tested against the Perm experience.

move to civilian production. The huge Lenin plant, which concentrated on shell production, faced a bleak future. It could only hope for money from outside for conversion.[35]

If privatization had a visible impact on urban life, this was not so in the countryside. A small number of private farms appeared and the majority of the 450 collective and state farms were reorganized as cooperative or share-holding companies, which theoretically gave their members the right to sell their share and leave. This did not, however, change the way the farms operated, and the single village shop remained the single village shop. Rising costs steadily increased the differential between rural and urban incomes. Discontent among the farmers was reflected by the rural deputies who passed a vote of no confidence in the oblast administration in early 1993, by the Peasant Union's threat of action, and by an unsuccessful 'milk' strike.[36] The soviet was prepared to subsidize the farmers directly and to keep the cost of bread down in the towns.[37] It was not just that it was apprehensive of doing otherwise but that local authorities, party and soviet, had long been responsible for running agriculture and feeding their population. Shops might be privatized but the ultimate responsibility for providing the population with bread lay with the administration.[38] This attitude did not disappear overnight, any more than did the commitment, on the part of the authorities, to state welfare. It is not important that the supply of food had always been rudimentary and welfare services poor or inadequate. What is relevant is that their provision by the authorities was ingrained, part of the job, and seen as such by rulers and ruled alike. The rulers might well seize the assets but this did not mean their abandoning old roles. The committed marketeers in Moscow and St Petersburg might stress the need to privatize everything but even the Gaidar government continued to talk in welfare terms and to maintain a huge state service sector, and the need for welfare grew as the economic situation worsened.

Local rulers tried to reconcile old ways of behaving with the new philosophy blowing down from Moscow. Their acquiring control over the valuable resources (which, it was argued, would bring economic benefits

[35] Podvintsev, 'Report'; interviews with journalists and political activists, March 1994.
[36] See below, p. 196.
[37] *Zvezda*, 3 February 1993, p. 1; Podvintsev, 'Report'. In September 1992 delays in deliveries of bread had caused a small riot in the centre of town, and the authorities were well aware of the importance of bread to the consumer. There was trouble again in January 1993 when the oblast soviet voted to subsidize the price of bread but failed to authorize the payment of the subsidy to the shops, petrol prices went up, the price of bread rose, and the shops put up the prices. The little council had to take emergency action.
[38] *Zvezda*, 26 May 1993, p. 1.

to all) could the more easily be justified, in their own eyes, by their continuing to take responsibility for food and welfare. The larger the role allotted to the private sector the more difficult it became to maintain this position. In Tatarstan and Sakha state regulation remained much more extensive. In Perm the rulers found themselves struggling. Their attitude towards the agricultural sector revealed the conflict between existing conventions and new constraints most clearly, and this is not surprising. Despite all its claims to rest on the working class, party rule in the regions had meant running agriculture directly while industry came under the Moscow ministries. We find the chairman of the agricultural administration, L. Nikitin, announcing in 1993: 'The livestock plan will be fulfilled by 107 per cent . . . egg production will be 115 per cent higher than last year – 294 million eggs will be available' – a typical traditional statement – but adding 'the original suggestion' that perhaps, rather than subsidizing the farmers, the government should give food benefit to the neediest. The federal government had not abandoned old ways either. The same issue of *Zvezda* carried the announcement that the Russian government had agreed to issue 3,000 tons of sugar (1 kg per head) to the oblast from the state sugar reserve; what was different was that now the regional authorities had agreed not to fix the retail price. The soviet allocated 1.4 mlrd r. to the farmers at the beginning of July 1993 – a third of the farms were unable to feed their livestock – but the administration refused to allocate the money until the towns had paid their taxes or the promised federal credits had arrived.[39] In September, as usual, 16,000 students were due to go out to bring in the potatoes, but now the higher educational institutions made their own arrangements with the farms, which included paying the students and the institutions receiving farm products.[40]

Politics and society

So far I have made almost no reference to activities by political organizations or by individuals outside the elite. It seems one can write of political developments in Perm and leave society out. This reflects the fact that here there was very little interaction between elite politics and something that could be called a wider political society, and in this respect Perm was very different from Tomsk. When it came to elections, society would come into the equation but between 1991 and 1993 the population largely stayed out of politics.

[39] *Zvezda* 14 July 1993, p. 1; see also 7 July 1993, p. 1.   [40] *Zvezda*, 26 August 1993, p. 1.

In the autumn of 1991 no one had been sure that this would be so. DemRossia held a founding regional conference which was attended by 194 delegates: eighty-five were non-party, while others represented the region's different democratic party organizations. Now, they felt, they could influence the future. It was not only they who reckoned times had changed. Fil, the mayor-to-be, and even Fedorov, the police chief and RF deputy, attended the conference too. When, ten days later, the Movement for Democratic Reform held a founding meeting, both Fil and Bystriantsev attended, and expressed the hope that the organization would mobilize the people in support of the authorities.[41] Their actions revealed their conviction that all should be participating in a joint effort, authorities and people. What the role of parties in this novel environment should be was far from clear to many. New democratic authorities, either at central level or in St Petersburg, for example, had shown themselves to be sticklers for registration, with requirements for membership lists, office address, etc. – all necessary for a political party to acquire a legal personality. In Perm both regional and city administrations created departments to 'work with social and political organizations', and the officials in the city department, in true Soviet style, took their brief to be that of trying to encourage socio-political activity, now that it was deemed desirable.[42]

Yet none of the parties in the course of the next three years managed to build up anything approaching a following or to exert an influence on politics. The most active of the democratic parties, with a membership of perhaps fifty, was the Social Democrats. With the departure of its leader, I. Averkiev, to the party offices in Moscow, V. Zotin, a member of the city soviet, took over as leader and became the best-known radical in the city. The Republican Party, the Democratic Party of Russia, and the Christian Democrats had fewer than a dozen members each. Although they had little in common, they united, as DemRossia, to make Communist Party property an issue, and in February 1992 they signed an agreement with Kuznetsov to work together with the administration. They resolutely refused to have any dealings with the soviet leadership. Their support for the administration was, however, short-lived as they began to target slow privatization and corruption within the administration, and as their call

[41] Podvintsev, 'Report'.
[42] The young administration official responsible for 'developing socio-political activity' was concerned that the new entrepreneurs showed so little interest; he was finding it difficult to get them to create an organization. Why, I asked, was this important? His answer was that there had been a presidential decree stressing the importance of new forms of activity: interview, March 1993.

for the dismissal of Gorbunov from the property committee fell on deaf ears. Kaliagin, the president's representative, offered little encouragement. By the autumn they were badly split and Kuznetsov hardly grieved over their withdrawal of support.[43]

The Communists had rallied – by the end of 1991 they could attract between 300 and 400 to open-air meetings – and their various organizations could count on a total membership running into a few thousand, but they were no more successful at achieving results. A campaign in the summer of 1992 managed to collect only 6,000 signatures in support of Yeltsin's resignation. In February 1993 the different Communist Parties, whose leaders tended to come from among university or institute professors, held a joint conference but a follow-up meeting attracted only 200 people, including journalists and onlookers.[44] The reaction, or rather non-reaction, to Yeltsin's call for a referendum on 20 March 1993 revealed only too clearly the apathy of the activists as well as of the population. Tiny meetings were held.[45] Street surveys suggested that, while supporters of the president outnumbered his opponents by nearly two to one, seven out of ten had no interest at all in politics. But 60 per cent were still prepared to turn out to vote when the referendum was held in April. Although this was less than in the presidential election of 1991, the pro-president vote was almost identical, in both the oblast as a whole (76 per cent) and the city (81 per cent). The Permiaki would still turn out to vote for 'their' countryman.[46]

---

[43] In April a branch of NTS (the anti-communist Popular Labour Union, an underground organization that had existed in the post-Second World War Soviet Union) was founded, led by a certain L. Kuznetsov. The Berezniki DemRossia organization split off and formed a separate organization. At the centre the DPR formally left DemRossia, but in Perm its members initially retained their membership; some then set up a branch of Civic Union. The Christian Democrats moved to the far right. DemRossia managed to collect between 20,000–40,000 signatures for the land referendum and, in January 1993, in a by-election for a seat in the Russian Parliament, their candidate, the blind teacher Andreev, picked up more votes than either the Communist candidate or Bystriantsev – but since only 15 per cent of the electorate voted, the seat remained vacant: Podvintsev, 'Report'.

[44] Podvintsev, 'Report'. The monarchists sometimes demonstrated together with the Communists but relations between them were strained.

[45] The NTS marshalled between fifty and seventy at a meeting; the Communists responded with one of 150–200; the NTS followed this with a pro-presidential meeting, attended by 400–500. The oblast press tended to support the president, although *Zvezda* provided surprisingly even-handed coverage; the television, under administration control, came out strongly for the president, and the price of petrol was lowered as a vote-catcher on the eve of the referendum. *Zvezda* carried statements by both Zotin, the democrat, and V. Maltsev, who had emerged as leader of the Communists: 23, 24 March 1991, p. 1.

[46] Yeltsin's economic policy was supported by 69 per cent and 73 per cent respectively. Of those who voted, 40 per cent were in favour of early presidential elections, and 73 per cent favoured Congress elections (24 per cent and 44 per cent of the electorate): official election returns; *Zvezda*, 28 April 1993, p. 1.

It was not that there was little discontent among the population, rather that the political parties seemed unable to focus or organize it. Nearly half a million people, approximately 16 per cent of the population, were below the recognized poverty line in January 1993. Surveys suggested that those who rated their families to be suffering real hunger and need rose from 6 per cent to 10 per cent between July and October 1992; those who felt they lived well hovered around 5 per cent. Key concerns were high prices and rising crime. Almost all felt a high level of insecurity; approximately half were alienated from politics and had no confidence in any of the political leaders or institutions. More than half saw the best survival strategy as one of working on their allotments, although the percentage seeking alternative or additional sources of income was rising slightly. The most popular recipe for coping with the high prices was for the local authorities to punish the traders.[47] Although rising prices and crime continued to dominate the list of popular concerns, by late 1993 the fear of unemployment had climbed into third place. By 1994 the percentage of those who considered that they were eating better than in 1993 was increasing, the percentage who saw no change was increasing (to about half), and those who felt they were eating worse was falling – to a third. The percentage of those who viewed the future with some hope had risen gradually since the summer of 1992 (from 26 per cent to 46 per cent) but the overwhelming majority (over 70 per cent) considered the socio-political situation in the region to be unstable or threatening. As might be expected it was the better-off who found life more bearable and the environment less threatening. Just over a quarter considered that their circumstances had become unbearable. However, rich and poor reacted almost identically when asked what action they might be prepared to take in order to remedy their situation, and over time their responses did not change. Between 60–70 per cent stated they would take no action whatsoever. Among those who were prepared to consider some form of protest, those employed in state or rented enterprises, the unemployed,

---

[47] The standard of living in the oblast was roughly average for the Russian Federation: *Zvezda*, 3 February 1993, p. 1; *Nasha zhizn' segodnia*, sector of sociological monitoring, Perm administration, July, October 1992. As of January 1993 there were just over 4,000 registered unemployed in the city; by the summer 20,000 were unemployed, but only 3,000 registered; by the autumn 20,000 were registered, and the period out of work was increasing – approximately half of those drawing benefit had been out of work for four months or more. But, even by the spring of 1994, the huge defence plants were still shedding labour very slowly. Real wages, in the oblast as a whole, fell by 15 per cent during the course of 1993, but by the spring of 1994 the original food stores had a reasonable supply of products, and stalls had appeared around the tram stops. The prices were, however, out of the reach of many: administration report; observations by author. Industrial production fell by 20 per cent in 1992, and again in 1993, and by 28 per cent in the first quarter of 1994: *Zvezda*, 8 September 1993, p. 1; 30 April 1994, p. 1.

pensioners, and those from the smaller towns without high education pre-dominated.[48]

What kind of activity might they undertake? Writing letters to the authorities and participating in a strike or a demonstration were claimed to be the most popular options. If organized political activity remained the preserve of a tiny minority, spontaneous demonstrations of angry shoppers blocking the main street became a regular occurrence. The first occurred in the summer of 1991 when supplies of tobacco ran out. Between the end of September and the end of October, in different parts of the city, the trams were stopped thirteen times and the trolleybuses nine times by crowds protesting against the shortage of alcohol, sugar, or bread. The response of the authorities was to get supplies to the spot as quickly as possible, which encouraged the view that this was an effective form of action. In September 1992 a rise in the price of bread brought panic-buying, shortages, and demonstrations. In both the autumn of 1991 and the spring of 1992, schoolteachers and health workers engaged in short-lived strikes to which the authorities responded by either making or promising wage rises.[49] The spring months of 1992 were ones of heightened tension as a whole, as prices rose and wages were delayed. On 1 May, the traditional holiday, 5,000 joined a demonstration to register their discontent with rising prices, and non-payment of wages, but as wages began to be paid more regularly (perhaps it helped that Gosznak, the state mint, was in Perm), the action subsided.

Tension rose again in the summer of 1993, with protest meetings held in some of the defence plants. There were threats of action, token strikes in some of the mines in August and September, and a protest meeting held in Perm in mid-September.[50] The Peasant Union, in protest at low milk prices, held up supplies of milk products into the city in August but the action was half-hearted, and brought no results.[51] During 1993 there was perhaps as much action from non-political organizations as from the parties. The Afgantsy, an association of Afghan war veterans, with a membership of perhaps thirty, surfaced from time to time and threatened to take measures to clean up the market. Among their demands was one for closing the frontiers of the oblast, given the porous state of Russia's

---

[48] *Zima-94*, 1–4, 1994, Perm oblast administration, survey.

[49] By the end of 1993 average salaries in health, education, and culture, dependent on the state budget, were 55–60 per cent of those in industry, only 1.5 times that of the minimum subsistence requirement: Podvintsev, 'Report'.

[50] A visit from Soskovets, chair of the federal metallurgy committee, which included a closed meeting with directors of the defence plants, and a promise of federal funding for conversion may have helped diffuse the discontent in the plants: *Zvezda*, 9, 23, 27, 30, 31 July 1993, p. 1; 7 August 1993, p. 1; 7, 14 September 1993, p. 1.

[51] *Zvezda*, 23 July 1993, p. 1; 6, 7, 10, 11, 12, 13 August 1993, p. 1.

borders. In the summer of 1993 the incidents on the Tadzhik border brought demonstrations from the Soldiers' Mothers to which the soviet responded by sending a delegation to look into conditions at the front.[52]

By this time the democratic organizations, together with Civic Union, had grouped together in a bloc Prikam´e, but they had no common programme.[53] The Communists responded by setting up, together with the Christian Democrats, the Party of Labour, and the regional trade union council, an organization called the Patriots of Russia, to which Civic Union then transferred its allegiance. But neither had grass-roots support nor represented any serious activity. Neither were any of the region's leading politicians associated with them. Yeltsin's announcement of 21 September on the dissolution of the Russian Parliament found the democrats divided. There was no upsurge of democratic activity. As the December elections for the federal assembly approached, the Communists showed themselves to be the better organized: they brought 200 of their members to a meeting of the Electors' Club, set up by the democrats in 1990 but open to all electors, voted in a new leadership, and secured the funds.[54] It remained to be seen how the two sides would fare in the elections.

Tomsk: pluralist politics

> On the political map of Russia Tomsk is above average – in spirit, in its approach, in the state of its local organs of power, in their agreement with the reforms. In its political convictions and social awareness, in the regrouping of its political forces, Tomsk is ahead of Moscow.

So argued Sulakshin, the president's representative, in April 1993.[55] The contrast with Perm was marked. In Tomsk there were active groups who held sharply opposed ideological positions, and whose spokesmen occupied leading posts in the soviets or administration; policy-making was accompanied by sometimes bitter debate; relations with Moscow were complex and often confrontational; individuals fought openly for power and influence. Here an ideologically divided elite struggled with the issues of furthering the region's interests (over which they did not agree) and over who should be responsible for policy in the region.

The discussion of developments in Tomsk will be briefer, partly

---

[52] Podvintsev, 'Report'; *Zvezda*, 18 June 1993, p. 1.
[53] Divisions among the democrats were exacerbated by revelations that L. Kuznetsov, the leader of the NTS, had four prison sentences behind him, for theft and assault, not political convictions; he ran unsuccessfully in the December elections; further damaging material appeared in January 1994, leading to his arrest: *Zvezda*, 16 July 1993, p. 1; 15 January 1994, p. 1.   [54] *Zvezda*, 23 October 1993, p. 1.
[55] *TM ekspress*, 23 April 1993.

because there is less data, and partly because several of the issues raised by elite behaviour in Tomsk are present in St Petersburg. We shall look at them there in more detail. Here I take, first, the question of privatization, then look at the relationship with Moscow, which involved political, institutional, and personal interests. We do not have enough data on the composition of the administration and soviets to see how far reaching the changes between the old and new orders were in personnel terms. It is certainly true that new individuals came in to play a key role at leadership level in both oblast and city soviets, and that some of Kress's key appointments within the administration were outsiders. Sulakshin made the job of president's representative a far more interventionist one than did Kaliagin in Perm. That much we can say. Data on the subsequent careers of the obkom and gorkom members of 1988 suggest that the very large number of institute heads and academics (as befitted a scientific centre) seemed, like their counterparts elsewhere, largely to have remained in post. There was some movement from the party and soviet administration into business, but here there are too many gaps in the data to draw comparisons with Perm or Krasnodar. More retired in Tomsk (possibly a consequence of an ageing conservative apparatus) but, unlike in Perm, a number of leading Communists, associated with the previous regime, remained as active figures in the soviet and in political life. A. Pomorov, for example, the first secretary, who became director of a plastics enterprise, was one; B. Yachmenev, who had defended the buro's actions in August 1991, was another. Tomsk provided more leading lawyers to defend the CPSU in the celebrated law case than any other legal centre in Russia.[56]

Privatization

Privatization, we saw, had become an issue in Tomsk as early as 1991 when the little soviet attempted to draw up a brief for the property committee. The events of August, followed by the uncertainty over who was to be the chief administrator, meant no further action that year. Kress, the ex-raikom secretary and soviet chair, was appointed to the post in December, and G. Shamin, a young, largely colourless individual with a background in civil defence, who had been a USSR deputy, replaced him as chair of the oblast soviet. Its members divided roughly as follows: agri-

[56] Pogodaev, 'Tomsk', August 1993, p. 119, draws attention to the split between those members of the apparatus, such as Pomorov, who continued to defend the socialist way, and others, such as Kozlovskaia, also in industrial management, but now an ardent supporter of income incentives and inequality: interviews with Tomsk lawyers, including those who had participated in the hearing, March 1993.

cultural lobby, forty; Democratic Tomsk, thirty; the Action group, twenty; Communists, twenty; industrial lobby, fifteen. The supporters of Action could, however, marshal a majority on the little soviet, the body which sat permanently and made recommendations to the soviet.[57] Sulakshin could exert no direct influence over decisions, something which, given his strong views and personality, he found unsatisfactory. However, there were individuals, in key posts, associated with either the Republican Party (the strongest democratic party in Tomsk) or with DemRossia with whom he was politically associated. A. Cherkasskii, chair of the city soviet was one; V. Bauer, a member of the Republican Party, appointed by Kress as one of his deputies was another, as was B. Shaidullin, a democratic activist, and chair of the soviet committee on foreign economic relations. But it proved to be far from easy for the democrats to work together. Political and personal differences drove them into opposite camps. Over privatization, the original split between Action and DemTomsk opened up again.

Essentially the dispute was over the form privatization should take. The Action group favoured leasing rather than outright privatization. In the summer of 1991 some of the soviet branch administrations (in the supply and trade sector) had been turned into commercial structures under the property committee. This was clearly illegal. The reasoning, however convoluted, that had prompted deputies to favour leasing rather than selling was that it enabled the soviet to retain control rather than allowing these crucial services to slip into dubious hands. Their opponents argued that the officials in the sector favoured leasing because they retained control – although formally responsible to the oblast structures, they in fact had a free hand – and that the executive committee favoured the arrangement because it was an easy option. In early January 1992 the regional soviet discussed the government's proposals on privatization. A. Petrov, chair of the property committee, argued that they denied the labour collectives any say; Kushelevskii criticized the government's programme, on the grounds that it was affecting production. The soviet voted to operate a 'Tomsk variation' of leasing rather than privatization until 1993, and not to implement the president's decree.[58] The city soviet, in contrast, voted in favour of privatization and drew up a list of properties for privatization.[59] The government intervened, calling a conference on the progress of privatization in Siberia, and sent a

[57] Interviews with members of the Action group, and with deputies of the other democratic fractions, March 1993. Note that the composition of the little soviet was not representative of the larger soviet, a phenomenon not unique to Tomsk (see below, p. 256).

[58] *Tom. vestnik*, 25 January 1992, p. 1; *Respublika*, 3 (1992), p. 3.

[59] *Tom. vestnik*, 14 February 1992, p. 5; 20 February 1992, p. 3; 25 February 1992, p. 1.

top-level delegation headed by A. Chubais, the chair of the property committee. He declared himself satisfied in general with the privatization programme, insisted that auctions and commercial competition should be its main planks, and praised the Tomsk committee for doing what it could in the face of a conservative soviet. Members of Action felt that they had been deprived of a proper hearing, and that their position had been distorted, but Chubais's intervention undermined their stance and in April the Supreme Soviet resolved that the Tomsk variant was illegal.[60]

Privatization proceeded slowly all the same. While the city soviet supported privatization, the chair of its executive committee, Gonchar, held up proceedings and only after his removal in October was there some movement forward. In the whole of 1992 only 56 out of the 464 retail trade and catering outlets were privatized, and only 1,675 were employed in the private sector by December.[61] An American consultancy firm was brought in to speed up the process and help with auctions. The property fund, responsible for organizing them, finally set up in December 1992, was the last to be established in Russia. It perhaps did not help that 70 per cent of Tomsk industry belonged to the defence sector.[62] In early 1993, according to the supporters of economic reform, the property committee was still dragging its feet. It favoured the privatization of, for example, the big Tomsk oil-chemical plant – but as a single unit, which would mean it retained its monopoly position. By the end of 1993 the committee claimed that 73 per cent of municipal trade and service enterprises had been privatized, and that this was enough.[63] The administration, claimed its democratic opponents, still thought in terms of controlling and disposing of resources and were apprehensive of a situation in which they could not do this. Yet, by the autumn of 1993, the new businesspeople (who included Kushelevskii) had appeared in sufficient numbers and strength to form an organization to defend their interests in the political

[60] *Tom. vestnik*, 20 March 1992, pp. 1–2; interviews with members of the Action group, March 1993.
[61] *Tom. vestnik*, 12 (1993), p. 3; slightly different figures (63 privatized out of a planned 246) were given at the city council meeting on 10 March 1993: *Tom. vestnik*, 10 March 1993, p. 3; oblast administration programme for 1993. It is important to bear in mind that shops and service outlets hardly existed, except in the centre of the city: there might be only one shop to serve a new housing estate, and to privatize it made little sense. Most of the town population shopped in the market.   [62] *Tom. vestnik*, 34 (1993), p. 4.
[63] *Nezav.*, 10 February 1993, p. 4; Pogodaev, 'Tomsk', December 1993. The auctions failed to attract many buyers, and the prices realized were low, which made those responsible suspect that a small informal consortium had agreed among themselves to divide the property: interviews with deputies and representatives of the city property committee, March 1993.

arena, and Tomsk's major resource – oil – had been reorganized as a stock-holding company, Tomskoil.[64]

Regional independence

Moscow had managed the region's oil resources, and determined the industrial profile of the region, heavily based on the defence industry. This included Tomsk-7, the defence city which did not appear on any maps, and where the accident in the chemical products plant in April 1993 sent a radioactive cloud into the atmosphere. Eight large plants accounted for a third of production. Higher education and research, all also on the federal budget, were the other major employers. Although the region produced milk, grain, and eggs, 60–5 per cent of its food supplies and consumer goods (and chicken feed) traditionally came from outside the region. With the freeing of food prices, the existing budget became quite inadequate (even if the food could still be obtained) while prices for raw materials, only a small residue of which came under local authority control, initially remained fixed. The regional authorities found themselves having to barter in order to bring in supplies for their population under extremely unfavourable and, in their eyes, unfair terms of trade.

In 1991–2 it was government institutions which became the first traders. They still thought in terms of how many thousands of tons of poultry feed were needed for the region's poultry, and how many thousands of eggs for the population. But now they were having to strike deals, barter, and bargain on a scale that they never did before. Deals were always a part of the Soviet system and, in this respect, the barter phenomenon simply built on old practices, but it now began to involve foreign partners, and from there it was but a short step to striking commercial deals involving the region's resources (such as the Siberian Forest scandal, for example, already referred to).[65] Whether it was for personal gain or to benefit the population, the regional authorities in Siberia saw no reason why Moscow should continue to dispose of their resources. This was what had lain behind the Siberian Accord.

With the Soviet government gone, the Accord found the Russian government distinctly less friendly. The Accord registered its association in Novosibirsk, not Moscow ('As long as I am in office', Makharadze was quoted as saying, 'you won't be registered') and found all its economic

---

[64] Pogodaev, 'Tomsk', September 1993. When the city centre was razed in the 1970s to build the huge white civic and party buildings, three were built: in the centre was the combined party and soviet building, to the right the theatre, and to the left the building of the oil administration.   [65] See p. 168 above.

agreements blocked by the Council of Ministers.[66] In theory joint action by the Siberian regions would strengthen their hand, but it was more complex than that: they were also competitors with each other for Moscow's favours. Many of the regions had the same raw materials to sell, and therefore were in competition with each other. Given Moscow's control over the budget, it was vital to make claims on behalf of the individual region. Tomsk, for example, and Novosibirsk, as the two major centres of academic research and higher education, could only view each other as competitors for allocations from the science budget. Tiumen, with its oil and gas reserves, could strike deals with Moscow but Tomsk was terribly dependent upon the centre to support its higher education and science institutes, and its defence industries. In 1993 its allocation for basic science was cut by half. By early 1993 60 per cent of its population were reckoned to be living below the official poverty line.[67] A strident line on independence could well incur disfavour; on the other hand, a lack of action was hardly like to bring concessions either.

In early 1993, with a new prime minister in office, the regional representatives planned a meeting, to be held in Tomsk. The federal authorities, in conflict with each other, were now anxious to find allies among the regions, and the Accord was registered in Moscow. Shamin, chair of the oblast soviet, visiting Moscow to ask for financial help with the scientific-educational complex and conversion, invited Khasbulatov from the Supreme Soviet to attend the meeting. He did not come but Chernomyrdin, the prime minister, flew in with a high-level delegation. To everyone's dismay, at the opening session he stated in no uncertain terms that the notion that strong regions meant a strong Russia was mistaken; 'not a single region can do anything if it is on its own', he said, and referred to the consequences of Baltic separatism for the fate of the Soviet Union. Although he softened his comments in a local broadcast the following morning the damage was done: Moscow, in the eyes of the Siberians, was still unprepared to yield its control. Maybe as part of damage limitation, E. Panfilova, minister of social security, and the deputy minister of health came to Tomsk a month later for a meeting with Siberian administrators to discuss the region's health and welfare problems.[68]

[66] Perov, 'Sibirskii paradoks', p. 54; *Ross. gaz.*, 27 July 1993, p. 4.
[67] January–November 1992 saw a fall in industrial production of 23 per cent, agricultural output by 12–15 per cent, and retail trade sales by 37 per cent. The fall continued throughout 1993 but unemployment remained low, and fewer than 5,000, lower than predicted: oblast administration programme; Pogodaev, 'Tomsk', December 1993; on poverty, see *Tom. vestnik*, 39 (1993).
[68] *Tom. vestnik*, 21 (1993), p. 3; 37 (1993), p. 1; 38–9 (1993), p. 3; *Deistvie*, 2 March 1993, p. 1; *Kr. znamia*, 20 March 1993, p. 1.

By this time the conflict between president and Supreme Soviet was reflected in their separate attempts to determine the content of the new constitution. A key issue was the rights of the republics as opposed to the regions. As we saw, in the example of Sakha and Tatarstan, the republics wanted their privileged status to be, at the very least, confirmed, and the regions wanted equality. The president, at this time, was seeking allies among the republican leaders; the Supreme Soviet, partly in consequence, partly because of its composition, became the champion of the regions. One tactic for a region was to claim or gain republican status. During 1993 the loudest champion of this was Sverdlovsk, advocating the creation of a Urals republic. The Perm leadership by and large kept out of it, although by the summer Kuznetsov began to make supportive statements while continuing to affirm his loyalty to the president.[69] In Perm, however, neither the issue nor Kuznetsov's statements prompted much debate: no one wished to stick their neck out or to take up positions. In Tomsk it was very different.

In March 1993 the Action group had drawn up a draft constitution for the region which, based on the principles of 'people's power, federalism, and the division of powers', referred to Tomsk oblast as 'a fully fledged [*polnopravnyi*] and equal [*ravnopravnyi*] subject of the Federation, whose population is the source of all the rights of the state organs of power' and proposed a category of Tomsk citizenship: 'a citizen of the Russian Federation living permanently in the oblast is a citizen of the oblast'. It further reaffirmed that 'the population (people) of the oblast is the owner (source) of all rights and powers'.[70] Although the draft was voted down by the oblast soviet, the issue came back on the agenda as the conflict, which now involved local politicians, deepened over the federal constitution. By supporting the case for the regions, an institution or political grouping was necessarily taking the Supreme Soviet side. Aspiring politicians needed to make choices, and Shamin, chair of the soviet, decided to gamble on the Supreme Soviet. He was an example of a politician with no personal or political following thrust into a position (chair of a regional soviet) that allowed him to play a role on the Russian stage. If he wished to pursue a political career, he had to act, and his choice of action was largely determined by the immediate political environment in Tomsk and his assessment of a highly unpredictable situation at federal level. It was a gamble for these aspiring politicians: make or break. They had no

---

[69] See above, p. 184. Two chief administrators who did maintain a consistent anti-presidential line were V. Mukha of Novosibirsk and E. Rossel from Sverdlovsk, but they were exceptions. Subsequently dismissed, but then re-elected as chief administrator, Rossel switched allegiance and in 1996 became a vocal Yeltsin supporter.

[70] Draft constitution. 'People' and 'source' were proposed as alternatives in the draft.

political party behind them, no nomenklatura network to support them. Even if they had individual political programmes, these would not ensure their future.

'Why should a citizen of the Russian Federation living in Tomsk have fewer rights than a citizen of the Russian Federation living in Tatarstan?', he asked, on the pages of *Nezavisimaia gazeta*. On no account should republican rights be diminished, but the regions should be given equal rights.[71] In June Shamin was among those who walked out in protest with Khasbulatov at the constitutional conference. The draft constitution found no greater favour among the regional soviets than among the republican ones. Although the proposed regional representation in the federal council was now back on a par with the republics (two from each), there was to be no change in their status vis-à-vis the republics. So Tatarstan was to keep 40 per cent of its oil, and Tomsk only 3–5 per cent of its? A referendum on the status of the region, argued its advocates, was the only way for Tomsk to a gain control over its resources. In July the oblast soviet returned to the question and this time voted in favour of holding a referendum on Tomsk acquiring republican status, and on a project to base the dismantling of nuclear warheads in the region.[72] (In 1992 the federal government, despite a vote against by the oblast soviet, had chosen Tomsk as a place for storing and then reworking disused nuclear warheads. The ecological groups had been campaigning ever since for the cancellation of the project, and a new organization, calling itself the Tomsk People's Movement, a grass-roots, left-oriented group, had also taken up the cause.) The decision to hold a referendum on republican status immediately attracted opposition. The city soviets of Tomsk and Tomsk-7 and a further nine town and district soviets voted against holding it. The oblast administration formally requested the soviet to rescind its decision, and initially stated its unwillingness to participate in carrying it out; the procurator unsuccessfully lodged a protest against the decision; DemRossia attempted to query the decision before the courts. A number of different reasons came into play, ranging from the constitutionality of such a step, its feasibility, and the cost of the referendum, to the inability of the region to survive without federal funding for its science and higher education complex and its defence plants.[73] But it

[71] *Nezav.*, 20 March 1993, p. 3. By 1993 the question of tax revenues, and the federal authorities' softer attitude towards the heavily subsidised republics was extremely contentious. For one account of the relative differences, see L. Smirniagin, *Ross. vesti*, 26 March 1993, p. 2.   [72] *Nar. trib.*, 17 June 1993, p. 1; 10 July 1993, p. 6.

[73] *Izv.*, 6 August 1993, p. 1; *Ross. gaz.*, 14 September 1993, p. 2; *Nar. trib.*, 28, 30 September 1991, p. 1. At the end of August the soviet reaffirmed its decision in favour of a referendum, and Kress agreed, unenthusiastically, to implement it: Pogodaev, 'Tomsk', August 1993.

was also that the holding of the referendum could only be seen as an anti-president act and, as such, a political statement. It was becoming almost impossible to separate political position from institutional loyalty.

If Shamin took on the defence of the Supreme Soviet, Sulakshin was the president's champion. During the summer he had organized a new group, Solidarity and Reform, to support the president and economic reform. This had caused tension within the Republican Party which, with its 400 members, was the strongest democratic organization in the region and had previously supported Sulakshin. It was now parting company with him over policies and questions of leadership. Although the Republicans did not support the referendum on regional status, they were opposed to the warheads project in principle, whereas Sulakshin was not.[74] Among the Tomsk democrats were several well-known figures who commanded respect – A. Kobzev, for example, a professor from a research institute, RF deputy, and leader of the Republicans – and who were finding it increasingly difficult to work with Sulakshin. They united in September 1993, just, over the presidential decree dissolving the Parliament but thereafter split irrevocably.[75] Predictably the oblast little soviet voted that Yeltsin's decree was unconstitutional, and received the backing of the full soviet. Members of Action and the Communists led the campaign to support the Supreme Soviet. The little soviet of Tomsk city council agonized (as did other democratic soviets) and finally adopted an extraordinarily convoluted resolution which blamed both sides, favoured new elections, and requested the speedy adoption of new constitutional legislation, but urged the continued existence of all organs of power. Its chair, Cherkasskii, was prepared to support the president. Kress, the chief administrator, produced an argued statement in support of the president's action, and in favour of early re-elections of Congress and president. The professors split into two camps, publishing their disagreement in letters to the press. Sulakshin queried Shamin's claim that the business community was behind the soviet decision. Memorial came out in support of the president; the Communists organized a committee to defend the constitution.[76]

Both the referendum and the wider issue of regional rights were now entangled in the conflict between president and Supreme Soviet. At a meeting of representatives of the soviets of the Siberian and Far Eastern regions, held in Novosibirsk on 29 September, Kushelevskii, representing

[74] Pogodaev, 'Tomsk', August 1993.

[75] The Economic Freedom group, headed by Shaidullin, split with the other democrats over the presidential edict: its members advocated a return to the status quo before 21 September; they also supported the idea of republic status.

[76] Nar. trib, 28, 29, 30 September 1993, p. 1; Pogodaev, 'Tomsk', September, October 1993.

Tomsk, suggested that a way of defending Siberia from 'the dictatorship' of Yeltsin was to create 'a Russian republic' in Siberia. More alarming, from the president's point of view, must have been the meeting's resolution which demanded a return to the status quo ante by 3 October and stated that, if this condition was not met, the Congress of People's Deputies could be offered a venue in a Siberian city; it also threatened the non-payment of taxes, the halting of energy supplies and transport, and non-participation in elections.[77] Against this background, the referendum attracted little attention. Whether under other circumstances more would have participated is impossible to say. As it was, only 24 per cent of the electorate bothered to vote, the majority in favour of republican status, and a further 5,000 voted against the nuclear warheads.[78] Then followed the October events in Moscow, and the supporters of regional autonomy and the soviets suffered a double blow.

Kress moved swiftly, together with Sulakshin, to propose the dissolution of the soviets, the closure of *Narodnaia tribuna*, the soviet paper, and its television channel, and new elections for both soviets and chief administrator. Although the fate of the town and district soviets was sealed with Yeltsin's decree of 9 October which dissolved them, the oblast soviet sought to preserve its existence.[79] Shamin argued for a compromise: the soviet should not rescind its decision that the presidential decree had been unconstitutional, but it should vote for a new one-chamber assembly, to be elected simultaneously with the federal assembly, and until then the little soviet should remain. His proposal was adopted, with the added clause that if the little soviet was unable to operate, all powers should pass to its chair. Kress responded by closing the soviet. Shamin attempted to dispute the decision before the courts, but then withdrew the suit. No action was taken against *Narodnaia tribuna*, which declared itself an independent paper.[80]

By now all attention was concentrated on the forthcoming elections to the federal assembly, and those for new local assemblies were put off until March. The idea of re-electing the chief administrator faded in line with presidential policy, and Kress strengthened his position by convincingly winning a seat to the Council of the Federation in the December elections. Towards the end of the year he announced a new collegial

---

[77] *Nar. trib.*, 30 September 1993, p. 1; 1 October 1993, p. 1.

[78] See Shamin, *Nar. trib.*, 15 October 1993, pp. 1–2.

[79] Under the presidential decree (no. 1617), oblast soviets remained, although they were obliged to prepare new regional constitutions and procedure for elections; the powers of the chief administrators were increased: *Sobranie aktov Prezidenta i Pravitel'stva RF*, 41 (1993), no. 3924. Some soviets dissolved themselves; others were effectively shut by the administration; others remained for the time being. See below, chapter 8, p. 262, and n. 45.   [80] *Nar. trib.*, 12, 14, 15, 16, 26, 28 October 1993, p. 1.

administration which, he suggested, would facilitate a more effective taking and executing of decisions. It included the chief administrator, his first deputy, and seven deputy chief administrators, the secretary of the administration, the administrators of Tomsk and Tomsk-7, head of the oblast internal affairs department, head of the regional financial administration, and the regional representative of the Central Bank, heads of the regional health and education departments, and a representative of the rectors of the higher education institutions.[81] This sounds like the kind of administration of which Perm politicians would have approved (and, one might add, party politicians of an earlier generation). Other personnel changes resulted from election outcomes. The two most important were the need to find a new deputy chief administrator and president's representative, given Bauer's and Sulakshin's election to the Duma. In place of Bauer, Kress appointed V. Khokhlov, originally chair of the trade union committee of the geology faculty in the university, then chair of the regional trade union council, and now of the trade union People's Bank. If this brought a sigh from the democrats, the decision on the president's representative brought outrage. Their candidate, and indeed the obvious democratic candidate, was A. Kobzev, RF deputy and leader of the Republicans. Yeltsin had already approved the choice when Sulakshin intervened. He had now broken completely with the democrats, with Russia's Choice, Bauer, and Shaidullin, he was critical of Gaidar, and moving to an alliance with enterprise directors. He succeeded in halting the appointment, and proposed instead his long-time assistant, L. Eftimovich. With her in post he would retain a voice in Tomsk affairs. The situation became farcical: a commission sent from Moscow was met at the airport by Kress, Sulakshin, and Kobzev. It failed to reach a decision and, three months later, Eftimovich was still 'acting' representative.[82]

A free press

The extent to which the local press had published adventurous or critical articles before 1991 varied greatly from region to region, with Leningrad at one end of the spectrum and a rural region such as Kursk or Belgorod at the other. The ending of party rule brought freedom and opportunity for the journalists and editors but, for many, it also brought a profound sense of disorientation. Local authorities and editors were unable to judge where power lay and what line to adopt. It was unclear to whom the papers belonged, and who would pay for them. Although this was a

[81] *Nar. trib.*, 23 December 1993, p. 2.   [82] Pogodaev, 'Tomsk', January, March 1994.

sector, unlike that of industry or agriculture, where the employees were ready and anxious to interpret their job differently – to write as they pleased – there was no agreement on what the role of the press should be. Was it to provide news, or information, or criticism, or to defend a political line? Gradually, and not surprisingly, those who financed the press began to answer these questions in the way that seemed to them appropriate. And where the press became dependent for its survival upon local authority or company subsidies, the journalists fell back in line. Only in a place such as St Petersburg, where there were both alternative sources of finance and a highly developed publishing world, could the press, by 1994, maintain an independent line and constant criticism of the regional authorities.

During the period 1991–4 the existence of different financial sponsors, defending or associated with different interests, determined whether the population received not so much different political perspectives on current developments as any criticism of soviet or administration behaviour. In Kazan it existed because of the independent Tatar press, and the *Telegraf*. In the company towns it was out of the question. In Krasnodar several newspapers survived, and the existence of the unresolved struggle for power, together with the contenders' ability to draw upon resources, provided some insights into local politics and criticism of the administration. In Perm it was *Zvezda*, the party paper, still under Trushnikov, its original editor, with one deeply conservative deputy editor, the other increasingly democratic, which emerged as the liveliest and critical paper. The paper was jointly owned by the oblast soviet and its own collective (as was the more reformist *Permskie novosti*); its traditional reputation and oblast-wide readership allowed it to attract advertising and to maintain a circulation of nearly 200,000, and an appearance five days a week. Its financial independence allowed it, in October 1993, to sever its connection with the soviet.[83] In contrast *Permskie novosti*, the more adventurous newcomer, lost ground and became wholly dependent on the soviet subsidy. Features on Memorial, historical pieces, and environmental issues continued to appear but none of these were any threat to the authorities.[84] *Vechernyi Perm*, the city soviet newspaper, heavily dependent upon its subsidy, opted for 'providing information'.

---

[83] *Zvezda*, 8 October 1993, p. 1.
[84] Memorial became well established as a research centre, with four rooms (two in the pedagogical institute), some technology, and a 2 mln r. grant from the regional soviet in 1992. It set up an archive and a prison camp open museum, and began to organize tours and conferences. The aim was to combine ventures that brought in revenue with research, and help for those who suffered under repression.

Zvezda developed no clear political line (given the composition of its editorial leadership this was hardly surprising) but it tended to be pro-president. It gave equal space to DemRossia and the Communists during the constitutional crisis. Unlike most of the provincial press it continued to report DemRossia activities but its coverage of the December 1993 elections was curiously muted. The party issue was avoided by its limiting coverage to the programme outline put forward by the insignificant ecological party; a few individual non-party and democratic candidates were featured, as was Kuznetsov, the chief administrator.[85] It was, however, in its pages that articles critical of the administration and elite appeared. They were largely the work of an individual journalist. Were they a threat to the authorities? Would it not have been relatively easy to silence him? Two factors were at work: the journalist had an established reputation, and a good party background. But, surely more importantly, if organized opposition that is capable of ousting those who rule does not exist and if there are no independent courts prepared to act against corrupt rulers or defend citizen rights, a critical press is something that rulers can afford to tolerate. They still may prefer to limit it. In November 1993 *Zvezda* published details of sugar deals under which Sapiro, then deputy chief administrator, had authorized the issuing of large bank credits to unreliable agencies for sugar which never materialized; at the very least the implication was one of unprofessional behaviour. Sapiro, using television, accused the paper of unethical behaviour, and of acting on behalf of commercial concerns. The paper responded by bringing a libel case against him. The case was still pending in April 1994 when Sapiro, in his new post as chairman of the regional assembly, announced that it was important that the administration and assembly had *its* newspaper to ensure that official announcements were published; he was not in favour of establishing a new one, given the expense, but of working with an existing one; and subsidies would only be forthcoming for those papers of which the assembly was a co-owner.[86] In other words *Zvezda* could not expect any financial support. For the time being it was safe, given its resources, although it had been deprived of its office in the House of Soviets to make space for the startling reappearance into political life of V. Surkin, ex-obkom second secretary, as chair of the department for the effective use of the region's precious metals and stones, an area in which he was not known to have any expertise. Could it be, asked *Zvezda*, that Chernyshev too was planning a comeback?[87] It seems clear that without

---

[85] See *Zvezda*, 10 December 1993, p. 2, for its final reporting.
[86] *Zvezda*, 20 November 1993, p. 2; 3, 23 December 1993, p. 1; 5, 9 April 1994, p. 1.
[87] *Zvezda*, 5 February 1994, p. 1; 12 April 1994, p. 1.

its campaigning journalist *Zvezda* too might become little more than a purveyor of local news and information.

In Tomsk the press developed very differently. *Krasnoe znamia*, the party paper, now jointly owned by its collective, a transport agency, and an information centre (and with a subsidy from the big chemical plant), survived on its traditional oblast circulation, conservative and dull. It had become a champion of press freedom – which meant criticizing the new democrats.[88] Its main competitor was the soviet-financed *Narodnaia tribuna* which gradually shifted to the right and, by the summer of 1993, was supporting the Supreme Soviet. As noted, Kress and Sulakshin wished to shut it after the October days. But the *Tribuna* had allowed the supporters and the opponents of the referendum to put their case on its pages, and its shutdown would have drastically restricted the reporting of political issues. The most interesting, and critical, of the papers was *Tomskii vestnik*, a new city soviet paper, very dependent upon its subsidy but with an editor, himself a member of the soviet, who argued the case for the paper preserving an independent line. By 1993 the more conservative section of the soviet was in favour of using its money 'more usefully' but the vote on the budget item went in favour, at least for one more year.[89]

In retrospect the period from 1991 to 1994 may appear as a short lively interlude in the history of the local press in Russia: subsidies from the central government and local authorities were still forthcoming, the shifting political situation and lack of clarity on the role of the press allowed those who wished to experiment. In some regions a spectrum of political views found a voice, but newspaper readership fell drastically and, for

[88] An editorial of 14 July 1992 announced that it had received complaints from the procurator and police for having published photos of the Memorial pickets demanding that 'Kress, Ponomarev, and Vladimirov must answer for their covering up the crime in Tomskstroi.' 'Never', argued the editor, with a curious lapse of memory, 'even in his worst nightmare during the worst period of *zastoi* [stagnation] did an editor ever dream that a newspaper could be blamed for publishing photographs of *something that had actually taken place.*' The original Komsomol paper, renamed *TM ekspress*, had become quite a lively publication; it was also believed to be subsidized by the chemical plant.

[89] Its opponents criticized its 'erotic photographs' and the poor coverage of the Communists, and suggested that the subsidy would be better spent on a voluntary militia. E. Nilov, the editor, disputed the eroticism, asked the Communist deputies to send in more materials, and defended the cheap rate for pensioners on the grounds that *Krasnoe znamia* had always been cheaper for veterans; the existence of the paper, he argued, made for stability in the city; if the soviet did not subsidize it, someone else would step in and change the content: author's notes from city soviet meeting, 10 March 1993. (Three years later with the paper still under his editorship, but now subsidized by the administration, his prediction had been borne out: the critical campaigning had gone from its pages.)

political coverage, people turned to the national press: *Argumenty i fakty*, followed by *Izvestia*, topped the subscription list for the more democratic public; *Trud*, the conservative trade union paper, maintained its readership among other sections of the population. Local politics was of much less interest. The future will surely see a reduction in the number of local newspapers. Either, as in many countries, they will provide local news, items of information, and very little on local politics or they may combine this with acting as the administration's paper, a more familiar role in the Russian context.

It is instructive to compare the fate of two key policies in the government's new agenda, privatization and press freedom, both of which involved cutting back state control and freeing up private initiative. The regional authorities reacted very differently towards them. Privatization was helped not only by the fact that it benefited officials, but also because it was a policy that required *more* state administration – departments, officials, licences, documentation – to implement it.[90] It could be accommodated within the prevailing administrative culture. Press freedom, on the other hand, required the removal of control. But is it also that some types of policy are intrinsically more 'government-friendly' than others? That, regardless of the specific conventions that influence rulers' behaviour, governments will find it easier to pursue some types of policy rather than others which are inherently 'government-hostile'? If we accept that the task of government is to make binding rules for society, to administer them, and to maintain order, it can be argued that governments will be predisposed towards policies that allow for regulation and control. The extension of state ownership, education, and welfare caused no problems for governments. The moves back, first by several western governments and then by those in post-communist states, to privatization and cutting welfare, are evidence that it is quite possible for governments to release certain activities from under their direct control, while managing and attempting to regulate the process. Allowing the management of physical resources to pass to other hands may be one thing. The pursuit of policies which threaten a government's ability to control the implementation of policy and to maintain order – i.e. those which affect certain functions directly tied up with *ruling* – may be another. The creation of an independent legal system, the defence of individual rights, and press freedom are perhaps inherently 'government-hostile' activities. They do not provide scope for increasing government administration and they bring

---

[90] When I asked Gorbunov, the chair of the property (privatization) committee in Perm, how he felt about heading a committee that would become redundant once privatization was complete, he smiled, 'we can always find something that needs doing'.

no bonuses for rulers – on the contrary, they offer only potential dangers.[91] Although inherited conventions will play an important role here too, perhaps these kinds of rights can only be won *from* rulers, not be granted *by* them, as can property rights.

Facing the electorate

In both Perm and Tomsk the December 1993 elections to the federal assembly and the referendum on the constitution were followed, the following March, by local elections. How might we have expected rulers and ruled to conduct themselves? In Tomsk, given organized political parties or movements, well-known figures, and open political debate over issues, we could have predicted ideological campaigns and that the electorate would split between democrat and Communist candidates. It is much more difficult to predict the type of the campaigns in Perm: on what basis might we have expected candidates to oppose each other, what kinds of choices could the electorate be offered, and how would it react? Perhaps loyalty to the president would be the determining factor.

The campaigns did differ, more in December than in March. In Tomsk well-known candidates adopted clear and very different political positions; in Perm the elections attracted little interest, organized political activity was minimal, and there were no popular well-known figures.[92] Yet in both cases the popular response was muted. The electorate responded in its own way, as though it was following some other rules, its own rules. Let us look first at the different choices offered the two electorates in December.

In both Perm and Tomsk the election brought a final rift in democratic ranks. In Tomsk Sulakshin stole a march on DemTomsk and the Republican Party by persuading the Moscow leadership of Russia's Choice to adopt himself and Bauer as the official candidates on the party list and as Russia's Choice candidates in the single-member constituencies in which they also stood. It was an extraordinarily high-handed act

---

[91] Control of communications and adjudication of disputes between citizens or between citizens and the state have over time and to varying degrees been wrested out of the state's grasp and become arenas where state, political organizations, and society confront each other. In the post-Soviet context, thanks to an extremely fortuitous set of circumstances, communications were captured initially by political society, then partly regained by the state; the legal system remained enmeshed with the state and, in the absence of powerful interests concerned to make it act as counter to the authorities, any victories remained individual and unconsolidated.

[92] According to the public opinion surveys, admittedly done a year earlier, October 1992, very few could name any of the local leaders; only 10 per cent managed to name Kuznetsov, the chief administrator.

on Sulakshin's part.[93] Subsequently other well-known democrats also gained Russia's Choice backing for the constituency seats but the consequence was that the democrats entered the election quarrelling and in disarray. Sulakshin did not contest a Council of the Federation seat but two of the original democratic RF deputies, D. Dobzhinskii and Kobzev, stood along with Cherkasskii, chair of the city soviet. O. Popov, a leading democratic deputy at regional and city level, and Shaidullin, a Yabloko candidate, completed the list of democrats. They faced Kress and A. Filimonov, deputy minister for gas and oil between 1987 and 1991, and now general director of Tomskoil.[94] In Tomsk there were only two Duma seats to be contested. Sulakshin stood in the more rural constituency, one of six candidates, among whom were Shamin (who had identified himself with Shakhrai's PRES, Unity and Accord) and Zhvachkin, an ex-party instructor, a supporter of strong government.[95] Bauer stood in the other, also one of six, among whom Yachmenev, the well-known Communist, featured as well as Tirskii, one of the original democratic activists.

In Perm too the democrats split. DemRossia had come to life, in the aftermath of October, and begun to discuss candidates for the Russia's Choice list when Kaliagin, the president's representative, intervened. He produced a list which included some from DemRossia, some from the Democratic Party of Russia, and others favoured by the administration (for example, Volchek, the young director of television) and had this recognized by the Moscow leadership as the official party list.[96] 'Russia's Choice or the administration's choice?', asked disillusioned democrats. This left the democratic activists – Averkiev and Zotin in particular – out in the cold, and forced to run as independents.[97] Kaliagin also led a campaign to rally support behind the 'democratic team' competing for the two Council of the Federation seats. This consisted of Kuznetsov, the chief administrator, and Zelenkin, the democrat from the aviation institute, who was working for an international investment and privatization agency. Not surprisingly, this evoked little response in general and scorn from the democrats. The third contender was A. Levitan, a 31-year-old ex-Komsomol secretary, member of the regional soviet, and president of a new business concern Nostromo. How the political positions of these three candidates differed it was difficult to say. In Perm there were four

---

[93] The Tomsk account is based largely on Pogodaev, 'Tomsk', October, November, December, 1993.   [94] The eighth candidate was A. Savin (background unknown).
[95] See below, p. 287, n. 48 for his views.   [96] *Zvezda*, 7, 20, 21 October 1993, p. 1.
[97] Kuznetsov, from the NTS, also stood, although his activities were already under investigation by the police.

constituencies, and again no shortage of contenders.[98] Most candidates had been members of the CPSU (as in Tomsk, a fact of life for provincial professionals); many who had never been associated with any political organization since adopted a party label in this period because it might help in obtaining office (who knew how the electorate would react?). Although the original democratic activists stood, the lists were dominated by directors of privatized companies, the occasional banker, lawyer, academic, and collective-farm chairman.

In Tomsk, as might be expected, the Communists organized a bloc, Power to the Toilers, which linked the left-oriented Tomsk People's Movement, Labouring Tomsk, and more patriotically inclined groups. They were led by experienced politicians – Pomorov and Yachmenev – and could count on the backing of a vocal part of the professoriate, and a better press. In Perm the Communist Party had made a re-appearance, led by V. Maltsev, a professor of philosophy from the Institute of Culture. It provided the core of a bloc of the left-patriotic organizations – Patriots of Russia and the Workers of Prikama – but its members too could not always agree on their candidates or campaign tactics.[99] In both regions these blocs supported individual candidates competing in the constituency seats. In neither did the patriots proper play anything but insignificant roles.

Turnout was low in both regions, and the results both unexpected and difficult to interpret. Turnout was slightly higher in the rural regions, and there the constitution just went through. In one of the Perm city constituencies turnout was only 42 per cent, in the other 44 per cent; in Tomsk fewer than 40 per cent voted in the urban constituency. Had the Permiaki abandoned the president? Yet in Perm Russia's Choice led the party list comfortably in all four constituencies. Zhirinovskii's Liberal Democratic Party came second in each. Was this a protest vote from a population offered no clear choice? The party figures were Russia's Choice 26 per cent, the LDP 14 per cent, and Women of Russia 12 per cent; Shakhrai's PRES came fourth with 9 per cent, Yabloko fifth with 8 per cent, and the Communists got just under 7 per cent. Russia's Choice and Yabloko tended to fare better in the larger towns, particularly in Perm city where together they picked up roughly 40–5 per cent of the vote; in the smaller towns and rural areas they could muster no more than 20–30 per cent. The Liberal Democrats fairly consistently pulled in 11–14 per cent, with a high of 19 per cent in Perm-76, the local garrison, and the Women of Russia ran strongly throughout.

In Tomsk the party results produced a major shock. The results put the

[98] I exclude the Komi–Permiak constituency.   [99] Podvintsev, 'Report'.

Liberal Democrats just ahead of Russia's Choice with 21 per cent to 20 per cent of the vote, Yabloko received 10 per cent, the Communist Party 10 per cent, the Women of Russia 8 per cent, and PRES 5 per cent. The LDP vote shattered any ideas of an electorate divided between the democrats and the Communists. Although the combined democrat vote looked more respectable, neither they nor the Communists could take much comfort from the result. Was this a protest vote against those who had dominated Tomsk politics for the past three years? Had all the debates, hard-won decisions, and open politics not meant anything to those who voted for the LDP and those who simply stayed away?[100]

In both Perm and Tomsk those strongly identified with the democrats, with the exception of Sulakshin, fared badly. In Tomsk Kress came out an easy leader for the Council of the Federation, and Filimonov a good second. None of the democrats came anywhere close. If one of them had stood instead of four and, if the electorate had voted along political lines, a democrat might have beaten Filimonov for second place. In Perm the Russia's Choice label failed to help Kuznetsov. Although the results were very close, Zelenkin topped the poll for the Council of Federation, and Levitan, the young businessman, took the second seat.[101] Whatever else the returns indicated, they suggested a marked lack of enthusiasm among the Perm electorate for their chief administrator. Somehow Kress had managed to acquire a reputation, but Kuznetsov had not.[102]

The lack of any correlation between party vote and that for candidates showed up even more clearly in the returns to the single-member constituencies. In Perm each of the four constituencies produced a clear winner but not because of their party affiliation. M. Putilov, a collective-farm chairman, officially a Civic Union candidate (although closer to the Agrarian Party) and backed by the left-patriotic bloc, won his rural constituency comfortably although neither the Civic Union nor the Agrarian Party vote correlated with that for him. V. Zelenin, professor, soviet deputy, and Communist Party member, won one of the Perm city constituencies (defeating the deputy director of a commercial bank) with

---

[100] We should bear in mind that only 39 per cent of the electorate voted for the party list. The results were reported in the local press as percentages of the whole electorate (to soften their impact) whereas in most places they were given as percentages of the vote cast. I have recalculated them, approximately, to make them comparable with those for other regions.

[101] Official electoral returns. The most complete published data are in *Zvezda*, 16 December 1993, p. 1.

[102] All seven district administrators of Perm city felt sufficiently emboldened to publish a critical open letter to Kuznetsov in February 1994 (*Zvezda*, 8 February 1994, p. 1), and his position in the new monthly *Reiting* carried out by *Zvezda* came way below many others: 15 February 1994, p. 1; 11 May 1994, p. 1, has Trutnev, director of EKS Ltd, leading.

25 per cent of the vote, although here Russia's Choice had polled 40 per cent to the Communist Party's 6 per cent. The other Perm city constituency was won by the Russia's Choice candidate, V. Pomelkhin, director of a private research institute, but the remaining seat went to an outsider, defeating both the democratic and Communist candidates (who did miserably) and the young director of the Stock Exchange. Here too the more outspoken democrats failed to attract a following.

The December results had revealed little that could help aspiring candidates except that party labels did little, and a reputation as a radical democratic activist even less. The electorate's behaviour was unpredictable. How could it be otherwise in Perm, one might ask? No key issue had been put before the electorate, the only ideological positions came from the radical democrats and the Communists – and neither was popular – and the majority of candidates, if they expressed their views, barely differed from one another. They tended to argue that the task of the Duma must be 'to act as a stabilizer, to guarantee stability, to agree the interests of different groups in the population'.[103] Zelenin, from the Communists and more ideological than most, argued that the Duma must be 'a legislative organ, and not a political one or it loses its rationale'; the government should 'concern itself with economics, and not politics, and with the producing of laws', while the president 'the father of the nation', should stand above and, 'during the present transitional period, actively intervene to achieve reconciliation between the conflicting sides'. On what basis then could one expect a voter to choose between candidates, even supposing he or she knew anything about them?

But much the same seemed to be at work in Tomsk. Although Bauer and Sulakshin won their seats quite comfortably, was it so clear that this was a democratic vote, and why had the Communists failed to make a showing? Their spokesman, Yachmenev, came fourth, and Tirskii, the democratic activist, polled very few votes in the urban constituency. Sulakshin's nearest contender was Zhvachkin; the advocate of strong government, Shamin from the soviet, came third.[104] Ideological politics seemed out of favour. The population cast their votes for the chief administrator, the most powerful director in the region, a dynamic and erratic popular politician, and a deputy chief administrator with a reputation for fairness and effective leadership.

V. Zotin, the leader of DemRossia in Perm, suggested that the democrats should recognize that they had had nothing to offer the people, and think

---

[103] Quotations taken from candidate survey; see details in appendix 4, pp. 327–8.
[104] The Tomsk press reporting of the results was poor. See *Nar. trib.*, 18, 23 December 1993, p. 1; and Pogodaev, 'Tomsk', December 1993, for the details.

again before participating in the local elections.[105] However, in the spring, he and a handful of other democrats stood for both regional and city assemblies. The left-patriot bloc, nothing daunted, fielded a candidate in nearly every constituency. Their leaflet spoke of:

the destruction of our native, Russian [*Rossiiskii*] way of life, the imposition of American ways and religion, alien to Russia, the destruction of the spiritual aspect of Russian life – the propaganda of a cult of envy and force, speculation, pornography, the almost legal creation of a network of brothels, the open entrapment of girls into prostitution (with the connivance of the administration, procuracy, and Internal Affairs department), the destruction of one of the best education systems in the world (as recognized, incidentally, by the American president, Clinton).

But this kind of language had nothing like the resonance in Perm that it did in Krasnodar. Kaliagin hesitated and, at the last moment put out a Russia's Choice list that included such administration candidates as Sapiro and Fil, the mayor. Here we see the dilemma facing a president's representative who had no personal or political following: either join forces with the unpopular minority of opposition democrats, critical of an administration that had, in their eyes, sold out to the old establishment, or link up with the administration. Two new groups fielded candidates; one, called Region, led by Levitan, riding high on his recent election to the Federal Council, and consisting largely of energetic ex-deputies and members of the business community, advertised themselves as being above party and supporters of the regional interest.[106] Rather more surprisingly *Zvezda* itself put forward four members of the paper's staff and gave them heavy coverage.[107] Most candidates, however, stood as independents, in particular, the new businessmen and district administrators. Bankers and entrepreneurs were well represented. Teachers, lawyers, and doctors featured, but relatively few industrial directors and farm chairmen. Ex-party officials stood (twelve of those who had been members of the obkom or gorkom in 1988) and twenty deputies sought re-election.[108]

In Tomsk, too, those who had stood as Russia's Choice candidates in December, nothing daunted, put together a slate, including three well-known democrats, for the local elections. Sulakshin's organization, Solidarity and Reform, participated as a separate group. His candidates were described by his opponents as 'a nomenklatura bloc of administrators and directors'. The Communists formed a group, For Labour and

---

[105] *Zvezda*, 25 December 1993, p. 1.
[106] See *Zvezda*, 15 March 1993, pp. 2–3, for their big spread.
[107] See, e.g., 18 March 1994, p. 2.
[108] *Zvezda*, 26 February 1994, p. 2. Laptev, obkom secretary for agriculture (but an independent in 1994), and Khlebnikov, chair of the city soviet, both from the 1988 obkom, won their seats.

Justice, in which the Agrarian Party participated, as did the trade union federation. Roughly 30 per cent of the electorate voted, and almost all the seats were filled. Of the political groupings only one, Solidarity and Reform, could claim any success: five of its candidates went through, four of them industrial directors or entrepreneurs, and the last the chairman of the labour collective at the chemicals plant where the explosion had occurred in April. Russia's Choice obtained only a single seat, and that was won by the one district administrator among their candidates. The Communists got two, the Agrarians two – directors of agricultural enterprises – and the trade union candidate, the general director of shareholding company, Tomskenergo, won a seat. The administrator of Tomsk went through, as did three other district administrators. The new Duma was dominated by economic managers (nine) and government administrators (five). There was one academic and one journalist but, as *Narodnaia tribuna* noted with relief, no 'pure politicians'. The opening session revealed that, despite careful preparatory work by the organizing committee, it took three votes before the Solidarity and Reform candidate, the director of a construction company, could win the chair. It looked, the paper commented, as though there were going to be urban–rural disagreements, and also possibly a directors' lobby versus the rest.[109]

And in Perm? Turnout was officially declared at over thirty per cent,[110] and the results essentially reaffirmed those of December. Party or even group affiliation did not help. A known name seemed to improve a candidate's chances. Zotin himself won a seat to both regional assembly and city duma but democrats and the Communists did poorly.[111] The left-patriots won five seats in the regional assembly (Bystriantsev was one of the victors) and three in the city duma. Both Sapiro and Fil, from the administration, were elected, along with five other Russia's Choice candidates. The Region group made no impact and Levitan, who had defeated Kuznetsov for the prestigious Council of the Federation seat, failed to get the miserly percentage needed to win a local seat. (The same was to happen, as we shall see, in St Petersburg.) None of the *Zvezda* candidates

---

[109] The town duma looked rather different: ten women among the eighteen, five deputies from medical institutions, six in education, two entrepreneurs. Seven of the candidates had been supported by the communist bloc or the trade union federation. Russia's Choice won not a single seat: *Kr. znamia*, 3 February 1994, p. 1; 2, 24, 29, 30 March 1994, p. 1; 16 April 1994, p. 1.

[110] Apart from in three districts where it fell below the required 25 per cent. The returns in one district were declared invalid but most assumed that in general the returns were inflated, and infringements fairly common. See *Zvezda*, 1 March 1993, pp. 1–2, for complete list of candidates; *Vech. Perm*, 5 April 1994, for the city duma; Podvintsev, 'Report'.

[111] The newly founded LDP, whose leader A. Chulkov made extravagant claims after the December elections, failed to find followers: *Zvezda*, 18 January 1993, p. 1.

won a seat. Trutnev, young director of the retail chain, EKS Ltd, and two of his associates, who had canvassed heavily, however, went through.[112] The result was a regional assembly dominated by former Communist Party supporters, many from rural districts on the one hand and representatives of the administration and new entrepreneurs on the other. As in Tomsk, a new business contingent had arrived, to compete for power with the administration and the rural elite.

The new assembly elected Sapiro as its chair, and he appointed Deviatkin (with twenty-five years' experience as a district soviet and party administrator behind him) as his deputy.[113] For the past three years Igumnov and Sapiro had worked together as Kuznetsov's deputy administrators. Now Igumnov was priming himself to step into Kuznetsov's shoes, and his colleague Sapiro moved over to lead the legislative body. Administration and assembly could work in tandem together again, and in the future. But some things had changed. Trutnev, the young ex-Komsomol entrepreneur, argued that power was beginning to move away from those who used to wield it, and demonstrated what he meant. The assembly set up four committees, with Trutnev getting the chair of economic and tax policy and another EKS Ltd employee, S. Chikulaev, the chair of the property commission in the city duma. Following his election, Trutnev moved fast to propose, and get passed by the assembly, a reduction in the level of taxation on business; the administration, and Sapiro, were caught unprepared and failed in their attempt to stop the measure going through.[114] Perhaps a new kind of politics was on the agenda.

How should we characterize it? Semi-state corporatist is not a bad description. The state element was still very strong, and business interests had entered the political arena, but the unions were absent. Labour's voice was crippled, given the choice between the fading Communists or the patriots. This outcome seems unsurprising in Perm, given the compact, pragmatic elite, and the new policy of privatization. We would

[112] *Zvezda*, 1, 5, 15, 23 March 1994, p. 1; N. Filippov and N. Andreev, *Zakonodatel'noe sobranie Permskoi oblasti* (Perm, 1994). Only one woman was elected to the assembly, and one to the city duma. Eleven of the fourteen duma seats were filled: Trutnev and Zotin sat on both. Four patriots went through (three low-level management officials and a schoolteacher); the remainder were all independents – two from EKS Ltd, a doctor, a director of a construction company, two from the banking sector, and one (a woman) from a charitable organization (electoral returns). According to its constitution, drawn up by the regional authorities, the duma was to be chaired by the mayor (appointed by the chief administrator) but its members voted to have a chair instead, and voted in Bezfamilnyi, a banker.

[113] He received twenty-one votes to Bystriantsev's eight, and Khlebnikov's four. See *Zvezda*, 30 March 1994, p. 1; 2, 5, 6 April 1994, p. 1, for the politicking and votes; see 8 April 1994 for Bystriantsev's comment that he was happy to see Sapiro, with his experience in the administration, as chair; see 5 May 1994, p. 1, for Deviatkin.

[114] *Zvezda*, 12 March 1993, pp. 1–2; 25, 29 March 1994, p. 1; 8, 15, 23 April 1994, p. 1.

not have expected ideological parties or deep political divisions in this community. 'Politics' was a matter for 'them', above; either one went along with what was expected or, at most, from the safety of the voting booth one voted against an unpopular leader. And the choices on offer, to those who wished to make a choice, were largely institutional (for the administration or against) or for individuals who declared themselves to be opponents of strongly held political positions.

In Tomsk, in contrast, there was an ongoing debate, and there were active political organizations which influenced decisions taken by the authorities. Yet the outcome was very similar. It seems that the very real open politics had failed to involve a substantial part of the community. Many remained as alienated from these 'elite' activities as their counterparts in Perm. What of those who were involved in politics? Could we say that what we saw in Tomsk, in the aftermath of communist party rule, was competition between the democrats, the champions of pluralist politics, and the 'statists' – a fair battle – and the democrats lost? Those who did vote voted them out. But why did they fare so badly? Was it that the policies with which they were associated – privatization, in particular – had failed to create a voting constituency, while giving birth to new corporate business interests? Or was it that they had shown themselves to be hopelessly divided? Tomsk suggests that both new and old ideological parties found it difficult to survive in the post-communist environment, and this is something I shall take up in the final chapter. The Tomsk democrats themselves would have pointed to another factor. The administration remained in the hands of Kress, a representative of the nomenklatura, who ruled through his own people and who, in October 1993, acted, as might be expected from a raikom secretary, to reassert executive power. The democrats remained at a disadvantage. If, in Perm, a united elite succeeded fairly quickly in welding the separate structures together, in Tomsk it required an ex-party secretary, a presidential decree, and the electorate's help. Surely, then, it would be different in St Petersburg?

7 St Petersburg: a democratic alternative?

The sheer importance of St Petersburg, economically, culturally, and politically, distinguishes it from all other Russian cities (except Moscow) in two respects. First, it has always enjoyed a unique status vis-à-vis the central government and, despite its dependence, has always been anxious to assert its independence. For this reason I shall not dwell on the St Petersburg–central government relationship: it was too different from that of our other regions. Secondly, the city's overshadowing of the surrounding region in terms of population and economic significance made for an unusual city–region relationship. Although until 1990, when obkom and gorkom were merged, the party structures followed the normal pattern with the obkom overseeing activities in region and city, the city soviet was not subordinate to the oblast soviet; instead, it had the status of an oblast soviet. Relations between city and regional authorities were therefore quite different from those in Krasnodar, Perm, or Tomsk. The focus of our attention is the city, renamed St Petersburg in 1991, with a population of over four million, equivalent in status and importance to a region, and recognized as such in the Federal Treaty.

If, in all our regions (except partially in Tomsk), the rules of the game introduced after August 1991 were a Moscow invention, imposed or introduced into hostile or sceptical environments, this was not so in St Petersburg. Here the city's own reforming politicians, elected with a sizeable popular mandate, had already put new structures in place. They had believed it important to separate executive and legislative functions, to provide for checks and balances, and for constitutional safeguards. The city's leaders shared a belief in the importance of economic reform and privatization. The new Yeltsin government was their government. Here then was the most auspicious environment for new structures of democratic government to shape relationships both within the elite and between elite and people. Yet, by the end of 1993, after continual conflict between the mayor's office and the soviet, the soviet had been dissolved and, for nearly a year, the city was without a representative assembly, ruled simply by its mayor. Fewer than 20 per cent of the citizens had turned out to vote for a new city assembly. The press was still lively and independent, but the citizens were apathetic. Political parties were no more in evidence here than elsewhere, although a new kind of lobby politics had emerged, focused round the mayor's office.

In our other regions the re-establishment of executive dominance can be attributed to the continuation of old practices by incumbent politicians, by the weakness of a democratic opposition, or by presidential moves against the soviets. Such explanations will not do for St Petersburg. Government policies may have played their part in weakening support for a 'democratic soviet' associated with the new course, but in St Petersburg executive dominance emerged despite a city leadership committed to new ways, and before presidential intervention. Here too an even more politicized and divided community than Tomsk failed to produce organizations that could command popular support.

The similarity between developments in St Petersburg and those at federal level suggests a complex set of factors at work, one which could include the new institutional rules themselves. Relationships at the centre were even more complex, and the conflicts sharper – those involved had more resources and more to lose – but similar patterns of behaviour can be observed. St Petersburg was not a microcosm of the federal centre but developments in the city help us to identify those factors which, even given willing actors, worked against the strengthening of representative institutions. I focus on two areas of activity, both crucial to the working of a democratic order, and where problems arose. First I consider the endeavours of the new rulers to create a workable legislative–executive relationship, then I look at the attempts to create new intermediary institutions to link society with its elected rulers. A brief profile of the city, including the developments that led to the election of a democratic city soviet and mayor, sets the scene.

St Petersburg, traditionally considered the most westernized of Russian cities, was founded by Peter the Great in 1703. Built at enormous cost in the marshes of the Finnish Gulf, with its port linking it to Europe, and its palaces and streets designed by western architects, the new imperial capital was intended to wrench Russia westwards, away from the conservatism of old Russia that emanated from Moscow. Although it lacked a natural resource base, the city became the country's leading industrial centre and, by virtue of being the capital, the centre of culture and science. In 1917 its citizens led the way first in bringing down the tsar and then in supporting the Bolsheviks. With the move of the capital to Moscow in 1918 St Petersburg's pre-eminence was ended but, throughout the Soviet period and, despite the devastating impact of the siege of Leningrad in the Second World War, the city retained its importance as

Russia's 'northern capital', an industrial and cultural magnet that drew people and resources from all over the Union. Because of its potential as a political rival, Leningrad's relationship with the central authorities in Moscow was always an uneasy one. The Brezhnev period witnessed the expansion of its huge industrial plants and network of research institutes, ever more closely tied to the defence sector (which employed, depending on definition, one-half to two-thirds of the labour force), but a shrinking of the central allocation of investment for the municipal economy. Leningrad politicians were not appointed to leading central posts, resulting in little turnover of the party and soviet elite. Meanwhile the cultural and educational institutions continued to replenish the ranks of the city's professional intelligentsia.

By the mid-1980s the consequences of damaging policies were becoming ever more apparent. The building of a dam which had disastrous ecological consequences contributed to the pollution of the water supply; the concentration of resources in the defence sector led to the deterioration of the physical and social infrastructure of the city (the transport network, roads, buildings, and educational and health facilities), and the stifling of innovation, both technological and cultural, and political repression brought isolation and backwardness. While the city authorities could claim, with some justification, that responsibility for all key decisions lay with the central government, not with them, and that Leningrad continually subsidized the central budget, there is little evidence of any effort on their part to alter the course.[1] Leningrad politics during the perestroika years until and including August 1991 have been widely reviewed.[2] I concentrate here on those aspects which distinguish the city

[1] For background on the city in the 1980s, see B. Ruble, *Leningrad* (Berkeley: University of California Press, 1990); 'Konceptciia razvitiia leningradskogo raiona v usloviakh radikal'noi reformy', working paper, Leningrad, FBT Leningradskaia, 23 March 1990.

[2] See McAuley, 'Politics, Economics'; V. Gel'man and M. McAuley, 'The Politics of City Government: Leningrad/St Petersburg, 1990–1992', in T. Friedgut and J. Hahn (eds.), *Local Power and Post-Soviet Politics* (New York: M. E. Sharpe, 1994), pp. 15–42. Where not otherwise noted, references can be found in these two articles. Further works include 'Obshchestvennye dvizheniia i stanovlenie novoi vlasti v Leningrade (1986–1991): predvaritel'nye materialy', unpublished working paper, Sector of the Sociology of Social Movements, Institute of Sociology, RAN, St Petersburg, 1991; V. Kostiushev (ed.), *Sotsiologiia obshchestvennykh dvizhenii: empiricheskie nabliudeniia, issledovaniia*, 2 vols. (St Petersburg, 1993), especially the contributions by E. Zdravomyslova, pp. 110–31, N. Kornev, pp. 154–81, and V. Gel'man, pp. 182–214.; A. Duka, N. Kornev, V. Voronkov, and E. Zdravomyslova, 'The Case of Leningrad', *International Sociology*, 10 (1995), pp. 83–99; P. Duncan, 'The Return of St Petersburg', in G. Hosking, J. Aves, and Duncan (eds.), *The Road to Post-Communism* (London: Pinter, 1992), pp. 121–37; R. Orttung, 'St Petersburg: Economic Reform and Democratic Institutions', *RFE/RL Research Reports*, I, 1992, and his more recent *From Leningrad to St Petersburg: Democratization in a Russian City* (Basingstoke: Macmillan, 1995); J. Andrews and A. Vacroux, 'Political Change in Leningrad: The Elections of 1990', in Friedgut and Hahn, *Local Power*, pp. 43–72.

from our other regions and which are important for the understanding of subsequent developments.

As in Tomsk, conflict between the soviet and its executive committee emerged before August 1991, but in Leningrad it was not rooted in political and policy disagreements, and it led to the redesigning of city government itself. Political activism was far more widespread here than in any of the other regions. Popular discontent with the ever-worsening conditions of everyday life and the identification of the apparatus with privilege, corruption, and political repression laid the basis for the party's electoral defeats in 1989. In 1990 the willingness of members of the city's professional and technical intelligentsia to take the opportunity offered by glasnost to fight for access to the media, to organize, and to challenge the apparatus resulted in a resounding democratic victory in 1990. The existence of a city party organization whose membership and apparatus produced both conservatives and democrats willing to do open battle with each other was relevant too. Here there was a parallel with Tomsk. During 1988–90 informal organizations, representing a wide range of political views, had emerged, unofficial journals and broadsheets had multiplied, and sections of the city's press had become increasingly radical and outspoken in favour of furthering the reform process. By 1990 both the People's Front, a loosely organized association embracing most of the democratic activists in the city (many of them reform-minded Communist Party members), the conservative nomenklatura, and the recently formed patriot organizations were anxious to participate in the elections. Democratic Elections-90, an offshoot of the People's Front, identified and publicized democratic candidates, offered rudimentary support, and warned electors against nomenklatura candidates. In turn a United Council of Russia supported the patriotic candidates who aimed at recreating a powerful Russian nation and described the People's Front as being composed of 'denationalized intellectuals who all lived well during the period of stagnation'. In all 2,500 gained nomination for the 400 seats. The campaign became tense with fears that the authorities were trying to foment clashes between democrats and patriots to create an excuse to halt the reform process, and disagreements over tactics divided the democratic camp. The democrats managed, however, to hold together and produced a list of Democratic Elections-90 candidates which *Smena* (the Komsomol newspaper, which had turned radical) published a few days before the election, followed by a second list for the run-offs.

Of the 400 seats in the Leningrad city soviet, 240 were won by candidates supported by the Democratic bloc. The patriots, with 5 per cent of the vote, picked up only two; the United Workers' Front and 'private entrepreneurs' won four seats each; the industrial lobby had its representatives (in the person of powerful directors), as did the police and military. The party apparatus was almost entirely absent, although more than twenty of the deputies were members of the obkom or of raikoms. Sixty percent of the deputies, including some of the leading democrats, were party members but only a third of them could be counted on to support the official party line.[3] In April 1990, therefore, the city had a soviet in which a democratic majority, its legitimacy established by the ballot box, faced a demoralized party opposition and set out to remedy the city's ills. By the time of the attempted putsch in August 1991 Lensoviet, as it was known, had, however, achieved very little and had lost the confidence of the majority of the city's population.

The soviet's initial ineffectiveness should not surprise us. Given the dependence of the city upon the federal authorities, its scope for action was severely limited. In February 1991, faced with a critical food situation, ever-worsening city services, and plummeting popularity,[4] Lensoviet laid part of the blame on its executive committee's failure to take preventive measures and on its own preoccupation with long-term plans rather than with immediate problems. It noted, however, that 'the crisis in the city's economy is the result, to a significant degree, of the general political and economic crisis in the USSR'.[5] This was only too true. There was little either soviet or executive committee could do to remedy this until the struggle for power between the Russian and the Union authorities was resolved. As in all the regions the main policy guidelines and the major part of the city's budget were determined in Moscow. Seventy percent of the budget came from federal allocations. Key institutions, such as the police, the KGB, and the procuracy came under Union jurisdiction, and much of Leningrad industry was controlled by the Union ministries. None of this changed with the 1990 elections.

Although under the old system any key decisions were taken in Smolny, the Leningrad party headquarters, a fairly clear division of responsibilities for city affairs existed. While the party oversaw personnel

---

[3] B. Gidaspov, the obkom secretary, requested a meeting of the Communist Party fraction but was rebuffed. The democrats also swept home in the seats for the Russian Parliament, winning twenty-five out of thirty-three; see McAuley, 'Politics, Economics', for more details.

[4] Only 23 per cent of the respondents to a telephone survey, conducted in February 1991, expressed any confidence in the soviet (*Len. pravda*, 20 February 1991, p. 2), but no more than 20 per cent were in favour of its resignation (*Smena*, 19 February 1991, p. 2).

[5] 'O prognoze i vazhneishikh pokazateliiakh plana kompleksnogo ekonomicheskogo i sotsial'nogo razvitiia Leningrada na 1991 goda . . . ', *Reshenie Leningradskogo gorodskogo soveta*, 26 February 1991, no. 12; *Vestnik Lensoveta*, 1 (1991), pp. 14–15.

appointments in all spheres and the means of communication and propaganda, the executive committee of the soviet was responsible for the financial and practical aspects of city administration. Management of the military-industrial complex belonged to the directors. Security lay in Moscow's hands, but the telephone lines linked up to Smolny. Following its electoral defeat the obkom continued to oversee a reduced party apparatus from Smolny. Although its buro had lost control over the city's policy agenda, and over the means of mass communication and appointments, the law enforcement agencies and the garrison still reported directly to Smolny, and the informal links between leading soviet and party officials were as strong as ever. The corridors might be empty but Smolny was still there, a shadow government which, through its connections, still exerted influence over city affairs. But times had certainly changed. In November 1990 the soviet voted to replace G. Voshchinin, the ex-party-apparatus police chief, with a professional policeman, A. Kramarev, and succeeded despite opposition from the obkom, the Union Ministry of Internal Affairs, and from A. Sobchak, its own chair. Both sides argued their case forcefully in the local press. But the victory of the soviet was a consequence of the Russian minister of internal affairs' control over regional appointments at a time when the Russian ministries were flexing their muscles against the Union leadership. When, in the spring of 1994, Sobchak wished to dismiss Kramarev he succeeded all too easily, given that he had support from on high.[6] Here we see an early example of what was to become a common practice – the turning to patrons at the centre for support in struggles with opponents at local level. In 1990–1 the existence of Union and Russian governments encouraged the practice but it did not disappear together with the USSR.

Traditionally the soviet had been a largely decorative institution among whose deputies it was not uncommon to find permanent city officials. Its commissions were meant to oversee the work of the executive committee departments, but in fact they did little. The new democratic deputies, in contrast, saw their job to be a full-time one. They, as the representatives of the people, would be the policy-makers and the executive would be the servant of the people. In 1990 when the new city soviet was elected, the executive committee was chaired by V. Khodyrev (who also chaired the soviet). He was flanked by three first deputy chairs, six deputy chairs, and a further twelve members of the executive committee. The chair and his deputies, and the secretary, each had their own secretariat. The executive

---

[6] Gel′man and McAuley, 'Politics of City Government'; for further discussion, see below, p. 238, n. 11.

was served by a number of service departments (organization, personnel, legal) and oversaw a complex structure of main administrations, administrations, committees, and associations, with a staff of perhaps 2,000. This small army of officialdom occupied the rabbit-warren of buildings stretching back from the Mariinskii Palace, seat of the soviet, spilt over into buildings in the neighbouring streets, and into offices scattered across the city. The executive committee was concerned primarily with the maintenance of city services and the administration of existing programmes, but also with the devising of policy proposals and drawing up the budget for the city. Its activity was heavily concentrated on managing the city's physical resources – roads, housing repair, building maintenance, transport (although culture and education featured too) – whereas communal services, social security, and the environment occupied a lowly place. Its key body was the planning commission, headed by A. Bolshakov, with an array of departments responsible for everything from city planning to transport, construction materials, and foreign links, and a staff of 350.[7]

As was customary, Khodyrev invited the newly elected deputies to a meeting to set up an organizing committee to draw up the new soviet's agenda. The series of meetings required before agreement could be reached were an early indication of the deputies' difficulty in finding consensus among themselves, and of the inability of soviet and executive committee to work together. The election of the chair of Lensoviet proved even more contentious. After weeks of stalemate the deputies turned to Anatolii Sobchak, a Leningrad university law professor and popular USSR deputy. By winning a by-election, he became eligible, and was elected as chair by a two-thirds majority. From the executive's point of view the soviet was a quarrelsome, fractious body with which it was difficult to deal. The deputies, in their turn, were deeply distrustful of Khodyrev and his staff of officials, and convinced that the executive, whoever staffed it, should simply execute soviet decisions. Such a view was shared by Sobchak, but in his view it should execute *his* decisions. Faced with this novel situation, the executive committee simply marked time. Khodyrev did nothing. By June 20 per cent of the officials (but fewer among the top administrators) had left. Those who remained were no less hostile than those who resigned to what they considered to be politically undesirable and amateurish deputies, most of whom had very little

---

[7] These were separate from the administrations or committees which existed in many of these areas, and presumably coordinated their activity with those in the planning commission: *Leningradskii gorsovet narodnykh deputatov, ispolnitel'nyi komitet: spisok telefonov*, Leningrad, 1989; interviews with deputies, April and September 1990, and with Shchelkanov, November 1992.

knowledge of how the city was run or of how a city might be run. In the eyes of the deputies and Sobchak (for once in agreement), the officials not only stood in the way of change but were poor administrators. In mid-June the soviet elected A. Shchelkanov, another popular USSR deputy, as the chair of the executive committee, and he began the slow process of recruiting a new team of top administrators, while the departments again began to prepare policy documents. The planning commission had its staff cut by more than half but, for the time being, A. Bolshakov remained in office with responsibility for preparing the budget.

The continued conflict between soviet and the executive committee owed something to a personality clash between Sobchak and Shchelkanov. There was also the incompatibility of Sobchak's interventionist presidential style of decision-making (and his impatience with any checks or attempts to control his actions) with Shchelkanov's wish to see rules of behaviour established and observed. But the conflict also had institutional roots. The deputies, while objecting to Sobchak's approach, wished to exercise control over an apparatus of officials who, they had every reason to fear, administered resources in their own interests. According to Shchelkanov, the deputies strove to take decisions great and small and to limit the officials' functions to the most unrewarding and menial tasks. Officials responded by simply not executing soviet decisions, and the soviet's only recourse was to propose their dismissal, hardly desirable at a time when Shchelkanov was involved in trying to recruit a new team.[8] The situation was further exacerbated by the inability of the new and old members of the executive committee to act together as a collegial organ. By the spring of 1991, Shchelkanov, convinced that existing arrangements were unworkable, put forward the first proposals for a new structure of city government which would include a mayor, separate from the soviet. This was the solution that was adopted, not without conflict, in early summer.

The new institutional arrangements included a popularly elected mayor, heading a city administration, and a city council with control over the budget and policy. Legislative proposals could come from either the mayor's office or the city council. These arrangements provided a partial blueprint for the federal authorities to bequeath to other regional authorities, with the difference that in the regions the chief administrator, at least initially, was appointed by the president. They were also very similar to those between the federal institutions, at central level, although here presidential power was greater.

Following Sobchak's election, with a handsome 66 per cent of the vote,

---

[8] A. Duka, 'Formirovanie novoi lokal'noi politicheskoi elity – na primere Leningrad/St Peterburga', unpublished ms., 1995, p. 12, suggests that 30 per cent of the top and middle-level officials had left by this time.

Shchelkanov left office. Now, it was hoped, administration and soviet could develop a working relationship. It was noticeable, however, that although the talk was of a separation of powers the soviet's concern throughout had been to subordinate the executive to its control and, even before becoming mayor, Sobchak had been anxious to strengthen mayoral rights. In May 1991 he succeeded in obtaining a ruling from the praesidium of the Supreme Soviet which, while it left the structure of the soviet and its control over the budget unchanged, gave the mayor the right to appoint the heads of the city administration. Following his election, he suggested further reducing the role of the soviet. The deputies responded by submitting a proposal to the Supreme Soviet that would have given the soviet the right to confirm appointments and administrative structures. The Supreme Soviet confirmed its original ruling, in its essentials, including the soviet's right to determine its own structure, but suggested that some internal reorganization might be helpful. The soviet had, in the meantime, already voted to streamline its activities and had elected A. Beliaev, a 37-year-old economics lecturer and middle-of-the-road supporter of DemRossia, as its chair. Sobchak subsequently attempted, again, to reduce the role of the soviet but, until it was dissolved in December 1993, the deputies retained the right to vote on the budget, to pass city legislation, and to determine their own structures.

We shall look at the way the relationship between mayor's office and soviet developed between 1991 and 1993 in the following chapter. Here it is important to note that, although, by the time of the attempted putsch in August, new structures, signalling a separation of powers, were in place, there were already indications that neither side was happy with the arrangements.[9]

As in Krasnodar, in August 1991 both supporters and opponents of the GKChP among the city's rulers and activists were prepared to declare themselves. General Samsonov, the military commander, formed a local emergency committee as required by the GKChP, and appeared on

---

[9] One issue on which they did see eye to eye was oversight of the district soviets, the sub-unit in local government. The conflict in Perm between oblast and city soviet – over property and taxation – repeated itself in Leningrad between city and district soviets. Lensoviet was convinced that property would be distributed unscrupulously by district officialdom; Sobchak too did not hesitate to make it known that he considered the district soviets an unnecessary link in the city structure. In early 1991 Lensoviet took the initial step of claiming jurisdiction over land, housing, and non-residential property, while leaving for the districts a share of the administration; when this was followed by the appointment of heads of the district administration by the mayor, the district soviets were rendered largely redundant. They still adopted the budget, but this was little more than a formality. All that remained was the right of passing a vote of no confidence in the head of the district administration, but the mayor was not obliged to make a replacement. For more details, see Gel'man and McAuley, 'Politics of City Government'.

television. The soviet assembled on the 19th and, almost unanimously, declared its unqualified opposition to the putsch. Sobchak returned to the city by midday, immediately confronted the committee, spoke from the Mariinskii Palace balcony and by evening had made his famous television attack on 'the former ministers'. Although, without doubt, his qualities of leadership, dynamism, and considerable oratorical skills were crucial, the actions of those in charge of law and order and of the media were no less so. It is revealing that it was evening before the soviet managed to gain access to television or lift the censorship of the press: those most 'reconstructed' institutions proved easily controllable. Journalists had to resort to running off broadsheets and handing them out on street corners. In contrast Kramarev, the police chief, refused to carry out Samsonov's orders on preventing street demonstrations, and sided openly with the soviet, while the KGB adopted a neutral position. This allowed individuals or institutions to take up positions, and reactions were indicative of power and ideological orientation.

Enterprise management proved able to counter any spontaneous protests from its labour force and, in the defence plants under Union jurisdiction, tended to act in this way. The new entrepreneurs, in contrast, were among the most active in offering financial and other aid to Lensoviet. B. Gidaspov, the obkom secretary, participated in the emergency committee but failed to give a clear lead to the Communist Party, which proved itself incapable of independent action. Although a survey, and the large meeting of the 20th in Palace Square, suggested overwhelming disapproval of the GKChP among the population, those prepared to take an active part in protests were limited to the original democratic activists, now joined by some youthful supporters. It was they who responded to the call at midnight of the 20th for able-bodied men to come to defend the Mariinskii Palace. If, therefore, one had to identify one action as the most significant in determining activities within the city, it would be Kramarev's stance against the GKChP. It allowed the expression of protest (whether the small demonstrations of the 19th or the huge meeting of the 20th) and thus undermined Samsonov's confidence that the situation could be controlled without bloodshed. From all accounts this factor weighed the most heavily with him. It resulted in his keeping the troops out of the city, and influenced his relationship with the leaders of the putsch (and their future behaviour). By the morning of 21 August the danger was over, and the democrats could celebrate.[10]

The most immediate consequences of the putsch were the disappear-

[10] A. Veretin, N. Miloserdova, and G. Petrov (eds.), *Protivostoianie* (St Petersburg, 1992), for the most complete documentary account; see also A. Sobchak, *Khozhdenie vo vlast'*, 2nd edn (St Petersburg, 1992).

ance of the Communist Party, the taking over of its property by the mayor's office and the soviet, and the renaming of the city as St Petersburg.[11] Sobchak moved the mayor's office out of the Mariinskii Palace and into Smolny, remarking that it would be foolish, at least for the time being, not to make use of the technical facilities that Smolny possessed, including the direct lines to all the key agencies. With him went many of those departments which the mayor's office had inherited from the soviet's executive committee. Some of those housed in the buildings near the palace remained where they were. Some of the Smolny staff lost their jobs; others became part of the new mayoral administration. The soviet, renamed Petrosoviet, remained in the Mariinskii Palace.[12] DemRossia, together with other democratic organizations, acquired a raikom building. Sobchak took over *Leningradskaia pravda*, the party newspaper, claiming that it was normal practice for a mayor's office to have its newspaper, and renamed it *Sankt Peterburgskie vedomosti*. (The soviet had founded its newspaper, *Nevskoe vremia*, earlier in the year. *Smena*, the Komsomol paper, now became wholly independent.)[13] Far more important, however, were the consequences of the changes at federal level. St Petersburg politicians would henceforth be dealing with one central authority, the Russian government, a government which included among its leading members Petersburg activists committed to the introduction of economic reform and privatization, and they could now proceed with a reform agenda.

[11] Although a referendum in June 1991 had gone in favour of 'St Petersburg' by a small majority, this had had no legal force. After the failed putsch, the praesidium of the RSFSR Supreme Soviet, on 6 September 1991, ratified the name change.

[12] In September 1991 Iu. Yarov, chair of the oblast soviet and RF deputy, was appointed as president's representative, but in November he was elected as deputy chair of the Supreme Soviet. Ten months later S. Tsyplaev, a physicist and former USSR deputy, was appointed as president's representative. Although he was a respected individual, the combination of the failure of the office of representative to establish itself as a key one, and the existence, in St Petersburg, of several important political figures, worked against Tsyplaev's playing a significant role in city politics.

[13] *Vechernyi Leningrad*, later *Vechernyi Peterburg*, originally a city soviet, as opposed to an oblast soviet, paper continued under its own collective sponsorship. The organization and fortunes of the city's press deserve a study in themselves but, for reasons of space, I can only touch on key differences between St Petersburg and our other regions.

8   The reassertion of executive power

'Why does one need a parliament at all?', asked *Komsomol'skaia pravda* in October 1993, and gave as the answer:

It works out the laws. And although practice shows that it is quite possible to get by with presidential decrees, all the same it is impossible not to have a parliament, in the West they wouldn't understand . . . What distinguishes the new Parliament, the federal assembly, from the Supreme Soviet? The absence of a Congress. And the fact that the deputies are now simply deputies, not people's deputies.[1]

In different regions of the country soviets had interpreted their powers granted under the law 'On the krai, oblast soviet of people's deputies and the krai, oblast administration', of March 1992, very differently.[2] Some had remained obedient adjuncts to the executive; others, of different political complexions, had asserted themselves. At federal level the Parliament had locked horns with the president and government. Assertion led to conflict with the executive, stalemate at the centre, the closing of the Parliament by force, and the subsequent dissolution of recalcitrant soviets, including Petrosoviet. By the end of 1993, and confirmed in the new constitution, the executive had reasserted itself as the dominant institution in the system. Yet even before this the soviets had lost ground to the executive and none of them, neither the Parliament nor even Petrosoviet, the most professional of the regional soviets, had managed to operate at all effectively as policy-makers, and all had lost any base of popular support. The two questions I address here are, firstly, the nature of and the reasons for the conflict between executive and soviet and, secondly, the soviets' failure to become effective and popular legislatures. St Petersburg is the case study but developments there shed light on those at the centre.

---

[1] *Komsom. pravda*, 29 October 1993, p. 1.
[2] The law had given soviets wide-ranging powers: the administration could only disburse property and finances within the limits and according to rules set by the soviet; the soviet had the right to ratify the structure of city administration, and the appointment of certain officers (the chair of the finance committee, the property committee, and the police chief) and to pass a vote of no confidence in the head of the administration and to appeal for his removal both to the president and to the Constitutional Court: *Ross. gaz.*, 20 March 1992, pp. 4–6.

Executive–legislature conflict

A strong, but still disputed, case has been made that a presidential system is prone to conflict between executive and legislature which is difficult to resolve. All too often this results in either a presidential assumption of power, or military intervention, or a breakdown into open violence. Reasons advanced include the existence of two separately elected bodies (president and assembly), each able to claim it represents the people; the fact that disagreement over policy cannot be resolved by changing the head of government (the president) peaceably because he has a fixed term of office; and policy deadlock encouraging a president to try to override the assembly, which responds by attacking the president. It has been suggested that, paradoxically, the system works with less conflict if the president has the backing of a majority party in the assembly, but then the element of checks and balances it was meant to provide is lost.[3] What can the Russian experience contribute to this debate? Here a presidential system, or what has been described as a semi-presidential system (where the prime minister has to have the support of the assembly), was adopted. Here too conflict between Congress and president brought deadlock, broken only by presidential intervention, armed conflict, and the adoption of a constitution tipped heavily in the president's favour. By identifying the factors that produced such an outcome, we should be able to say whether Russian experience bolsters or weakens the argument that constitutional arrangements can make or break the chances of democratic consolidation. This will require us to ask what else might explain institutional conflict and a battle which was won by the executive. Ideological differences? Personalities? Conventions of behaviour, a clash between different interests? If none of these seem relevant in the Russian case, an argument for the structures themselves will gain weight. But even then it would be desirable to demonstrate how the structures produced the conflict and the deadlock.

Perhaps the conflict between president and Parliament that steadily worsened throughout 1993 can be easily explained. Many, on both sides, assumed that it was simply the political ideas and intransigence of the

---

[3] A. Lijphart (ed.), *Parliamentary Versus Presidential Government* (Oxford University Press, 1992), is a good introduction. See J. Linz, 'The Perils of Presidentialism', *Journal of Democracy*, 1 (1990), pp. 51–69; M. Shugart and J. Carey, *Presidents and Assemblies: Constitutional Design and Electoral Dynamics* (Cambridge University Press, 1992); A. Stepan and C. Skach, 'Constitutional Frameworks and Democratic Consolidation: Parliamentarism Versus Presidentialism', *World Politics*, 46 (1993), pp. 1–22; S. Mainwaring, 'Presidentialism, Multipartism, and Democracy', *Comparative Political Studies*, 26 (1993), pp. 198–228; M. Duverger, 'A New Political System Model: Semi-Presidential Government', *European Journal of Political Research*, 8 (1980), pp. 165–87; F. Riggs, 'Conceptual Homogenization of a Heterogenous Field: Presidentialism in Comparative Perspective', in Dogan and Kazancigil, *Comparing Nations*, pp. 72–152; G. O'Donnell, 'Delegative Democracy', *Journal of Democracy*, 5 (1994), pp. 55–69.

opposing side that was responsible. The president's camp saw themselves as the reformers battling against a 'red–brown' alliance of pro-communist nomenklatura and quasi-fascist patriots. The majority in the Congress saw themselves as defending the people and country from disastrous economic policies and an increasingly dictatorial president. But was it ideological differences that made the presidential system unworkable, or was it that the system could not work in an ideologically divided environment because it empowered both sides? Without doubt, at federal level, there was a gulf between the market reformers and the pro-communist opposition, but ideological positions have to be institutionalized to carry weight. The question is whether the institutions allowed or encouraged the political disagreements to become incapable of resolution. It clearly would be inappropriate to hold the federal institutions themselves responsible for creating the ideological divide – the strongest variant of the structural argument – but it may be that they created interests which sought justification in ideological positions.

This is where the experience of St Petersburg is relevant. Here both executive and legislature were controlled by democrats, and both favoured privatization and marketization. Yet the relationship between the two was highly conflictual. If ideological differences were not responsible, which factors were? By identifying them we may be able to see to what extent the institutional arrangements themselves, whether in St Petersburg or at the centre, played a part. I begin by looking at the way the democratic St Petersburg authorities approached privatization in order to show that ideological differences were not responsible for the hostility between mayor's office and soviet.

Privatization and policy disputes

As might be expected from the flagship of free enterprise, the St Petersburg authorities ran one of the most successful privatization campaigns in the country. A. Chubais, the deputy prime minister responsible for privatization, was from St Petersburg, as were P. Filippov and S. Vasil'ev, two leading advocates of privatization at federal level. Both the mayor's office and the soviet were fully behind the Gaidar reforms, and anxious to lead the way. Sobchak spoke of St Petersburg becoming a major international centre of commerce, finance, and tourism; the democratic deputies dreamt of the conversion of the defence industry, the creation of new industry and of a healthy environment, and the city's rebirth as a scientific and cultural centre. A reorganized property committee, KUGI, was set up in the mayor's office, staffed by younger economists and district representatives. It was responsible for drawing up a programme for privatization (to be approved by the soviet) and for

taking decisions on the form privatization was to take and the procedures to be followed. The soviet's role was one of monitoring the
process. The relationship was slightly more complicated than this would
suggest, and the way the process was organized had several consequences unforeseen by either KUGI or the soviet, but both sides supported the privatization programme. The conflicts occurred over
individual cases of privatization or over deals struck by the mayor, on
which the soviet felt it should have been consulted. They were over
implementation rather than principle.[4]

If by the beginning of 1994 the policies of economic reform were
beginning to change the life of the city, the results were far from those that
had been hoped for. Any idea of the city's population benefiting as a
whole had to be relegated to a far distant future. For the great majority of
the city's population the years since 1990 had brought financial hardship,
a fall in the standard of living, and a worsening environment. In the
official reports the years 1990, 1991, and 1992 all qualified as those of
deep crisis. In 1990 food and consumer goods had disappeared from the
shops and markets. In 1991 industrial production began to fall, primarily
in the consumer goods industry. Money incomes doubled, and savings
trebled; food prices also doubled, but goods themselves became scarcer
and scarcer. The city's supplies of basic foodstuffs and soap were down to
20–30 per cent of the previous year's levels, and retail trade fell by one-
half to two-thirds for some items. Crime figures rose by 16 per cent and
the murder rate tripled. By the winter of 1991 people were hungry. By
1992 the consequences began to show up in the birth- and death-rates,
and in sickness. The birth-rate was only 7.7 per thousand, down 17 per
cent on the previous year's figure, and by 1993 it had fallen a further 17
per cent. Meanwhile the death-rate was running at 13.4 per thousand in
1992, up to approximately 18 by the end of 1993, pensioners now made
up a quarter of the city's population. Between 1990 and 1994 the city's
population fell from five to four and a half million.[5]

If 1991 was the year of the goods famine, 1992 was the year when price
rises far outstripped wages – and goods were still in short supply. Real
wages fell by half. Crime leapt by an alarming 62 per cent. Housing
construction was almost at a standstill, back at the level of 1953. Only
10,000 new flats came into circulation in a city where half a million were

---

[4] Gel'man and McAuley, 'Politics of City Government'.
[5] In 1990 the city's ageing population was 5.3 million; by 1991 1.7 million of its citizens
were either pensioners or invalids. The city data are taken from *Len. pravda*, 15 February
1991, p. 2; *Nev. kur'er*, 5 (1991), p. 6; *St Pbg ved.*, 29 January 1992, p. 5; 28 January 1993,
p. 2; 2 July 1993, p. 3; *Gorod Sankt Peterburg, 1993* (St Petersburg, 1994), pp. 9–32; *Chas
pik*, 24 August 1994, p. 6. For an account of various aspects of city life, see *Peterburg
nachala 90-kh: bezumnyi, kholodnyi, zhestokii* (St Petersburg, 1994).

on the housing list, and a third of the population still lived in communal flats. Industrial production fell by 20 per cent, down to the level of 1977. Over 50,000 people were laid off; another 400,000 changed their jobs. Workers in one of the more militant shops in the Kirov plant, whose members had been active in setting up a workers' committee and supporting the Yeltsin presidential campaign in 1991, sent a letter with 1,500 signatures to the VII Russian Congress in December 1992:

> We, the workers of the Kirov plant, being part of that very people thanks to whom our country has to this day remained independent, and therefore we have the right to ask you:
> Why do the peoples of Russia suffer today from your actions, why is there weeping and bloodshed?
> Who is directing the black dealings in the Russian state in which suddenly arbitrariness and illegality rules more and more? Why is the powerful economy dying?
> We, the workers, are sick to death of the propaganda directed against the people . . . he who loves his motherland, Russia, never causes her pain and suffering . . . If the Congress won't end the Yeltsin–Gaidar reforms directed against the people, the only recourse for us will be a political strike.[6]

No action followed, although no visible improvement occurred. Privatization began to make inroads into trade and services, and to a lesser extent in industry, but this made no impact on the standard of living. By the end of the year 15 per cent of the labour force were in the private sector and 27 per cent of retail trade was going through private hands.

Industrial production continued to fall in 1993 until, by mid-1994, it was only half that of 1991. Unemployment was estimated as being in the order of 120,000 but four-day weeks and extended unpaid holiday had become the norm in the defence industry plants. As many as 20 per cent of the city's enterprises were reckoned to be loss-makers, still living off government credits, and debts. By now only 50 per cent of the labour force was classified as working in the state sector; over 40 per cent of the large and medium-sized industrial plants had been privatized.[7] Retail trade, catering, and services were largely in private hands. The percentage of the labour force employed in trade, in credit, finance, and insurance, and in city administration saw substantial increases while most other branches declined. The best-paid sector became banking, the worst-paid culture and education. Incomes and prices continued to rise, but by now incomes were running slightly ahead of prices, and food and consumer goods (predominantly imported goods at very high prices) reappeared in the shops and markets. The new-rich appeared – foreign cars, luxury

---

[6] Leaflet distributed at the Congress.
[7] See *Izv.*, 13 March 1993, p. 5, on St Petersburg as the flagship of privatization. See also *Nezav.*, 11 January 1993, p. 2, on the Kirov plant, followed by *Izv.*, 26 January 1994, on its uncertain future.

apartments, electronic equipment, designer clothes, and foreign holidays – all became visible and accessible to a very small percentage of the population. Housing construction began again. A larger percentage, perhaps as many as 20 per cent of the population, began to live better than in the preceding years but the numbers of the really poor increased too. The old and sick, the beggars, and the child prostitutes round the railway stations became a feature of city life.[8]

Although preoccupied by the possibility of widespread social protest or the refusal by substantial sections of the population to pay rents and rates, neither mayor's office nor soviet weakened in their commitment to reform. Many of the city's problems stemmed from years of neglect of the infrastructure and the environment, followed by a food crisis, and could not be laid at the door of the new authorities. There was no way that, with its existing revenue, the city could maintain its services, let alone make improvements to its ever-deteriorating fabric or provide new amenities for its citizens. In 1993 the city government estimated that it would be able to finance only 25 per cent of its expenditure unless fares and rents were raised substantially, and throughout 1993 and 1994 fares, in particular, doubled and tripled. But, as was the case with all the regions, the city was hostage to federal policies on taxation. With its huge and declining defence sector, and numerous science and education institutions, it was in no position to hold the federal authorities to ransom. All it could use as bargaining chips were its importance to the future of Russia and its international image, the contacts between its industrial directorate and the government, and contacts between St Petersburg politicians and those at the centre. By 1993 it was allowed to retain a much larger share of the taxes it collected, but it was still dependent upon a subsidy from the federal government, and even then was running a substantial deficit. Projects such as the unfinished metro extension could only be continued if federally funded.[9]

Bargaining with Moscow over the budget did not cause dissension

[8] Official figures suggested a slight decrease in reported crime – 149 crimes per 10,000 of the population – but the actual crime rate was difficult to establish; in popular perception the danger to persons and to property had steadily increased in the face of a helpless or conniving police force. For a personal account of the changing life of the city from the 1960s to the 1990s, as seen through western eyes, M. McAuley, 'From Leningrad to St Petersburg', ms. (St Hilda's College, Oxford, 1993).

[9] The major items of expenditure were housing, capital investment, and socio-cultural expenditure, followed by transport. In 1992 the city retained 41 per cent of the tax collected (profits and VAT, primarily); in 1993 it was 69 per cent. These two items made up the largest part of the city's revenue, with income tax coming third. The subsidy accounted for 11.7 per cent of budget in 1992, 6.5 per cent in 1993. See Gel'man and McAuley, 'Politics of City Government'; Kudrin, St Pbg ved., 2 July 1993, p. 3. Sobchak used the money for the metro to finance the costly Goodwill Games (there was no city soviet to oppose the decision) which, when it subsequently became known, provoked a major scandal.

between the mayor's office and the soviet. Beliaev, chair of the soviet, was as anxious to get as good a deal as possible for the city on the budget as was Kudrin in the mayor's office.[10] In the autumn of 1993, when president and Supreme Soviet were at loggerheads, Beliaev was active in organizing the meeting of regional representatives (an action that was more pro-Supreme Soviet than pro-president). Mindful of possible budget implications, he did not wish St Petersburg to be seen as an enemy of the Supreme Soviet, but his fellow deputies' reactions to the president's dissolution of the Parliament (which I look at in a moment) owed more to ideological than to practical considerations. In St Petersburg both mayor's office and soviet were sufficiently self-confident to maintain their stances vis-à-vis each other and towards the federal authorities regardless of quarrels at the centre. And conflict between Sobchak and the soviet, despite their sharing common policy aims and their both being supporters of the Yeltsin government, continued throughout the whole period. What, then, prompted it?

The city elite: different constituencies?

The deputies complained that Sobchak was autocratic, vain, fearful of competitors, and an incompetent administrator. He could also be gratuitously offensive when he wished. He revealed himself to be an impetuous decision-maker, whose edicts too often were in contravention of the law. The mayoralty seemed no better able than the original executive committee to devise a city strategy. Its committees worked in an ad hoc manner while documentation issuing from the mayor's office, relating for example to the budget or to proposed reorganizations of city administration, was ill prepared. Some blamed this on Sobchak's ineptness and his failure to structure decision-making on a collegial basis; others on his poor choice of personnel, his preference for individuals whose only necessary quality would be their loyalty to him.[11] But was the problem primarily one of personality? Many of these criticisms were simultaneously being directed against other chief administrators, including the chief of them all and his office. Whereas Yeltsin responded by accusing the Parliament of being dominated by supporters of the communist past, Sobchak described the

[10] See *Vech. Pbg*, 13 January 1993, p. 1, on Beliaev turning to the Supreme Soviet.
[11] By 1994 he had replaced Kramarev, the respected police chief, D. Filippov, the head of the most efficient tax inspectorate in the country, and D. Sergeev, an able administrator in the economics committee, with less competent individuals. He continued to support a deputy mayor, L. Savenkov, who was charged with the illegal export of caviar to his own German firm, and metals via Finland, and who claimed, in his defence, that he was acting for the good of the city even if the documentation was not in order: M. Makarevich, 'St Petersburg: Leningradskaia oblast'', *Pol. monit.*, January 1994. A. Vinnikov, 'The End of Soviet Power in St Petersburg: An Insider's View', *Europe–Asia Studies*, 46 (1994), pp. 1215–30, provides a deputy's view.

soviet as a set of amateurish, marginal individuals, often interested in private gain and unrepresentative of the electors, who were unable to agree on anything except opposition to the mayor. There was certainly some truth in this. Particularly in the first year of its existence the soviet conducted its business in an often chaotic and quite ineffective fashion. But although personality may have played a part, and ineptness is irritating, to explain institutional conflict simply in these terms seems hardly satisfactory.

Could it be that the institutions reflected different constituencies? The mayor's office, it was sometimes suggested, was dominated by officials of the old order, different in kind and political conviction from the intelligentsia democrats in the soviet. What evidence is there on this? The data are not as good as one would like. They are sufficient, however, to cast doubt on a straight sociological explanation. A comparison of the structure of the mayor's office in 1993 with that of the executive committee of 1989 shows that both major restructuring and personnel change had occurred. In 1989 Khodyrev had chaired an executive committee of three first deputy chairs and six deputy chairs, all with wide-ranging briefs, and twelve further members, and with the planning commission as the dominant body. In 1992 the mayor's office was headed by the mayor and the vice mayor (popularly elected) and five deputy mayors responsible for economic development, trade and catering, social welfare, foreign relations, and property administration. Only the first two of these committees had existed previously; and of the original ten deputy chairs of the executive committee, only one was still in place, and one other still in city administration.[12]

In 1994 the structure was reorganized as shown (brackets refer to previous occupation).[13]

Mayor A. A. Sobchak (law professor)

First deputy chairs
Committee for Administration of the City V. A. Yakovlev (chief engineer, housing administration)
Committee for Foreign Links V. V. Putin (KGB)
Committee for Economics and Finances A. L. Kudrin (economist, colleague of Chubais)

---

[12] Data on the structure and personnel of the soviet, executive committee, and mayor's office are from *Leningradskii gorsovet: spisok telefonov*; *Organy gosudarstvennoi vlasti i upravleniia Sankt-peterburga: tel. spravochnik* (St Petersburg, 1992); *St Petersburg Report*, 2–3 (St Petersburg, 1992); *Gorod Sankt-Peterburg, 1993*; for biographical data on obkom/gorkom members 1988–93, see appendix 2, pp. 322–3.

[13] Instruction of mayor, 16 March 1994, no. 241. Note the disappearance of the vice mayor, following Sobchak's 'dismissal' of Shcherbakov (see below, p. 296, n. 66).

Deputy chairs

Committee for Social Welfare V. L. Mutko (district administration)

Head of the Government Apparatus V. I. Malyshev (district administration)

Committee for Property Administration M. V. Manevich (research economist)

Members of the government

Committee for Culture V. P. Yakovlev (university professor)

Committee for Trade and Food A. G. Stepanov (canteen administration, deputy head, City Food Supply Administration)

Justice Administration Iu. M. Novolotskii (defence lawyer)

Committee on Architecture and City Planning O. A. Karchenko (deputy head, city administration)

Administration of Internal Affairs A. G. Kramarev (replaced by Iu. Loskutov, head of the Fire Brigade Training School)

The structure of committees and administrations, which had become extremely complex under the old system, had been simplified. Some were simply abolished – agro-industry and people's control, for example. Others were elevated from administration to committee status (for example, labour, social welfare, foreign links) and, as privatization took place, trusts and supply agencies became stock-holding companies.[14] If we compare personnel in 1993 with those in 1989, we can, as a rough approximation, say the following: in almost all cases the more important committees or departments had a new head who had come from outside, but they included among their staff, sometimes as deputy head, two or perhaps three individuals from the original committee or administration (exceptions were internal affairs, education, and land). New committees – press and communications, youth, property, citizens' complaints – did not seem to draw upon staff from previous departments. Some may have come from obkom departments. The mayor took over the higher party school – now the higher school of administration – and created a council for science and higher education, again traditional party concerns. Part of the obkom's administration department, including its former head, staffed the mayor's administration department.[15] Sobchak's apparatus was headed by one of Khodyrev's assistants, and included the assistants to two of the former executive-committee chairmen; similarly the protocol, administration, and control departments were run by their original heads. Press and information were new departments.

The more technical the department or administration the greater likeli-

---

[14] The committees were as follows: labour and employment, investment, legal, housing, land reform and use, amenities and roads, health, transport and communications, education, press and mass communication, youth, sport.   [15] Duka, 'Formirovanie', p. 13.

hood of the carry-over of the same head and his deputies (capital construction, supplies, roads, housing repairs, parks, bakeries, pharmacy, veterinary services, hotels, flood prevention, dachas, civil aviation, railways, etc.). Some of the departments or administrations which became corporations or stock-holding companies retained their original heads: the construction committee became, for example, the State Stock-Holding Construction Corporation of St Petersburg under its previous head, Iu. Khozhukovskii, now with the title of president. Others rose in size and status with privatization – the tax inspectorate, for example, to which D. Filippov, the able obkom secretary, was appointed as head. On the basis of these data the mayor's office looks, despite the carry-overs, substantially different, both in structure and personnel, from the original executive committee.

What, however, if we ask a different question? Soviet officials who were members of the obkom/gorkom tended to be classic nomenklatura figures. Did they move out of city government or did they remain in post? The members of the original executive committee, by 1993, were employed as follows:

Khodyrev	Director, commercial concern; consultant, Tetrapolis
Bolshakov	President, AO Highspeed Network
Maksimov-Rogovtsev	Director, concern Nord
Avdeev	Deputy chair, property committee
Arkhipov-Gubkin	Director of bank, Gavan concern
Zakharova	Management, commercial publishing
Serova-Shishkin	Chair, committee on trade

Bolshakov subsequently moved on to become minister for cooperation with the CIS. Here there was little continuity with the past. However, when we widen the survey to include all the soviet administrators who had been members of the obkom or gorkom in 1988, we find a pattern very similar to that in Perm. Among the military/legal personnel, most made a normal career move, with the exception of a leading KGB official who had become a consultant in Astrobank. Of those in civilian administration, nearly half remained at their previous post (head of an administration, of the railways) or of its refashioned counterpart (Gossnab to Lenglavsnab), and a small clutch moved into the new construction corporation. The occasional individual again moved up to Moscow or to oblast administration, or remained in district administration. Demotions were rare. There were those who moved out of soviet administration to a different kind of government post – from the cultural department to the directorship of the Mariinskii theatre, for example, or from a deputy chair in the executive committee to the manager of the Dinamo sports club. But a larger group moved into new commercial structures: to a bank directorship, to a Russian–Finnish joint venture, and then back into the mayor's administration, to general directorship of the north-west association of regional cooperation.[16] The picture is one of stability accompanied by a movement out to commerce.

What though of their party colleagues? Of those in the obkom/gorkom apparatus, perhaps a third moved into government administration, at different levels. Two moved upwards to the central government, a few moved sideways to city or oblast administration – one to the mayor's office, three to the tax inspectorate, including to its chair, and one to a consultancy post in the St Petersburg construction corporation; one to the oblast administration, one to head the oblast branch of the central bank. In this group were those who moved to such posts as prorector of the Ministry of Internal Affairs Institute, director of ITAR-TASS agency, or head of the Fire Service Training School. Gidaspov, the first secretary, moved back to head of a project institute. The largest single group, however, fourteen in all, moved into leading positions either in new commercial ventures (eleven) or to new organizations (like the association of industrial enterprises) or to a newspaper editorship.

Of the raikom and oblast gorkom secretaries, roughly a third moved into government administration – again two to Moscow, the majority to posts in district administration in city and oblast, one to the mayor's office. Although in general they preserved their status, the odd demotion occurred – from party secretary to lesser posts in district administration. The great majority of these secretaries (fourteen in all), however, moved into deputy directorships, occasionally the directorship, in large plants in the defence industry sector, some of which had become or were in the process of becoming stock-holding companies. Here we see very clearly the close ties that existed between the party and the directorate. Leading city raikom secretaries, such as A. Aleksandrov, moved to head the association of industrial enterprises (he took with him another district secretary). Fewer of this group moved into commerce, although one set up an international business centre, one became a bank director, and another the director of a new concern Avgustina.[17] As was the case in Perm, government, industrial, and professional institutions absorbed the

---

[16] The chair of the trade union council had joined the board of a joint venture, Viktoria, which specialized in hotel management.

[17] Of the nine primary party secretaries for whom I have information, two remained as lecturers in their institutes; the other seven had risen to posts of dean, rector, or head of department in their academic institutes; two to deputy directorships in their industrial enterprises; and one had become the president of a Russo-German joint venture.

displaced party apparatchiki, and took them in at levels equivalent to their status. More marked in St Petersburg, and reflecting the greater opportunities in the vanguard city, was the move by a group of leading soviet and party officials into the new world of commerce at a top level. When two or three moved together, the hierarchy of positions was preserved in the new venture.

The industrial and cultural directorate saw little change. Of the twenty leading enterprise directors in 1988, only one, G. Khizha, had moved by 1993, and that was to join the government; of the thirteen institute or university heads, all were in place, and two department chairs had taken down the label 'scientific communism' from the door and put up 'sociology' instead; of the seven from the cultural elite, one had risen, one slipped down, and one moved sideways, while the rest remained in their previous posts. The data do not allow us to see who the newcomers were, at lower levels, and who staffed new institutions, and hence they may overemphasize continuity. But at least we can say that if the city administration had a new committee structure, where the chairs were largely newcomers, and where new areas of activity – property, foreign relations (foreign investment and business deals), and social welfare – had become key concerns, and a commercial and business sector had emerged, the overall picture for the city is one of a remarkably stable elite. Other sectors remained in the hands of those who had run them under the old regime. In the five years since 1988, a period which had seen radical political change, there was little movement among those who were in charge of the city's most important industrial enterprises, and its scientific, educational, and cultural institutions. Nearly half the leading government administrators remained in place; the rest moved to new posts in the state sector and into commerce. The redundant party apparatchiki fanned out between government administration, industrial directorships, and new commercial structures.

That a similar type of elite stability (although with differences at the edges) can be observed in St Petersburg, in Tatarstan, and in Perm strengthens the case for looking for systemic causes. A 'nomenklatura conspiracy' is not of itself an explanation, while the claim that these were the people with leadership skills and administrative competence is simply unverifiable. We need, instead, to think in terms of a political system which, during the Brezhnev period, had produced patterns of long tenure – those who finally achieved their long-awaited promotion under perestroika expected no less for themselves – and a system of personnel appointment which was both party- and network-dependent. Open competition for posts, in whatever field or institution, was no part of Soviet practice. With the party's disappearance, existing incumbents were freed from control from outside, and there was no alternative appointment system to hand. Most simply stayed in place. Newcomers, such as Sobchak, resorted to the same traditional practices as did all in positions of authority, whether they were government administrators, bank presidents, university professors, or industrial directors: reliance on personal contacts, and existing networks. Sobchak drew from the university, then turned to the party apparatus, loyal deputies, reform-minded administrators, and the directorate.[18]

Systems of recruitment based upon personal networks were as much part of the deputies' world as that of the nomenklatura. Was it, however, to return to the sociological hypothesis, that their networks were very different, those of a non-nomenklatura public? Certainly Petrosoviet was a body with very little nomenklatura or elite presence. Those of its members who were of the heavy brigade moved out and away – Khizha, for example, to the Council of Ministers, or Filippov, the ex-obkom secretary, to the tax inspectorate; some were drafted into the mayor's office – for example, V. Malyshev, with a district party and soviet background; others, of whom the prime example was Khodyrev, the former chair of the soviet, moved into commerce, and away from the soviet.[19] The nomenklatura, in effect, abandoned the soviet as an institution. It remained a body even more dominated by 'outsiders', members of the technical and academic intelligentsia, some who had risen in their profession, others who had not. In this respect, unlike the soviets in most of the country, Petrosoviet broke with tradition and with the elite. Studies have drawn attention to the high proportion of intellectuals among the deputies, and particularly among the most active. In an analysis of members of the first two praesidia, Duka reaffirms this and suggests that there were three different types among them. These were the activist-protesters (those who had played a key part under perestroika), the individual truth-seekers (the lone dissidents), and 'the decent chaps', with no political past but nominated by their institute to challenge a nomenklatura figure.[20]

Although in St Petersburg the two institutions did then have different socio-political profiles, it would seem wrong to put too much weight on this as an explanation of the conflict between them. Among key members of the city administration it was not only Sobchak who came from the academic intelligentsia; in his appointments he drew upon individuals

[18] Duka, 'Formirovanie', p. 13, suggests five different sources of recruitment.
[19] Although Khodyrev held no formal posts in the administration, he was still reckoned in 1993 to wield immense influence over city decisions.
[20] Duka, 'Formirovanie', pp. 10–11; T. Protiasenko, 'Intellektualy v politike: profes-sional'naia kar'era i put' v deputaty', Regional'naia politika, 1 (1992), pp. 23–31; V. Rumintsev and M. Makarevich, Dvadtsat' pervyi (St Petersburg, 1994), give a bio-graphical portrait of the members of the little soviet.

with very different institutional backgrounds, including from the university. Some among the democratic deputies moved to work in the administration – for example, S. Beliaev, lecturer from the polytechnic institute, who headed the important new property committee until co-opted into the central government – and others moved to Moscow to work for the government (P. Filippov and S. Vasil´ev, for example).[21] The avidity with which non-nomenklatura individuals took up the defence of executive institutions, whether in St Petersburg or in the federal government, suggests that the idea of an entrenched nomenklatura successfully warding off blows to its ways of doing things is far too simple.

The movement out of Petrosoviet by some of the more able and moderate figures did, however, have consequences for the relationship between the mayoralty and the soviet. When, in 1992, the soviet voted for its little soviet, they did not stand. It was the radical People's Front fraction, a group of relatively young members of the professional intelligentsia, which succeeded in getting almost all its candidates elected and whose leader, S. Egorov, became the majority leader in the little soviet.[22] In March its members supported a motion 'to consider it expedient to remove A. Sobchak from office'. Although the vote of 148 in favour was far fewer than the 267 votes required for a two-thirds majority (and even then the president was not obliged to remove the office-holder), the action set a precedent. The soviet in Krasnodar krai, as well as those in some other regions, subsequently used the same legislative provision to real effect. Sobchak responded by trying to obtain a presidential edict which would make the mayor's office more similar to that of a republican presidency. Both sides canvassed for support in high places, and the draft edict disappeared somewhere in a government office. Although Petrosoviet's chair, A. Beliaev, succeeded in maintaining a reasonable relationship with Sobchak, the soviet became even more hostile towards the mayor.[23] Sometimes, given individuals within the mayor's office who had good personal relations with soviet colleagues, decisions could be reached behind the scenes without the usual public squabble. But in and of themselves neither social composition nor personalities were sufficient to account for the conflict. Nor did a soviet have to be led by a group of radical intellectuals to be locked in battle with its administration. Witness the Supreme Soviet as the prime example.

[21] By 1996 S. Beliaev had been elected on the Chernomyrdin party list and led its fraction in the Duma. Rather differently, a deputy such as Bella Krukova, the television producer, became a national figure and rarely appeared at the soviet.

[22] Ten members of the People's Front and March fractions, four from the Free Democratic Party, two from the combined Social Democrats and Republican parties, and twelve who did not belong to any fraction were elected: *Reiting*, 5 (1992), p. 6.

[23] See Gel´man and McAuley, 'Politics of City Government', for further details.

The struggle for power and executive victory

To understand the conflict between the two branches of government, whether in St Petersburg or at the centre, we need to step back and see what they were fighting over. If during 1990–1 the conflict was over the redistribution of power between executive and legislature, by 1992 Smolny had again become the dominant institution. Its mayoral officials were far less powerful than their predecessors in the obkom. The mayor's office controlled an incomparably smaller number of appointments. Higher education, science, sections of the cultural world, the means of mass communication, social organizations, unions, and religious organizations no longer lay within the grasp of the city authorities, although they retained considerable financial leverage over many institutions. The mayor's office controlled neither the press nor the judiciary, and its decisions could be and were queried before the courts. The soviet existed as a point of criticism and a check on its activities. Institutions in St Petersburg had contacts and friends in high places in Moscow. They could obtain rulings or financial support independent of the mayor's office. The elite might be as stable as in Perm but sections of it, and some of the new business concerns, were not reliant on the administration's goodwill in order to prosper. In all these respects St Petersburg differed from most regions in the country. It had a sufficiently developed network of organizations which were not dependent upon the administration to make opposition possible. A great deal still depended upon the federal authorities. If an institute lost central funding, it was doomed. If a defence plant failed to get a subsidy, it was in trouble. Both would work with Sobchak if it seemed that his intervention could help – and the military-industrial directorate preserved its links with Smolny – but many had better connections at the centre than Sobchak (and how long would he be in office?). The changing situation at the centre meant keeping one's options open.

The mayor's powers were considerable, however. Firstly, as the chief executive in a system which gave much individual power to the incumbent, he could exercise his powers of appointment and take decisions affecting properties, business deals, relations with foreign companies, and proposals for new ventures. Secondly, despite the city's financial problems and its dependence upon the federal budget, the amount of money at the city's disposal was substantial and had increased. The extra-budget fund was controlled by the mayor. His office's ability to find money for projects or for those newspapers he wished to support gave it considerable power. Thirdly, and most importantly of all, privatization of the city's buildings, enterprises, and services put enormous power into the hands of its property committee, and into those of all its officials dealing with licences, permits, and legal documentation. To summarize: the sources of power had passed from centralized political control over appointments and communications to an elected executive with control over a substantial administrative apparatus and responsibility for the distribution of valuable resources.

How, in such a situation, would its officials act? Conventional ways of behaving assumed the management and distribution of resources according to instructions from above – and now these were to privatize. Suddenly there were scores of claimants, both from outside institutions and from those which were part of the administration; there were deals to be done, promises of political support, fortunes to be made. It may be that the process in St Petersburg was better regulated than in many places, because of both a more honest property administration and the vigilance of the soviet, but it could not but result in corruption and administrative misdemeanours. Those in the city offices, often merely following the example of their superiors, found it difficult to distinguish the public from their own private interest. The state apparatus did not shrink but expanded, as it attempted to manage and regulate a lucrative process. As in Perm a quango-land of agencies and concerns emerged. The existence of a large bureaucratic apparatus, controlling and dispensing patronage, made the mayor's office a focus for lobby groups – from new business, commercial concerns, district administrations, pressure groups. Meanwhile those in office, the leading officials, were only too aware of a changeable situation, one that was unpredictable and difficult to control, and in which they were continually required to react to sudden crises. Long-term planning, even if there had been officials capable of doing it, was practically impossible. They needed to take decisions, and they also wanted to safeguard some kind of future for themselves. In such a situation they were necessarily susceptible to pressure from those who could offer either short-term solutions or future financial security. We should not think that this applied only to officials in the administration. By the time they left office most of the soviet deputies, it was estimated, had ensured for themselves either employment or access to financial resources by virtue of their deputy status.[24]

Until we have a proper study of administrative behaviour it is impossible to know the extent to which traditional patterns of behaviour held

[24] Interviews with deputies and journalists, 1993–4. Duka, 'Formirovanie', pp. 23–5, suggests that 10 per cent of the deputies had improved their housing illegally, and that the average bribe to those on commissions responsible for accepting tenders or allocating property was $2,000 in 1994; of the twenty-four in his survey who were still active in politics after the soviet was dissolved, sixteen had raised their social status.

(and we need to know more of what *they* were) and to what extent they underwent change. We can see how the new environment did nothing to encourage the observance of legal procedures. It is still surprising quite how easily Sobchak, a professor of law, found it to take decisions contravening the law when he thought it necessary (for example, at the time of the March 1994 elections).[25] It is also surprising quite how poor the administration was at preparing documentation to put before the soviet. But regardless of this we can see how executive actions would inevitably lead to conflict with an elected assembly whose members saw themselves responsible, at a minimum, for acting as a check upon the executive while simultaneously devising policies to benefit the city. This brings us back to the constitutional arrangements. In such a situation a legislature which attempted to control executive behaviour could not but find itself acting as a permanent 'objector'.

During 1992 and 1993 the soviet prevented the sale of particular cultural institutions for commercial use; it successfully obtained court rulings against illegal mayoral decisions. The numbers were not large – in 1993 6 per cent of the mayor's decisions were rescinded[26] – but one could argue that the existence of a critical soviet, prepared to challenge the administration's decisions and query the budget, acted as a curb on potential illegality. Sobchak considered both activities unhelpful. Not surprisingly the drafting of a new city constitution, as required by law, and whose content was a matter for the soviet, fuelled the conflict still further. The soviet draft provided for stringent controls over the administration. Sobchak responded with a compromise document, hoping to split the more moderate deputies who were tired of confrontation, and their chair, Beliaev, away from the more radical. It clearly had a chance of being accepted but it was overtaken by the events of September 1993.

Conflict at federal level

In the light of the above we can see why the situation was so much worse at federal level. Here were concentrated vast resources, powerful vested interests, and the federal budget. Even before privatization began, the Union government was the target of ministerial, regional, and institutional claimants. Ryzhkov, described as the weeping prime minister and

---

[25] See below, pp. 295–6.

[26] The soviet also stopped the spending of city money on the dam across the Finnish gulf (but the federal authorities found it elsewhere). See Gel'man and McAuley, 'Politics of City Government'; M. Gornyi and A. Shishlov, 'Organizatsiia vlasti i upravleniia v Sankt Peterburge', St Petersburg, Strategiia paper, 1994; A. Sungurov, *Gorodskoi sovet Leningrada, Peterburga* (St Petersburg, 1994); interviews with deputies, 1993, and ex-deputies, 1994.

deluged with demands, spoke of the 'throat' or 'shout' economy. Once the Russian government had taken over much of the federal inheritance and economic reform got underway, the ministerial and regional scramble for control of the valuable resources took off with a vengeance, and the clamour for subsidies from the defence sector grew deafening. We have seen examples of this from our republics or regions, and they need to be multiplied tenfold. New corporations, quangos, and banks emerged, able to target the presidential apparatus, the Council of Ministers, and the Supreme Soviet. It became difficult to see where government institutions ended and lobbies began. An article in *Izvestia* suggested:

Against the backdrop of political pluralism and market relations in the economy, but in the absence of laws on state power, political parties, the civil service, corruption, and organized crime, and in the absence of a law on the phenomenon itself, lobbyism presents a threat to the democratic order itself that was chosen by the country.

This is the context in which we need to place the new institutions and the constitutional rules according to which they were meant to be operating. By the spring of 1992 three structures at federal level were vying with each other: the presidency (with its administrative apparatus, system of presidential representatives, and network of advisory councils and centres),[27] the re-formed Council of Ministers (with a fast-growing apparatus based in part on the old Central Committee apparatus, subordinate to the prime minister), and the Supreme Soviet (with its speaker, committees, apparatus, and advisory centres).[28] Simplifying again, at central level an executive committed to economic reform and privatization, finding it increasingly difficult to work together with a more conservatively minded Congress and Supreme Soviet, resorted to using, wherever possible, executive prerogatives to introduce policy changes. The Congress, in turn, swung between the role of policy-maker (committing the government to further financial expenditure) and one of trying to block or control the executive.

But was it primarily policy differences that accounted for the ever more strident opposition to the government on the part of the Supreme Soviet

[27] In the autumn of 1993 discussion in the press suggested that the president's administration employed 2,000 people.

[28] Gaidar began the process of building up a prime-ministerial administration of newcomers, able to counter conservative ministries; Chernomyrdin inherited these new structures and extended them to bring in his own people. Published work on elite data at federal level is still scant. See O. Kryshtanovskaia, 'Transformatsiia staroi nomenklatury v novuiu rossiiskuiu elitu', *Obshchestvennye nauki i sovremennost'*, 1 (1995), pp. 51–65; N. Ershova, 'Transformatsiia praviashchei elity Rossii v usloviakh sotsial'nogo pereloma', in Zaslavskaia and Arutiunian, *Kuda idet Rossiia?*, pp. 151–4, provides some preliminary findings.

and Congress? It was undoubtedly true that the social consequences of economic reform provided a cause around which opposition could rally and, in this sense, they played a part. It is also true that the policies raised the stakes and simultaneously provided the means for both sides to battle with each other. They changed the nature of politics. But this is something different from seeing the conflict in terms of one institution pushing privatization and another opposing it. By the summer of 1993, having lost to the president in the referendum, having lost any claim to be the voice of the people, the Congress was defending its rights as law- and constitution-maker with even greater vigour. It was in effect defending its existence as an institution.[29]

Although the struggle for institutional power was waged under the slogan of a separation of powers, with all declaring themselves anxious merely to ensure that power was not monopolized, both sides were actually insisting that they should control policy-making. A clear delineation of function had failed to emerge. The deputies saw themselves as the only defence, the only means of controlling the activities of often corrupt and otherwise unaccountable officials in whose hands lay huge resources; they should make the laws, and control the executive. In turn the leaders of the executive structures saw the assemblies as far from representative bodies, their members endlessly quarrelling among themselves, unable to produce coherent legislation, concerned with their own private and also sometimes corrupt interests, and yet demanding that they should be the locus of decision-making. Both claimed to be representing the people. The predictions of the negative consequences of choosing a presidential system seemed to be borne out with a vengeance.[30]

Yet is it so clear that this is right? The existence of two independent institutional structures (and the Council of Ministers which gained ground in its own right until it perhaps was pre-eminent in its control of resources) encouraged conflict. But if a parliamentary system, with the head of government elected by the parliament and able to be dismissed by it, had been chosen instead, would it have been more workable? It is difficult to see that it would. It might have led to less conflict but more corruption. Perhaps it would just have led sooner to executive pre-eminence. As it was the executive could, and did, employ the weapon of co-

---

[29] By this time policy initiatives had become subordinated to the conflict over jurisdiction. The question of who should control the central bank, for example, took precedence over what financial policy should be pursued. As one commentator observed: 'The president publishes decrees as though the Supreme Soviet did not exist, and the Supreme Soviet stops the decrees as though there was no president.'

[30] E. Huskey, 'Democracy and Institutional Design in Russia', *Democratization*, forthcoming, provides a useful discussion of the consequences of adopting a semi-presidential system in the Russian context, and takes the analysis on through 1995.

optation to weaken deputies' loyalty to the legislature and, given its control over financial resources, bought off lobbies or used the threat of withholding resources in order to weaken opposition. This practice revealed itself most blatantly, after the decree of 21 September 1993, in Yeltsin's offer of jobs within the executive offices to any parliamentarian willing to abandon the Supreme Soviet. Under a parliamentary system the executive would have redoubled its efforts and resources to buy a majority within the Congress and, if Yeltsin had been unsuccessful and voted out of office, his successor would have done the same – because there were no stable political majorities on which anyone could rely, not even those composed of 'democrats' or 'conservatives'.

The most we can say is that constitutional arrangements which insist that independent institutions should share in policy-making, at a time when huge resources are being redistributed and there are no established conventions of legality and accountability, will result in a relationship dominated by a struggle for power and authority. The only circumstances under which this will not occur are when the legislature refrains from exercising its rights. This was not so in St Petersburg or at the centre.

Legislative weakness

Should we be surprised that active, popularly elected bodies proved unable to establish themselves as equal partners in the political arena? Was the Russian lack of experience responsible? Such an answer would clearly be inadequate. Representative assemblies, with no prior experience, can quickly develop into powerful institutions. It may be that certain circumstances favour this outcome – and they were absent in Russia – but there is no pocket-book guide on this.[31] Were there features of the Russian situation which favoured one or the other? In any system the executive starts with the stronger hand – control of the means of force and implementation of decisions – and the legislature is the challenger. In the aftermath of communist party rule the legislature had a large bonus of popular support, facing an unpopular and discredited government

---

[31] The fortunes of legislatures that came into existence two centuries ago is no guide. An environment which includes a restricted suffrage and the acceptance of a limited role for government implies an institution of a very different type from that of a legislature in a democratic welfare state. It may be, and I shall argue this, that the absence of political parties is a factor that weakens the development of the legislature in the contemporary world; it clearly could not be so argued a hundred years ago. Nor can we look to long-lived legislatures of today to tell us what is necessary or unnecessary for a newly born institution to survive: once an institution is firmly established it may be able to maintain itself by quite different mechanisms from those required for one starting out as a new institution.

apparatus. But, in a state-run and state-controlled society, the executive directs a vast array of resources, both coercive and financial, which it can use to defend itself. In such a context, with its accompanying administrative culture, a policy of privatization, at least in the short run, strengthens the executive's position – as the disburser of property and the source of power – and allows an expansion of the administrative apparatus. Another feature of the post-communist environment that privileges the already privileged position of the executive is the system of appointment to offices rather than open recruitment.

The choice of a presidential system does not have obvious consequences for legislative strength one way or another. On the one hand, the assembly has to share the role of the people's representative with the president, and it does not have direct responsibility for creating the government. On the other, as a body wholly independent of the executive, its members are in a stronger position to act as creative legislators in their own right. Much will therefore depend on what the members of a new legislature see their role to be. While legislatures may all be described as representative assemblies elected by the people to pass the laws of the land, their roles and those of their deputies differ markedly. The legislature may be the source of policy-making or the scrutinizer. The deputy may see his role as that of defending constituency interests or advancing those of a group; as carrying a party mandate, or as elected, like the Burkean parliamentarian, to use her judgement as she thinks fit. To take but two examples: in the United States most legislation emanates from within Congress, much is blocked, and members of Congress are first and foremost representatives of their constituency interests; in Britain, the executive is the source of almost all legislation, most is assured of passage, and the members of the House of Commons' first loyalty is to their party. While the role played by the legislature will be influenced by other factors too, the deputies' perceptions of their role will affect their behaviour. In St Petersburg, as at the centre, the deputies saw their role in maximalist terms: setting the legislative agenda, drawing up and passing the laws, and exercising a check on the executive.

There is nothing built into the legislative–executive relationship per se that will influence the ability of deputies to do this. Whether they will be effective policy-makers, if this is what their members wish to be, will depend upon their ability to organize their activities. Either a committee system and an organizational structure able to translate legislative proposals into majority decisions, or a party system which can produce a coherent majority, would seem to be necessary. If both are present the legislature will work well as policy-maker; without either there will be serious problems.

As an institution which checked executive activity Petrosoviet did not perform too badly; as a policy-maker it was much less successful. Its members did draft and pass new legislation for the city – for example, covering the process of privatization, health insurance, or the sale of apartments. In this respect its activities were not negligible (and the draft for health insurance became the basis for the subsequent Russian law) but they did not have a visible impact upon the lives of the citizens, nor were they vote-winners. After the soviet's dissolution its members could make but modest claims for their achievements as policy-makers.[32] Admittedly, given executive control of resources and economic collapse, the environment was inauspicious. But to see the failure of the soviets, at all levels, to defend their newly won rights and to develop into strong representative institutions in terms of the people's Davids battling against an executive Goliath would be to ignore both in-built weaknesses in the soviet structure and deputy perceptions of their role. They may have been Davids but they chose the wrong terrain on which to fight, and they came armed with sticks instead of slings. It was the absence of either a party system or an organizational structure and effective procedures that was to prove so destructive of decision-making and of their popularity. St Petersburg serves as the case study.

Petrosoviet: organization and factionalism

In 1990 the democrats had shared only the vaguest of platforms: opposition to apparatus rule, and the conviction that a democratic city government should put the rights and welfare of its citizens at the top of the agenda. The People's Front began to fade once the election had been won. Just as importantly, however, there were no mechanisms to bind a deputy to the Front and, on the part of the deputies, no sense that they were or should be representatives of a party or organization, bound by its programme, and in turn able to draw upon it for support. Lensoviet opened with an individualistic democratic majority facing small ideological oppositions (orthodox Communists and patriots) and an interest-based industrial lobby, some of whose members were far from enthusiastic at the thought of devoting time and energy to what they had envisaged as a largely honorific job, and who began to absent themselves from the daily sessions. During 1990–1 soviet proceedings were characterized by chaotic and lengthy disagreements within its democratic majority. Its members united in response to national crises but could agree on little else.

---

[32] Discussions with deputies, 1993.

They inherited an organizational framework and procedures from their Soviet predecessor. For a start Lensoviet was a large body – 400 deputies who now decided they should work full-time. The rules provided for an elected chair (who doubled as chair of the executive committee) and a praesidium. The deputies voted to separate the two offices and to form the praesidium of the elected heads and deputy heads of twenty-seven commissions, created to oversee and devise new policy in different areas. Some of these were devoted to traditional spheres of city administration – transport, education, health – others demonstrated the commitment to change – economic reform, glasnost, human rights. The commissions had memberships of fifteen to twenty-five deputies (individuals could belong to more than one), and were to make recommendations to the praesidium. There was no institution to organize a legislative agenda. Inevitably, given the structures and the lack of leadership, the praesidium either simply accepted the recommendations or acted in a quite arbitrary fashion. With the creation of a mayor's office, and Sobchak's departure from the chair, the soviet floundered still further. It had already decided to hold shorter sessions and, in the spring of 1991, had moved to elect a smaller praesidium on an individual basis.[33] But by the autumn of 1991, as was true of soviets more generally, Petrosoviet was in deep trouble: struggling under the leadership of Beliaev, the moderate democrat, to become more than an ineffectual talking shop. Those who were still anxious to play an active role as deputies now began to consider electing a smaller soviet, to work full-time. This idea, rather than that of holding new elections, was approved by the federal authorities, and Petrosoviet reorganized its structure. The whole soviet would meet briefly every three months to decide key issues while a little soviet, elected from among the 400 deputies, would work full-time through its commissions, themselves reduced in number, and the praesidium would coordinate the work.

In January 1992 Petrosoviet, with difficulty, after three ballots, elected thirty-eight deputies to serve on the little soviet.[34] It was, as noted, the radical People's Front fraction which, as a consequence of its stricter internal discipline, succeeded in getting almost all its candidates elected.

---

[33] The deputies received 150 r. a month while retaining their place of work and salary; the first session ran nearly full-time until the end of June. Thereafter it was agreed to hold short, few-day sessions, initially bi-monthly, and then monthly (see *Vestnik Lensoveta*, 1 (1991), pp. 6–13, for the sessions and decisions taken, April 1990–May 1991). For further detail, and references where not otherwise given, see Gel′man and McAuley, 'Politics of City Government'.

[34] For the members of the little soviet, see *Vech. Pbg*, 25 January 1992, p. 1; on the election, *Vech. Pbg*, 16 January 1992, p. 1; *Smena*, 15 January 1992, p. 1; M. Dmitriev and V. Ludin, in *Reiting*, 5 (1992), p. 6.

There was now a second wave of politicians who had cut their teeth as politicians in the soviet but were not particularly well known or popular outside its walls. Until the end of 1993, the little soviet of thirty-eight, its thirty-odd commissions and committees, and a small permanent staff remained in the Mariinskii Palace. No more than one or two deputies worked full-time at the head of each commission, and their staff was small, as was the apparatus serving the chairs and deputy chairs. The Palace, with the departure of the mayor's office to Smolny, became a strangely empty place. The larger soviet assembled once every two or three months for six to eight days to take key decisions. At the beginning of 1993 it voted to abolish the praesidium; it also re-elected the little soviet, which lost a few of its more radical members. Its structure was as shown.[35]

Chair   A. Beliaev
Deputy chair   B. Moiseev

Praesidium
Administration   Foreign Links
Information   Legal department
Organization department   Personnel
Press Centre   Secretariat[36]

Little soviet
Permanent commissions and committees
Blockade, Veterans,
    Repression Victims★   Foreign Links★
Building and Land Use   Glasnost and Mass Media★
City and District Government★   Healthcare
Communications   Housing
Control   Human Rights★
Culture and Heritage   Industry
Ecology   Law Enforcement
Economic Reform★   Legislation★
Education   Mandate
Family and Childcare   Military-Industrial Conversion★
Food★   Planning and Budget

[35] *St Pbg Report*, pp. 40–1; Sungurov, *Gorodskoi sovet*, p. 25; interviews with ex-deputies, 1994.
[36] These departments were staffed primarily from the original executive committee: the organizational department drew from the original secretariat, the head of the administration came from the original general department. There were more newcomers in the legal department, and in the press centre, information, and foreign links.

Property*	Trade and Services
Science and Higher Education*	Transport
Social and Political Organizations*	Youth and Sport
Social Policy	

* Commissions created since 1990.

Although by 1992 the environment for policy-making was much more favourable these changes did not bring the desired results. The preparation of agenda items and policy documents improved, but institutionally the soviet remained flawed. Until 1993 the praesidium retained the right to take mandatory decisions, thus partly duplicating the role of the little soviet. Even without it, the relationship between the little soviet and Petrosoviet became, in practice, similar to that between the Supreme Soviet and Congress: a group of deputies, better informed (but at the same time more easily controlled by the leadership) acted de facto in place of the soviet. The group was not, however, representative of political opinion within the soviet, still less of the electorate. A five-tiered hierarchical structure developed consisting of, at the base, 359 deputies (as of 1 September 1992), 123 of whom worked full-time in the commissions, a little soviet of thirty-eight, a praesidium of fifteen (elected on an individual basis), and, finally, the chair.

The chair, who had the right to issue instructions (*rasporiazhenia*), could in practice be likened to the director of an enterprise. He had the right to employ and dismiss its officials, to sign *kommandirovki* (authorizations for official travel), to award (or not to award) bonuses both to deputies and to officials, and so on. This inevitably led to a degree of patronage and political clientelism, regardless of the intentions of the holder of the post. Travel abroad, for example, justified as enabling deputies to acquire foreign expertise, and sponsored by western governments and institutions, was greatly sought after. In the case of the Supreme Soviet, Khasbulatov used his powers and the Soviet's financial resources blatantly and extensively. The procedure for discussion and voting, at the Congress, also allowed scope for manipulation by the chair. A further practice inherited from the previous system, the selecting of a commission from among the deputies to note the amendments and proposals during debate and then to produce the final resolution, also lent itself to manipulation and heightened tension while being an extraordinarily inefficient way of producing decisions. If at the centre the powers of the chair, and the procedures, led to wide-scale abuse, and open conflict, Petrosoviet was a model in comparison. Here too, however, it was clear that patronage existed and that procedures for taking decisions were time-wasting and inefficient. Enormous amounts of time could be spent on preparing proposals when it was quite unclear whether they would stand a chance of being adopted or not. It should be added too that the soviet lacked both a drafting staff and technical and expert advisers. If there had been a well-organized committee structure, a procedure for organizing and keeping to a legislative agenda, and tight time constraints, perhaps more proposals would have come to fruition.

Structure, procedures, and organizational practices should not be held solely responsible for ineffective policy-making and the discrediting of the soviets as representative institutions. It was the absence of political parties or coherent political groupings that thrust the organizational burden upon structures that were ill suited to the task. Political and ideological differences between the Lensoviet deputies began to reflect themselves in fractions in 1990 (although not all belonged to a fraction), and this continued until the soviet's dissolution in 1993. Initially the groupings changed as the political environment did and the democratic fractions tended to be short-lived. In February 1991 a Democratic Russia bloc was formed which included deputies who belonged to no particular fraction and members of five democratic fractions. By the end of the year and through 1993, with a smaller number of active deputies, voting on key issues tended to split 150 democrats to 60 Communists.[37] With the exception of the People's Front fraction which produced policy proposals worked out by its leaders, all the fractions limited their political activity to issues concerning individual appointments or misdemeanours. It was the commissions that occupied themselves with policy-making. Hardly surprisingly in such circumstances the pursuit and realization of a coherent policy agenda was impossible. It is true that erratic and sometimes contradictory policy-making on the part of the federal government forced regional soviets to behave in a reactive fashion, but the absence of effective, firmly grounded political organizations either within the soviet or in the wider society essentially created deputies who were incapable of working out and realizing policies to meet the needs of the city. This is something I shall return to in the next chapter.

The Congress and the Supreme Soviet

We must remember that both soviets and Congress had been elected when the party was still in power and the role of the elected assemblies still quite unclear. Although in Leningrad the majority of deputies were

---

[37] The existence of strong personalities was relevant too in the early period: Marina Sal′e led a radical, anti-communist People's Front group while P. Filippov led a fraction, Constructive Approach, advocating free-market measures and a more gradualist approach, and emphasizing the importance of strict observance of the law. A conservative Rebirth of Leningrad fraction was led by V. Sazonov. Sungurov, *Gorodskoi sovet*, p. 11, suggests there were no more than 180 active deputies by 1992.

newcomers who advocated change, this was not so in most of the country, nor was it really true in the Russian Parliament. Although Yeltsin won the chair, just, the proportion of deputies holding party, soviet, and managerial posts was still significant.[38] Whereas in St Petersburg the nomenklatura figures abandoned the soviet, and other honorific deputies drifted away, the importance of the Congress and the perks that went with being a federal deputy meant that, to a much greater extent, it retained its membership. Roughly 10 to 15 per cent of the deputies, either confused or dismayed by the new politics, simply stayed away even when crucially important votes were being taken. But the majority who were prepared to exercise their mandate found it no easier to agree on a legislative programme than did the members of Petrosoviet, and for many of the same reasons. Despite much greater resources, and qualified backup, the legislative process was disorganized and long drawn-out.

It was not just that the fractions which abounded in the Parliament failed to develop either a disciplined membership or to become nuclei of new parties.[39] Very different concerns on the part of the deputies made for unstable majorities and manipulation by the leadership. A study of deputy behaviour at the end of 1992[40] suggested figures: perhaps only 10 per cent of the regular attendees would vote consistently with their fraction; only they could be described as holding an ideological position. A further 10 per cent whose primary interest was in a long-term political career, either as a deputy or in government, sought to adopt strategies most likely to advance their chances. Some opted for developing a high profile, catching the television cameras, although it was far from clear whether this strategy would be most effective. Perhaps as many as a quarter of the deputies looked upon the mandate primarily as a short-term ticket to another job, a way of improving their material circumstances or raising their status: not simply acquiring a Moscow apartment (although this was very important) but getting a post in a commercial firm or in the state sector. This was a time of uncertain futures for a great number of people. There were both those whose institutes and enter-

---

[38] V. Sheinis and A. Nazimova, untitled article, *Argumenty i fakty*, 17 (1990), p. 3.

[39] The fractions in the Supreme Soviet in 1993 were constituted as follows: DemRossia 49, Radical Democrats 50, Accord for the Sake of Progress 53, Left–Centre Cooperation 62, Free Russia 55, Sovereignty and Equality 49, Motherland 52, Change–New Politics 53, Industrial Union 52, Workers' Union–Reform Without Shocks 53, Agrarian Union 129, Communists of Russia 67, Fatherland 51, Russia 55 (V. Pribylovskii, *Politicheskie fraktsii i deputatskie gruppy rossiiskogo parlamenta*, 2nd edn (Moscow, 1993)). For party development, see pp. 273–4 below.

[40] V. Gel´man, 'Evoliutsiia predstavitel´nykh organov vlasti v sovremennoi Rossii', *Pol. monit.*, 11 (1992), pp. 154–76. See also T. Colton, 'Professional Engagement and Role Definition Among Post-Soviet Legislators', in T. Remington (ed.), *Parliaments in Transition: The New Legislative Politics in the Former USSR and Eastern Europe* (Boulder: Westview Press, 1994), pp. 55–73.

prises were likely to close, and others who could not survive on the salary at their original place of employment. Becoming a deputy, especially in Moscow but also in St Petersburg, provided the opportunity, through new contacts, to ensure some kind of future for oneself and one's family. Others desperately needed to retain the mandate to survive. For those who had risen high, leaving office meant losing everything: individuals did not have the backing of a party organization, an organized political following, a base on which a political career could be founded. A key example was Khasbulatov, but there were many others for whom the Congress was their life-blood.

The largest single group of deputies – perhaps 40 per cent in all – did not view the job as their primary occupation. Among them were regional politicians, industrial directors, and farm chairmen, and ministerial officials. For them Congress was a place to further or defend regional interests, to discuss matters of common concern, and to lobby for sectional interests; but, perhaps even more important, attendance provided an opportunity for a trip to Moscow to visit the more important ministerial officials. Although the Supreme Soviet's control over the budget was an important weapon enabling its leadership to gain supporters among regional officials, the executive–legislative conflict worked against the legislature becoming the sole, or even a major, site for the promotion of regional or other interests. This in turn worked against the deputy being seen as the key defender of the constituency interest: others from the region (the chief administrator, the soviet chair) could lobby more effectively at ministerial level, and we have seen them actively doing this.

This combination of interests, and the organizational and procedural inheritance, could not produce an effective policy-making body. It did, however, mean an institution which a skilful chair, like Khasbulatov, could control. His own political survival required his ability to manipulate its members. He used the same carrots and sticks as the executive – posts, money, apartments, foreign travel – to secure the allegiance of needy and 'upwardly mobile' deputies, and the budget to try to secure regional support. These were the only ways of building a majority, not necessarily for a legislative programme, but to defend the Congress. If those within a legislature are to mount a strong attack against the executive, they must have a solid basis from which to fight. It may (as in nineteenth-century England) be property and wealth; it may be the threat of electoral support. The deputies had neither. They did not represent solid constituencies; they had no roots outside the Moscow buildings. For some of the nomenklatura deputies, the system that had given them mandates had disappeared; many of the new deputies had won by chance, and all the by-elections showed that the electoral environment of 1990 was gone forever. Without party support and a following at constituency level, many deputies' only hope of survival or of a political career lay in the continued existence of the Congress. This had to be defended at all costs. It was the only issue which could unite a sufficient number of its members: those ideologically committed to the existence of a democratically elected legislature, those with personal interests, and those who saw it as a way of opposing the president. The decision by the parliamentary leadership to build up its own armed contingents to defend the Supreme Soviet was indicative of its inability to rely on other forms of support.

By the summer of 1993 the debate over the clauses of the new constitution (the relationship between executive and legislature, and the federal structures) and over the procedure for adopting the constitution, had, not surprisingly, become almost deadlocked.[41] Tempers were running high, and the language used by the two sides had become quite unrestrained. Kostikov, the president's press secretary, referred to the Congress as having turned into

a hellish machine for the annihilation of civil peace and political stability in Russia. The Congress has broken all conceivable and inconceivable rules of political decency and human morality: it ceaselessly insults the president, the ministers, the government, the whole of Russia . . . it has placed itself above the law, [and] left the bounds of a democratic and civilized Russia.

A. Nevzorov, the talented television producer, who would be elected as a member of the Duma in December, suggested that

Of all living beings rats suffer the longest death-throes. That fact is recognized by all observers of the animal kingdom. Rat power in Russia will doubtless suffer from drawn-out death-throes. All that is left to the rats is to use the remaining 10,000 or 15,000 fanatics and turn them against the people. Civil war – that's the only way Yeltsin can prolong his political life.[42]

The conflict ended with the president's dissolution of the Parliament, a defiant stand by a minority of the deputies, and bloodshed on the streets of Moscow.

The end of Petrosoviet

During the spring and summer of 1993 the attitude within the Petrosoviet towards the Yeltsin government had begun to shift. At the time of the

---

[41] The executive–legislative relationship was of course only one of the issues. As noted, the spokesmen for republics and regions were by now at loggerheads over their respective rights. For a good analysis of the different factors that led to the crisis of September–October 1993, see G. Breslauer, 'The Roots of Polarization', *Post-Soviet Affairs*, 9 (1993), pp. 223–30.

[42] ITAR-TASS circulated statement, 29 March 1993; *Den'*, 11 (1993), p. 2. The praesidium of the Supreme Soviet was also drafting statements that were hardly less vituperative.

April referendum the majority of the democrats united to support the president. Beliaev wavered but came down on the president's side. Sobchak himself continued to support the president, speaking at a rally in Palace Square, and, as was expected, the majority of the citizens who turned out to vote gave strong support to the president.[43] Some of the more radical members of the little soviet were, however, becoming fearful that a strong president might mean a stronger mayor; others had begun to feel a sense of solidarity with colleagues in the Supreme Soviet or that a balance of power at the centre allowed the regions greater autonomy. Yeltsin's dissolution of the Parliament was supported initially by only 100 deputies. Joint action by the People's Front fraction and members of the new Regional Party, both democratic fractions, and the pro-Communist deputies produced a majority in favour of a draft resolution critical of the president's action. DemRossia deputies decided to prevent its passing by making the session inquorate but Beliaev, now siding with the Supreme Soviet, called a meeting of the little soviet which passed the resolution. Neither side could muster enough votes in the full soviet (DemRossia had assembled 130) either to overrule or to support the resolution. Even without the regional issue high on the agenda as in Tomsk, many of different persuasions felt obliged to defend the legislature. The most democratic of the soviets had parted company with its president.

Following the October days, with great difficulty, and only after a personal request from the president to Beliaev, the soviet reviewed the matter and rescinded the resolution passed by the little soviet. Sobchak stayed his hand but, when the little soviet produced a draft constitution for the new city assembly which included its right to ratify administration structures, he proposed the dissolution of Petrosoviet. Not surprisingly, in a rare show of unanimity, the deputies voted overwhelmingly against the proposal and in favour of holding elections in March 1994 for a new assembly; they set 22 December as the date on which they would vote on a final draft of the city's new constitution. They never met to do so. On 21 December the soviet was dissolved by presidential decree, no. 2252, and its functions and property were handed over to the mayor's office. The powers of the new assembly, to be elected in March, were prescribed by the mayor's office and, not surprisingly, were much more limited.[44]

[43] In January Petrosoviet had hosted a democratic conference, advocating a constitutional assembly to resolve the question of a new constitution, but its democrats were already beginning to divide among themselves (author's notes from attendance at conference, rallies, Petrosoviet meetings). It was said that mayoral employees were notified, during the April crisis, that attendance at the rally in Palace Square was expected. See also Sungurov, *Gorodskoi sovet*, pp. 29–30.

[44] Sungurov, *Gorodskoi sovet*, pp. 31–3; Gornyi and Shishlov, 'Organizatsiia vlasti', pp. 3–4; author's notes from sessions.

Yet even where chief administrators or presidents (in the republics) were faced by docile soviets, the preference of some in the post-October environment was to reduce their powers still further. Both Krasnodar and Sakha are examples. This suggests a motivation other than one of self-defence or at least a calculation that it is wise to safeguard oneself, institutionally, against potential opposition. Alternatively it could be prompted by a simple belief that a unitary executive type of rule is the most appropriate one. Not all chief administrators acted in this way. Many moved cautiously, either not wishing to encourage confrontation, or preferring to be seen to be sharing responsibility for unpopular policies with an elected assembly. Kuznetsov in Perm was one such, whereas Kress moved against the Tomsk soviet.[45] And, in some cases where chief administrators did act in a high-handed manner, the consequence was to bring Communists and democrats together 'to defend the right of representatives'. Rights rather than policies emerged as the point at issue.

Could the soviets have prevented their marginalization at the hands of the executive in those instances where their members wished to play a major role? Let us think back to Petrosoviet. The existence of legislation which empowered it to act, of courts prepared to issue verdicts against the mayor's office, and of an independent press anxious to discuss city politics were all essential to its activities. But its ability to influence important city appointments (the head of the Security Forces, for example),[46] and indeed its own powers vis-à-vis Sobchak, stemmed primarily from the degree of support it enjoyed *from above*, from the president or from the prevailing distribution of power at the centre. The deputies claimed that they were the people's representatives. Yet, as the passive reaction to their dissolution and then the election of March 1994 showed only too clearly, the deputies had largely forgotten or never realized that without their electors they were paper figures.

Ideologically disposed against parties, lacking a constituency, and

---

[45] V. Gel'man, 'Formula mestnoi vlasti: gubernator vsegda prav', *Novaia gazeta*, 3 August 1994, pp. 4–5; A. Kasimov and O. Senatova, 'Moskovskoe porazhenie rossiiskogo federalizma', in *Vek XX i mir* (Moscow, 1993), pp. 183–91. The federal institutions in 1992 and 1993, however much their leaders criticized each other, had also found it useful to be able to attribute difficulties to each other's behaviour; it may be better not to be the sole policy-maker when things go wrong.

[46] In autumn 1992 when Colonel V. Cherkesov, a KGB official involved in investigations of dissidents in the 1980s, was appointed as regional head of the Ministry of State Security, the soviet registered a protest and appealed to the president to revoke the appointment, but to no avail: *Smena*, 21 November 1992, p. 1; *Nev. vremia*, 21 November 1992, p. 1. The soviet could pass a vote of no confidence in city officials, as it did in the case of the head of the housing committee in March 1992, but the mayor could ignore this (unless it involved one of four specified posts) and the housing official remained in post for a further year: Gornyi and Shishlov, 'Organizatsiia vlasti', p. 9.

finding a lobby role distasteful, many deputies were quite unclear whom or what they were representing. Without a community whose interests they were defending and which provided them with an identity, the deputies attempted to construct one within the new institution. At its worst the result was quite 'empty' politicians, unable to distinguish their private interests from public concerns. At best talented and committed individuals could not realize their aims.

In observing the Congress and soviets in different parts of the country at work during 1992 and 1993, I became aware how the interplay between old habits of thought, conventions, and procedures on the one hand, and attempts to do things differently, tackle new tasks, and introduce new ideas on the other, continually produced the unexpected, both for the observer and the participants. To describe the soviets as legislatures in transition would be very misleading because it would imply that they were in the process of becoming a recognizable 'thing'. In truth they were elected bodies struggling to find a role for themselves, and both the roles and their behaviour were *sui generis*. Just as the communist party state influenced the type of protest and the way informal organizations conducted themselves, often in ways that mimicked the very state they were challenging, so did new legislatures incorporate elements of the new informal world while striving to become 'state institutions'. It is possible that, over time, in bodies of more manageable size, the organization of coherent political majorities will develop. Voting within the Duma in 1994–5 was more disciplined than in the Congress or Supreme Soviet during 1992–3. But deputy behaviour will depend on the type of representatives the electorate returns to office and this, in its turn, will be influenced by the kind of political organizations that mediate between society and state. For these reasons the final chapter focuses on representation and organization.

9   Facing the electorate

At the time of the December 1993 elections *Izvestia* featured a one-page explanation of the electoral system, probably written in the president's administration. The basic task of the Duma, it stated, was 'to work out laws and control the activity of the government. For this reason professionals are needed to work in this chamber – lawyers, economists, and specialists in the sphere of administration, and also professional politicians, representing the most influential Russian political parties.' Those elected to a constituency seat should see themselves first and foremost as representing the district, with a duty to defend its interests; the party-list deputies should represent 'a particular political force [*sila*]'. In making his or her choices the voter should consider 'the experience, wisdom, and honesty of the candidate'.[1] The image conjured up is of an assembly composed of party politicians, constituency representatives, and a group of 'legislative specialists'. Whom the latter would be representing remains unclear, yet it was this notion of the deputy as 'a professional legislator' that dominated the perceptions of those seeking office. Some intuitively felt there was a problem. A candidate in St Petersburg suggested:

We should not forget that Parliament is not only a legislative but also a representative organ [emphasis added]. The deputy should not only write and pass laws, but also defend the interests of his electors. And for that, professionalism alone may be insufficient. It is necessary to have a feeling of responsibility and civic obligation.

Another, a Petrosoviet deputy, now standing for the Duma, advanced the idea that 'a certain proportion of the deputies should not be professionals but simply representatives of the people who elected them'.[2]

I suggested, at the end of the last chapter, that in their preoccupation with their role as law-makers the deputies simply forgot about their constituents. Partly because they had had no ties to begin with, partly because this did not interest them, they failed to build up grass-roots organizations. This was to have consequences both for the candidates'

---

[1] *Izv.*, 7 December 1993, p. 7.
[2] All quotations from candidates given in this chapter are taken either from the author's candidate survey or from a *Nevskoe vremia* survey. See below, pp. 266–72, and appendix 4, pp. 327–8 for details.

and the electorate's behaviour when it came to elections. In general, whether we are talking of political organizations reaching out from the legislature to potential voters or of organizations formed outside the legislature but interested in getting their candidates elected to it, the period from 1991 through 1994 saw very little action. In all our regions political parties remained tiny transient organizations. Although, since 1991, hundreds of organizations had registered as political parties, no consolidation occurred; on the contrary almost all had fractured even further. Commentators lamented that the so-called parties were little more than 'divisions among the upper crust of society', collections of endlessly regrouping members of the Moscow intelligentsia. Society failed to produce firmly grounded political organizations which linked it with the institutions of the state. Rather, as we have seen, loose socio-political movements, political machines, lobby groups, and short-lived electoral blocs featured as the intermediary institutions linking state and society.

If we think of the state as those institutions that make authoritative decisions and implement them through apparatuses that are hierarchical, staffed, and backed up by the means of coercion, society or civil society is characterized by relations 'marked by normative discourse aimed at reaching understanding between social participants', for example, voluntary associations or trade unions. Political society mediates between the two. Its institutions translate projects from society into 'policies adopted by the state', and can include both parties and parliaments. Some institutions, a socio-political movement for example, lie across the civil/political divide. Within such a framework Urban characterizes communist party rule as having an overdeveloped executive (state) and an underdeveloped civil society, with no scope for 'political society'. Gradually, after 1988, with political clubs, elections, and political parties, political society re-emerged to fill in the trench between the two, but the linkages between state, political society, and society were still frail.[3] Although schematic, such a framework helps to illuminate some of the developments we have observed.

If we extend the idea of institutions lying across a divide we can think of parliaments lying across the divide between political society and the state: they both represent the people, and make authoritative decisions. Under the Soviet system they were simply part of the state. After 1989 they began

[3] M. Urban, 'State, Property, and Political Society in Postcommunist Russia: In Search of a Political Center', in C. Saivetz and A. Jones (eds.), *In Search of Pluralism: Soviet and Post-Soviet Politics* (Boulder: Westview Press, 1994), pp. 125–39. He refers back to A. Arato for the framework. G. White, 'Civil Society, Democratization, and Development (I): Clearing the Analytical Ground', *Democratization*, 1 (1993), pp. 375–90, discussing a similar framework, refers to Stepan's putting legislatures and electoral systems under 'political society', whereas he would put them under 'state', n. 14. This underlines the point that some institutions and activities may lie across the thresholds and, possibly, that they are therefore particularly important as sites of negotiation.

to acquire a representative function but, as we have seen, the Russian Parliament was far more concerned with its 'state' role than with its representative function. It felt more at home on the state side of the divide than as part of society. Its members could identity themselves as state administrators, but only with difficulty as representatives. We have seen how, in different regions, it was the executive which played an active role in entering the new political arena as the people's representative, emphasizing a direct state–society link without political intermediaries. None of this, we might say, is surprising. If socio-political movements are, in Urban's words, 'born in civil society', in the Soviet environment their father was the state, and an overweening state. A picture of state, political society, and society as separated from each other may be misleading here. In the Soviet context state and society were bonded together. Political society, whether under perestroika or after the ending of communist party rule, was their joint offspring, and the new or aspiring parliamentarians were no exception. Let us begin with them, and then look at political organizations.

Neither representatives nor politicians

At the time of the December 1993 elections I conducted an interview survey of those standing as candidates for the Duma and the Federal Council from St Petersburg. Approximately half of the 124 candidates (and of those interviewed) had served as deputies at either federal or local level. Here then was a group of current and aspiring parliamentarians. *Nevskoe vremia* also polled the candidates for their views on a select number of questions. A similar questionnaire was used in Perm and Tomsk to see whether significant differences appeared. I also followed the candidates' television and radio broadcasts in St Petersburg, and attended election meetings.

I shall begin with views of the role of the deputy. Only a quarter of those interviewed mentioned representing their constituents. Half saw the deputy's role as one of producing legislation or, more narrowly, drafting laws; a few thought it to be deciding important questions of state policy. The notion of working back in the constituency with their electors, or in a party, had no place in their thinking. Answers to the question 'how will you keep in touch with your electors?' revealed that, although a minority had clear ideas, others had hardly thought about it. Some vaguely suggested through an aide (one had in mind the district administrator), or by occasional visits. Although only one stated that his ties with the electorate ended with the collecting of signatures for his candidature, and henceforth he would pursue his own ideas in Moscow, few had given any thought to creating a social constituency for themselves. One of the federal deputies, when asked at an election meeting why he had so rarely come back to meet with his constituents, replied that he had been almost wholly involved 'in using his expertise', working on legislation that would control the activities of the Ministry of Internal Affairs and KGB.[4] Although it is doubtless an important issue, it is far from clear that this was his electors' priority.

The inadequacy of the work of the executive branch and the absence of a qualified staff may have encouraged deputies, working full-time, to see their job as one of drafting legislation. But then they and the administration were doing the same job, preparing and re-drafting legislation. It is hardly surprising that they quarrelled over spheres of competence, and that administrative officials stood for election. A district administrator argued:

I am a logician by training and consider that that is appropriate for working on legislative proposals. Further, from working in the social sphere, I can see which parts of a draft or law will work and which will not.

Another suggested: 'From working in the administration I know at first hand how imperfect the laws are. It is important that they are all clearly and properly formulated and do not allow for different interpretations.'[5] This confusion over roles or at the very least an unusual perception of the role of the elected representative only becomes intelligible if placed in the ideological environment of post-communist Russia.

Although the great majority of candidates considered a multiparty system to be desirable, fewer than a quarter belonged to a political party.[6] They were asked how they would reach a decision in Parliament if faced

---

[4] N. Arzhannikov, author's notes from election meeting with candidates for the Federal Council, St Petersburg, Frunzenskii district, 8 December 1993.

[5] And an employee in the mayor's office argued: 'the deputy should be concerned with working out mechanisms for the executive but not interfering in its role, finding a normal balance . . . The government must work and not engage in politics . . . the president's role is like that of the speaker . . . he must create a situation such that the two branches of power do not quarrel but work together properly in order that there are results so that society moves forward.'

[6] Examples of statements in favour of parties: 'If there aren't political parties which express the interests of social groups which have formed, there's no structured public opinion and it can become the plaything of demagogues and populists'; 'Strong political parties express the views and interests of large groups of citizens, and consequently it becomes easier to agree on macro interests'; 'Democracy is competition; when there is no competition, movement slows down.'

Those against: 'Parties are formed with self-interested aims, or are concerned with achieving power, don't do any real work . . . the individual party member does not decide anything'; 'It is sufficient to have associations of the toiling people who will voice the interests (not necessarily political) of strata of the population'; 'Parties are a bad thing because they hinder the management of the state.'

Unfortunately the question on whether the existence of opposition is desirable was poorly worded: some interpreted it to mean in principle, but many (and it became apparent that many felt quite unsure answering questions of a general kind) simply related it to their view of the present government. The favourite answer was, of course, that there should be an opposition 'if it is a constructive one'.

by an issue that had not featured in the election campaign. If, as perhaps expected, three-quarters of the independent candidates said they would rely on their own opinion or 'good sense' (other answers included 'the electors' interests' and 'specialist advice'), more than half the 'party/bloc' candidates gave the same answer; only a quarter said they would be guided by their party or fraction and this regardless of the party or fraction to which they belonged.[7] The constituency everyone wished to represent, regardless of party, was 'the people'. The original nomenklatura had always thought of themselves as the vanguard, speaking for a collective unit, 'the people'. With the democratic victory, this dissolved into individuals, each with equal rights, and members of the original elite felt confused: where had their constituency gone?[8] Not surprisingly, they strove to re-create a collective electorate. But the democrats too felt uncomfortable in this unstructured environment. Yet who 'the people' were was dodged by all except some of the extreme patriots, prepared to identify who was *not* included: the Jews and the Caucasians. Even the Communists had a problem in deciding whom to claim as their constituents. Both the working class and the *trudiashchiesia* (the labouring masses) sounded too class-based, and fitted ill with patriotic rhetoric. The economic consequences of the Gaidar reforms had enabled them to claim a new constituency of 'the poor', and this they tried to make the basis for the nation.[9]

The desire on the part of everyone to escape from class interests encouraged the tendency to talk in terms of 'the common interest', to insist that the interests of all could be served. 'National consensus', the term most overused by all the politicians in the summer of 1993, was contrasted with its seeming alternative 'civil war' (although who the two sides

---

[7] But this is not surprising given that the association of many with a party or bloc was a purely tactical move to win a seat; see pp. 277–8 and 294 below.

[8] V. L. Tsymburskii, 'Ideia suvereniteta v posttotalitarnom kontekste', *Polis.*, 1 (1993), p. 30.

[9] Norton, *Reflections*, pp. 77–8, makes the point that workers (unlike peasants, who are attached to the land) are associated with other workers in a world economic system. 'If the nation has a sizeable working class, the figure of the worker, freighted with referential meaning, becomes divisive, for it is associated with a particular class and cannot supply a symbol for the whole.' Patriotic language will avoid its usage because 'the worker as a sign transcends nationality'. Party ideology, since Khrushchev, had spoken of the party representing the interests of the whole people, a concept which for some had acquired a patriotic and then a Union content. I noted how in Krasnodar, and also in Perm, a pro-communist orientation elided with a patriotic one. In St Petersburg, one of the leading Communist Party candidates argued that the role of the deputy is 'to be a citizen of his country', 'to defend "our country" from "their country", that of the cosmopolitans' (see n. 39 below). It is but a short step from this to the claims of the patriots that a deputy should 'be true to the fatherland' and 'serve the nation', and therefore not surprising that the Communists and patriots often appeared on the same platforms. A Pamiat slogan, 'Patriots of the whole world unite!', exemplifies the curiously confused ideological environment.

were to consist of was never specified). Sectional interests were considered divisive. Although the voice of the lobbyist could be heard ('the task of the deputy', according to one of the new millionaires, 'is to pass laws which secure the basis for private property'), it tended to be muffled. Candidates from Civic Union, the industrialists' lobby, preferred to talk of the deputy's task as one of 'passing laws which will ensure stability', 'preventing the passing of laws of an anti-*narodnaia* [anti-social] character'. But when directors are using the same words as their workforce, while acquiring ownership of the factories and granting themselves huge salary increases, political language has ceased to express the two sides' opposing interests. The spokeswomen for Women of Russia also refrained from making any socially divisive claims, still less any that were damaging to men; their appeal was for moderation and calm.

Disapproval of promoting narrow sectional interests had the ironic consequence that sectional interests were sometimes presented, in all good faith, as common interests. In St Petersburg this appeared in the insistence, particularly from the professional intelligentsia, that deputies should be specialists or 'professionals'.[10] They fully shared the *Izvestia* view that legislative specialists were necessary. A system of party rule that increasingly had come to denigrate professional competence and specialist expertise, yet emphasized hierarchy and status, had bred intellectual and professional elitism among its intelligentsia. Lenin's notion that cooks could participate in running the country could now be held up to ridicule. A lone voice argued:

Parliamentary professionalism does not mean that we should elect lawyers and economists and not housewives . . . a professional parliamentarian is a quite new profession in Russia . . . it requires a whole range of qualities which a lawyer may not possess . . . a housewife can become one if she has a good education, if she can read and compose a well-written document, and is able to express her point of view.

But very few would have agreed. Many conceded that, while 'specialist knowledge' was an essential attribute of the deputy, it was not sufficient in and of itself:

Yes, it's desirable that professionals work in the Parliament. But a diploma does not guarantee professionalism. Furthermore I am convinced that the very worst outcome is if the Duma is made up of very professional, very literate, very erudite but dishonest people.

And one pointed out: 'Of course professionals are needed but of what sort? The KGB also maintains that their people are professionals.' But of those who answered the newspaper survey, only a few (and none of those who had served as deputies) thought 'professionalism' should play no part. There was the occasional exception. A new entrepreneur stated:

[10] See also Colton, 'Professional Engagement'.

I think we should drive the professionals out. Let them find work for themselves in the economic sphere. Recently the word 'professional' has come to be used in place of 'official, bureaucrat'. The officials have recently been reproducing themselves faster and faster while thinking up ever new ways of enriching themselves at the expense of those who work creatively. They are gradually turning into common or garden parasites, living off those who do the real work and produce.[11]

Intellectual elitism, though, was not enough to explain the insistence by so many on the need for professional qualifications. There was, I suggest, the need to find another persona for the deputy who had no identity as a representative, and this is where the image of the deputy as a 'legislative specialist' was useful. One of the candidates, a defence lawyer, in his television campaign broadcast, argued that since the task of the Duma was that of a law-maker ('there should be no politics there'), its membership should consist solely of lawyers: then the Parliament would work professionally, and the country would get good laws.[12] This was but the extreme expression of a position that had many adherents. An economist argued that only the appropriate specialists should be elected: 'I am an economist, a specialist on economic reforms, I know how they should be done, and I managed to do a great deal in Gaidar's government.' Other answers to *Nevskoe vremia* included:

Yes. I am sufficiently competent in the sphere of legislation, in jurisprudence and economic questions, I have a certificate from the University of Houston in marketing and business, and experience of economic activity.

And:

Yes. I worked for sixteen years in an applied science institute . . . have a doctorate, more than 100 academic publications . . . and recently . . . experience in working on draft legislation. Furthermore I am completing a legal education . . . and the analysis of what happens in politics led me to [give] lectures in political science, first in a Californian university, and now in Petersburg.

Lawyers and economists were seen as the most appropriate candidates for politicians. Several of the St Petersburg candidates, already serving as deputies, were taking law degrees (while working as a full-time deputy?).[13] Others who were not lawyers and economists but shared the 'specialist' view stressed their particular expertise. An army officer argued

---

[11] The young representative of the nationalist Russian Party, Bondarik, shortly to be arrested on a charge of murdering a party colleague, argued that 'A parliamentary commission must, first and foremost, be honest and incapable of being bought. You can always find professional advisers.' A construction engineer suggested that the deputies should simply be 'People, who reflect the interests of the great majority of the working people, and who are subordinate to and controlled by them.'

[12] Television campaign broadcast, 26 November 1993.

[13] One of the candidates put her finger on the problem of the legislative specialist: 'If we elect lawyers, the Parliament will become one big institute of state and law – but we have already got one of those. Economists? We already had Gosplan, and the country did not flourish.'

that 'Parliament should contain economists, lawyers, sociologists, industrialists, and the military.' A trade union official supported the need for professionals: 'Yes. I am a specialist in labour law and social and tax policy.' Some of the new entrepreneurs or managers stressed their practical knowledge:

Who is more professional than the Russian entrepreneur? With their first-hand experience of both the carrot and the stick they know which laws Russia needs.

An industrial manager argued:

Without being modest, I objectively include myself in the ranks of the professionals – those who manage industry – and the economists. Both as regards macro and micro questions only we, the directors, who meet face to face every day with the workers – the fundamental and most important section of our society – know people's demands and ways of improving their lives.

Neither the view of deputy as 'legislative specialist' nor that of a parliament of specialists has any place in the classic literature on representation and deputy roles. Nor does it reflect the Burkean conception of the politician who, rising above the fray, seeks the common good.

In the absence of a party loyalty, or a function as spokesman for a group or a constituency, what is to make a deputy a good deputy? It would seem that only individual qualities can distinguish the candidates. 'First and foremost it should be selfless, honest, responsible, and cultured people who work in the Duma', argued one, and it was the quality of moral probity that was seen as most important for a deputy. 'Morality and honesty' was cited by nearly half, 'professionalism' came second, then 'cleverness, administrative ability', 'holding to a firm position, independence', and 'the ability to listen to others, to compromise'. The concern with morality was slightly more pronounced among the non-deputies. For many 'a morally upright specialist' should be descriptive of the deputy:

Yes, and my professional expertise is appropriate, but the matter does not consist of professionalism. The professional Gaidar dipped into our pockets, and robbed the people . . . very professionally. Today morality in politics should stand in first place, and not bare professionalism.[14]

From some of those who had already served as deputies, and wanted political careers, came a rather different claim. In their view a new profession had come into existence, that of the professional politician. A charge often laid against the deputies by the administration, and in the press, and one readily admitted by many of them, was of their lack of

---

[14] An unusual claim came from one of the new millionaires: 'The basis of professionalism is morality. Therefore I consider that, in the first place, parliamentarians must either be people, well known, to whom one would turn for the resolving of conflicts, or wealthy people because material wealth creates spiritual richness.'

'professionalism'. This, many argued, must be responsible for their inability to work effectively together. They lacked the expertise possessed by their western counterparts. The use of the word 'professional' is important. Whereas in a western context the word 'politician' may or may not have a pejorative connotation, in Russia it was wholly negative – a talker, with narrow, selfish, 'ideological' interests. In the words of one of the candidates: 'I consider that *in the Duma there should be fewer politicians* [emphasis added], and more who understand economics and law, experienced financiers, energetic and honest entrepreneurs.'

In a long-established democracy the term 'professional politician' has the connotation of someone who, as a result of experience and not necessarily very likeable talents, knows how and when to strike bargains, advance a political position, use influence, woo the electorate, cultivate allies, destroy enemies. He or she knows how to play the parliamentary or party game to advantage. The advocates of the term in Russia, however, meant something rather different. For some the image was closer to that advocated by Burke:

The professionalism of the deputy is of a particular kind. It consists of a breadth of vision, of an intellectual ability to work with others to reach decisions and, most important, to reconcile the interests of different social groups, and, finally, it includes elementary decency.

A deputy, one of the very few active in a political party, an engineer turned politician, who had picked up a law degree, argued:

I consider myself to have been a professional politician since 1989, I have experience of working in state institutions, I am a specialist in military matters, the defence industry, and in the administration of large systems, I am a deputy, and co-chairman of the city branch of the Republican Party. Parliamentary professionalism, in my view, must be based on a new profession – parliamentary professionalism, which requires considerable erudition and experience.

But even here it remains unclear as to what exactly this 'professionalism' is. During a pre-election discussion a deputy, replying to the question of what his party stood for, referred to 'professionals in politics; just as you intellectuals would want to be represented by a council of your best representatives, we want to see the "best politicians" elected'. When pressed as to what constituted a 'good', professional politician, his colleague answered that it was someone who can 'really work on the legislation, who can see that the poor drafts from the mayor's office and budget errors do not go through unamended, it is not the deputy who creates scandals, brings charges of corruption, is always in the news'.[15] The image is of an able, hard-working, committee member; it is almost entirely legislature-centred and has nothing to do with party, constituency, or electorate.

[15] Author's notes from meeting of *Peterburgskaia tribuna*, discussion club, 17 January 1994.

Putting choices before the electorate

In an established democratic system the electoral rules are agreed and state officials are responsible for administering an election. Simplifying, we can say that the state provides the framework and the rules, political society provides the players, and society, the electorate, picks the winners. It is important to bear in mind that this is a simplification of the electoral game in democratic systems given, on the one hand, varying degrees of state involvement ranging from intimidation, close links with one political party or another, to falsification of election results and, on the other, the existence of electoral rules that benefit particular participants and in their turn influence the organization of political society. The nature of the choices offered to the electorate crucially affects outcomes. In Russia, in the early 1990s, established and agreed electoral rules did not exist and the state was directly involved as a political actor. The political organizations that participated in the 1993 and 1994 elections were for the most part hastily assembled coalitions or groups. The majority of candidates competed as individuals. In other words, these were elections in which a tiny minority decided both the rules and the choices put before the electorate.

The 1993 election in St Petersburg

None of the parties that came into existence in 1990–1 (the Social Democrats, Christian Democrats, the Cadets, the Democratic Party of Russia, the Liberal Democratic Party, the Republican Party (reform communists), the militant communist parties, the monarchists, the Russian Party, the Anarchists) had developed into coherent national organizations with regional branches. All underwent splits, sometimes more than once.[16] Party activities in St Petersburg, rather than developing, dwindled

---

[16] There is a substantial literature, mostly informational, on the parties. See V. Krasnov, *Sistema mnogopartiinosti v sovremennoi Rossii* (Moscow, 1995); A. Salmin (ed.), *Partiinaia sistema v Rossii v 1989–1993 gg.: opyt stanovleniia* (Moscow, 1994). For a recent discussion, which contains a listing of parties post-1993, see S. Fish, 'The Advent of Multipartyism in Russia, 1993–1995', *Post-Soviet Affairs*, 11 (1995), pp. 340–83. For the regions, see V. Gel'man and O. Senatova, 'Politicheskie partii v regionakh Rossii', in Gel'man (ed.), *Ocherki rossiiskoi politiki* (Moscow, 1994), pp. 16–30; Gel'man and Senatova, 'Politicheskie partii v regionakh Rossii: dinamika i tendentsii', *Vlast'*, 5 (1995), pp. 39–48. The existence of a Social Democratic, as opposed to a Democratic Party of Russia or a Republican, group often depended on which democratic activist from Moscow had got there first. The links between Moscow and the provinces were very tenuous, if they existed at all. I spent the morning of 22 September 1993 (following Yeltsin's edict on the dissolution of Parliament and the holding of elections) in the office of the chair of the Kazan Social Democratic Party; the phone rang four times; it had not occurred to him that there was any reason to contact party headquarters or that they would contact him. The example may be slightly unfair: in Tatarstan the chances of meaningful voter turnout were slight, but I suspect the reaction to Yeltsin's announcement was the same throughout the provincial towns of Russia.

to little more than monthly meetings of a handful of activists. The democratic organizations had been given a building in the aftermath of the August days but its rooms remained almost entirely bare. DemRossia held monthly meetings here but the democrats were as divided in St Petersburg as in Tomsk. Despite the insistence by Yeltsin that new elections to a federal assembly should take place no later than the autumn of 1993, few either at the centre or in St Petersburg had shown signs of getting themselves organized or running a recruitment campaign in the summer.[17] Patriotic activities were very similar. Here too there were splits, and the organizations remained small: Pamiat, and Fatherland, and Lysenko's National-Republican Party. Among the patriots and communists recognizable ideological parties (the Russian Communist Workers' Party, Nina Andreeva's Bolshevik Party, the Russian Party, Russian National Unity) – either militant communist or nationalist-fascist – existed, and all had a clutch of supporters in St Petersburg. For a while the Front for National Salvation brought some of them together at national level, but by the summer of 1993 the strains within the organization were beginning to show.[18] Whether democrats, communists, or patriots, all were characterized by splintering and infighting. One party, the Communist Party of the Russian Federation, however, stood out. A returnee to the scene in 1992, it had a national organization and a respectable if elderly membership of original party members.

With the announcement that half the seats in the Duma would be elected by a party-list system, the party leaderships in Moscow were galvanized into action. They had to calculate their chances of collecting enough signatures to compete, and to decide who should feature in the party lists.[19] The Communist Party, concerned to 're-establish civil peace and legality, and to return the country to the rails of civilized development', and committed to recreate 'the Union by voluntary agreement', entered the election on its own.[20] So did the two that existed by virtue of

---

[17] Shakhrai, minister for nationality affairs, did form a new party, PRES, or Unity and Accord, and G. Yavlinskii began to take soundings among democratic activists, which gave birth to Yabloko.

[18] It included representatives of the Communist Party of the Russian Federation, Ampilov's Labouring Russia, Lysenko's National Republican Party, Makashov's Russian National Unity, Afanas'ev's Cadets, Baburin's Russian All-National Union, and Konstantinov from the Russia fraction in the Supreme Soviet. By July Lysenko and Baburin had distanced themselves.

[19] See appendix 3, pp. 324–6, for details on the rules and procedures for the December 1993 elections.

[20] The party stood for 'general state, general democratic priorities' but also for recognizing Russian national specifics; Stolypin was cited as a statesman: *Izv.*, 19 November 1993, p. 4; religion, according to Ziuganov, was a private matter (television broadcast, 23 November 1993).

their leaders, the Democratic Party of Russia under Travkin, and Zhirinovskii's Liberal Democratic Party. N. Travkin, now backed by Govorukhin, the patriotic film director, mounted a television campaign sharply critical of president and government. Govorukhin referred to the 'bloody constitution', to Yeltsin's having less education but more rights than Nicholas II, and claimed that, unlike Yeltsin in the aftermath of the storming of the White House, in the civil war the Whites had awarded no medals because they recognized that none could be won for shooting one's fellow countrymen.[21] Zhirinovskii put together a party list, a programme aimed at 'patriotic statists', and organized an election campaign that revolved around himself. Zhirinovskii, the posters claimed, 'will defend Russians across the territory of the whole country': 'I shall allow no one to insult Russians!'; 'I shall defend Russians!' Azerbaijanis would be deported, thus halting the flight of Russians from Azerbaijan ('Democracy also includes the use of force'); the standard of living would be doubled in six months by stopping conversion and selling arms, stopping the export of raw materials, and ending organized crime.[22]

Most of the other parties recognized that they had no chance of gaining electoral support. Their leaders therefore were interested, or rather desperate, to join an electoral bloc that might do well. Although there was some consistency in the choices (the regrouped Social Democrats tended to join up with Yabloko, for example), the issue of the October days split democratic organizations at all levels. The leaders of the two key democratic blocs – Gaidar and Yavlinskii – neither of whom belonged to a political party, both looked to past and present members of DemRossia and outside it. The drawing up of the party lists was sometimes highly contentious, and often shrouded in mystery. Their final composition was decided by the party or bloc leadership in Moscow and the voice granted the local organizations, where they existed, varied from party to party. Judging from the final lists, the voices from St Petersburg did not carry much weight.[23] Yabloko, a quite new organization, had no time to squabble – here the St Petersburg organization and a list of candidates was created in the space of a few days on the basis of phone calls from

---

[21] *Izv.*, 24 November 1993, p. 4; television broadcast, 23 November 1993.

[22] He was in favour of a strong state sector (but maintaining the market), of a strong national army, of 'patriotism, pride in Russia', but this should be 'the Russian state (not the Union of Soviet Socialist Republics or CIS) on the territory of the USSR': programme; *Izv.*, 30 November 1993, p. 4.

[23] The occasional candidate appeared high up a list (the director of the Kirovskii plant in the Civic Union, the leader of the Petersburg branch of the LDP high in its list, and O. Vasilashvili, the actor, in the Russian Movement for Democratic Reform), but the first Petersburg candidate in the Communist Party list (Iu. Sevenard) came in sixteenth place, A. Golov in fourteenth place in the Yabloko list and, even in Russia's Choice list, St Petersburg only came in twenty-sixth place with M. Molostvov.

Yavlinskii and Boldyrev to friends and activists from earlier days. Yabloko was 'for democracy with clean and strong hands', 'the values of freedom, property, and honest competition'. It too wanted 'a strong state' – but here Boldyrev in particular was at pains to stress the separation of powers, and the ending of corruption. Its main criticism of the government was for its too monetarist economic policy and for 'the soft dictatorship' of the constitution.[24]

Russia's Choice faced a problem. What was Russia's Choice? Was it DemRossia minus those who had deserted to Yabloko and, if so, should its list reflect all those parties which were members of the movement? Or was it a new bloc, a president's party led by Gaidar, embracing all who wished to join? The sessions held in the DemRossia headquarters in St Petersburg were long and heated. Alternative lists circulated; representatives of banking and commercial concerns demanded the inclusion of their candidates in return for financial support; bargains were struck. The final list sent to Moscow included DemRossia activists from the Russian Christian-Democratic Party and the Free Democratic Party, from Memorial, and non-party people, but the Moscow leadership (essentially Gaidar) made the final choice. Russia's Choice, closely identified with its leader Gaidar, the 'iron Winnie-the-Pooh', led off with the slogan 'Freedom, Property, Legality' and used as its television motif 'Your choice is the choice of Russia.'[25] The message was one of a government that had achieved much (stocking the empty shelves) and would now ensure 'a stable currency, a stable authority, and a stable state'. A strong state was needed, and for this the constitution was essential – without it, argued Gaidar, there was the danger of 'yet another dissolution of democracy in Russia'.[26]

Of the remaining parties or blocs, only three had a presence in St Petersburg. They were RDDR; the Russian Movement for Democratic Reform, which owed its existence to Sobchak's ability to maintain an organization based on the administration; and PRES, the Party of Unity and Accord, Shakhrai's creation, based on regional and republican administration with Chernomyrdin's unspoken support and Gazprom money. RDDR managed a video – with onion domes and songs –

---

[24] Author's notes from election meetings: Boldyrev, Oktiabrskii district, 4 December 1993; Frunzenskii district, 8 December 1993; television debate, 1 December 1993.

[25] A catchy slogan, but an unfortunate one given its association with the unpopular voucher campaign. For months the government, with US money, had been running an advertisement 'Your voucher – your choice', and concern was voiced in Washington that the two were connected.

[26] *Izv.*, 8 December 1993, p. 4; programme materials. Russia's Choice used a video of the bloody scenes in Moscow, with the background of a song 'God grant . . . ', to warn of the possibility of a communist–fascist revanche.

recruited a general to stress the theme of statehood, and a young singer to attract youth but its message was empty: it was for 'Hard realism in the place of fantasy and adventurism', 'the search not for enemies but for the like-minded', 'for Professionalism, Responsibility, and the Trust of the masses'.[27] PRES was for Unity and Accord, its constitution (written on the way to its founding meeting) stressed strengthening 'Russia as a modern industrial power', 'integrating the values of the spiritual and material culture of Russia into world civilization'. It was 'for stability . . . moving forward, but rejecting radicalism'. What did it stand for? 'We would like to be a conservative party', said one of its spokesman at a meeting, 'but the trouble is that at the moment we can't find anything worth conserving.' This prompted Beliaev, chair of Petrosoviet, seeking endorsement wherever possible, to suggest that this was what was so attractive about PRES: here was a party concerned solely with creating an organization, rather than concentrating on political issues.[28]

Civic Union was rather different again. It was the voice of the military-industrial lobby, headed by A. Volskii, president of the Russian Union of Industrial Enterprises. If Chernomyrdin stood behind the fabulously rich energy sector, Civic Union fought for subsidies and money for conversion. Its voice was that of the patriotic statists; it favoured 'A centrist position, conservatism, for compromise, against the danger of a social explosion'. Order featured strongly: 'Order in the state, in the economy, on the streets'. Russian capital and industry must be saved, and the break-up of Russia averted. But although a number of St Petersburg candidates had the backing of Civic Union, the organization had no city office nor activists campaigning on its behalf.[29]

A consequence of the hasty creation of parties or electoral blocs was that many who appeared on the party lists (apart from the Communists) had no prior association with the organization, and no previous experience of politics, still less any work at constituency level. Some had little interest in the programmes, which too often were hurriedly put together,

---

[27] Programme leaflets; television broadcast, 30 November 1993.

[28] *Zvezda* meeting, 25 November 1993.

[29] Volskii spoke favourably of the Chinese example, and of de Gaulle as a hero: television broadcasts, 23, 25, 30 November 1993; *Izv.*, 4 December 1993, p. 4. Yet the St Petersburg candidates hardly spoke with a coherent voice; one ex-raikom secretary, now a general director, favoured a strong two- or three-party system: 'parties express interests of groups of people and through them in organs of power try to ensure the carrying out of those interests . . . if there aren't fractions in the Duma we can't talk of democracy because society is divided between different interests and they must be expressed'. He sympathized with Ziuganov. Two others were doubtful or opposed to parties; one favoured autocratic rule (*samoderzhavie*); M. Goriachev, the young multimillionaire, argued that 'the interests of business are the interests of all!', and claimed to support the economic views of both Volskii and Yavlinskii.

and sometimes hardly distinguishable one from another. A total of 119 candidates from St Petersburg competed for the Duma places (forty-eight as independents) and five for the two Council of the Federation seats. The collecting of signatures was done, primarily, in institutions and apartments; both parties and individuals, where they had the money, paid canvassers (1,000 r. for a full sheet of signatures). Incidents of illegality began to surface: payment for a signature; students tricked into thinking they were signing a petition on student hardship. There was little the electoral commissions could do in the few days granted them to check out the lists and complaints. In a few cases individuals were disqualified, or withdrew.[30] New campaign methods appeared: the distribution of free drinking glasses, or oranges, free metro tickets, a lottery linked with an election leaflet. Complaints were voiced that the post office, which charged 25 r. per leaflet delivered, sometimes simply failed to deliver. The intense efforts of a few, poor organization or its almost total absence, small clusters of intense politicking, an unscrupulous use of the media and probably money, marathon tedious television sessions, and widespread lack of interest on the part of the electorate marked the election campaign.[31]

Who were the candidates? Before we consider key individuals, what kind of people had put themselves forward? Of the eighty-eight candidates interviewed (73 per cent of the total), only three were women. Half were between the ages of forty and fifty, the remainder split fairly evenly between the fifty-to-sixty and thirty-to-forty age brackets, with a sprinkling below the age of thirty. Almost all who stand for election in Russia today have higher education, and hold white-collar jobs. To try to identify whether social background was associated with different political posi-

[30] S. Tsypliaev, the president's representative, withdrew his candidature when it was revealed that fictitious signatures appeared in his list. Among his supporters, however, was the suspicion that their appearance and discovery was not accidental. Tsypliaev and Beliaev, the soviet chair, had agreed to pool their resources for the collection of signatures – a strategy that required good faith on both their parts – but some believed that Beliaev had taken the opportunity to ensure that a future rival was discredited. Success or failure could depend on the herculean efforts of a single individual. L. Kesel′man, the doyen of public opinion polling in the city, galvanized Russia's Choice and part of the press into campaigning on behalf of N. Arzhannikov, ex-policeman, democratic activist, and RF deputy, as a candidate for the Council of the Federation. Aspects of the Arzhannikov campaign were not unique to it: signatures gathered at the eleventh hour, money found to produce a professional video and a glossy campaign leaflet, but so late that the video was shown only twice and a million leaflets still lay in their packages in Russia's Choice headquarters after all was over.

[31] *Anon*, November–December 1993, p. 5. This also refers to the dailies not taking materials from the Communists or the LDP, whereas radio and television took LDP broadcasts. On a rather different scale: an *Izvestia* headline declared (24 November 1993): 'Chernomyrdin has found 100 mlrd r. for the miners [of western Siberia], Gaidar is looking for trillions and setting out for Vorkuta'. The prime minister and deputy prime minister were into the business of competition for the votes of the striking miners.

tions, I took parents' occupation. This suggested that those supported by Russia's Choice and the other four democratic parties or blocs had predominantly been brought up in professional families, whereas those supported by the other parties (Civic Union, Liberal Democratic Party, communists, patriots)[32] were more likely to come from families where the father had not received a higher education, and had worked in industry, or in the military. Among the independent candidates, the two types of social background was distributed equally. Social background did therefore have an echo, but only a faint echo, in what we can call political position (although, again, we must be wary of reading too much into electoral bloc affiliation).[33] The sons and daughters of the Petersburg intelligentsia, *if* they approved of political parties, were much more likely to be found on a democratic party list; those from the less professional backgrounds who took a party mandate were more likely to be found on the other lists. But type of social background did not make an aspiring politician more or less likely to align himself with a party.

Among the youngest, new types were represented – the wealthy director of a new commercial concern, the ambitious young economist, the lawyer committed to improving the environment, and the outspoken anti-semitic Russian nationalist – speaking in voices very different from those of the oldest generation. Among the latter the spectrum of opinion was no less wide: the monarchist, the 'soviet' trade unionist, a Communist Party official, an ex-dissident camp survivor, the energetic director of a machine-building enterprise. If members of the oldest generation instantly recognize each others' political positions, formed over the years, those of the youngest generation are still seeking theirs, and not looking to their elders for guidance. The youthful were less likely to have a party attachment but this means little. Most of those who appeared either on a party or electoral bloc list, or were supported by one for a constituency seat, were there by virtue of being approached or 'buying' a place on it and older candidates were more likely to have the necessary contacts or be known by those in the electoral bloc leadership. On such questions as the desirability of a multiparty system or the advantages of a strong or weak president, members of the oldest and youngest generations divided no differently.

But what of the thirty-five- to fifty-year-olds, who came to maturity

[32] Although certain parties were banned and could not participate under the party lists, an individual could stand for one of the majoritarian seats with the support of one of the banned parties.
[33] One of the LDP candidates, for example, had been approached by two of the communist parties, hesitated, but decided on this occasion to accept the LDP ticket. But then he would not have been approached by the democratic parties. On the other hand a candidate might stand on one ticket but, once in the Duma, abandon it for another (Mark Goriachev, for example).

during the period of *zastoi* or stagnation? Here were the original democratic activists of the perestroika period, almost all from the arts or scientific-research institutes, many of them having served in the soviet and now with a taste for politics. These tended to be western-oriented, convinced that they must learn from western experience, but not necessarily attached to a party. They were joined by lawyers and administrators, by new entrepreneurs with business interests, and by the occasional political activist, associated either with one of the communist parties or with Zhirinovskii. In general this generation seemed less politically literate than the older generation, less enterprising than the young.

There was little correlation between answers to questions on the deputy's role, reasons for standing, the role of political parties, the desirability of opposition, and the functions of the different federal institutions with social background, membership of the CPSU, deputy or non-deputy status, age, or party or non-party affiliation. Half the candidates, both those who had and had not served as deputies, had been Communist Party members, but this did not distinguish their answers from those who had never been. Not surprisingly, candidates supported by a political party stated that they approved of political parties in principle. Those who had served as deputies tended to emphasize the ability to compromise as a key quality for a deputy; those supported by the non-democratic parties tended to stress the ability to defend a firm position, and made no mention of compromise. Those towards the left of the political spectrum made more mention of the deputy's task as representing the interests of the electors, whereas those on the Russia's Choice list rarely did so.

Certain political positions could be identified – a democratic westerner, a patriot, a pro-communist – but the bearers of these did not necessarily have a party affiliation, while even among those who professed to share a political allegiance there was a variety of views on the role of deputies and the structure and role of government. For example, only the Communists had a consistent line among themselves on the presidency:[34]

A president is not needed; the consequence of introducing the presidency was the break-up of the Union, and a struggle of ambitions and sovereignties.
There should not be a president.
The president is a US import.

Here they parted company with the patriots, most of whom favoured a strong president. He should have an

[34] Of all who offered an answer on the presidency, forty-one favoured a strong presidential role, thirty-four a weak one; the responses did not correlate with any of the indicators, or other responses.

all-embracing role – be a political leader, a master [*khoziain*], he must feel that this is his country, land, and people.

Be a maker of peace; answerable for everything that happens in the country and not be afraid to take responsibility.

The president should have a dictatorial role and the deputies should support him.

Russia's Choice candidates were divided. He should:

be 'the real head of state' at a time of crisis but at normal times have a representative, decorative role.

In the future it will be necessary to move from a presidential to a parliamentary system.

He should determine the rules of the game; act against the authoritarian tendencies of top officials; decide the fate of democracy; effect reform.

The elections for the two places in the Council of the Federation and the eight single-member constituencies dominated the campaign. There were five candidates for the two council seats: N. Arzhannikov, supported by Russia's Choice; Beliaev, from the soviet, with the support of Russia's Choice, of Unity and Accord, and of the Movement for Democratic Reform; Iu. Buldyrev, the young deputy to the first Congress of Soviets, who had risen to become inspector general under Yeltsin and then been dismissed when, it was believed, he tried too hard to stamp out corruption, and who was now one of the leaders of Yabloko; D. Filippov, ex-obkom secretary for industry, who had earned a reputation as the creator of the cleanest tax inspectorate in the country before being summarily and unaccountably dismissed by Sobchak in the summer of 1993 after the inspectorate claimed misdemeanours on the part of the property committee in the mayor's office; and V. Shcherbakov, retired naval admiral, deputy mayor, supporter of the Supreme Soviet in the autumn, and backed by the Communist Party and the extreme right.

Among the single-member constituency seats for the Duma that for the central district was the most bitterly contested. Here A. Nevzorov, the popular patriotic television producer, was standing, and four democrat contenders threatened to split the vote against him. This became even more of a danger when the Liberal Democratic candidate stood down in favour of Nevzorov. One of the two Russia's Choice candidates stood down but, despite frantic and last-minute negotiations, the final line-up still included one candidate each from Russia's Choice, Yabloko, and the Movement for Democratic Reform. Nevzorov just won, narrowly beating the Russia's Choice candidate. Dismay and bitterness prevailed. A. Chernov, the Russia's Choice candidate who had stood down, wrote an unpleasant piece for *Moskovskii komsomolets*, implying cowardice and lying on the part of Yabloko activists, a piece sadly reminiscent of Soviet journalism.[35]

Yabloko's criticism of Yeltsin's action against the White House, of the constitution as dictatorial, and of the government's divisive economic policy provoked a very hostile response from some Russia's Choice activists. Bolshevik language resurfaced ('whoever is not with us . . .') on the lips of those who had never used it before. But in general, with the exception of LDP candidates and the occasional militant nationalist or radical communist, the language of the campaign was anodyne. Nevzorov used his television and radio time to give his version of the October days: the mowing down by the president of young Russian boys, trying to save the country from a corrupt government which was destroying the people and Russia. He quoted at length from a note to him, found in the hands of a dead defender of the White House, begging him to revenge their deaths, and those who had died defending the fatherland in Russian interests in Moldova. The October events he likened to the Spartacus uprising: 'a normal, popular uprising' against a repressive government that had driven the people to despair. Flashes of extreme nationalism, not usually allowed on the screen, emanated from individual candidates. Bondarik, from the Russian Party, argued that since 1917 a Zionist mafia had robbed and weakened the Russian people. He demanded that Russia 'be ruled by a Russian patriotic government which will defend the honour and dignity of the Russian people, of all native inhabitants of *Rossia*'.[36] One militant communist stood as an independent in order to get media coverage. But it was Zhirinovskii's voice and that of some of his supporters that stood out. These included Marychev, head of a factory club, an

---

[35] The use of opinion polls muddied the picture. L. Kesel'man, the leading opinion pollster and an emotional Russia's Choice supporter, produced data to show the Russia's Choice candidate was ahead; the others refused to admit their validity; Iu. Nesterov, from Yabloko, employed another pollster, who showed him in a strong position.

[36] The north Caucasian mafia, he argued, must be driven out. 'The Russian people have been completely deprived of power and property. Power in Russia . . . was seized by the international Zionist mafia. "Perestroika" of 1985–90 replaced the slogan on the face of an anti-Russian, anti-people regime from "socialism" to "liberalism" while preserving all power in the hands of the Zionist partocratic mafia' (leaflet; television broadcast; election meeting). Bondarik's candidature had the blessing of metropolitan Ioann, of the St Petersburg and Ladozhskii diocese. Similar sentiments came from a member of one of the monarchist organizations, who used his television time to show a video of a forbidden meeting on 9 May, which included the police arresting and handcuffing the demonstrators, against the background of the singing of a monarchist hymn, now, he claimed, banned. The leader of the People's Social Party, Iu. Beliaev, not among the candidates, and an advocate of paramilitary action (but not to defend 'that Chechen Khasbulatov or the time-server Rutskoi'), was quite open about the need to get his people into the police, the security forces, and the procuracy; they supported Russian business, and would create conditions under which the Jews would be forced to emigrate: *Nev. vremia*, 16 November 1993, p. 2.

able orator. He pleaded with the voters 'to give Zhirinovskii a chance' and, unlike most contenders, he was quite willing to criticize his opponents. The powerful and corrupt are allowed to go free, he argued, referring to Kharchenko, general director of the Baltic Shipping Co., involved in corruption charges, while Sobchak arrested the pensioners who protested at the removal of Lenin's statue from the railway station.[37] Tuinov, the writer, poured scorn on both the Communists and the democrats 'both politically impotent, neither able to run a country in a civilized manner. The first tried, for seventy years, to force us to be happy and, of course, deceived us; the latter tried, quickly, at our expense, to enrich themselves. It's insulting to a great power!' If, he argued, 'we vote for Gaidar or Shakhrai we cleanse them of the blood on their hands . . . it is to a monastery one should turn for forgiveness, and they are heading for the Duma'.[38]

But the debate had an ideological quality only at the extreme edges. Even though there were clear differences between the more moderate Communist Party candidates and the more patriotic, the Communist Party's message was as bland as the rest.[39] There was a heavy sameness about the statements. Foreign policy, immigration, Russians in the near-abroad, Chechnya, and Tatarstan were remarkably absent from the discussion. Almost all dwelt on the virtues of stability, safety, and social

[37] Radio broadcast, 22 November 1993; author's notes from Vyborg district meeting. Ivanov, a naval officer, argued that Russia had always found itself military saviours (his list included Alexander Nevskii, Suvorov, Stalin, and Zhukov) and that 'today Russia will only be saved by well-educated and informed people, brave, resolute, and crystal clear patriots of the fatherland, with experience of leading large contingents of people, and one such is M. N. Ivanov' (leaflet). Convinced of a plan to colonize the country and reduce the population to 30 million in the next century, he advocated strengthening Russian representation in government, increasing order, ending the export of raw materials, and ending 'the robbery of money-lending criminal interest rates'. All those who had lost their money would be compensated financially, housing would be found for workers, employees, and the police; he said, 'We shall NOT PERMIT our children and grandchildren to live in RESERVES like American negroes and indians!': *St Pbg ved.*, 30 November 1993, p. 4.

[38] *Vech. Pbg*, 29 November 1993, p. 2. We cannot, he argued, leave power in the hands of 'political vampires', responsible for the events of 3–4 October, and those in the ministries, clinging to their privileges: television broadcast, 6 December 1993.

[39] For Iu. Belov, ex-obkom secretary: 'People ask "where is my motherland?" How can this be? It is the democrats who, despite their emblem of Peter the Great, cannot hide their cosmopolitanism . . . We must save the country. There are only two blocs that matter – "theirs" (the cosmopolitans) and "ours", the statists': television broadcast, 29 November 1993. 'I am for the spiritual emancipation of Russia from the commercial surrogates of culture . . . I am against those who, behind their emblem of the Bronze Horseman, hide their cosmopolitanism, those for whom Russia is "that country"': *St Pbg ved.*, 8 December 1993, p. 3. E. Krasnitskii, however, a younger party member who gained a seat on the party list, was close to a social democratic position: interviews with Belov and Krasnitskii, November 1993.

calm. The question of property hardly featured except for the Communists' insistence that a strong state sector was vital, and everyone argued that the interests of domestic producers must be safeguarded. Almost no one insisted that privatization must be reversed; at most it should be done differently. All agreed that the question of land ownership was not something to be rushed and that it was important to prevent it falling into foreign hands. All were in favour of democracy; all wanted more law and order and a decrease in crime; all were in favour of helping the weak, elderly, and poor; all were in favour of a strong government, and an attack upon corruption.[40] 'Democracy' was already a second-order word, as was the term 'market relations'. These were no longer contestable concepts; discussion had moved on. But what had it moved on to? The key phrases, which all felt obliged to use (although some embraced different meanings) were: a strong state, stability, social welfare, order, legality, the unity of Russia. Human rights had been replaced by 'human worth'. Terms such as 'patriotism' or 'spirituality' featured quite frequently. But there was no competition between political languages, no advancing of clear political positions.

The campaign was perhaps most interesting for what it revealed of the struggle between older political conventions and new. Within a few days of the start of the television campaign, the president's team and Russia's Choice found themselves the target of nothing but criticism – on the economy, for the handling of the Supreme Soviet, and for the strongly presidential constitution. Nothing equivalent had been allowed on the air in the days following the storming of the White House. Taken aback and angry, the president's advisers struck out. V. Kostikov, his press secretary, announced that serious 'anomalies' had occurred in the way television had interpreted the presidential decree guaranteeing free access to the media:

The democratic instrument . . . is being used by a number of electoral blocs and individual candidates not as a means of putting forward their programmes but for

---

[40] For Yeltsin too the theme of stability was a key one and, like those in the Communist Party, he argued for 'returning life to a normal path, to create a healthy basis for the stable development of Russia'. All of this the constitution would do and the elections, if the voters chose aright, would produce 'a normal Parliament': *Izv.*, 16 November 1993, p. 3. It is interesting how the concept of 'normal' was used. The Communists now suggested that the pre-September situation was normal (although at the time they did not characterize it as such); for Yeltsin the existence of the Congress had meant that the situation was abnormal (it created conflict and opposition to reform for which the people had spoken), but in talking of a return to normalcy it is difficult to see what he could have in mind – to a *pre*-Congress period? Hardly. Yet in some sense this was what he was seeking: a peaceful society, without a battle for power between the government structures.

crude attacks on the president, the government, and opponents. Calls are being made to hate and to take revenge against those who defended democracy on 3–4 October . . . certain candidates make no mention of the need to find a national consensus, so much needed by society, but rather fan the dangerous wind of civil war. From the television screens a stream of lies, rumours, social demagogy, and plain rubbish is assailing the voters. The demagogic character of such appearances leads one to conclude that we are not faced with honest competition between different political platforms but with planned provocation, aimed at forcing the authorities to take measures in order to save the voters from disinformation, in order then to accuse the president and government of suppressing democracy.

'Society', he threatened, 'has the right to use instruments to safeguard democracy from destructive forces' when candidates, 'pretending they are seeking seats, openly disregard all the rules of the game'.[41] The democratic instruments he had in mind were the arbitration court, the electoral commission, the Ministry of the Press, and 'democratic organization'.[42]

The president held a meeting with leaders of the parties and blocs at which he expressed his concern at the criticism of the constitution and warned that, if candidates went beyond the limits of their programmes, they would be deprived of free television time. Although this warning, and Shumeiko's subsequent petition to the arbitration court that propaganda against the constitution should exclude a candidate or party from competing, brought a lull in the criticism, the court rejected the claim and the lull was short-lived.[43] Kostikov fell straight back into Soviet political rhetoric and Shumeiko clearly favoured limiting criticism but, despite his warning, Yeltsin then stepped back. Some television journalists felt obliged to warn candidates that criticism of the constitution would be reported to the electoral commissions, and tied themselves in knots trying to decide what kind of statements were admissible, but candidates disregarded the warnings and the criticism continued.[44]

If this was a political landscape little distinguished by ideological positions, it was peopled by recognizable political types. This was a particular feature of post-communist Russia. I have already referred to some of them: Egorov, the chief administrator, and Kondratenko, the nationalist

---

[41] *Nev. vremia*, 26 November 1993, p. 3.   [42] *Izv.*, 26 November 1993, p. 1.

[43] *Izv.*, 27 November 1993, p. 1; *Nev. vremia*, 1 December 1993, p. 3; *Izv.*, 3 December 1993, p. 4.

[44] It was noticeable at election meetings that those chairing became uncomfortable if heckling or interruptions occurred. 'Don't get so excited'; 'control yourselves'; 'conduct yourselves in a civilized fashion'; 'behave properly' – all were used as admonitions. Another chair proposed to the meeting a 'peaceful discussion . . . we don't want to hold a meeting here'.

politician, in Krasnodar, for example. If the Kondratenko type was rarely found in a position of authority in the post-1991 period, the Egorovs, I suggested, had either never left the scene or made a discreet comeback. They were *the pragmatic administrators*. In Perm they had a representative in Kuznetsov, the chief administrator, and in Tomsk one in Kress, the 46-year-old ex-party secretary and chief administrator, the cautious centrist whose answers revealed nothing of any policy orientation. He spelt out his reasons for standing for the Council of the Federation carefully: firstly, because the election would show whether those who live in the region have faith in the administration; secondly, because the regional administration must have 'real authority in order to defend the interests of the region' and the interests of the people of Tomsk. The deputy should be an upright, thinking individual, who cares about others, he said, and strives to introduce policies which are not destructive. Parties exist to express the interests of different strata but it was time that they worked together to find joint decisions; he was reserving judgement as to whether he might join a fraction. He opposed confrontation of any kind and saw the president's role as one of uniting the different institutions.[45]

In St Petersburg those with a background in administration who entered the political arena were more like *industrial barons*, those who in a different environment would have become captains of industry. D. Filippov, the ex-obkom secretary, and head of the tax inspectorate, was one. Although his grandfather had been a wealthy entrepreneur, he himself had risen through the Komsomol, industry, BAM (the Siberian railroad), and then party work to head its industrial department. 'I could have directed many departments', he boasted, and he was drawn to politics because he wanted to realize his potential. He had no nostalgia for old times, but the state must be responsible for the transition to civilized market relations, and that meant having people in charge who knew the old system and how to manage things. 'The market is not a bazaar and it's not the collapse of the economy. State and society are not objects for experimentation. We must take politicking out of the economy. Market relations must be built by responsible and competent people.'[46] The individual must be able to live. Privatization was a scandal, with corruption extending right to the top, including Chubais, chair of the federal property committee. The government should have the key role, and lead. He would not wish to join a party – parties were not normal – and the presence of numerous parties in the Duma would mean the endless sorting

[45] His and other answers from the interview survey, Tomsk, if not otherwise referenced.
[46] Leaflet.

out of positions, and nothing getting done.[47] Those who had risen in the world of industry were very similar. For Filimonov, the 59-year-old ex-oil minister, now president of AO Tomskoil and seeking election in Tomsk, the government should occupy centre stage. The main role of the deputy was 'to introduce correctives into the present government's policy', to act consistently in the interests of his electors; he saw his task as improving living conditions for the workers, oil employees, and the elderly, and as defending the interests of the region. The great danger today was that Russia might break up; political parties, therefore, must work to unite the people and to save industry from collapse; opposition to the government was undesirable at such a time. The Federal Council should be composed of professionals, and contain a powerful scientific lobby, not 'bought' deputies. The president should not interfere in the government; he should ease tension, not cause it. Although neither Filippov nor Filimonov had the backing of Civic Union, it would not have been surprising if they had.[48]

Among the *new entrepreneurs* a recognizable type emerged. These were sometimes the ex-Komsomol officials, such as Trutnev in Perm. In Tomsk they were represented by Il'in, a 33-year-old who in the last year and a half had organized twenty-two enterprises and built three factories, and was nominated by the local industrial business association. He saw the requirements for a deputy as being honesty, courage, youth, and administrative ability and the task as one of 'creating the conditions for an evolution towards the market, and the perfection of the tax system'. He favoured holding the country together without using force and encouraging production; he hoped to improve life for the people of Tomsk, to ensure that taxes remained in the region, and that there was no kowtowing to Moscow. The deputy must be independent; it was time to unite for action, not talk; parties existed because of the discontent of certain social

[47] Television broadcast, 3 November 1993; Frunzenskii district meeting; survey. *St Pbg ved.*, 4 December 1993, p. 2. At the Frunzenskii meeting his election speech bore similarities with earlier political speeches but this time he was rattling off the data on the administration's *failures*, not its achievements; at one point, he slipped back into 'we' and then corrected himself to 'they'.

[48] A more extreme industrial management position came from S. Zhvachkin, a 37-year-old ex-party instructor, now manager of a construction trust in Tomsk. For him the deputy should be an upright individual, concerned with the stability of the country; they should 'begin by depoliticizing Parliament; create a Parliament and not parties, express the interests of all the citizens'. 'It's time to introduce order in Russia. Those who were deputies, and represent political tendencies are again standing for election. That's bad. If they are elected, there will again be more talk than action. I have a feeling of civic hostility [*grazhdanskaia zlost'*] towards politicians, and parties.' The more parties there were, the more the people suffered. The deputy must be 'politically neutral', act independently, and not join political battalions.

strata. The Duma should create the laws, and the rest should see that they were carried out; opposition to the government was a bad thing. In St Petersburg the new entrepreneurs could be found in very different electoral blocs, from Civic Union to Russia's Choice, and standing as independents. They tended to stress the virtues of talent and initiative, and to have the haziest of political programmes. As a political group they were quite unstable.[49]

In contrast there was the non-party *defender of the people*, a type found more often in the regions than in St Petersburg. In Tomsk she was I. Bakhrusheva, the head of a first aid station, nominated by her colleagues, and with no previous experience in politics, who saw the role of the deputy as 'knowing and being able to defend the interests of the electorate, of those who work and their families'; she hoped to improve life for people. Parties, she considered, should play a secondary role in the Duma; they should cease fighting one with another, and unite because the same problems affected all; the key issue of the day was the unity of Russia. The Duma should know which laws are necessary, the Federal Council should help the Duma, and the government should not hinder it; the president should be concerned with very general questions of policy.

Then there were the *human rights democrats*. They came from among those who either had a dissident background or who had participated in the democratic movement in the perestroika period, and they included people of different generations and backgrounds. But there were no newcomers to politics among them: almost all had served as deputies either at federal or regional level. In St Petersburg, Arzhannikov, the ex-policeman, was one such. 'The individual is afraid of the state – that's not normal – the state must defend the individual . . . we must have a law to control the security services so that blood will not flow, a law to prohibit the creation of bugging devices and their sale.' They had a higher profile in St Petersburg than in our other regions, and tended to be associated with Russia's Choice or to stand as independents. They emphasized legal reforms, press freedom, open government, and legislative rights.[50]

---

[49] M. Goriachev was an example. Other candidates included G. Glagovskii, with an extraordinary election video of beautiful people doing nothing in particular in a *Twin Peaks* style; another new businessman featured himself sitting woodenly on a kitchen chair in a field of buttercups, from which he addressed the viewers. The reason they appeared on the different party lists was that the parties wanted their financial support. See also the example of Mironov, p. 294 below.

[50] Arzhannikov, television broadcast, 3 December 1993. Iu. Rybakov: 'the bureaucratic system continues to operate, oppressing and adapting the individual to itself'; the Duma had to decide 'not only problems of political freedom but in the first place those of the civil economic rights of the citizens of Russia'; it needed not only lawyers and economists but also the defenders of rights, 'whose experience and sensitivity' would help to produce more humane laws (leaflet). Others included M. Molostvov, B. Pustintsev, and Iu. Vdovin.

A rather different type was the *practical democrat*, typified by O. Popov, a 47-year-old journalist, democratic activist, soviet deputy, and Russia's Choice candidate for the Federal Council seat in Tomsk. He was standing because he was 'fed up with life as it is; the state is rotting with power; we must create representative power while there is still money left in the exchequer'. Parties stabilized political life; they were vital; it was good to have an opposition to the government; the Duma should elect a good government and create a legislative basis for reforms in the interest of the majority; the main role of the government should be to see that radical reform continued, and to take into account the interests of youth, pensioners, and those paid from the state budget; the president should be an arbiter. In St Petersburg there were many such among the Petrosoviet activists, and they were to be found in the ranks of Russia's Choice or Yabloko, or running as independents, but they shared no common political programme.

Our final type is a specific product of the post-Soviet environment: the *office (or position) politician*. This is not to suggest that we do not find individuals in most political systems who seem to draw any stature they have primarily from the holding of a post. But the post-communist environment was unusual in that a large number of individuals with no previous experience of politics or talents suddenly found themselves catapulted into positions. If Filippov was an able individual, striving to carve out a role for himself in a new world, there were others whom the political environment suddenly created out of nothing. They were essentially hollow figures, created by the holding of a post and who, lacking a base or a programme, would look for support wherever they could find it. In St Petersburg one such was V. Shcherbakov, who leaned to the right; the other was A. Beliaev, who came from the democrats. Shcherbakov – ex-nuclear submarine commander, rear admiral, doctor of military science, lecturer – had been elected to the soviet and then the post of vice mayor. His campaign video consisted of black-and-white photos, tracing his family and naval career. He claimed that his role had been important in ensuring that no blood had been spilt on the streets in August 1991 and October 1993; he was 'a convinced centrist, concerned for the rebirth of Russia on the basis of its genuine national and state interests'. He favoured 'the creation of a multilayered, socially oriented economy, in the centre of which stands a person with his daily needs; "Reforms for the people, and not at the expense of the people"'. This phrase echoed the Communist slogan, but he refrained from a direct call for the recreation of the Union. He could not but 'be sorry that the military christening of the newborn Russian army involved shooting at its Parliament building. I grieve for the losses, I am ashamed for the authorities and for the country.

At the same time, I understand that the abscess, developing for many months, had to burst sometime.' When asked about his relationship with Khasbulatov, the disgraced speaker of the Supreme Soviet, who had held the chair of the Council of the Interparliamentary Assembly, he declared that he was and remained an adviser to the holder of the *post* of chair of the Council, and that it would be up to the new chair to decide whether to retain him. Why had he entered politics? For the sake of his grandchildren and the fate of a great power.[51] Position or office politicians tend to avoid talking about their programmes because they were largely non-existent. Shcherbakov resorted to stating that he would not go into his ('believe me, it exists') and claimed that his record as deputy mayor (twenty conversion projects, saving jobs) was enough.

A. Beliaev, in contrast, the young political-economy lecturer, came from the centre-democratic group of deputies. As chair he strove to be above fractions, to maintain a dialogue with Sobchak, and with the Supreme Soviet and president. In September 1993 he tried to play a leading role among regional representatives without taking up a clear anti-presidential position. His programme was intended to appeal to all: he was 'for the combination of liberal market reforms with state support; [for] the scientific-technical potential of the country, including the defence industry; for culture; for helping those sections of the population most socially unprotected'. He had the support of Petersburg academics, businesspeople, and members of the cultural intelligentsia – and they appeared on his video. He gained the backing of PRES, DPR, RDDR, and Russia's Choice (but not Yabloko), although one would have thought it difficult to reconcile Travkin's and Gaidar's positions. Although the going had been rough, he claimed, there were now more goods in the shops and, 'most important, during these two years we have maintained peace and calm in Petersburg'. He would put his considerable financial and administrative experience to good use in the Council of the Federation. But at election meetings, he decided not to speak on his pro-gramme: it was enough that he was 'independent', and would defend the regional interest and aim to achieve a strong united Russia.[52]

These then were the political organizations and types of candidates who put themselves up for election in St Petersburg in December 1993. They were certainly a hotchpotch. Before we look at the response of this most democratically inclined of city populations, it bears saying that, although during 1991–4 the authorities were continually apprehensive that they might be faced with widespread social protest, none occurred. Tension

---

[51] Leaflet.
[52] Television broadcast, 3 December 1993; leaflets; Frunzenskii district meeting.

was appreciable at times but any protest was sporadic, uncoordinated, and short-lived. The angriest and most disruptive protest was over the disappearance of the owners of a fraudulent investment company, who made off with the savings and vouchers of a gullible, largely elderly public. Blocking main streets, as in Perm, and picketing Smolny and the soviet were the tactics adopted. Neither collective protest nor collective action to effect improvements in an increasingly difficult daily environment made an appearance.

Only 52 per cent turned out to vote. The constitution went through comfortably with 70 per cent in favour. Russia's Choice picked up 25 per cent of the party vote, Yabloko 19 per cent, and the LDP came third with 17 per cent; the Communist Party, as expected – and this was the only result that was expected – got its 6 per cent, Sobchak's RDDR got 9 per cent, Women of Russia 5 per cent, Travkin's DPR and Shakhrai's PRES 4 per cent apiece. The two places in the Council of the Federation went to Boldyrev and Beliaev, just in front of Arzhannikov. The constituency seats went to four Russia's Choice candidates (but of very different types, and in three of these districts the victor polled fewer votes than those cast against all the candidates), to the multimillionaire Goriachev, to the popular and patriotic Nevzorov, to a young free-market independent, and to a middle-of-the-road economist. There was no relation between party voting in a district and the success or failure of party-supported candidates for the constituency seats. From observation in three election stations, one might say that coherent voting was the exception, typical of maybe 5–10 per cent of the electorate. Occasionally one saw a middle-aged man fill in no to the constitution, yes for Nevzorov, Shcherbakov, and Filippov, and the Communist Party – and then do the same for his elderly mother's papers, or a youngish woman might tick Yabloko, Boldyrev, Nesterov, and no to the constitution. But these were the exceptions. A family, for example, sure only that they wanted to vote for Nevzorov, voted for the constitution, for Boldyrev, hesitated on the party list and opted for RDDR. A voter might vote for the LDP, for Nevzorov, against the constitution, and then for Arzhannikov. It was clear that the constitution presented few problems, many hesitated over the choice of party, and the lists of names for the Council of the Federation and for the Duma often meant nothing to the voter. If we relax the criterion of coherence (voting for an individual supported by the party voted for, and in keeping with the party's stance on the constitution), it is clear that pro-reform and more conservative voters could be distinguished and that, for many, the lists of individuals produced either scorn or despair. A working-class father and son voted for the LDP, for the constitution ('you can't live without a constitution'), and then crossed out all the individual names ('what can you expect from any of them?'). The way the election was structured, with its party and constituency lists, in the kind of candidate environment I have described, resulted in the electorate being presented with baffling and sometimes meaningless choices.[53]

The 1994 elections in St Petersburg

If the choice offered to the electors in December 1993 was unappealing, that for the new city assembly the following March was insulting. Only the Communist Party and the LDP competed as parties. Electoral blocs, hastily put together round a possible future candidate for mayor, and independents dominated the scene. Let us look at these developments in a little detail, although they are complex and the reader may be flagging, because they illuminate the general discussion on political organization which follows. They complete my analysis of the politics of St Petersburg.

Among the blocs three stood out. The Democratic Unity of Petersburg was led by A. Beliaev, confident after winning a seat to the Council of the Federation. He appeared at a DemRossia conference in January and announced his intention of standing for election to the new city assembly, and then for its chair. The conference elected him as 'leader' and the back-room bargaining over the list of candidates began. DemUnity included twelve deputies from the previous soviet, a few of the better-known democratic activists or cultural figures, and 'new money'. The leading figures here were the two Ananov brothers, one in the jewellery business, the other in fish-canning, both rich, and I. Baskin, reckoned by some to be the richest man in the city. One of his construction companies was engaged in the development of the ecologically threatening new port against which the Greens had recently won a court case. The argument used to justify his inclusion in the DemUnity list was simple: money is required to fight an election campaign, that is the way it is done in a civilized country, and hence Baskin is needed.[54] A second bloc, Beloved City,

---

[53] An analysis of voting by district suggested that the 1990 and 1993 referendum pattern repeated itself: the central district and the north in favour of reform, the south and the suburbs more conservatively. The LDP did best in Kolpino, a huge sprawling new estate to the south, and in Kronstadt. The Communist Party fared best in the old elite district of Smolny, but also in Vasil'evskii island and the Moskovskii district; there was no evidence that it was picking up a worker or communal apartment vote: A. Dombrovskii, *Chas pik*, 19 January 1993, p. 3. The problem was that the electoral system was hindering rather than helping the expression of this divide.

[54] On Baskin's inclusion, see also *Ross. gaz.*, 8 February 1994, pp. 1–2. DemUnity claimed the support of twenty-six political and social organizations, including the Russian Christian Democrats, the Free Democratic Party of Russia, the Republican Party, and the Party of Economic Freedom: Makarevich, 'St Petersburg', January 1994. Karaulov, the secretary of DemRossia, was not included in the list but, when an attempt was made to remove him from the secretaryship, he managed, with the help of a bloc of delegates from a ship-building institute, to defeat his opponents by a vote of fifty-six to forty-three. The DemUnity group then left the meeting, miscalculating that this would make it

included B. Moiseev, formerly deputy chair of Petrosoviet, and a strong contingent of fifteen former deputies, many of whom came from the original Popular Front fraction. This democratic bloc, however, also included Shcherbakov, the vice mayor, who could draw upon communist and patriotic support, and the wealthy director of the Eliseevskii food chain. Shcherbakov received a public blessing from the arch-nationalist Metropolitan Ioann.[55]

In our other regions, we noted the practice of the administration putting forward its candidates. In St Petersburg, after the poor showing of his party in the December elections, Sobchak's authority in the city, let alone his presidential aspirations, suffered a setback.[56] But there were others within the administration thinking ahead to the next mayoral election. Many reckoned that S. Beliaev, the former head of the property committee and now working for the central government, was the individual behind All Petersburg, a bloc that included the president of Astrobank, the representatives of other financial interests, M. Dmitriev, the young economist and ex-RF deputy, and a few former deputies and cultural figures.[57] The patriots, in their turn, appeared as a bloc, Great

inquorate; it did not and Karaulov retained control of the juridical entity. Henceforth two rival DemRossia councils met on alternate Mondays in the same building.

[55] Details on the blocs or candidates, where not otherwise stated, are from *Nev. vremia*, 16–18 February 1994, pp. 3, 4; *St Pbg ved.*, 3, 4, 6, 10, 11 March 1994; electoral lists. The Regional Party was a party of 'deputies' looking for a future after having to leave the Mariinskii Palace. It had thirty-six members and four full-time paid workers. Members paid one-third of the minimum salary as dues; they had to be recommended by three members, undergo a six months' candidate period, and were accepted on the basis of secret voting at the conference. Despite the attempt at strict party organization, the members quickly found themselves in disagreement one with another: Makarevich, 'St Petersburg', May 1994.

[56] His rating within the city had fallen from 78 per cent in August 1991 to 22 per cent in March 1994: Makarevich, 'St Petersburg', March 1994. An attempt to create a new party, the Party of Legal Statehood, led by Iu. Novolotskii, from the legal department of the mayor's office, failed to bear fruit; founding conference, 20 January 1994.

[57] See *Ekho*, 10 March 1994, p. 18, for D. Travin's analysis; 16 March 1994, p. 18, has interviews with representatives of the leading blocs on their budget strategies. But to think that the different democratic blocs had different ideological or policy programmes would be incorrect. Their leaflets resonated with the same kind of appeal: 'A way out of the crisis exists for Russia – it lies in a transition to a civilized civil society, and Petersburg can and must act as a leader in this process. Our aim is to create a strong representative authority in Petersburg, which will carry out reforms in the interests of the citizens. The city does not need "projects of the century", but housing repairs, good streets, transport that works, hospitals that are equipped, order and safety on the streets . . . The city must be run by PEOPLE whose RESPONSIBILITY, PROFESSIONALISM, and CULTURE meet the TRADITIONS of PETERSBURG . . . The city assembly will not be a "fig leaf" shielding the executive authorities. WE SHALL EXERT STRICT CONTROL TO ENSURE THE MAYOR'S DECISIONS ARE IN THE CITIZENS' INTERESTS': electoral bloc, DemUnity, *Nev. vremia*, 5 March 1994, p. 4. Compare this with: 'We have united our efforts in order to bring back traditional qualities and make them again part of everyday life: mutual respect between citizens, Petersburg style and Leningrad patriotism, clean and safe streets, pavements in good repair, trams and buses that run according to their

Russia, incorporating the Russian Party, the Russian National Assembly, and patriotically minded individuals.[58] Yet some of these could equally well have been sponsored by the Communist Party, which had discarded all calls for socialism in lieu of those for the return of the USSR. The 'true' communists, the radical splinter parties and organizations, the most important of which was the Russian Communist Workers' Party, banded together under the heading Motherland, yet even they included a banker and the director of a commercial firm among their candidates.[59]

To think of these blocs as organizations of like-minded people would be quite wrong: they were hastily scrambled together by leading individuals on the basis of expediency, and many of those who joined acted on the same basis. Some individuals collected sponsorship by more than one bloc. For example, A. Mironov, the 28-year-old president of an oil-supply company and director of a glass factory, claimed, in the half-page spread he purchased in *Nevskoe vremia*, that he was 'fed up with politicking. How can the city authorities engage in high politics when the city is drowning in mud? I am amazed that people who have not managed to do anything for the city should stand again, put forward programmes of general phrases – and nothing concrete.' The electors, the article claimed, would have little difficulty in recognizing him because of his remarkable likeness to the hero of the popular television serial *Santa Barbara*. He appeared, smiling, holding his two little daughters on his knee. Mironov had the backing of Democratic Unity (despite the fact that its leader, Beliaev, and many of its candidates were precisely those against whom his criticism would seem to be directed), and of the new Legal Party, based in the mayor's office and in competition with DemUnity, and of a third, smaller bloc.[60] Others either preferred or had no option other than to stand as independents.[61]

timetables, and much else that makes the city dear to its inhabitants, and life in it worth living . . . Most important is the RESTORATION OF LEGALITY and the SAFEGUARDING of CITIZENS FROM CRIME AND ARBITRARINESS . . . we are for REFORM IN THE INTERESTS OF ALL WHO LIVE IN THE CITY . . . we shall guarantee ORDER IN THE ADMINISTRATION OF THE BUDGET, LAND, AND PROPERTY . . . we consider that it is UNACCEPTABLE FOR ANY AUTHORITY TO USE EXTREMIST AND ILLEGAL METHODS, to "search for enemies" . . . ECONOMIC DEVELOPMENT MUST TAKE INTO ACCOUNT ECOLOGICAL PROBLEMS . . . We shall do all we can in order that our beloved city celebrates its 300th anniversary as a flourishing centre of science, industry, and culture': electoral bloc, Beloved City, leaflet, March 1994.

[58] Bondarik, leader of the Russian Party, was arrested shortly before polling day on a charge of murder of a rival within his party.

[59] *Nev. vremia*, 16, 17, 18 February 1994, pp. 3–4.

[60] *Nev. vremia*, 5 March 1994, p. 4; *St Pbg ved.*, 3 March 1994.

[61] In order to compete a party or bloc had to collect 35,000 signatures, an individual 2,000. In all, twenty-four parties or blocs attempted to collect signatures. For those with money, there was no problem: it was reckoned that DemUnity paid most for a signature, up to 400 r.: *Nev. vremia*, 16 February 1994, p. 3; Makarevich, 'St Petersburg', January 1994.

In all, two parties and fourteen blocs put up candidates. Only DemUnity, Beloved City, and Motherland put up someone in each of the forty districts. Of the 754 candidates, 152 stood as independents. In terms of gender and age, the candidates were very similar to their counterparts in 1990 – 87 per cent male and with an average age in the mid-forties; still nearly 30 per cent from the academic world and culture, a handful of workers, police, and doctors. The difference was that in 1994 business stepped forward (a third of the candidates came from the new economy), and the engineers and economic administrators of 1990 had largely disappeared.[62] Although the overwhelming majority of the 754 candidates were newcomers, seventy-seven were former deputies of the Petrosoviet or the Parliament, scattered between the blocs, and a further twenty were unsuccessful candidates from 1990. Here was a new group of aspiring professional politicians. The former deputies can be split between those who, formally, had retained their original job (as a research worker, a lecturer, a docker); those who had set up new ventures (a foundation to support business, an institute on privatization, an independent law firm, a press agency, a bank); and those, a few, who had moved to work full-time for a political party or club. For many of them getting re-elected was the equivalent of keeping a job.

There was almost no campaigning, none on television. DemUnity brought out pink and blue leaflets for their candidates, and described themselves as the Electoral Bloc of Aleksandr Beliaev, hoping to attract voters with his name. Incidents of threats or violence against individual candidates by small groups of heavies (stopping and smashing up the Memorial mini-bus, for example) and bomb threats before concerts were reported.[63] By the time the ballot boxes closed on 20 March, fewer than 20 per cent of the electorate had turned out to vote, well below the required 25 per cent. Sobchak extended voting by a further day and announced that out-of-town students and non-resident soldiers would be eligible to vote. The procurator's protest against the legality of the

[62] The share of 'elite' positions (leading in the profession) had risen from a fifth to more than a third. In these respects the differences between the blocs were not large, although those of a more patriotic-left hue (but not the Communists) had fewer business and elite candidates: L. Kesel'man and M. Matskevich, analysis, ms., 1994. The Communist candidates – thirty-six in all – born between 1936 and 1948, came in large part from higher-education institutions.

[63] *Nev. vremia*, 18 March 1994, p. 1; *Izv.*, 22 March 1994, p. 4. An element of farce was introduced by Sobchak's hasty decisions in changing the electoral rules during the course of the campaign, and their contestation in court. The most striking example was a decision that those holding office as mayor, vice mayor, deputy of the Council of the Federation, procurator, judge, and police officials could not stand for election or, if elected, should resign their posts. The ruling affected his two main competitors in a future mayoral election: Beliaev and Shcherbakov. The legality of such a ruling was successfully challenged in court: Makarevich, 'St Petersburg', January, March, 1994.

extension was rejected by Sobchak; ten of the electoral blocs protested against the extension, and several candidates subsequently turned to court. By Monday evening the required turnout had been achieved in twenty-four of the fifty districts (not enough to produce a quorate assembly), but in each case (because of the rule that a candidate should receive 50 per cent to win on the first round) all went to the second round.[64] Of the forty-eight candidates who went through to the second round, nineteen were supported by DemUnity, and twelve of them had led in their district; Beloved City and All Petersburg had five apiece. Not a single Communist Party candidate, LDP candidate, or patriot made it through. Eighteen were former deputies or worked in government administration; academics, new business (Baskin was there), and enterprise management were all represented. Both Shcherbakov and A. Beliaev went through.[65] Beliaev had come ahead of A. Shchelkanov, the democratic chair of the soviet executive committee in 1990, running as an independent, whom he now faced in the run-off. Shchelkanov suggested that they should together declare the election invalid, given the original turnout, but DemUnity supported Sobchak's decision.

For the second-round voting in April, there were no rules on minimum turnout. As in March, roughly 18 per cent came out to vote. DemUnity was shattered to find it had won only three seats, and Beliaev lost to Shchelkanov (with a 16 per cent turnout). Beloved City and All Petersburg got five and four seats respectively. Ten independents won. Of the twenty-four deputies, only one was a member of a national party, two belonged to DemRossia, and three to a regional St Petersburg party. Half of the members of this small non-quorate group had experience as deputies (and among them members of the scientific intelligentsia were well represented), and five in city or district administration. They included Shchelkanov and Shcherbakov, the vice mayor.[66] The directors of construction firms and of new corporations or associations featured, but none of the really wealthy bankers or entrepreneurs went through, nor the big enterprise directors. Money, after all, did not determine the outcome, and Beliaev's strategy had backfired badly.[67] The Perm scenario

---

[64] *Nev. vremia*, 22, 23, 24 March 1994, p. 1.   [65] *Nev. vremia*, 26 March 1994, p. 4.

[66] Sobchak then dismissed Shcherbakov from his post. Shcherbakov appealed the legality of the decision to the procurator who concluded that, since the legislation did not allow for the dismissal of the vice mayor, Shcherbakov's claim was justified but that, since the legislation contained no procedure for removing a vice mayor, he could not rule, and the matter should be resolved by a court: *Nev. vremia*, 13 May 1994, pp. 1–2, for interview with Shcherbakov, and 25 May 1994, p. 1, for the procurator's answer.

[67] *Smena*, 5 April 1994, p. 1, was the only one of the four dailies to provide both turnout and percentage vote for all candidates. At a press conference Beliaev argued that the block had obtained 30 per cent of the total but its getting only three seats showed the imperfection of the system, and the low turnout should be blamed on the executive which 'had done nothing to encourage people to come and vote': Makarevich, 'St Petersburg', April 1994.

had repeated itself. A local politician could win election to the prestigious Federation Council seat (and could believe he commanded a personal following) and then be ignored by the electorate when it came to the local election. In Beliaev's case this meant that his mayoral aspirations were killed and his standing in the Federal Council undermined. Suddenly he found himself alone: a politician without a programme, a party, or financial backers.

The city limped through without an assembly until the following November, when the vacant seats were contested. This time Gaidar's party entered the arena. DemUnity was no more.[68] Thirty percent turned out to vote, and the Communists did well. But again first-round fortunes were poor predictors: at the second round (down to a 19 per cent turnout again), the Communists collected only three seats, Beloved City another three, Gaidar's party two, and All Petersburg one. The new assembly was very similar to its counterpart in Perm and Tomsk in its inclusion of both the new rich, administration officials, and a few Communists; it differed in having a slightly larger contingent of the former deputies, now set on a political career.[69]

Political organizations: parties, blocs, and lobbies

If this was multiparty politics, it was multiparty politics of a rather peculiar kind. In the summer of 1990 the Committee to Support Democratic Russia had produced a prognosis for 1991: the present division between the democrats and the patriotic–communist alliance would be replaced by 'new political forces, oriented towards social groups, and their distinguishing character will be their relationship to social conflicts produced by transition [to the market]'.[70] Although the authors did not foresee the break up of the USSR and the emergence of an independent reform-minded Russian government, these should have encouraged the tendencies they predicted. Most analysts, whether in Russia or the west, would have agreed with them. Once the market began to produce its winners and losers, political organizations would emerge to defend the

---

[68] DemRossia finally split in May over the question of whether to participate in Gaidar's new party, Russia's Democratic Choice. Karaulov sided with the Ponomarev–Starovoitova–Yakunin group who did not favour joining Gaidar's party and who held the leadership of DemRossia. In June a conference of Russia's Democratic Choice in St Petersburg was attended by eighty-four people, a constitution was adopted, and a council (proposed by the organizing committee, with the request that no changes be made) was elected: Vdovin, Godunov, Gordin, Zhuravskii, Derevianko, Eremeev, Molganov, Pustyntsev, Reznik, Rybakov, Shtamm, Sychev.

[69] *St Pbg ved.*, 4, 22 November 1994, p. 1; *Vech. Pbg*, 1 November 1994, p. 1.

[70] Leningradskii komitet podderzhki dvizheniia DemRossii, *Sbornik*, 1, July 1990, St Petersburg Archive of Social Movements.

different interests. Yet in 1993 and 1994 parties and electoral blocs could hardly be understood in these terms. Although there was a party of the new entrepreneurs – Borovoi's Economic Freedom Party – it failed to collect enough signatures to compete, and none of the 'left' parties had any serious constituency in the working class. If anything, the introduction of market reforms had been accompanied by a downturn in party activity and an increasingly strident and abusive debate over who had the right to call themselves the defenders of the people.

If we think of a political party as an organization that puts forward candidates at central and regional level, with a leadership, a membership, an organizational structure (this may be centralized or decentralized), and some programmatic goals, then, of the thirteen contenders in the 1993 elections, only one – the Communist Party of the Russian Federation – would qualify. It was the one organization with a membership across the country, a leadership recognized by the local branches, a programme, and publications, the only organization that could field candidates at federal and regional level and win seats at both. How can we characterize the others?

Party/bloc	Leader
Political party	
Communist Party of RF (KPRF)	Ziuganov
Leader-centred movement	
Democratic Party of Russia (DPR)	Travkin
Liberal Democratic Party (LDP)	Zhirinovskii
Electoral bloc	
Russia's Choice (VR)	Gaidar
Yabloko	Yavlinskii, Boldyrev, Lukin
Government/sectional lobbies	
Movement for Democratic Reform (RDDR)	Popov, Sobchak
Unity and Accord (PRES)	Shakhrai
Agrarian Party	Lapshin
Civic Union	Volskii
'New' associations	
Future of Russia	Lachevskii
Women of Russia	Fedulova
Ecology movement (KEDR)	Panfilov
Dignity and Charity	Grishin

Travkin's DPR and Zhirinovskii's LDP were wholly focused around and dependent upon an individual; Russia's Choice and Yabloko were electoral coalitions, hastily assembled around an individual and the issues of the moment; RDDR and PRES had their roots in the administration. Civic Union and the Agrarian Party, in contrast, were classic sectional lobbies. If Civic Union was the heavy industry lobby, the Agrarian Party was based on the farm chairmen and local agricultural officials. It opposed 'disturbing' land ownership, argued for subsidies for agriculture and a halt to the import of foreign food.[71] Neither it nor Civic Union had any difficulty in collecting signatures, but there, because the two sectors were structured very differently, the similarity ended. The Agrarian Party had no need of a membership, or a press – the local press lay in the hands of the local administration, the rural population was accustomed to voting for the farm chairmen and, anyway, theirs was a message of which the voters approved. The industrial directors, in contrast, could ensure that signatures were collected but they could not persuade their work-force to vote for them, and they did not. We might ask why the heavy industry lobby bothered to compete. If representation in the Duma would strengthen the Agrarian lobby, and allow it to exert influence on future presidential candidates, a Duma presence would seem less impor-tant to the military-industrial complex. Its ability to lobby the govern-ment did not lessen after its failure to pass the 5 per cent barrier in the elections. But as far as individuals were concerned, a seat in the Duma would raise their status and possibly their leverage in their own regions.

Very different were Russia's Future and the Women of Russia. These were organizations created for the elections, whose leaders' networks were based on largely defunct Soviet organizations. Russia's Future drew from an ex-Komsomol network but also received money from Gazprom. Chernomyrdin, thinking ahead to a presidential campaign, was prepared to support more than one organization. The smart young leaders had no programme to offer, except the claim that the electorate should place a wager on youth. The Women of Russia drew from the original women's organizations.[72] Finally there were two strange organizations – Dignity and Charity – which may have drawn upon trade union and veteran organizations, and KEDR, the ecology party, but consisting of a group of largely elderly individuals, unrelated as far as one can tell to the grass-roots environmental groups.

Not surprisingly, given the reasons why they had come into existence, almost nowhere did these political organizations compete in the regional elections in 1994. Again the exception was the Communist Party which fielded candidates across the country, and won seats. In Krasnodar the Liberal Democratic Party, after its December successes, came into

[71] *Izv.*, 27 November 1993, p. 4.   [72] *Izv.*, 2 December 1993, p. 2.

existence, participated, and won seats in the following November, but nowhere else in Russia were LDP candidates successful.[73] As we have seen, the pattern at regional level was competition between local interests: the administration, particular business interests, ex-deputies, sometimes left-patriotic candidates, and plenty of independent candidates. The intermediary institutions that had emerged as the links between society and state were a motley collection of president-oriented groups, governmental or quasi-governmental lobbies, business groups, and a fringe of tiny ideological 'parties'. If different political environments produce different types and different combinations of political organizations, why was post-soviet Russia producing this combination?

Explaining political organization

Several scholars have focused on the reasons for the failure of political parties to put down roots during this period.[74] Explanations, drawing on the comparative literature on party formation, have concentrated on their premature emergence, the lack of defined social cleavages, and cultural factors. I am interested in something rather different: in understanding the types of political organizations that *did* come into existence. But, by way of introduction, it is helpful to review, briefly, the factors that worked against parties becoming the dominant type of political organization. Political parties, we are reminded, tend to develop once the identity and authority of the state has been established, and once groups within a legislature begin to reach out to a constituency, or when groups within society recognize the feasibility of advancing their interests through representation. In Russia none of these conditions were present.

In a survey carried out in the Russian Federation in 1993 only 41 per cent of the respondents claimed to feel themselves to be citizens of Russia.[75] It is probably true that most states persist despite the inability of either the majority or substantial sections of the community to recognize their citizenship. However, when a state collapses in a literate community in the modern world, the inability of rulers or ruled to agree on the basis for citizenship may place a serious obstacle in the way of creating a stable state, and hence party formation. In Russia post-1991 the federal authorities struggled with the problem. Yeltsin tended to stress 'all the Rossiane'

---

[73] Gel´man, 'Novaia mestnaia politika', in Gel´man, *Ocherki rossiiskoi politiki*, p. 85.

[74] A. Dallin (ed.), *Political Parties in Russia* (Berkeley: University of California Press, 1993); M. Weigle, 'Political Participation and Party Formation in Russia, 1985–1992: Institutionalizing Democracy?', *Russian Review*, 53 (1994), pp. 240–70.

[75] L. Gudkov, 'Russkoe natsional´noe soznanie', in Zaslavskaia and Arutiunian, *Kuda idet Rossiia?*, p. 179.

(i.e. 'all the peoples of the Russian Federation') as being the basis for the state; yet at the same time he would claim that the Federation upheld the principle of national self-determination for all its peoples. Although guardedly, he would refer to the special responsibility that lay with the Federation for the 'Russian-speaking population in the near-abroad'. Meanwhile, leaders of the national republics claimed an ethnic basis for their states, while suggesting that the rights of all who lived in them would be respected.

We might want to argue that the Russian Federation began its independent existence with an impossible task. How could one expect the leaders or people of a huge multiethnic territory, itself the dismembered torso of an empire, to fashion a shared identity among themselves? Quite apart from the legacy of empire, and ethnic identification, the institutional structures inherited from the Soviet past were hardly helpful. The curious asymmetrical federal arrangements which privileged the national territories and encouraged ethnic consolidation, and the less-than-clear separation of powers between president and Parliament created a framework which encouraged conflict – and hence made it more difficult for the rulers to play a united part in creating a new sense of national identity.[76] This, the institutional factor, brought into play elites who started structurally divided and who, by squabbling among themselves in pursuit of their own interests, made the sense of citizenship and community even harder to achieve.

The lack of an agreed political identity has consequences for party formation. Parties presuppose the recognition of the community of which one is a *part*, i.e. the recognition that one is defending interests separate from those of others while sharing a common identity. If, however, the boundaries of the community are unclear, opponents cannot be distinguished from 'outsiders' or enemies, and political organizations begin to claim to be speaking for the nation. It was not accidental that in Krasnodar everyone, including the democrats, had to be 'patriots'. President and Parliament saw in each other the enemy of 'the nation'. At the time of the December 1993 elections Yeltsin appealed to the voters to choose those who sought neither confrontation nor their own ambitions; he was expecting deputies of different persuasions to be elected and he was prepared to work with all reformist and democratic organizations in whose hands the future of Russia lay.[77] Yet this very wording implies that there are others who belong to 'another Russia' and whose challenge can

---

[76] See Breslauer, 'Roots of Polarization', on the role played by the unresolved issues of statehood and nationhood in a context of imperial dissolution, combined with the lack of clarity surrounding the roles of the different branches of government.

[77] *Izv.*, 10 December 1993, pp. 1–2; television broadcast, 9 December 1993.

only come in those terms. In turn, some among the Communists openly claimed to be representing 'our Russia' against 'their Russia'. Both president and Parliament insisted they spoke for 'Russia' – to which Russia did one then belong and to whom did one owe allegiance?[78]

It was not just that this was an environment that lacked legitimate opponents; it was also that its politicians neither represented nor spoke for recognized collective identities. As we saw, among those standing for office, including those on a party ticket, the majority wished to represent 'the people', not a sectional interest, or a social constituency, a regional or ideological interest. This in turn encouraged them to claim that they spoke on behalf of the 'nation'. The lack of different stable collective identities not only left ethnic identification as the main contender; it also made it difficult to think of 'nation' in any other way. Where were the counter-ideologies? To whom could one appeal as the voice of the nation? Church and tradition had little to offer; perhaps it should be the army as representing the interests of the community, or the state institutions themselves? None of these were capable of playing such a role.

Had the central authorities managed to establish themselves as effective rulers, capable of exerting their authority, they might have been seen as the bearers of state power. In this respect Russia's international position and place in the world economy continually undermined the new state's claim to be able to defend its citizens. Even when a community with a strong shared sense of identity gains political independence, the ability of its newly elected authorities to defend their citizens' interests is highly questionable in today's integrated world. Other players will take decisions that may have a greater impact upon their lives.[79] Where little sense of a shared identity exists, the weakness of the state will be ascribed to its rulers' not representing its people and, where great expectations are had of the state, the rulers' problems are compounded. In the Russian context the choice of 'western' policies by the new rulers made it even harder for them to escape an identification with 'the west' and to fashion a distinct and shared Russian identity.

[78] See M. Urban, 'The Politics of Identity in Russia's Postcommunist Transition: The Nation Against Itself', *Slavic Review*, 53 (1994), pp. 733–65; see also his 'December 1993 as a Replication of Late-Soviet Electoral Practices', *Post-Soviet Affairs*, 10 (1994), pp. 127–58, for examples of past political conventions determining electoral practices.

[79] Small compact communities, able to identify with their newly won independence, will find it easier to be able to believe in their sovereignty. Multiple identities need not necessarily pose a threat – citizens may feel themselves both Catalan and Spanish – but not all dual identities – Spanish–Basque, for example – are so accommodating. A much longer time period than that of the few years following the break-up of the Soviet Union and the gaining of their independence by the countries of Central Europe will be needed before we know whether any of them will give rise to stable states and political identities. See pp. 314–15 below.

The unresolved issue of the identity of the political community not only made it difficult for groups to recognize each other's legitimacy, it also placed a series of highly contentious issues on the political agenda – the nature of the federation, the issue of the Russians abroad, and the renewal of the Union – which split the supporters and opponents of economic reform, and produced unstable alliances.[80] But this draws our attention to a basic requirement of a democratic order: those who compete for office must recognize each others' political identities and agree on the rules for deciding conflicts. To put it another way: although its constituency is the people, *for democracy to work, the people needs to be composed of distinct political constituencies.* If the first requirement for a democratic order is the recognition of the rightfulness of the unit itself,[81] the second is the recognition by its citizens that they differ one from another. The problem facing Russia was not, therefore, the lack of 'democratic culture' or 'democratic attitudes' but *the absence of identity-making ideologies.* The democrats, brought into existence by the electorate as 'those who are against the nomenklatura', provide a good example. They were not helped by finding themselves, once the Communist Party was banned, without an opponent who would compel them to define themselves. As many of their early assumptions proved to be false – the economic crisis was far worse than imagined; so were national conflicts, the refugee problem, corruption, poverty, crime – and it became clear that they shared no common policy programme, they needed the red–browns to bolster their self-identity.[82] Without an opponent it was not clear who they were nor whom they represented, and this was reflected in the hasty alliances with new business interests and others at the time of the regional elections.

In referring to the absence of organized political or social constituencies, and the anti-ideological environment, I have already introduced factors that others have held responsible for weak party development. Post-communist society, it has been argued, was a flattened, state-dominated society, where social, ethnic, or religious cleavages had not acquired organized social voices. Antipathy towards ideological identification with

[80] Urban, 'State, Property, and Political Society'.   [81] See above, p. 112, n. 10.

[82] For some, this led to the argument that on 3–4 October the president had saved the country from the danger of a 'national-Bolshevik dictatorship'. When Iu. Boldyrev, from Yabloko, suggested that the present government, because of its divisive economic policy, was a greater danger than the opposition because it was laying the ground for a red–brown comeback, some within Russia's Choice could not contain their anger. Boldyrev was portrayed as the new Rutskoi, the traitor from democratic ranks. How could he accuse democrats of being 'worse than red–brown'? See also V. Pastukhov, 'Rossiiskoe demokratichnoe dvizhenie: put′ k vlasti', *Polis.*, 1 (1992), pp. 8–16, for an interesting analysis of the democrats' ideological weakness.

a political organization was a further element in the post-communist inheritance. Rather differently, it has been suggested that certain strategic choices – decisions not to hold a founding election for the new state in the autumn of 1991 or to create a presidential party of reform, or to move faster to a proportional representation system – all contributed to weak party development.[83] My rather different concern – to explain the types of political organization that *did* emerge – leads me to emphasize rather different features of the post-communist environment, and other important strategic choices. I would argue that it was a combination of particular policies and institutional choices within the ideological environment described above, and within a heavily state-structured society whose groups had interests to defend, that resulted in the curious assortment of political organizations.

The most important institutional choice was the decision to adopt a presidential system of government. In the post-communist context the prize is the executive – the central state institutions that control the apparatus of coercion and law and order, and administer the economic resources, including the budget on whom all depend. Not only the military-industrial complex, but agriculture, the universities, pensions, the media – all are financed by the centre. The question becomes: who is to control and disburse these huge resources? The introduction of a presidential system concentrates attention on capturing control of the government through the presidency, and for that a different kind of political organization (a coalition around a leader) is required from one whose aim is primarily to capture seats in an assembly. A presidential system, in a collectivist culture, encourages the perceived need to have a leader, standing above the fray, representing the whole people. It was for this reason Yeltsin had argued, when he became president, that he should belong to no party. Within the legislature itself groupings tend to develop along 'for or against the executive' lines rather than on the basis of policy differences, and coalitions 'to defend the legislature' override political divisions. In some CIS states (and in Tatarstan), the president created his own party – the 'king's party', intertwined with the executive structures. In Russia Yeltsin did not do this, although from time to time he suggested that he might,[84] and some have argued that, had he done so, on the basis of DemRossia in 1991, this would have given a powerful

---

[83] See sources in n. 74.

[84] A revealing proposal came from Chubais, the leading liberal economic reformer left in the Yeltsin administration by 1993. At a meeting of heads of the regional (i.e. state) property committees in May 1993 he urged them to put forward candidates in the forthcoming elections: see V. Gel'man, in *Nezav.*, 9 June 1993, p. 2.

impetus to party-building. This is, however, very doubtful. The lack of agreement over a policy agenda and over political identification would have persisted. But, more than this, the creation of a presidential party in an executive-dominated system tends to weaken the legislature – and hence interest in party-building by its members or by the community outside.

If the structural arrangements did little to encourage the development of parties within the legislature reaching outwards to the electorate, why was society itself unable to create them? The political activities that had emerged during 1987–91 were of two kinds: first, small groups putting forbidden issues on the agenda – ecology, religion, civil rights, political discussion – and, second, loosely linked movements advancing new social identities – the people, the individual, the nation. The unexpected collapse of nomenklatura rule brought the democrats to power with a programme of marketization, privatization of state property, and of deregulation – the rolling back of state institutions – accompanied by demands for press freedom and individual liberty. This was to be implemented in the name of a new social constituency which did not yet exist: the middle class. The policies would create the constituency which would then underpin them.[85] But society was already structured in a quite different way. To see it as flattened or atomized is to miss the solid institutional interests that existed. There were territorial regional elites, corporate sectoral institutional interests (the military-industrial complex, energy, agriculture, science, etc.), official institutions such as the procuracy, army, the security forces, or the media, and a variety of quasi-governmental agencies, offices, organizations from the trade unions to cultural organizations, and veterans' and youth associations. All looked to the state budget. All remained after the ending of party rule. What happened? On the one hand the original state institutions were not slow to obtain slices of state resources for themselves: state agencies became corporations, industrial directors and farm chairmen acquired controlling packets of shares. Huge quango-like corporations, partly state, partly private, began to replace the original state structures.[86] On the other hand, a private commercial sector began to emerge, very uneven in geographic terms: banks, finance houses, insurance companies, stock exchanges. These restructured or new 'economic' interests organized

[85] J. Staniszkis, 'Main Paradoxes of the Democratic Change in Eastern Europe', in K. Poznanski (ed.), *Constructing Capitalism* (Boulder: Westview Press, 1992), pp. 179–97.

[86] See S. Peregudov, 'Business Interest Groups and the State in the USSR and Russia: A Change of the Model', paper presented at XV World Congress of International Political Science Association, Berlin, August 1994.

themselves differently. The agricultural managers formed an open political 'party'; the heavy industry/defence sector organized itself primarily
into a lobby for pressurizing government behind the scenes, but also tried
to enter the electoral arena. The energy lobby, in contrast, worked only
behind the scenes, and did not link its fortunes with any one political
organization. The banks, perhaps because they were new institutions,
preferred to support political individuals; they were courted by those of
all political persuasions and spread their largesse between them. They
were still seeking an appropriate host. To explain these developments in
terms of corruption or greed, either on the part of officials, deputies, or
the new entrepreneurs is to miss the point. It was not that 'we don't have
proper businesspeople' or that 'deputies think only of themselves' or 'the
nomenklatura simply want to hold on to property' – although all that may
have been true – but that the attempt to introduce 'a free market' into the
post-communist environment necessarily had this result. In the absence
of a legal system of contacts, binding rules, and trust, and without a
secure livelihood for officials or politicians, all were defending their interests as best they might.

The new policies encouraged the original economic institutional interests to organize themselves as political lobbies, while creating new business and commercial interests which began to look for political
representation. The first targeted and partly invaded the executive structures, while not ignoring the legislature as an arena; the second, the
newcomers, who were less experienced, began to look to the legislatures
(casting their money between political groups) as a possible place to
advance their interests. If this was one consequence of the policies, the
second was that, far from producing a middle-class constituency as a
basis for a liberal party, they created a wide social division that did not
lend itself to 'party representation'. Who were the beneficiaries of
privatization? The old nomenklatura, new bankers, young traders, industrial directors, top artists – but not the small entrepreneurs, who in the
sociological imagination of the reformers began to substitute for the
middle-class as the social base of reform, and who were hammered by
the tax system and by a lawless environment, and certainly not the
impoverished intelligentsia. On whom was his new party, Russia's
Democratic Choice, to be based, Gaidar was asked in the spring of
1994? Was it the new rich or not? If the former, why should they be concerned with liberal values, and the Federation? He found it difficult to
answer. Inadvertently, the policies recreated a broad division between
'the people' and 'them' – seen as a corrupt and incompetent elite, furthering western interests – and this lent itself to expression either in a

social movement or in protest votes for the outsider rather than in organized political constituencies.[87]

What kind of a party, we might ask, could represent the urban intelligentsia? By and large a supporter of democratic rights, freedom of speech,
and civil liberties, the intelligentsia found itself struggling. It had always
defined itself as the moral voice, the political spokesman for the people,
for Russia. Now it found itself supporting a government whose policies
had not only sent the standard of living plummeting, but whose members
paid scant heed to civil liberties, and seemed to care little for intelligentsia
values. In an established democratic order the intellectuals would align
with different political programmes; here they were still concerned with
creating a democratic community. But if they succeeded, they dug their
own grave: their role would disappear and with it their self-identification.
The irony was that, if they failed, and an authoritarian regime emerged,
there would be a place for them.

Might one have expected the attack on social welfare and the threat of
unemployment to have produced a social democratic constituency? In
theory, yes, but in practice a number of factors worked against this. First
the Communist Party still had the loyalty of part of its constituency (the
elderly); second, the ideology of socialism was too tarnished to attract
support and had few promoters; third, the trade unions still existed,
institutionally and with resources, but were too bureaucratized and discredited to spearhead a movement; and finally, and not specific to post-
communist society, it seems to be easier to organize for social rights than
in defence of them.

In conclusion we see that a policy agenda of privatization, under presidential rule, encouraged lobbies, corporate bargaining concentrated on
the executive, the representation of economic sectional and commercial
interests, and the underrepresentation of the poor, white-collar workers,
the elderly, and the young. The broad division that existed between those
in favour of continuing with economic reform, 'liberalization', and press
and political freedoms, and those favouring a stronger patriotic leadership and more state intervention did not find its reflection in the political

---

[87] See H. Kitschelt, 'Social Movements, Political Parties, and Democratic Theory', *Annals
of the American Academy of Political and Social Science*, 528 (1993), pp. 13–29, for an interesting attempt to explain the emergence and role of different types of political organizations in established democratic systems in terms of their focus on direct or on
representative mechanisms. In post-communist systems, I would argue, both social
movements and political parties may be simultaneously concerned with creating democratic institutions of different types and with furthering interests; they are both similar to
and different from their namesakes in established democratic systems in origins, functions, and interaction.

institutions. Ideological groupings – the free-marketeers versus the Communists for example, the Russian patriots versus the liberal intelligentsia – existed only as bumps on a landscape. Nor did socio-economic divisions produce society's political face. Politically it was a landscape of executive structures, lobbies, individuals, new political types, and an abused electorate. Three years, it may be argued, were hardly long enough for new social interests to coalesce and give birth to coherent political organizations – this was still a society undergoing such change that it had not yet found a political face. Maybe, but where were the new ideologies that were going to be able to organize collective activity in such an environment?

Conclusion

More than three years have passed since the bitter struggle between president and Parliament ended in bloodshed. The Communist Party made substantial gains in the elections to the Duma in December 1995 but, in the presidential election six months later, Yeltsin made a surprising comeback and won a clear victory over Ziuganov, his Communist opponent. Time moves fast in post-Soviet politics. Do recent developments lead me to reassess the analysis offered here? No, but in writing the conclusion, I find myself wanting to give certain points even greater weight.

First, I would emphasize the importance of short-term concerns to both rulers and ruled during those years. With the collapse of the old order, and the appearance of an uncertain future, immediate concerns came to the fore. This was a politics of the short term. This is one important reason why it was difficult to predict developments at the time, and why it would be foolish to think that we could do so for the future. This is not to say that we cannot identify certain trends, or that everything became unpredictable, but rather that we need to be very aware of the limits to predictability. By way of example, let us look briefly at the 1995 and 1996 elections. This also allows us to bid farewell to our regions in the summer of 1996, rather than leaving them in 1994. First, and confirming the analysis in chapter 9, the 1995 Duma elections witnessed what can only be described as a rash of political organizations, putting individuals forward for election under the party ticket. Some of the parties or blocs that had existed in 1993 were still there, but not all, and only three of them made the 5 per cent barrier (the Communist Party, Zhirinovskii's LDP, and Yabloko) as did one newcomer – the government party, Our Home Is Russia, led by Chernomyrdin, the prime minister. The Agrarians did no better this time than Gaidar's new party; a party of beer-lovers did better than Shakhrai's PRES, now no more popular than an Association of Advocates and a Party to Defend Pensioners. Altogether forty-three groups, several simply named after a leader or leaders, competed.[1]

---

[1] Electoral data is from *Vybory deputatov Gosudarstvennoi Dumy. 1995. Elektoral'naia statistika* (Moscow, 1996) for the 1995 Duma elections; for the presidential elections I have used the data of the electoral commission, unconfirmed at the time of writing.

Communist gains were predicted and confirmed. But the seemingly secure Agrarian vote collapsed. The popular General A. Lebed, already tangling with P. Grachev, the defence minister, who entered the arena as part of a patriotic coalition, showed no sign of replacing Zhirinovskii as the scourge of the establishment. And Chernomyrdin's party did even worse than expected. How far could our regions' past history have helped us to predict their electoral behaviour in 1995? In all five (I exclude Tatarstan where no party-ticket voting took place in 1993), the combined democratic vote fell. It fell least in St Petersburg (predictable), and most in Perm, the only region where the LDP held its electorate (quite unexpected). The Communists moved into first place in Krasnodar (predictable), in Tomsk (perhaps not surprising), and in Sakha (was Nikolaev sleeping?). In Tatarstan, as one might have predicted, Shaimiev's new-found loyalty to the Russian government was reflected in a substantial vote for Chernomyrdin's Our Home Is Russia. But why had Nikolaev then failed to get the required support from the Sakha population?

In the first round of the presidential election six months later, Yeltsin, with 35 per cent of the vote, and Ziuganov, with 32 per cent, emerged as the two leaders; General Lebed, the outsider, came third with 20 per cent, and joined forces with the Yeltsin team. In the second round Yeltsin won comfortably with 53 per cent to Ziuganov's 40 per cent. How did the electorate of our regions behave? In St Petersburg and Krasnodar it was as I would have predicted. From the start, Yeltsin was the clear winner in St Petersburg, Ziuganov in Krasnodar, and at the second round each picked up the extra votes that might have been expected. So some things are predictable. If St Petersburg had voted like Krasnodar and vice versa, we would be talking of a world where nothing remains constant, and where no ideological positions exist. But this is not so. Five years after the ending of communist party rule, there were some stubborn ideological bumps on the landscape. There has also been a tendency for the west and south to vote more conservatively than north and east but, within all but a very few regions, this general tendency could be reversed by the presence of personalities or sudden, short-term factors.

Tomsk now looked no different from a score of regions with no democratic past. At the first round Yeltsin received 35 per cent of the vote, the country-wide average, Ziuganov 22 per cent, and Lebed an impressive 20 per cent; at the second round Yeltsin scored 59 per cent, Ziuganov 34 per cent – a very average result. In Perm the LDP and Communist vote of December 1995 collapsed, and Lebed did not benefit: instead Yeltsin, the local boy, picked up a handsome 55 per cent at the first round and 71 per cent at the second. On this count Perm became one of the leading 'democratic' regions. But what if the candidate had not been Yeltsin? And how might Perm vote in future? We could not say. It would be even more unwise to think ahead for Sakha or Tatarstan. In Sakha, in the first round, Yeltsin received more than 50 per cent of the vote, Ziuganov only 20 per cent, whereas in Tatarstan, despite all the publicity surrounding Shaimiev as a peace-maker in the Chechen war, Ziuganov beat Yeltsin into second place. Something had gone wrong there. It was put right at the second round – the vote in Tatarstan for Yeltsin leapt from 34 per cent to 64 per cent and, most unusually, the vote for Ziuganov fell by more than 10 percentage points. It was almost identical to the Sakha vote. Here we surely see evidence of either manipulation or compliant electoral behaviour, but also signs that voters may be prepared to be disobedient.

Elections, it has rightly been argued, introduce the element of uncertainty into the polity. But there is a qualitative difference between an element of uncertainty in an environment in which other features of life have a predictability or constancy and one where they do not. Choosing rulers means one thing where rules governing everyday behaviour are known and observed, or broken with knowledge of the consequences; where laws remain in force, at least for a while; where rights are recognized, and transactions are either based on trust or there is assurance of enforceability. Where none of these conditions exists, the consequences of choice are quite uncertain, and the future opaque. In May 1996 in St Petersburg, and against all expectations of even a month before, Sobchak, the seemingly unassailable candidate in the mayoral election, was narrowly beaten by one of his deputy mayors, the lacklustre and little-known V. A. Yakovlev. Lobby politics, personalities, ideological positions, and protest votes probably played a part. If this was post-Soviet politics at its best – an incumbent politician was defeated in a fair election – the election videos sank to a new low in character defamation and, in the televised debate between Sobchak and Yakovlev, the discussion degenerated into trivia and character assassination. 'I had hoped', said the chair, 'we were going to hear a debate about your programmes.' But even had Yakovlev spoken of his programmes, no one would have been able to predict what his term of office would bring.

By the summer of 1996 the presidents or chief administrators in all six of our regions came from the original party or soviet administration. Shaimiev and Nikolaev were still safely in place. Yakovlev in St Petersburg came from the original housing administration of the soviet executive committee. In Perm, Kuznetsov, his days numbered after failing to win a seat to the Federal Council in 1993, linked his fortunes to Chernomyrdin's party in 1995 and went through to the Duma. As expected, Igumnov, the experienced Soviet administrator, stepped into his shoes. In Tomsk Kress, former raikom secretary, was re-elected as chief administrator, and noisy democratic politics were no more than a memory. In Krasnodar, by the end of the year, Kondratenko would be elected. They all had considerably more autonomy vis-à-vis Moscow, and they were less powerful within their regions than their party predecessors, but the executive's dominant position was secure.

The ability of regional elites to bend or blur new rules, and to adapt institutional structures to their advantage, needs emphasizing. Their members were surprisingly agile in their dealings with Moscow, adept at retaining control over resources and gaining new prizes, and largely successful at remaining in power. Moscow's role in determining these outcomes was far from negligible. The lack of a coherent policy towards the regions and the divisions at the centre allowed scope for autonomous action; short-term considerations of power on the part of the presidential team helped strengthen local administrations, weaken representative bodies, and drive competitive politics off the agenda. But, as we have seen, politics was not everywhere the same. Where there was pressure from below, either nationalist or democratic, and individuals existed who were able to lead or provide a focus for such aspirations, competition occurred. The new institutional structures and rules gave scope for an open politics, concessions were won, and, occasionally, the incumbent rulers were dislodged. But everywhere such challenges faded away. The nationalist movements lost momentum as the ethnic nomenklatura made itself the people's representative; the democrats undermined themselves by unpopular policies, ineffective government, and disregard for their constituents. The party of power, of the administration, emerged as the dominant authority. Again there were differences. If the company towns remained monoblocks, clans, political lobbies, and corporate interests brought an element of competition in the regions or cities where control over resources was shared or disputed. But none of these were grounded in social constituencies. All the social movements were weak, transient; none developed into serious organizations. If, in the early 1990s, politics at federal level and in St Petersburg or Tomsk had common traits, by 1996 the political infighting around a sick president had become far more similar to the clan violence of that earlier period in Krasnodar. As an explanatory model of developments at the centre, Krasnodar now seemed the more appropriate.

What do we conclude? The Soviet past still cast a long shadow. There is still a good deal more post-*Soviet* politics to be got through. Changing the institutional rules – a separation of powers, competitive elections, press freedom – makes a difference in the short run if there is pressure from below or a divided resource base. The institutional changes will not in themselves create an open and competitive politics. On the contrary they may well allow an existing elite to secure its position and, at a time when rule enforcement breaks down and the future is uncertain, inherited conventions of behaviour will play a crucial role. To empower the people, meaningful alternatives must exist and they require both a language and organizational forms. In the absence of a language to structure political relations, ethnicity can fill the emptiness and an elite defend the virtues of good management. Political society is made up of clans, lobbies, and individuals. The ruled have no real choices. Perhaps the intelligentsia is badly needed after all?

I suggested in the introduction that the politics of Russia in the early 1990s provide us with the opportunity to observe struggles to resolve the most basic of issues: the identity of the community, the establishment of political rights, of rule enforcement, and the safeguarding of interests. The coincidence of these issues clearly makes for an extremely difficult agenda. Whether it is a manageable one must remain an open question, particularly in the global environment of today.

Voices arguing that the nation-state, existing within a geopolitical order of states, is already slipping into history, are not new.[2] And in post-communist developments the stubbornness of the independent state is apparent. But international economic agencies, the movement of international capital, the multinationals, and nuclear weapons cannot but undermine the importance of territorial boundaries and the ability of political rulers to control physical space. Civil war is the antithesis of the state. Yet, in both new and old states, we observe seemingly irresolvable outbreaks of civil war, with interventions of limited success by the international community, and the emergence of no-go areas. Law and order cannot always be maintained. Private forces move in to replace the state. Crime has developed an international self, as have weapons sales. The emissions of nuclear power plants are no respecters of borders either. The increasing sophistication of detection instruments cannot prevent the traffic in nuclear materials or in narcotics. Transnational companies (no longer with a homebase in any single state) have budgets larger than those of small countries, financial markets can make or break governments, and international agencies – World Bank, IMF – spell out terms to those struggling to survive economic crisis. The electronic revolution creates an international network of communications whose impact upon political developments we are only beginning to assess while the movement of

---

[2] The literature is huge; I draw attention to one contribution, which is concerned with the consequences for sovereignty: J. Camilleri and J. Falk, *The End of Sovereignty? The Politics of a Shrinking and Fragmenting World* (Aldershot: Edward Elgar, 1992).

people – in search of survival or a decent life – runs counter to notions of creating states based on nations. In such a world the Russian Federation's borders may be porous but they are hardly exceptional.

At most, in today's world, elected rulers may be able to play a part in taking some decisions that affect their citizens' lives. Recognizing rulers' limitations does not entail denying the very real and justified importance people ascribe to gaining their independence. If we take the former Soviet republics or the countries of Central Europe as an example, there has been a qualitative and quantitative increase in independent decision-making in the hands of the new rulers. The distinction between those communities where the people and the rulers of their choice take decisions, albeit limited, and those where no such choice exists remains an important one if one believes in the right of people to participate in decision-making that affects their lives. But the question remains: what kind of representative institutions and political forms are the most appropriate to achieve a people's aspirations in the new global environment? The political institutions of long-established liberal democracies may not be the relevant ones. They may still be 'working', up to a point, in communities knitted together by a functioning bureaucracy, a legal system, and predictable patterns of exchange and commerce. It may be these other institutions that allow them to survive. But what were once radical and liberating political arrangements may now be playing a conservative role in their societies of origin, and may hold no answers for societies striving to find ways to meet today's concerns.[3] They may hinder the emergence of new forms of representation, ways of solving conflict, and a more just distribution of society's goods. They perhaps stand in the way of transnational governments, social movements, or the blurring of state/private administration.

Perhaps we are finally witnessing the dismantling of the state. Not only the instability which characterizes many new states – those in Africa, for example – but also developments in long-established states perhaps

---

[3] William Connolly, in his *Identity/Difference: Democratic Negotiations of Political Paradox* (Ithaca, N. Y., and London: Cornell University Press, 1991), pp. 217–20, refers to 'the double-bind of late-modern democracy: its present terms of territorial organization constrict its effective accountability, while any electoral campaign within this territory that acknowledged the import of this limitation would meet with a predictable rebuff at the polls . . . Defined *within* the terms of sovereignty, the alternatives are these: either democracy remains confined to the territorial state and becomes increasingly a conduit for converting global pressures into disciplines and burdens for its most vulnerable elements, or the terms of sovereignty itself are extended to supranational institutions that progressively widen the gap between the scope of democracy and the source of policies governing people.' He continues: 'today democracy is the living ideal through which the territorial state receives its highest legitimation. But to confine the ethos of democracy to the state today is to convert the state into the penitentiary of democracy.'

herald a future in which the identity of citizenship tied up with a political authority, with voting, payment of taxes, and a particular territorial unit will be replaced by allegiances to different authorities. It would not be surprising if it was where the large state of the twentieth century found its apogee, in communist party rule, that the collapse begins. And, not for the first time, the departure of a political form is accompanied by the most desperate attempts to re-create it once more. In the case of Russia, with a long tradition of a state that dominates society, it would be foolish to underestimate the staying power of the state. But, while it would be unwise to ignore the weapons, it would be equally unwise to ignore the insidious and audacious challenges to them on the part of society. Maybe we are simultaneously witnessing two things: one of the last attempts to create a democratic state and one of the first to create something new.

Could it then be that in the post-communist world we shall observe new, post-sovereign, post-representative democratic forms of organizing political rule? But can a society skip stages and move straight on to 'post-state' forms? What might we mean by this? That, in contrast to the unity of territory and authority, and the one-dimensional citizenship of the modern state, different and overlapping 'territories', depending upon sphere of activity, and multidimensional allegiances would become the order of the day. Rule-making in the financial/economic sphere would not coincide with that in the environmental; weapons control would be different yet again, as would decisions in the world of culture and education. If this is a possible future, or rather if this is already partly with us, the question then arises: what kind of political forms will fit this new world and how will they emerge?

Appendices

Appendix 1   Political actors

The list includes those who appear more than once in the text; they are classified either as federal figures or by region, in order to aid quick referencing.

FEDERAL

Vadim Bakatin	USSR minister of internal affairs under Gorbachev, 1988–90; reform communist candidate for the RF presidency, 1991
Viktor Chernomyrdin	prime minister, RF, December 1992–; from the gas industry
Anatolii Chubais	chair, property committee, RF; deputy prime minister, 1992–5; economist from St Petersburg
Nikolai Egorov	minister for nationalities and regional politics, RF, 1994–5; head of president's administration, 1995–6; from Krasnodar
Egor Gaidar	prime minister, RF, 1992; leader, economic reform; leader, Russia's Choice, then Russia's Democratic Choice; economist from Moscow
Mikhail Gorbachev	general secretary, CPSU, 1985–91; USSR president, 1990–1
Ruslan Khasbulatov	chair, RF Supreme Soviet and Congress of People's Deputies, 1991–3; economics lecturer from Moscow
Egor Ligachev	Secretariat from 1983, then Politburo member, CPSU; from Tomsk
Valerii Makharadze	inspector general, 1991; deputy prime minister, 1992; plant director and soviet chair from Volgograd

Nikolai Ryzhkov	prime minister, USSR, 1985–90; Communist candidate for RF presidency, 1991
Sergei Shakhrai	minister for nationalities and regional politics, 1992–4; deputy prime minister, RF, 1991–2, 1993–6; leader of PRES; lawyer from Moscow
Vladimir Shumeiko	deputy prime minister, RF, 1992–3; speaker, Federal Council, 1994–6; plant director from Krasnodar
Oleg Soskovets	chair, committee on metallurgy, 1992–3; first deputy prime minister, 1993–6
Nikolai Travkin	RF deputy; director of construction trust; founder and leader of DPR
Arkadii Volskii	president, Russian Union of Industrial Enterprises, 1991–; leader, Civic Union, 1992–3; from Central Committee CPSU
Grigorii Yavlinskii	leader of Yabloko; economist from Moscow
Gennadii Ziuganov	leader, KPRF; from CPSU apparatus

KRASNODAR

V. Diakonov	chief administrator, 1991–2
N. Egorov	deputy chief administrator, 1991–2; chief administrator, 1992–4; then to Moscow
S. Glotov	left-patriotic RF deputy, 1990–3, 1993–5; organizer of Fatherland
V. Gromov	ataman, VKV Cossacks
E. Kharitonov	chief administrator, 1994–
N. Kondratenko	chair, krai soviet 1990–1; dismissed August 1991; won seat to Federal Council 1993; leader of Fatherland
E. Nagai	ataman, KKV Cossacks
V. Samoilenko	mayor, Krasnodar, 1991–3
A. Zhdanovskii	chair, krai soviet, 1991–3

LENINGRAD/ST PETERSBURG

N. Andreeva	leader, (Stalinist) VKPB party
N. Arzhannikov	RF deputy; Russia's Choice candidate in Federal Council election, 1993
A. Beliaev	chair, Petrosoviet, 1991–3; elected to Federal Council 1993; led DemUnity bloc in 1994 municipal elections

S. Beliaev   Lensoviet deputy; joined Property Administra-
                               tion 1991; moved to Moscow, 1993
Iu. Boldyrev   USSR deputy, 1989–91; inspector general,
                               1992–3; joint leader of Yabloko, 1993–5; elected
                               to Federal Council, 1993
A. Bolshakov   head, planning commission of soviet executive
                               committee, 1988–90; moved to ministerial post
                               in Moscow, 1994
D. Filippov   head, tax inspectorate 1991–3; from obkom
P. Filippov   Lensoviet deputy; RF deputy; moved to Analytic
                               Centre, president's administration, 1991–4
G. Khizha   defence industry director; Lensoviet deputy;
                               moved to ministerial post in Moscow, 1991–2
V. Khodyrev   chair, soviet executive committee, 1983–90
A. Kramarev   police chief, 1990–4
A. Kudrin   deputy mayor; chair, economics and finance
                               committee, 1992–6
A. Nevzorov   television producer, *600 Seconds*
A. Shchelkanov   USSR deputy, 1989–91; head, Lensoviet execu-
                               tive committee, 1990–1
V. Shcherbakov   Lensoviet deputy; vice mayor, 1991–4
A. Sobchak   USSR deputy, 1989–91; elected mayor 1991–6;
                               led RDDR in 1993 elections
S. Tsypliaev   president's representative, 1992–
S. Vasil´ev   Lensoviet deputy; economist; moved to Moscow
                               with Chubais, 1991

PERM

I. Averkiev   leader, Social Democrats
M. Bystriantsev   chair, oblast soviet, 1991–3; re-elected as deputy
                               1993
E. Chernyshev   first secretary, obkom, 1988–91
V. Fil   mayor, Perm, 1992–4
V. Gorbunov   chair, oblast property committee, 1990–
G. Igumnov   deputy chief administrator, 1991–5; then chief
                               administrator
S. Kaliagin   president's representative, 1991–
B. Kuznetsov   chief administrator, 1991–5; elected to Duma on
                               Our Home Is Russia ticket, 1995
A. Levitan   entrepreneur; elected to Federal Council, 1993;
                               led Regional bloc in 1994 elections

V. Maltsev	leader, KPRF 1993–5
V. Petrov	chair, soviet executive committee, 1990–1
E. Sapiro	deputy chief administrator, 1991–4; elected chair of oblast assembly, 1994
R. Shvabskii	chair, oblast soviet, 1990–1
V. Trutnev	president, EKS Ltd
V. Zelenin	Communist oblast soviet deputy; elected to federal Duma, 1993, 1995
V. Zelenkin	Democratic oblast soviet deputy, 1990–3
V. Zotin	town deputy; leader, DemRossia, 1991–3; elected to assembly and town duma, 1994

SAKHA

M. Nikolaev	president, 1991–
L. Safronov	managing director, Yakutalmaz/Almazy-Rossii-Sakha
V. Shtyrov	vice president, 1991–

TATARSTAN

Z. Agliullin	leader, radical VTOTs, 1993
R. Altynbaev	mayor, Naberezhnye Chelny, 1991–
F. Bairamova	Tatar nationalist leader; poet
R. Belaev	gorkom secretary, Naberezhnye Chelny, 1969–85
I. Grachev	Soviet deputy; leader, Consensus; elected to federal Duma on Yabloko ticket, 1993
R. Khakimov	founding member, TOTs; president's adviser, 1992–
V. Likhachev	vice president, 1991–
M. Miliukov	leader, TOTs, VTOTs, 1988–93
F. Mukhametshin	speaker, Supreme Soviet, 1991–
M. Sabirov	prime minister, 1991–
M. Shaimiev	president, 1991–
Iu. Voronin	deputy chair, Council of Ministers, 1990; RF deputy, 1990–3

TOMSK

| V. Bauer | deputy chief administrator, 1992–3; Russia's Choice candidate elected to federal Duma, 1993 |
| A. Cherkasskii | chair city soviet, 1990–3 |

V. Gonchar	chief, city administration, 1991–
A. Kobzev	RF deputy; leader of Republican Party and DemRossia in Tomsk
V. Kress	chair, oblast soviet, 1991; then chief administrator; elected to Federal Council, 1993; re-elected chief administrator, 1995
A. Kushelevskii	soviet deputy; elected chair of executive committee, 1991
A. Pomorov	obkom secretary, 1991
R. Popadeikin	soviet deputy; elected chair of executive committee, 1990; resigned, 1991
G. Sapiro	deputy chair, city soviet, 1990–3
S. Sulakshin	USSR deputy, 1989–91; president's representative, 1991–3; Russia's Choice candidate elected to federal Duma, 1993
B. Yachmenev	leading Communist spokesman, 1991–
V. Zorkal'tsev	obkom secretary, 1988–90; elected to federal Duma on KPRF ticket, 1993

Appendix 2   Elite study personnel data, 1988/1993

The table provides data on the numbers of those members and candidate members of the regional and city party committees elected in 1988 who held nomenklatura positions and whose occupations could be identified in 1993.

	Krasnodar			Perm			Leningrad/St Petersburg		
	Krai/gorkom 1988	Of whom, position known in 1993	%	Ob/gorkom 1988	Of whom, position known in 1993	%	Ob/gorkom 1988	Of whom, position known in 1993	%
Party apparatus									
Krai/ob/gorkom apparatus	34	30		31	31		40	35	
Raikom secretaries	40	30		27	24		20	19	
Primary party secretaries	17	1		11	11		19	9	
Soviet apparatus									
Civilian posts	69	51		33	26		51	39	
Military/security/legal	11	10		7	7		16	9	
Professional									
Industry/farm directorate	49	20		29	23		20	20	
Scientific/academic directorate	11	6		13	10		16	13	
Culture and media	12	9		9	9		7	6	
Total	243	157	65	160	141	88	189	150	79
Rank-and-file members	106	–		138	–		120	–	
Total	349	–		298	–		309	–	

Appendix 3   Electoral laws of October 1993 and political parties

The decree of 21 September 1993, dissolving the Parliament, announced the holding of elections for a new federal assembly. This was to consist of a State Duma, to be elected on 12 December, and a Council of the Federation, whose formation was not specified: *Ross. gaz.*, 23 September 1993, pp. 1–2. On 1 October the electoral arrangements for the Duma were finalized in a decree. Half of the 450 deputies were to be elected by a party-list system, half by a simple majority system (single-member constituencies). For a party or bloc to participate, its organizers had to present its list of candidates and 100,000 signatures in support (not more than 15,000 from one region) by 6 November. The 225 party seats would be distributed among those parties which obtained at least 5 per cent of the vote, and in proportion to their percentage of the vote: *Ross. gaz.*, 8 October 1993, pp. 3–5.

During the October days Yeltsin had banned a number of patriotic and communist parties and organizations, thus, it seemed excluding them from the election. As of 4 October these included: the Front for National Salvation, the Russian Communist Workers' Party, the Communist Party of the Russian Federation, the Union of Officers, Shield, the United Workers' Front, the Communist Youth organization, Labouring Russia, Freedom, and Russian National Unity. By 21 October the Communist Party of the Russian Federation and a small organization, Freedom, had been unbanned. When the lists closed on 6 November, twenty-one of the thirty-five starters who had attempted to collect the required number of signatures had succeeded. The one surprise failure was Borovoi's Economic Freedom Party. After verification eight hopefuls, from both the right and the liberal wing, were disqualified. They included: Cadets, Baburin's Union, New Russia, the Russian Christian Democrats, the Association of Independent Professionals, the Party of Consolidation, the National-Republican Party, and the Association Transformation/Resurrection: *Izv.*, 7 October 1993, p. 2; 13 October 1993, p. 4; 21 October 1993, p. 2; 9 November 1993, p. 2. This left thirteen parties or electoral blocs competing under the party-list system.

324

They were:

Agrarian Party	Lapshin
Civic Union	Volskii
Communist Party of the Russian Federation (KPRF)	Ziuganov
Democratic Party of Russia (DPR)	Travkin
Dignity and Charity	Grishin
Ecology Movement (KEDR)	Panfilov
Future of Russia	Lachevskii
Yabloko	Yavlinskii, Boldyrev, Lukin
Liberal Democratic Party (LDP)	Zhirinovskii
Unity and Accord (PRES)	Shakhrai
Movement for Democratic Reform (RDDR)	Popov, Sobchak
Russia's Choice (VR)	Gaidar
Women of Russia	Fedulova

For the majoritarian seats, a candidate had to collect 2,000 signatures by 14 November. The only conditions for election were that 25 per cent of the electorate should vote, and that the winner should collect more votes than those cast against all the candidates. The fate of the Council of the Federation remained uncertain until 11 October when it was decreed that it would be an elected body: two members were to be elected from each of the republics and regions, and the cities of Moscow and St Petersburg of the Russian Federation. They could stand on a party basis or as individuals; each candidate was required to submit signatures equivalent to 1 per cent of the local electorate by 14 November. A simple majority system was to determine the outcome, again provided that 25 per cent of the electorate voted, and that the number of votes cast against all the candidates did not exceed the number cast for the leading candidate: *Ross. gaz.*, 19 October 1993, pp. 4–5. In early November a further decree abolished the qualification, for both Duma and Council of the Federation, that a candidate could not be elected if she or he collected fewer votes than those cast against all the candidates. This received little media attention and the relevant, now meaningless, box remained on the ballot paper. Those who marked it simply wasted their vote. (In three of the eight St Petersburg constituencies a majority of the electorate voted in this way which, under the original rules, would have resulted in a new election: *Nev. vremia*, 17 December 1993, p. 3.)

Finally, on 15 October a decree announced that voting for or against a new constitution would also take place on 12 December. Here a 50 per cent turnout was required for the result to be valid and, for the constitution to pass, a simple majority of those voting was required: *Ross. gaz.*, 19 October 1993, pp. 5–6.

The electorate then was being offered four choices: firstly, to vote for or against a constitution, drawn up by the president's administration; secondly, to vote for a political party or bloc from among a list of thirteen; thirdly, to vote for two individuals (some backed by a party, some independents) to represent the region in the Council of the Federation; and, fourthly, to vote for one individual (either party-backed or an independent) to represent the district in the Duma.

Among the small democratic parties which featured in the regions between 1991–4, the most important were the Republican Party (which had grown out of the Democratic Platform in the CPSU), the Social Democrats, the Christian Democrats, the Cadets (whose Moscow leadership shifted to the right), and the Free Democratic Party of Russia (led by Sal'e from St Petersburg). Once the Communist Party was unbanned in 1992, several competitors emerged: the Communist Party of the RF (a centrist organization, led by Ziuganov), the Russian Communist Workers' Party (more militant), and the All-Union Communist Bolshevik Party (VKPB) led by Nina Andreeva. Patriotic organizations (as opposed to sympathies) barely existed in our regions, except for in St Petersburg. Here the most important were probably Fatherland, the National Republican Party (led by Lysenko), the Russian Party (Bondarik), and the fascist People's Social Party (Iu. Beliaev). Following the success of Zhirinovskii's Liberal Democratic Party in 1993, some local LDP organizations appeared.

Appendix 4   Candidate survey, December 1993

Candidates could both stand in one of the single-member majoritarian constituencies and be included in the federal party-bloc list for the Duma seats. In St Petersburg more than half those on the party list also stood in the single-member constituencies. In all 119 people stood for election. There were also the two Federal Council seats: here there were five candidates. Of the 123 standing, 85 were interviewed. Of the thirteen party/blocs which competed, five either had no Petersburg candidates or no regional organization (and only four candidates, who could not be traced). Of the eight parties or blocs which did compete, the only one for which fewer than two-thirds of the candidates were interviewed was the Movement for Democratic Reform or RDDR (four out of ten). During the course of the campaign a few withdrew from the campaign; a few picked up party support. Depending upon where one places such candidates the numbers in the different categories vary slightly, but not so as to affect the nature of the sample. Interviews were carried out in the first week of December, on the basis of a prepared questionnaire, by the author and a team of interviewers, organized by the Institute for Political Research, St Petersburg.

State Duma

	Candidates	Interviewed	Elected
Single-member constituencies			
Independent	48	38	3
Nominated/supported by party/bloc	42	39	5
Total	90	77	8
Federal/regional			
Party/bloc list			
St Petersburg candidates not also competing			
in single-member constituencies	29	9	7
Combined total	119	86	15

Note: Twelve of the fifteen elected were interviewed.

Council of the Federation

	Candidates	Interviewed
Independent	3	1
Party/bloc supported	2	1
Total	5	2

Note: Of the two elected neither was interviewed.

The *Nevskoe vremia* survey appeared during 2–11 December 1993. It included fifty-eight of the candidates standing for the Duma.

In Perm all eleven candidates for the two city constituencies were interviewed, as were twelve of the nineteen party-list candidates and two of the three competing for the Council of the Federation. In their responses, the Perm candidates showed themselves to be very similar to their Petersburg counterparts. The spectrum of opinion among the Petersburg candidates was wider – with a minority of radical opinion (be it Liberal Democratic, patriotic, communist, democratic, or highly idiosyncratic) making its appearance – while the Perm contestants, regardless of their political affiliation, tended to cluster in the middle. As in Petersburg, the candidates valued uprightness, professionalism, intellectual ability, and the ability to compromise as the most desirable qualities for a deputy. They were even more agreed on the desirability of political parties, which they saw as reflecting the social interests of different groups in society, but they showed no greater willingness to be guided by party discipline. Rather more frequently they expressed the view that the Duma was no place for politics.

In Tomsk only ten of the twenty candidates standing for the Duma under the plurality system or for the Federal Council were interviewed. Given the small numbers I do not attempt comparisons but see pp. 286–9 for examples of candidate positions.

Bibliography

I RUSSIAN PERIODICALS AND NEWSPAPERS

JOURNALS AND PERIODICALS

Kuban
Narodnyi deputat
Novoe vremia
Obshchestvennye nauki i sovremennost'
Politicheskie issledovaniia
Politicheskii monitoring
Politika i mysl'
Predely vlasti
Regional'naia politika
Svobodnaia mysl'
Tatarstan
Vash vybor
Vestnik Lensoveta
Vlast'
Voprosy filosofii

NATIONAL NEWSPAPERS

Den'
Izvestiia
Komsomol'skaia pravda
Moskovskie novosti
Nezavisimaia gazeta
Novaia gazeta
Rossiia
Rossiiskaia gazeta
Rossiiskie vesti
Sovetskaia Rossiia

KRASNODAR

Iug
Kazach'i vesti

Komsomolets Kubani
Krasnodarskie izvestiia
Kubanskie kazach´i vedomosti
Kubanskie novosti
Kubanskii kur´er
Sovetskaia Adygeia
Sovetskaia Kuban (later *Vol´naia Kuban*)
Vol´naia Kuban (formerly *Sovetskaia Kuban*)

LENINGRAD/ST PETERSBURG

Anon
Chas pik
Ekho
Leningradskaia pravda (later *St Peterburgskie vedomosti*)
Nevskii kur´er
Nevskoe vremia
Reiting
Sever-zapad
Smena
St Peterburgskie vedomosti (formerly *Leningradskaia pravda*)
Vechernyi Peterburg

PERM

Permskie novosti
Positsiia
Vechernyi Perm´
Zvezda

SAKHA

Mirnyi rabochii
Respublika Sakha
Sotsialisticheskaia Yakutiia (later *Yakutiia*)
Yakutiia (formerly *Sotsialisticheskaia Yakutiia*)
Yakutskie vedomosti

TATARSTAN

Chelny izvestiia
Izvestiia Tatarstana
Kazanskie vedomosti
Kazanskii telegraf
Molodezh´ Tatarstan
Nezavisimost´
Respublika
Suverenitet

Vechernyi Kazan
Vestnik NF

TOMSK

Gorodskaia gazeta
Krasnoe znamia
Narodnaia tribuna
TM ekspress
Tomskaia tribuna
Tomskii vestnik
Vestnik SSRP

II BOOKS AND ARTICLES

Akhiezer, A., 'Rossiia kak bol'shoe obshchestvo', *Vop. fil.*, 1 (1993), pp. 3–19.
Rossiia: kritika istoricheskogo opyta, 3 vols., Moscow, 1991.
'Sotskul'turnaia dinamika Rossii', *Polis.*, 5 (1991), pp. 51–64.
Akhmetov, I., 'Tatarstan', *Pol. monit.*, May 1994.
Altynbaev, R., 'Politicheskie, ekonomicheskie, i sotsial'nye kharakteristiki g. Naberezhnye Chelny', Unesco conference, 'The Culture of Young Towns', September 1993, Naberezhnye Chelny.
Andreev, A., and E. Panasiuk, 'Kazach'e dvizhenie', *Polis.*, 3 (1993), pp. 57–61.
Andreev, A., et al., *Politicheskaia stsena Kubani: kto est' kto*, Krasnodar, 1994.
Andrews, Josephine, and Stoner-Weiss, Kathryn, 'Regionalism and Reform in Provincial Russia', *Post-Soviet Affairs*, 11 (1995), pp. 384–98.
Andrews, Jo, and Vacroux, Alexandra, 'Political Change in Leningrad: The Elections of 1990', in Friedgut, Theodore, and Hahn, Jeffrey (eds.), *Local Power and Post-Soviet Politics*, Armonk, N. Y.: M. E. Sharpe, 1994, pp. 43–72.
Bahry, Donna, and Way, Lucan, 'Citizen Activism in the Russian Transition', *Post-Soviet Affairs*, 10 (1994), pp. 330–66.
Baklanov, G., 'Svoi chelovek', *Znamia*, 11 (1990), pp. 7–120.
Beissinger, Mark, 'The Persisting Ambiguity of Empire', *Post-Soviet Affairs*, 11 (1995), pp. 149–84.
Bienen, Henry, and Herbst, Jeffrey, 'Authoritarianism and Democracy in Africa', in Rustow, Dankwart, and Erikson, Kenneth (eds.), *Comparative Political Dynamics: Global Research Perspectives*, New York: Harper Collins, 1991, pp. 211–32.
Breslauer, George, 'The Roots of Polarization', *Post-Soviet Affairs*, 9 (1993), pp. 223–30.
Bunce, Valerie, 'Should Transitologists Be Grounded?', *Slavic Review*, 54 (1995), pp. 111–27.
Busygin, E. P., *Etnodemograficheskie protsessy v kazanskom povolzh'e*, Kazan, 1991.
Busygina, I., 'Regional'noe izmerenie politicheskogo krizisa v Rossii', *MEMO*, 5 (1994), pp. 5–17.
Camilleri, Joseph, and Falk, Jim, *The End of Sovereignty? The Politics of a Shrinking and Fragmenting World*, Aldershot: Edward Elgar, 1992.

Carnaghan, Ellen, 'Alienation, Apathy, or Ambivalence?: "Don't Knows" and Democracy in Russia', *Studies in Public Policy*, 237, University of Strathclyde, 1994.

'Chto znachit byt' demokratom segodnia?', *Polis.*, 4 (1991), pp. 47–61.

Chubb, J., *Patronage, Power, and Politics in Southern Italy*, Cambridge University Press, 1982.

Colton, Timothy, 'Professional Engagement and Role Definition Among Post-Soviet Legislators', in Remington, Thomas (ed.), *Parliaments in Transition: The New Legislative Politics in the Former USSR and Eastern Europe*, Boulder: Westview Press, 1994, pp. 55–73.

Connolly, William, *Identity/Difference: Democratic Negotiations of Political Paradox*, Ithaca, N. Y., and London: Cornell University Press, 1991.

Dahl, Robert, *Democracy, Liberty, and Equality*, Oslo: Norwegian University Press, 1986.

Dallin, Alexander (ed.), *Political Parties in Russia*, Berkeley: University of California Press, 1993.

Danilov, Iu. G., *Tret'e izmerenie Yakutii*, Yakutsk, 1991.

Di Palma, Giuseppe, 'Legitimation from the Top to Civil Society: Politico-Cultural Change in Eastern Europe', *World Politics*, 44 (1991), pp. 49–80.

Diligenskii, G., 'Dinamika i struktirovanie politicheskikh orientatsii v sovremennoi Rossii', in Zaslavskaia, T., and Arutiunian, L. (eds.), *Kuda idet Rossiia?*, Moscow, 1994, pp. 70–9.

Dmitrieva, O., *Regional'naia ekonomicheskaia diagnostika*, St Petersburg, 1992.

Dragunskii, D., 'Naviazannaia etnichnost'', *Polis.*, 5 (1993), pp. 24–30.

Duka, A., 'Formirovanie novoi lokal'noi politicheskoi elity – na primere Leningrad/St Peterburga', unpublished ms., 1995.

Duka, A., Kornev, N., Voronkov, V., and Zdravomyslova, E., 'The Case of Leningrad', *International Sociology*, 10 (1995), pp. 83–99.

Duncan, Peter, 'The Return of St Petersburg', in Hosking, Geoffry, Aves, Johnathon, and Duncan (eds.), *The Road to Post-Communism*, London: Pinter, 1992, pp. 121–37.

Duverger, Maurice, 'A New Political System Model: Semi-Presidential Government', *European Journal of Political Research*, 8 (1980), pp. 165–87.

Dybrin, S., and Platonov, Iu., 'Naberezhnye Chelny v zerkale obshchestvennogo soznaniia ego zhitelei', Unesco conference, 'The Culture of Young Towns', September 1993, Naberezhnye Chelny.

Eisenstadt, S., and Lemarchand, R. (eds.), *Political Clientelism, Patronage, and Development*, London: Sage, 1981.

Eisenstadt, S., and Roniger, L. 'Patron–Client Relations as a Model of Structuring Social Exchange', *Comparative Studies in Society and History*, 22 (1980), pp. 42–77.

Ekiert, Grzegorz, 'Democratization Processes in East Central Europe: A Theoretical Reconsideration', *British Journal of Political Science*, 21 (1991), pp. 285–313.

Ershova, N., 'Transformatsiia praviashchei elity Rossii v usloviakh sotsial'nogo pereloma', in Zaslavskaia, T., and Arutiunian, L. (eds.), *Kuda idet Rossiia?*, Moscow, 1994, pp. 151–4.

Evans, Geoffrey, and Whitefield, Stephen, 'Identifying the Bases of Party

Competition in Eastern Europe', *British Journal of Political Science*, 23 (1993), pp. 521–48.

Farukshin, M., 'Politicheskaia elita v Tatarstane: vyzovy vremeni i trudnosti adaptatsii', *Polis.*, 6 (1994), pp. 68–77.

Filippov, N., and Andreev, N., *Zakonodatel'noe sobranie Permskoi oblasti*, Perm, 1994.

Fish, Stephen, 'The Advent of Multipartyism in Russia, 1993–1995', *Post-Soviet Affairs*, 11 (1995), pp. 340–83.

Fomenko, O., 'Tatarstan', *Pol. monit.*, May 1992.

Forrest, Joshua, 'Asynchronic Comparisons: Weak States in Post-Colonial Africa and Mediaeval Europe', in Dogan, Mattei, and Kazancigil, Ali (eds.), *Comparing Nations: Concepts, Strategies, Substance*, Oxford and Cambridge, Mass.: Blackwell, 1994, pp. 260–96.

Ganelin, R. (ed.), *Natsional'naia pravaia prezhde i teper'*, 3 vols., St Petersburg, 1992.

Garipov, Ya., 'Sotsial'no-etnicheskaia struktura rabotnikov i mezhnatsional'nye otnosheniia na KamAZe', in *Sovremennye natsional'nye protsessy v respublike Tatarstan*, Kazan, 1992, pp. 70–4.

Geertz, Clifford, *The Interpretation of Cultures: Selected Essays*, New York: Basic Books, 1973.

Local Knowledge: Further Essays in Interpretative Anthropology, New York: Basic Books, 1983.

Gel'man, V., 'Evoliutsiia predstavitel'nykh organov vlasti v sovremennoi Rossii', *Pol. monit.*, 11 (1992), pp. 154–76.

'Novaia mestnaia politika', in Gel'man (ed.), *Ocherki rossiiskoi politiki*, Moscow, 1994, pp. 67–96.

Gel'man, V., and McAuley, Mary, 'The Politics of City Government: Leningrad/St Petersburg, 1990–1992', in Friedgut, Theodore, and Hahn, Jeffrey (eds.), *Local Power and Post-Soviet Politics*, New York: M. E. Sharpe, 1994, pp. 15–42.

Gel'man, V., and Senatova, O., 'Politicheskie partii v regionakh Rossii', in Gel'man (ed.), *Ocherki rossiiskoi politiki*, Moscow, 1994, pp. 16–30.

'Politicheskie partii v regionakh Rossii: dinamika i tendentsii', *Vlast'*, 5 (1995), pp. 39–48.

Glezer, O., et al., 'Sub''ekti federatsii: kakimi im byt'?', *Polis.*, 4 (1991), pp. 149–59.

Gornyi, M., and Shishlov, A., 'Organizatsiia vlasti i upravleniia v Sankt Peterburge', St Petersburg, Strategiia paper, 1994.

Gorod Sankt Peterburg, 1993, St Petersburg, 1994.

Gudkov, L., 'Russkoe natsional'noe soznanie', in Zaslavskaia, T., and Arutiunian, L. (eds.), *Kuda idet Rossiia?*, Moscow, 1994, pp. 175–87.

Hahn, Jeffrey, 'Reforming Post-Soviet Russia: The Attitudes of Local Politicians', in Friedgut, Theodore, and Hahn, Jeffrey (eds.), *Local Power and Post-Soviet Politics*, Armonk, N. Y.: M. E. Sharpe, 1994, pp. 208–38.

Higley, John, and Gunther, Richard (eds.), *Elites and Democratic Consolidation in Latin America and Southern Europe*, Cambridge University Press, 1992.

Hirschman, Albert, 'The Search for Paradigms as a Hindrance to Understanding', *World Politics*, 22 (1970), pp. 329–43.

Hughes, James, 'Regionalism in Russia: The Rise and Fall of Siberian Agreement', *Europe–Asia Studies*, 46 (1994), pp. 1133–61.

Huskey, Eugene, 'Democracy and Institutional Design in Russia', *Democratization*, forthcoming.

Il'in, M., 'Sobiranie i razdelenie suvereniteta', *Polis.*, 5 (1993), pp. 144–7.

Iskhakov, D., 'Neformal'nye ob''edineniia v sovremennom tatarskom obshchestve', in *Sovremennye natsional'nye protsessy v respublike Tatarstan*, Kazan, 1992, pp. 5–52.

'Sovremennoe tatarskoe natsional'noe dvizhenie: pod''em i krizis', *Tatarstan*, 8 (1993), pp. 25–31.

Jowitt, Ken, *New World Disorder: The Leninist Extinction*, Berkeley: University of California Press, 1992.

'Soviet Neotraditionalism: The Political Corruption of a Leninist Regime', *Soviet Studies*, 35 (1983), pp. 275–97.

Kara-Murza, A., 'Chto takoe rossiiskoe zapadnichestvo', *Polis.*, 2 (1993), pp. 90–6.

Kasimov, A., and Senatova, O., 'Moskovskoe porazhenie rossiiskogo federalizma', in *Vek XX i mir*, Moscow, 1993, pp. 183–91.

Khagurov, A. A., and Tleuzh, A. Kh., *Agrarnaia reforma na Kubani problemy i perspektivy*, Moscow, 1993.

Kirkow, Peter, 'Regional Politics and Market Reform in Russia: The Case of the Altai', *Europe–Asia Studies*, 46 (1994), pp. 1163–87.

Kitschelt, Herbert, 'The Formation of Party Systems in East Central Europe', *Politics and Society*, 20 (1992), pp. 7–50.

'Party Systems in East Central Europe: Consolidation or Fluidity?', *Studies in Public Policy*, 241, University of Strathclyde, 1995.

'Social Movements, Political Parties, and Democratic Theory', *Annals of the American Academy of Political and Social Science*, 528 (1993), pp. 13–29.

'Konseptsiia razvitiia leningradskogo raiona v usloviakh radikal'noi reformy', working paper, Leningrad, FBT Leningradskaia, 23 March 1990.

Kordonskii, S., 'Intelligentsiia v roli natsional'noi intellektual'noi elity', *Predely vlasti*, 1 (1994), pp. 134–52.

Kostiushev, V., 'Obshchestvennye dvizeniia v postkatastrofnom obshchestve: protsessy sotsial'noi sub''ektivatsii', in Alekseev, A., Kostiushev, and Zdravomyslova, E. (eds.), *Sotsiologiia obshchestvennykh dvizhenii: kontseptual'nye modeli*, St Petersburg, 1992, pp. 61–71.

Kostiushev, V. (ed.), *Sotsiologiia obshchestvennykh dvizhenii: empiricheskie nabliudeniia, issledovaniia*, 2 vols., St Petersburg, 1993.

Krasner, Stephen, 'Sovereignty: An Institutional Perspective', *Comparative Political Studies*, 21 (1988), pp. 66–94.

Krasnov, V., *Sistema mnogopartiinosti v sovremennoi Rossii*, Moscow, 1995.

Kryshtanovskaia, O., 'Transformatsiia staroi nomenklatury v novuiu rossiiskuiu elitu', *Obshchestvennye nauki i sovremennost'*, 1 (1995), pp. 51–65.

Lapidus, Gail, and Walker, Edward, 'Nationalism, Regionalism, and Federalism: Center–Periphery Relations in Post-Communist Russia', in Lapidus (ed.), *The New Russia: Troubled Transformation*, Boulder: Westview, 1995, pp. 79–113.

Lehmbruch, Gerhard, 'The Organization of Society, Administrative Strategies,

and Policy Networks', in Czada, Roland, and Windhoff-Héritier, Adrienne
   (eds.), *Political Choice: Institutions, Rules, and the Limits of Rationality*, Boulder:
   Westview Press, 1991, pp. 121–58.
Leningradskii gorsovet narodnykh deputatov, ispolnitel'nyi komitet: spisok telefonov,
   Leningrad, 1989.
Levada, Iu., 'Problema intelligentsii v sovremennoi Rossii', in Zaslavskaia, T., and
   Arutiunian, L. (eds.), *Kuda idet Rossiia?*, Moscow, 1994, pp. 208–13.
Lijphart, Arend (ed.), *Parliamentary Versus Presidential Government*, Oxford
   University Press, 1992.
Linz, Juan, 'The Perils of Presidentialism', *Journal of Democracy*, 1 (1990), pp.
   51–69.
Linz, Juan, and Stepan, Alfred, 'Political Identities and Electoral Sequences:
   Spain, the Soviet Union, and Yugoslavia', *Daedalus*, 121 (1992), pp. 123–39.
McAuley, Mary, 'From Leningrad to St Petersburg', ms., St Hilda's College,
   Oxford, 1993.
   'Politics, Economics, and Elite Realignment in Russia: A Regional Perspective',
   Soviet Economy, 8 (1992), pp. 46–88.
McFaul, Michael, 'Russian Centrism and Revolutionary Transitions', *Post-Soviet
   Affairs*, 9 (1993), pp. 196–222.
   'State Power, Institutional Change, and the Politics of Privatization in Russia',
   World Politics, 47 (1995), pp. 210–43.
Mainwaring,   Scott,   'Presidentialism,   Multipartism,   and   Democracy',
   Comparative Political Studies, 26 (1993), pp. 198–228.
   'Transitions to Democracy and Democratic Consolidation: Theoretical and
   Comparative   Issues',   in   Mainwaring,   O'Donnell,   Guillermo,   and
   Valenzuela, J. Samuel (eds.), *Issues in Democratic Consolidation: The New South
   American Democracies in Comparative Perspective*, Notre Dame, Ind.:
   University of Notre Dame Press, 1992, pp. 294–341.
Makarevich, M., 'St Petersburg: Leningradskaia oblast'', *Pol. monit.*, 1994.
Mandelshtam, M., and Vinokurova, V., 'Nationalism, Interethnic Relations, and
   Federalism: The Case of the Sakha Republic (Yakutia)', *Europe–Asia Studies*,
   48 (1996), pp. 101–20.
Mann, Michael (ed.), *The Rise and Decline of the Nation State*, Oxford: Blackwell,
   1990.
Marks, G., and Diamond, L. (eds.), *Re-examining Democracy*, London: Sage,
   1992.
Mayall, James, *Nationalism and the International Society*, Cambridge University
   Press, 1990.
Meiklejohn Terry, Sarah, 'Thinking About Post-Communist Transitions: How
   Different Are They?', *Slavic Review*, 52 (1993), pp. 333–7.
Minnibaev, T., *Politicheskaia kar'era provintsialov*, Kazan, 1991.
Mukhariamov, N., 'Tatarstan', *Pol. monit.*, 1994.
Mustafin, M. R., *Novye tendentsii v rasselenii naseleniia Tatarii*, Kazan, 1990.
Mustafin, M. R., and Khuzeev, R. G., *Vse o Tatarstane*, Kazan, 1992.
North, Douglas, *Institutions, Institutional Change, and Economic Performance*,
   Cambridge University Press, 1990.
Norton, Anne, *Reflections on Political Identity*, Baltimore: Johns Hopkins
   University Press, 1988.

Obshchestvenno-politicheskie dvizheniia i organizatsii v respublike Tatarstan, Kazan, 1992.

'Obshchestvennye dvizheniia i stanovlenie novoi vlasti v Leningrade (1986–1991): predvaritel´nye materialy', unpublished working paper, Sector of the Sociology of Social Movements, Institute of Sociology, RAN, St Petersburg, 1991.

O'Donnell, Guillermo, 'Delegative Democracy', *Journal of Democracy*, 5 (1994), pp. 55–69.

Olson, Mancur, 'The Logic of Collective Action in Soviet-Type Societies', *Journal of Soviet Nationalities*, 1 (1990), pp. 8–27.

Organy gosudarstvennoi vlasti i upravleniia Sankt-peterburga: tel. spravochnik, St Petersburg, 1992.

Orttung, Robert, *From Leningrad to St Petersburg: Democratization in a Russian City*, Basingstoke: Macmillan, 1995.

'St Petersburg: Economic Reform and Democratic Institutions', *RFE/RL Research Reports*, I, 1992.

Pastukhov, V., '"Novye russkie": poiavlenie ideologii', *Polis.*, 3 (1993), pp. 15–26.

'Rossiiskoe demokratichnoe dvizhenie: put´ k vlasti', *Polis.*, 1 (1992), pp. 8–16.

Peregudov, S., 'Business Interest Groups and the State in the USSR and Russia: A Change of the Model', paper presented at the XV World Congress of the International Political Science Association, Berlin, August 1994.

Perov, V., 'Sibirskii paradoks', *Narodnyi deputat*, 3 (1992), pp. 51–5.

Peterburg nachala 90-kh: bezumnyi, kholodnyi, zhestokii, St Petersburg, 1994.

Petrov, N. V., 'Chto takoe polietnizm?', *Polis.*, 6 (1993), pp. 6–15.

Petrov, N., et al., 'Sotsial´no-politicheskii monitoring Rossii', *Politika i mysl´*, 1 (1992), pp. 10–41.

Pizzorno, Alessandro, 'Interests and Parties in Pluralism', in Berger, Suzanne (ed.), *Organizing Interests in Western Europe: Pluralism, Corporatism, and the Transformation of Politics*, Cambridge University Press, 1981, pp. 247–84.

Podvintsev, O., 'Report on Developments in the Perm Region, 1991–1994', ms.

Pogodaev, N., 'Tomsk', *Pol. monit.*, 1993, 1994.

Pribylovskii, V., *Politicheskie fraktsii i deputatskie gruppy rossiiskogo parlamenta*, 2nd edn, Moscow, 1993.

Priestland, David, 'Ideological Conflict Within the Bolshevik Party, 1917–1939', DPhil. thesis, University of Oxford, 1991.

Protiasenko, T., 'Intellektualy v politike: professional´naia kar´era i put´ v deputaty', *Regional´naia politika*, 1 (1992), pp. 23–31.

Przeworski, Adam, *Democracy and the Market: Political and Economic Reforms in Eastern Europe and Latin America*, Cambridge University Press, 1991.

'Some Problems in the Study of the Transition to Democracy', in O'Donnell, Guillermo, and Schmitter, Philippe (eds.), *Transitions from Authoritarian Rule*, 3 vols., Baltimore: Johns Hopkins University Press, 1986, vol. I.

Putnam, Robert, *Making Democracy Work*, Princeton University Press, 1993.

Riggs, Fred, 'Conceptual Homogenization of a Heterogenous Field: Presidentialism in Comparative Perspective', in Dogan, Mattei, and Kazancigil, Ali (eds.), *Comparing Nations: Concepts, Strategies, Substance*, Oxford and Cambridge, Mass.: Blackwell, 1994, pp. 72–152.

Roeder, Philip, 'Varieties of Post-Soviet Authoritarian Regimes', *Post-Soviet Affairs*, 10 (1994), pp. 61–101.

Rosenau, James, 'The State in an Era of Cascading Politics', *Comparative Political Studies*, 21 (1988), pp. 13–44.

'Rossiiskaia modernizatsiia: problemy i perspektivy', *Vop. fil.*, 7 (1993), pp. 3–39.

Ruble, Blair, *Leningrad*, Berkeley: University of California Press, 1990.

Rumintsev, V., and Makarevich, M., *Dvadtsat' pervyi*, St Petersburg, 1994.

Said, Edward, *Culture and Imperialism*, London: Chatto and Windus, 1993.

St Petersburg Report, 2–3, St Petersburg, 1992.

Salmin, A., 'Soiuz posle soiuza', *Polis.*, 1–2 (1992), pp. 34–55.

Salmin, A. (ed.), *Partiinaia sistema v Rossii v 1989–1993 gg.: opyt stanovleniia*, Moscow, 1994.

Savva, M., *Mezhnatsional'nye otnosheniia: teoriia, praktika, i problemy Kubani*, Krasnodar, 1993.

Sbornik zakonodatel'nykh aktov respubliki Adygeia, 1, Maikop, 1993.

Schmitter, Philippe, 'Corporatism Is Dead! Long Live Corporatism!', *Government and Opposition*, 7 (1989), pp. 54–73.

'Dangers and Dilemmas of Democracy', *Journal of Democracy*, 5 (1994), pp. 57–74.

'Interest Systems and the Consolidation of Democracies', in Marks and Diamond, *Re-examining Democracy*, pp. 156–76.

Schmitter, Philippe, with Karl, Terry Lynn, 'The Conceptual Travels of Transitologists and Consolidologists: How Far to the East Should They Attempt to Go?', *Slavic Review*, 53 (1994), pp. 172–87.

Scott, James, 'Corruption, Machine Politics, and Political Change', *American Political Science Review*, 63 (1969), pp. 1142–58.

Sergeyev, Victor, and Biryukov, Nikolai, *Russia's Road to Democracy: Parliament, Communism, and Traditional Culture*, Aldershot: Edward Elgar, 1993.

Shapovalov, V., 'O kategoriiakh kul'turno-istoricheskogo protsessa v Rossii', *Svob. mysl'*, 6 (1993), pp. 68–78.

Sheinis, V., 'Natsional'nye problemy i konstitutsionnaia reforma v Rossiiskoi Federatsii', *Polis.*, 3 (1993), pp. 45–50.

Sheinis, V., and Nazimova, A., *Argumenty i fakty*, 17 (1990), p. 3.

Shreider, Iu., 'Rossiia v mire XXI v.', *Polis.*, 2 (1993), p. 36.

Shugart, Matthew, and Carey, John, *Presidents and Assemblies: Constitutional Design and Electoral Dynamics*, Cambridge University Press, 1992.

Sik, Endre, 'Network Capital in Capitalist, Communist, and Post-Communist Societies', *International Journal of Urban and Regional Research*, 18 (1994), pp. 73–93.

Slider, Darrell, 'Federalism, Discord, and Accommodation: Intergovernmental Relations in Post-Soviet Russia', in Friedgut, Theodore, and Hahn, Jeffrey (eds.), *Local Power and Post-Soviet Politics*, Armonk, N. Y. : M. E. Sharpe, 1994, pp. 239–69.

Slider, Darrell, Gimpel'son, Vladimir, and Chugrov, Sergei, 'Political Tendencies in Russia's Regions: Evidence from the 1993 Parliamentary Elections', *Slavic Review*, 53 (1994), pp. 711–32.

Smyth, Regina, 'The Russian Parliament and Political Consolidation', in Blum, Douglas (ed.), *Russia's Future: Consolidation or Disintegration?*, Oxford and Boulder: Westview Press, 1994, pp. 31–45.

Sobchak, Anatolii, *Khozhdenie vo vlast'*, 2nd edn, St Petersburg, 1992.

Sobianin, A., and I'urev, D., *Rasstanovka sil v korpuse narodnykh deputatov RF po itogam trekh dnei raboty vneocherednog VIII s''ezda (10–12 marta 1993 g.)*, Moscow, 1993.

S''ezd narodnykh deputatov RSFSR v zerkale poimennykh golosovanii, Moscow, 1991.

VI s''ezd narodnykh deputatov Rossii: politicheskie itogi i perspektivy, Moscow, 1992.

Soleivchik, S., 'Demokratiia pod voprosom', *Novoe vremia*, 30 (1992), pp. 49–51.

Sovremennye mezhnatsional'nye protsessy v TSSR, Kazan, 1991.

Staniszkis, Jadwiga, 'Main Paradoxes of the Democratic Change in Eastern Europe', in Poznanski, Kazimierz (ed.), *Constructing Capitalism*, Boulder: Westview, 1992, pp. 179–97.

Stavrakis, Peter, 'State Building in Post-Soviet Russia: The Chicago Boys and the Decline of Administrative Capacity', Kennan Institute Occasional Paper No. 254.

Stepan, Alfred, and Skach, Cindy, 'Constitutional Frameworks and Democratic Consolidation: Parliamentarism Versus Presidentialism', *World Politics*, 46 (1993), pp. 1–22.

Streeck, Wolfgang, and Schmitter, Philippe, 'From National Corporatism to Transnational Pluralism: Organized Interests in the Single European Market', *Politics and Society*, 19 (1991), pp. 133–64.

Sungurov, A., *Gorodskoi sovet Leningrada, Peterburga*, St Petersburg, 1994.

Suny, Ronald, 'Ambiguous Categories: States, Empires, and Nations', *Post-Soviet Affairs*, 11 (1995), pp. 185–96.

The Revenge of the Past: Nationalism, Revolution, and the Collapse of the Soviet Union, Stanford University Press, 1993.

Tarasov, Iu. 'Praviashchaia elita Yakutii: shtrikhi k portretu', *Polis.*, 2 (1993), pp. 171–3.

Tatarstan na pereskreste mnenii, Kazan, 1993.

Tatary i Tatarstan, Kazan, 1993.

Teague, Elizabeth, 'Russia and Tatarstan Sign Power-Sharing Treaty', *RFE/RL Research Report*, 3, 8, April 1994, pp. 19–27.

Tishkov, V. 'Etnonatsionalizm i novaia Rossiia', *Svob. mysl'*, 4 (1992), pp. 19–24.

'O prirode etnicheskogo konflikta', *Svob. mysl'*, 4 (1993), pp. 4–15.

Tsymburskii, V., 'Ideia suereniteta v posttotalitarnom kontekste', *Polis.*, 1 (1993), pp. 17–30.

'Ostrov Rossii', *Polis.*, 5 (1993), pp. 6–23.

Unger, Roberto, *Plasticity into Power: Comparative-Historical Studies on the Institutional Conditions of Economic and Military Success*, Cambridge University Press, 1987.

Urban, Michael, 'December 1993 as a Replication of Late-Soviet Electoral Practices', *Post-Soviet Affairs*, 10 (1994), pp. 127–58.

The Ideology of Administration: American and Soviet Cases, Albany: State University of New York Press, 1982.

'The Politics of Identity in Russia's Postcommunist Transition: The Nation Against Itself', *Slavic Review*, 53 (1994), pp. 733–65.

'State, Property, and Political Society in Postcommunist Russia: In Search of a Political Center', in Saivetz, Carol, and Jones, Anthony (eds.), *In Search of Pluralism: Soviet and Post-Soviet Politics*, Boulder: Westview, 1994, pp. 125–50.

Varese, Frederico, 'Is Sicily the Future of Russia? Private Protection and the Rise of the Russian Mafia', *Archives européenes de sociologie*, 35 (1994), pp. 224–58.

Veretin, A., Miloserdova, N., and Petrov, G. (eds.), *Protivostoianie*, St Petersburg, 1992.

Vinnikov, A., 'The End of Soviet Power in St Petersburg: An Insider's View', *Europe–Asia Studies*, 46 (1994), pp. 1215–30.

Volkov, V. K. 'Etnokratiia – nepredvidennyi fenomen posttotalitarnogo mira', *Polis.*, 2 (1993), pp. 40–8.

Vybory deputatov Gosudarstvennoi Dumy. 1995. Elektoral'naia statistika, Moscow, 1996.

Walker, Rob, *Inside/Outside: International Relations as Political Theory*, Cambridge University Press, 1993.

Wallerstein, Immanuel, *Geopolitics and Geoculture: Essays on the Changing World-System*, Cambridge University Press and Editions de la Maison des Sciences de l'Homme, Paris, 1991.

Weigle, Marcia, 'Political Participation and Party Formation in Russia, 1985–1992: Institutionalizing Democracy?', *Russian Review*, 53 (1994), pp. 240–70.

Welch, S., *The Concept of Political Culture*, London: Macmillan, 1993.

White, Gordon, 'Civil Society, Democratization, and Development (I): Clearing the Analytical Ground', *Democratization*, 1 (1993), pp. 375–90.

Whitefield, Stephen, and Evans, Geoffrey, 'The Russian Election of 1993: Public Opinion and the Transition Experience', *Post-Soviet Affairs*, 10 (1994), pp. 38–60.

Zakiev, M. Z., 'Nationalism and Democratism in Tatarstan: The Ethnonym of the People', in *Tatarstan Past and Present*, London: SOAS, 1992, pp. 1–14.

Zaslavskii (Zaslavsky), V. 'Nationalism and Democracy in Transition in Postcommunist Societies', *Daedalus*, 121 (1991), pp. 97–122.

'Rossiia na puti k rynku: gosudarstvenno-zavisimye rabotniki i populizm', *Polis.*, 5 (1991), pp. 65–79.

Zubov, A., and Salmin, A., 'Soiuznyi dogovor i mekhanizm vyrabotki novogo natsional'no-gosudarstvennogo ustroistva SSSR', *Polis.*, 1 (1991), pp. 42–57.

Index